Advanced Textbooks in Economics

Series Editors: C.J. Bliss *and* M.D. Intriligator

Currently Available:

Volume 2 : *Lectures on Microeconomic Theory* (Second Revised Edition)
E. MALINVAUD

Volume 5 : *Applied Consumption Analysis* (Second Revised Edition)
L. PHLIPS

Volume 11: *Collective Choice and Social Welfare*
A.K. SEN

Volume 12: *General Competitive Analysis*
K.J. ARROW and F.H. HAHN

Volume 14: *Distributed Lags* (Second Revised Edition)
P.J. DHRYMES

Volume 15: *Notes and Problems in Microeconomic Theory*
P.B. DIXON, S. BOWLES, D. KENDRICK, L. TAYLOR and M. ROBERTS

Volume 17: *Stochastic Methods in Economics and Finance*
A.G. MALLIARIS and W.A. BROCK

Volume 19: *International Trade and Resource Allocation* (Second Revised Edition)
A.D. WOODLAND

Volume 20: *Introduction to the Use of General Equilibrium Analysis*
R.R. CORNWALL

Volume 22: *Lectures in Econometrics*
L.R. KLEIN and W. WELFE

Volume 23: *Public Enterprise Economics* (Second Revised Edition)
D. BÖS

Volume 24: *Optimal Control Theory with Economic Applications*
A. SEIERSTAD and K. SYDSAETER

Volume 25: *Capital Markets and Prices: Valuing Uncertain Income Streams*
C.G. KROUSE

Volume 26: *History of Economic Theory*
T. NEGISHI

Volume 27: *Differential Equations, Stability and Chaos in Dynamic Economics*
W.A. BROCK and A.G. MALLIARIS

Volume 28: *Equilibrium Analysis*
W. HILDENBRAND and A.P. KIRMAN

ECONOMICS OF INSURANCE

ADVANCED TEXTBOOKS IN ECONOMICS

VOLUME 29

NORTH-HOLLAND
AMSTERDAM • NEW YORK • OXFORD • TOKYO

ECONOMICS OF INSURANCE

K. BORCH †

Norwegian School of Economics and Business Administration, Bergen, Norway

Edited and Completed after Professor Borch's Death by

Knut K. AASE *and* Agnar SANDMO

Norwegian School of Economics and Business Administration, Bergen, Norway

1990

NORTH-HOLLAND
AMSTERDAM • NEW YORK • OXFORD • TOKYO

ELSEVIER SCIENCE PUBLISHERS B.V.
Sara Burgerhartstraat 25
P.O. Box 211, 1000 AE Amsterdam, The Netherlands

Distributors for the United States and Canada:
ELSEVIER SCIENCE PUBLISHING COMPANY, INC.
655 Avenue of the Americas
New York, N.Y. 10010, U.S.A.

ISBN: 0 444 87344 9

PRINTED IN THE NETHERLANDS

INTRODUCTION TO THE SERIES

The aim of the series is to cover topics in economics, mathematical economics and econometrics, at a level suitable for graduate students or final year undergraduates specializing in economics. There is at any time much material that has become well established in journal papers and discussion series which still awaits a clear, self-contained treatment that can easily be mastered by students without considerable preparation or extra reading. Leading specialists will be invited to contribute volumes to fill such gaps. Primary emphasis will be placed on clarity, comprehensive coverage of sensibly defined areas, and insight into fundamentals, but original ideas will not be excluded. Certain volumes will therefore add to existing knowledge, while others will serve as a means of communicating both known and new ideas in a way that will inspire and attract students not already familiar with the subject matter concerned.

The Editors

PREFACE

When Karl Borch died in December, 1986, he was working on the manuscript of a textbook on the economic theory of insurance, the area which had been his main interest throughout his academic career. The manuscript had not been finished; we know that he planned to add at least one additional chapter, and it may well be that he would have expanded on the chapters which had already been written. But even in its unfinished form the manuscript does give a very readable and fascinating overview of the field to wich Borch made so many pioneering contributions since his first publications around 1960. We have therefore decided to publish these chapters more or less in the form in which they were to be found at Borch's death; only minor editing has been undertaken.

Given the incomplete nature of the manuscript we have further decided, in consultation with the series editors, to add a selection of Borch's articles in the economics of insurance. We have naturally chosen the articles with a view to their complementarity with the textbook exposition, so that they may be seen also as a selection of readings to be studied along with the main text. We hope that the book as a whole will serve as a stimulating introduction to the economics of insurance.

We are glad to be able to publish this book as a memorial to a scholar who was not only a leader in his field, but also an important source of inspiration and support to a large number of colleagues and students, both at the Norwegian School of Economics and Business Administration and at many universities and research institutions throughout the world.

Bergen, March 1989

Knut K. Aase　　　　Agnar Sandmo

CHAPTER 1

INSURANCE AND ECONOMICS

1. Insurance and Economic Analysis

1.1 It is not possible to give a definition of insurance which is short and precise, and at the same time completely satisfactory. A number of definitions can be found in the insurance literature, but they tend to be long and involved, and usually one can find some kind of insurance that does not quite fit the definition.

For the present purpose it is sufficient to consider an *insurance contract* as described by two elements:

(i) $P =$ the premium paid by the insured when the contract is concluded.

(ii) $x =$ the compensation which the insured receives if specific events occur when the contract is in force. Clearly x is a random variable, and must be described by a probability distribution $F(x)$.

The essential objective of a theory of insurance is to determine the relationship between the two elements, i.e. how the premium P depends on the properties of the probability distribution $F(x)$. A pair $(P, F(x))$ can obviously also be interpreted as a gamble, or as a risky investment. This means that results in the theory of insurance may be relevant in the study of uncertainty in general economics and finance. It also means that methods developed in economic and financial analysis may have applications in insurance.

1.2 Insurance is an economic activity, and an important one. Most authors of general economic texts discuss insurance, usually in a separate section. In his *Wealth of Nations*, (Book I, Chapter 10) Adam Smith (1776) writes that the insurance "premium must be sufficient to compensate the common losses, to pay the expense of management, and to afford such a profit as might have been drawn from an equal capital employed in any common trade". This is a very good statement of how insurance premiums must be calculated, and we shall return to it in later chapters.

On the effect of insurance Adam Smith writes (Book V, Chapter 1): "The trade of insurance gives great security to the fortunes of private people, and by dividing among a great many that loss which would ruin an individual, makes it fall light and easy upon the whole society. In order to give this security, however, it is necessary that the insurers should have a very large capital". He does not say how large this capital should be, nor does he discuss how much of his money an entrepreneur would be prepared to risk in the insurance business. Adam Smith does however observe (Book I, Chapter 10) "the universal success of lotteries", and compares it with the "very moderate profit of insurers". In modern terms this means that Adam Smith considered people's desire to gamble as a more important element in the economy than their "risk aversion", i.e. their willingness to pay to get rid of risks.

1.3 The passages quoted above show that more than 200 years ago Adam Smith had a good insight into the essentials of insurance. In the following century there was a rapid development in economic theory, which did not seem to have led to any deeper understanding of insurance. The three main centers of this development were Cambridge, Lausanne and Vienna. At the time the theories developed at these centers were considered as different "schools". Today the differences between them seem less fundamental, and it is convenient to refer to the three schools as the "neo-classical" theory.

1.4 In Vienna Carl Menger, the founder of the Austrian School does not seem to have anything important to say about insurance. His most brilliant student and successor, Eugen Böhm-Bawerk did however write his dissertation (Habilitationsarbeit, 1881) about the value of contingent claims. Apparently it did not occur to him that the obvious application of this theory was to insurance premiums. The owner of an insured ship has a claim against the insurer if the ship is lost or damaged at sea. The value, or the price he pays for this contingent claim is clearly the premium demanded by the insurer. Böhm-Bawerk does not seem to have returned to the problems of his dissertation at any later stage. His purpose was apparently to show that values, or "certainty equivalents" could be computed for contingent claims, and hence that one could confidently proceed with the development of a theory based on complete certainty.

It was obviously a fairly difficult mathematical problem to compute the value of a complicated contingent claim, and the solution was probably beyond the mathematics of Böhm-Bawerk. In the second half of the nineteenth century Austrian and German actuaries developed a "risk theory". The purpose of this theory was essentially to determine the capital which an insurer had to hold in order to give adequate security to the buyers of insurance contracts. If actuaries could solve this problem, Böhm-Bawerk could with some justification ignore the uncertainty inherent in any contract involving contingent claims. The effect of this division of labour was however that an economic theory of insurance would have to be based not only on standard economic analysis, but also on a "risk theory" beyond the grasp of most economists.

1.5 In Lausanne Leon Walras (1874) saw insurance as a device for removing the uncertainty inherent in all other economic activities. This made it reasonable to develop a theory for general economic equilibrium under full certainty, leaving the insurance sector as a special subject to be studied separately.

This is of course essentially the same conclusion as the one reached by Böhm-Bawerk, although with a slightly different interpretation. To Walras the link between the two sectors is the "prime d'assurance", which a modern business economist will recognize as the "cost of capital" to business of different risk classes.

1.6 In Cambridge Alfred Marshall came close to develop an economic theory of insurance. In his *Principles* (1890) he discusses insurance premiums as the price one has to pay to get rid of the "evils of uncertainty". In the Mathematical Appendix to the book he mentions the work of Daniel Bernoulli 150 years earlier as an "interesting guess", and he seems to recognize that the Bernoulli principle may be the key to the problem of insurance premiums. Marshall did not himself develop this idea, and nobody in Cambridge seemed to take the hint.

Marshall wrote about the "evil of risk", and believed that people were willing to pay to get rid of this evil. He noted that businessmen paid insurance premiums "which they know are calculated on a scale sufficiently above the true actuarial value of the risk to pay the companies' great expenses of advertising and working, and yet to yield a surplus of net profits". This means of course in modern terms that Marshall believed that the important decision makers in the economy were "risk averse".

It is interesting to compare Marshall's views with those expressed by Adam Smith more than 100 years earlier. At Marshall's time people were no longer allowed to organize lotteries for their own profits. Gambling seems to have flourished in the Victorian era, and had at least a snob appeal, even if it was not quite respectable. People's willingness to gamble was however not worthy of the study by serious economists, who focused their interest on the prudent risk averse investor. This attitude does not seem to have changed during the last 100 years, and this is in a way surprising. Governments in many countries have made increasing use of people's propensity to gamble to increase revenue by state lotteries and to borrow at low interest rates by premium bonds. The revenue obtained by exploiting "risk lovers" is already a fairly important element in public finance, and the attitudes of these people seem to deserve serious study.

1.7 The Bernoulli principle and its implications will be discussed in the next chapter, but it may be useful to give a brief outline already at the present stage. In the early days of the calculus of probability it was taken as granted that the value, and hence the fair price of a gamble was the mathematical expectation of the gain. If the probability of a gain x is $f(x)$, the fair price would be

$$E\{x\} = \bar{x} = \sum_{x=0}^{\infty} x\, f(x)$$

Applied to insurance this means that the fair premium for a risk described by the probability distribution $f(x)$ would be

$$P = \bar{x} = \sum_{x=0}^{\infty} x\, f(x)$$

The counter example given by Bernoulli (1738) has become known as the St. Petersburg Paradox. He considered a game in which a coin is tossed until it shows heads. If the first head appears at the n'th toss, a prize of 2^n is paid. The expected gain in this gamble is

$$E\{x\} = \sum_{n=1}^{\infty} (1/2)^n 2^n = \infty$$

Bernoulli argued that no rational person would be willing to pay an arbitrarily large amount for the right to participate in this gamble. As an alternative Bernoulli suggested that the person would assign the "moral" value or utility of $\log x$ to a physical gain of x. The value of the gamble is then the moral expectation:

$$E\{\log x\} = \sum_{n=1}^{\infty}(1/2)^n \log 2^n = \log 2 \sum_{n=1}^{\infty} n(1/2)^n = 2 \log 2$$

1.8 Bernoulli gave his own justification for setting the moral value of a gain of x equal to $\log x$, but from his correspondence it is clear that he was willing to replace $\log x$ with some other concave function, such as $u(x) = \sqrt{x}$, or $\log(c+x)$. This means that the utility assigned to a gamble described by a probability distribution $f(x)$ would be

$$E\{u(x)\} = \sum_{x=0}^{\infty} u(x)\, f(x) \tag{1}$$

where $u(x)$ is an arbitrary increasing concave function, i.e. the inequalities $u'(x) > 0$ and $u''(x) < 0$ hold.

From Jensen's inequality it follows that

$$E\{u(x)\} < E\{x\}$$

Hence a person will pay less than the mathematical expectation for the right to play a gamble. Similarly an insurer will demand a "risk premium" in addition to the expected loss in order to cover a risk.

Bernoulli assumed that the function $u(x)$ was concave. This implies that the person considered is risk averse, and that he will pay less than the expected gain for a lottery ticket, and more than the expected loss for an insurance contact covering the risk. If $u(x)$ is convex, i.e. $u''(x) > 0$, the person will be a "risk lover", and he will buy lottery tickets even if the price is higher than the expected gain. He will however not buy insurance if the premium is above the expected loss. If $u(x)$ is linear, the person will be "risk neutral".

1.9 Marshall in Cambridge was aware of these possibilities of generalizing the Bernoulli Principle, and he was not the only one. Bernoulli's work, originally published in Latin, was translated into German in 1896 by a prominent mathematician, Alfred Pringsheim. The translation was published with an introduction by the philosopher Ludwig Fick, and had the title "Grundlage der modernen Werthlehre", (Foundation of the Modern Theory of Value).

This title was however premature, by about 50 years. The economists who developed the neo-classical theory of value, continued to ignore the Bernoulli hypothesis. They put it to work only after von Neumann and Morgenstern (1947) had proved the hypothesis as a theorem. In fact they proved that if a person had a consistent preference ordering over the set of all games described by probability distributions, there exists a function $u(x)$ such that (1) gives the utility assigned to the gamble described by $f(x)$. This result has become known as the *Expected Utility Theorem*, and it is indeed the foundation of the modern theory of value.

1.10 It is a little surprising that economists did not apply the Bernoulli hypothesis before it had been proved as a theorem. It had been endorsed as an interesting guess by the leading Cambridge economist, and Austrian and German mathematicians, i.e. Czuber (1904) had shown how it could be used to determine insurance premiums. Usually economists have been willing to explore the implications of heroic assumptions which seem reasonable on intuitive ground. It is not easy to see what held them back when it came to insurance, although one may guess that they had accepted that this activity required special methods of analysis.

The breakthrough was made by Arrow (1953), who showed how the values of contingent claims were determined by market forces, and that these made demand for risk-bearing services equal to the supply in the market. Arrow's model is quite general, but the application he has in mind is the prices of securities in a stock market. It is however clear that the model can also be interpreted as an insurance market, and this interpretation will be discussed in the following chapters.

2. Insurance in the National Economy

2.1 In all industrial countries insurance is an important sector of the economy. In the U.S.A. there were in 1984 about 5000 insurance companies. They collected more than 250 billion dollars in premiums, and provided employment for about 2 million people.

Insurance is about equally important in other industrial countries. International comparisons are difficult, since the statistical definition of insurance varies from one country to another. In most countries the primary source of insurance statistics is the reports of the governmental supervisory authority, which naturally tends to focus on the statistics it needs to check that the insurance companies under supervision are solvent. In other

Table 1.1: Insurance premiums in 1984 in U.S. Dollars, at the exchange rate at the end of 1984.

	Total business		Non-life business		Life business	
	Dollars Millions	World share %	Dollars Millions	World share %	Dollars Millions	World share %
1. U.S.A.	253395	50.88	159262	56.58	94133	43.48
2. Japan	73585	14.78	21829	7.76	51756	23.91
3. W. Germany	32508	6.53	19178	6.81	13330	6.16
4. Great Britain	26464	5.32	10813	3.84	15651	7.23
5. France	19077	3.83	13296	4.72	5782	2.67
6. Canada	15796	3.17	8604	3.06	7192	3.32
7. Australia	8730	1.75	6151	2.19	2579	1.19
8. Italy	7369	1.48	6362	2.26	1007	0.47
9. Netherlands	6178	1.24	3398	1.21	2779	1.28
10. Switzerland	5664	1.14	2833	1.01	2831	1.31

Source: *Sigma*, April 1986.

countries the main source of insurance statistics is publications by different insurance trade associations, which usually will cover only the members of the associations. Attempt at international comparisons are usually frustrating, and different authors have arrived at different results.

2.2 The following four tables are taken from the monthly newsletter *Sigma*, published by the Swiss Reinsurance Company. The newsletter is generally considered as the most reliable source of comparable insurance statistics. The statistics covers only the whole non-communist world.

Table 1.1 gives the figures for the 10 countries which account for more than one per cent of the world's insurance premiums. Together they account for about 90 per cent of the total. The table contains few surprises, it consists of the 10 major OECD countries in about the order one would expect, and the order would not change, even if there should be fairly substantial variation in the exchange rates.

The exchange rate of the U.S. Dollar was close to its all-time peak at the end of 1984, so the table does to some extent exaggerate the importance of insurance in the United States.

2.3 In Table 1.2 the influence of the size of the country is eliminated, and this does bring in some changes in the order, i.a. two Scandinavian countries find their place among the top ten. The countries included have similar social security system, so the large differences in per capita life insurance premium may seem surprising. They can probably be explained by differences in statistical coverage.

Pension plans set up by private companies and local governments are important in all the countries, but their legal positions are different, and they are not always included in the insurance statistics.

2.4 In Table 1.2, the two first countries stand apart from the rest. The differences between the other 8 countries are small, and the order between them can be completely reshuffled by minor fluctuation in exchange rates. Effects of this kind are eliminated in Table 1.3, which gives insurance premiums in per cent of GNP for the years 1979 and 1984. The most surprising aspect of this table may be that Ireland and Great Britain in 1984 had moved to the top of the list. The explanation may be that these two countries have experienced relatively slow economic growth in the five-year period. It would be tempting to speculate on a number of other aspects of the table, and seek explanations of some of the differences, but this would in most cases be pure guesswork.

2.5 The three preceding tables indicate that insurance is not defined in quite the same way in the countries included. This is brought out even more strongly in Table 1.4, which gives the number of insurance companies in 15 important countries. At first sight it may seem normal that the U.S.A. which accounts for about 50% of the world's insurance premiums should also have about half the insurance companies in the world. It is however surprising that the U.S.A. should have almost 150 times more insurance companies than Japan which accounts for 15% of the world's insurance premiums. The Table may reflect differences in the structure of the insurance industries in different countries, but most of the differences are probably due to differences in legislation and statistical coverage.

Most of the older insurance countries had a large number of small — usually mutual — insurance companies which wrote fire insurance for a local community, or insured fishing vessels and livestock for local fishermen and farmers. Most of these small companies cooperate among themselves, and in some countries they have formally merged into a major company. Other small companies operate virtually, but not formally as subsidiaries of major insurance companies.

Table 1.2: Insurance premiums per head of population in 1984, in US Dollars at exchange rates at end of 1984.

	Total	Non-life	Life
1. U.S.A.	1071	673	398
2. Switzerland	880	440	440
3. Canada	628	342	286
4. Japan	613	182	431
5. Australia	562	396	166
6. West Germany	531	313	218
7. Norway	484	287	197
8. Great Britain	468	191	277
9. Sweden	435	208	227
10. Netherlands	428	235	193

Source: *Sigma*, April 1986

Table 1.3: Insurance premium in per cent of GNP.

	1979	1984
1. U.S.A.	7.25	6.91
2. Switzerland	6.16	6.47
3. Ireland	5.97	8.52
4. Great Britain	5.83	7.05
5. Netherlands	5.55	5.56
6. West Germany	5.10	5.87
7. Australia	5.08	5.48
8. Canada	5.06	4.95
9. Japan	4.89	6.19
10. South Africa	4.78	6.78

Source: *Sigma*, April 1986

It may be worth while to stress once more that international insurance statistics is a frustrating subject.

2.6 In general one needs a license to sell insurance contracts, and in most countries these sellers have to operate under government supervision or

Table 1.4: Number of Insurance Companies in some Countries in 1983.

	Life	Non-Life
U.S.A.	2048	3474
Great Britain	188	381
Canada	104	161
W. Germany	94	306
France	73	245
Colombia	23	34
Japan	23	14
Belgium	22	93
Denmark	22	154
South Africa	22	22
Italy	21	109
Philippines	21	90
Switzerland	21	57
Spain	15	429
Sweden	13	240

Source: *Sigma*, December 1985

regulation. The main objective of this supervision — which we shall discuss in detail later — is to make certain that the insurers are solvent, i.e., that they have sufficient financial resources to pay claims, even if things should take an unfavorable turn.

In general private persons are not allowed to sell insurance. The only important exception is Lloyd's of London, where more than 25000 rich people accept insurance at the risk of losing their whole personal wealth, presumably in the hope of making profits. In most countries insurance is sold only by stock companies and mutual insurance companies. Usually insurers of both types compete in the same markets, and none of the groups seems to have any special competitive advantage. This raises some intriguing questions about the objectives of management in insurance companies. The usual assumption that the task of management is to maximize the wealth of stock-holders makes little sense as the objective of a mutual company. On the other hand it is not easy to spell out the objectives of a mutual insurance company, and one is inevitably led to the problem of "equity between generations". Should a mutual insurance company pay its profits out as dividends to the owners, i.e. to the current policy holders, use it to profits back to provide additional

e

er private persons or business firms. may differ from one case to another, ful in general. In order not to get lost t to divide the field into three classes rately.

d ordinary life insurance with payment at death.

(ii) *Business insurance*, the insurance bought by businessmen, covering commercial risks of all kinds.

(iii) *Household insurance*, bought by the ordinary consumer as protection against the risks in everyday life.

There are at least three reasons which make it convenient to study these three classes of insurance separately:

(i) Each class seems to require its own special types of theoretical analysis.

(ii) In the market each class of insurance faces different types of competition.

(iii) The government, through its supervisory or regulatory authority often takes different attitudes to these three classes of insurance.

3.2 Life insurance is essentially a form of saving, and it is natural to analyse it with the methods developed for the study of the consumption-saving decisions.

In the market life insurance competes with other forms of savings. There are no obvious limits to how much people could — or should — save. Apparently Americans have during the last decade saved less than people in most industrial countries, less even than people in some highly developed welfare states, where the need to save for a rainy day should be much smaller. In the U.S. it should therefore be possible to increase the sale of life insurance quite substantially. The problem for the seller is then, first to convince people that they should save more, and secondly that life insurance is a good form of saving.

Life insurance companies are in a sense the custodians of the savings of widows and orphans, and it seems to be generally agreed in most countries that these companies must be subject to strict supervision by the government. The companies are usually not allowed to engage in risky investments, and the government will in some way try to make certain that the premiums are adequate, i.e. sufficient to meet long-term liabilities.

3.3 Business insurance is bought by businessmen, or their companies, usually from insurance companies run by businessmen, and can be seen as a method of risk sharing, or reallocation of risk within the business community.

Insurance is however only one of many possible ways to arrange risk sharing, and in the market the sellers of business insurance compete with the promoters of such arrangements. The market for business insurance can clearly be expanded if insurers show imagination and ability to develop insurance contracts which businessmen find more attractive than alternative schemes for risk sharing.

There is no strong or obvious need for government supervision and regulation of business insurance. Usually the contracts are concluded between corporations and insurance companies which can negotiate on almost equal terms, and neither party is likely to ask the government for help or protection. In general they would probably be satisfied if the government limited its activity to prevent fraud and to maintain law and order.

3.4 Household insurance is bought by the "little man", and usually his choice will be limited to a few standard contracts. This kind of insurance is clearly sold in a mass market, and the conventional economic theory of competitive markets should be applicable to this kind of insurance. Some difficulties do however, occur, and we shall discuss these in a later chapter.

In most countries there seems to be keen competition in the market for household insurance, but this competition is essentially among insurance companies. The ordinary consumer has no real alternative to insurance when he wants protection against a risk.

Governments have for a long time been concerned with household insurance, and much of the insurance legislation is designed to protect the buyer, who generally will be the weaker party to the insurance contract. During the last decade the consumers' movement has in general led to a demand for stricter supervision and regulation by the government.

3.5 The classification of insurance activities indicated is summarized by the table below:

	Life insurance	Business insurance	Household insurance
Theoretical analysis	Consumption & saving models	Bargaining models and game theory	Competitive market models
Competition and marketing	Other forms of saving	Other forms of risksharing	Competition among insurance companies
Government attitude	Supervision to maintain solvency essential	No strong need for regulation	Increasing demand for regulation

In some countries an insurance company is allowed to write any kind of insurance, but usually a company can sell either life insurance or non-life insurance. There seems however to be a tendency towards a further specialization, to the effect that a company will sell exclusively either business or household insurance.

A short survey of these three classes of insurance, and their specific problems has been given in a recent paper by Borch (1981).

3.6 The relative importance of the three classes of insurance may differ from one country to another, depending on the definitions used in the statistics. The following two tables give some summary information from Sweden and the U.S.A.

The two tables are surprisingly similar. If the premium for automobile insurance in Sweden is divided between business and household insurance, in the same proportion as in the U.S.A., the two classes become about equal in both countries.

3.7 The observation by Adam Smith cited at the beginning of this chapter, implies that an insurance premium consists of three components:

$$P = E + A + R$$

Here the first term is expected claim payment under the insurance contract, and it is convenient to write $E = E\{x\}$.

The second term A represents the administrative expenses of the insurance company.

Table 1.5: Direct insurance premiums received by Swedish companies in 1983. Millions of Swedish kronor.

	Life insurance	Business insurance	Household insurance
Pension plans	7492		
Other life insurance	9106		
General property and liability		3931	1886
Automobile insurance			4074
Marine insurance		1159	
Aviation insurance		25	
Credit insurance		180	
Livestock insurance		115	
	16598	5410	5960

Source: Private Insurance Companies 1983. Official Statistics of Sweden.

Table 1.6: Net Premiums received by U.S. Insurers in 1984. Millions of Dollars.

	Life insurance	Business insurance	Household insurance
Life insurance	134804		
Automobile insurance		8675	43307
General liability		8254	
Fire insurance etc.			4853
Homeowners multi peril			13213
Commercial multi peril			9016
Workers Compensation		15107	
Marine insurance		4565	
Other business insurance			7337
	134804	52954	61373

Source: Insurance Facts 1985–86. Insurance Information Institute.

The third term R is usually referred to as the "risk premium". It represents the reward to the insurer for his service as risk-bearer.

In household insurance A is often substantial. On the other hand, since the sums insured usually are modest, R will be relatively small, and can often be ignored.

In large business insurance contracts, one cannot assume that $R = 0$, but A may be of little significance.

This makes it convenient to study business and household insurance separately.

3.8 The decomposition of the premium suggested by Adam Smith indicates a natural "division of labour".

To compute the first term, the expected claim payments $E\{x\}$ is essentially a statistical problem, and this has traditionally been handled by actuaries. The problem can be extremely difficult, for instance if changes in legislation make most statistics from the past irrelevant.

The second term, the administrative expenses A, presents a problem in cost accounting, and is clearly the concern of the accountants. There is obviously some difficulties involved in allocating general overhead costs among the individual insurance contracts.

The risk premium R, which is the last term in the formula, is determined by supply and demand in the market. To calculate this term economic analysis is required, and this will be the subject of this book.

References for Sections 1–3

Arrow K.J. (1953): "Le rôle des valeurs boursières pour la répartition la meilleure des risques." *Colloques Internationaux du CNRS, XL*, 41–48. English translation (1964): "The role of securities in the optimal allocation of risk-bearing," *Review of Economic Studies 31*, 91–96.

Bernoulli D. (1738): "Specimen theoriae novae de mensura sortis." *Proceedings of the Imperial Academy 5*, 175–192. St. Petersburg. English translation (1954): "Exposition of a new theory on the measurement of risk," *Econometrica 22*, 23–36.

Böhm-Bawerk E. (1881): *Rechte und Verhältnisse vom Standpunkte der Volkswirtschaftlichen Güterlehre*, Innsbruck.

Borch K. (1981): "The three Markets for Private Insurance," *The Geneva Papers on Risk and Insurance 20*, 7–31.

Czuber E. (1904): *Wahrscheinlichkeitsrechnung und ihre Anwendung*, Vienna: B.G. Teubner.

Marshall A. (1890): *Principles of Economics*, London.

Neumann J. von, and Morgenstern O. (1947): *Theory of Games and Economic Behavior*, Second edition, Princeton University Press.

Smith A. (1776): *The Wealth of Nations*, Edinburgh.

Walras L. (1874): *Eléments d'Economie Politique Pure*, Lausanne. English translation (1954): *Elements of Pure Economics.*

4. The Place of Uncertainty in the Theories of the Austrian School*

1. *Uncertainty* was introduced at a very early stage by the founder of the Austrian School. In the first chapter of Carl Menger's *Grundsätze* we find a paragraph on Time and Error (§4 *Zeit-Irrthum*). In the revised edition of 1923 the paragraph reappears, without substantial changes, but now in the second chapter, and split in two parts, one on the Time element (§5a *Das Zeitmoment*) and one on the Uncertainty element (§5b *Das Moment der Unsicherheit*). Menger does not say anything in this paragraph that strikes today's reader as remarkable. It is, however, remarkable that he should have felt it necessary to introduce Time and Uncertainty so early in the work, and also that he should find it natural to discuss the two elements together.

When Menger published his Grundsatze, there were hardly any mathematical economists. The only mathematicians who worked on problems connected with economics were actuaries, and to them it was quite natural to treat Time and Uncertainty in a symmetric manner. The present value of an amount M payable after t years if a certain person is still alive, is $(1+r)^{-t}p_tM$, where r is the rate of interest, and p_t the probability that the person shall be alive. Such calculations have been routine for more than 200 years, and the more advanced actuarial mathematics of the second half of the nineteenth century was to a large extent developed in Vienna.

Without some mathematical concepts at the back of one's mind, it is hard to see why Time and Uncertainty should call for symmetric treatment in economic analysis. It is, therefore, surprising that Menger and the early Austrians, with their clear aversion to mathematics, should find such treatment natural. A connection between Time and Space should have been more obvious to them. This idea has been developed by many economists, and it is attractive because it makes it possible to treat transportation and storage as productive activities — producing unchanged goods available at a different place and a different time.

2. The idea of a symmetry between Time and Uncertainty has persisted in the Austrian School, although it was never stated very clearly how such a symmetry could be exploited in economic analysis. The idea may simply have sprung from Menger's intuition, or it may have been based on knowledge of the work done by his distinguished colleagues at the Vienna

---

* Reprinted from *Carl Menger and the Austrian School of Economics*, J.R. Hicks and W. Weber (eds.), 1973, pp. 61–74, copyright (c) Clarendon Press, Oxford.

Technische Hochschule. There is, however, no evidence that indicates that Menger was familiar with the basic principles of actuarial mathematics.

Much of Böhm-Bawerk's work is centred around the time element. In his *Positive Theorie* Uncertainty enters only as the third element (*Die Kürze und Unsicherheit des Lebens*) of the Second Reason for a positive interest rate — or rather for a general undervaluation of future goods. In the obituary article on Böhm-Bawerk by Schumpeter, the idea is summed up as follows: "...that future satisfactions always have to be multiplied by a certain coefficient, which expresses the probability of the expected utility (a "risk premium")" (O.U.P, (1951)). The article was written in 1914, and translated into English in 1951 with the co-operation of Haberler. The English text is an almost modern formulation of the actuarial principle, and may be due to hindsight. One cannot help feeling that two younger Austrians have tried to express what Böhm-Bawerk really wanted to say.

The Uncertainty element plays an important part in Böhm-Bawerk's 'Habilitationsschrift' (Böhm-Bawerk (1881)), and it is a little surprising that it should yield almost completely to the Time element in the *Positive Theorie.* In his first book Böhm-Bawerk discusses 'immaterial goods', and what we today will call 'conditional claims'. He discusses whether such *Rechte und Verhältnisse* shall be considered as real goods (*echte Güter*), and how their value shall be determined. Much of the discussion is quaint to a modern reader. Böhm-Bawerk argues that love, friendship, honour, and character must have a value — for instance, because it may increase one's creditworthiness. Behind the discussion there are, however, ideas which are important, and which have been developed only in the last two or three decades.

Böhm-Bawerk's objective is to calculate a person's wealth (*Vermögens-komputation*) because this wealth, correctly assessed, will determine his economic behaviour. The idea is that a person's actions are motivated not only by his visible or tangible wealth, but by all his assets, including uncertain income which he expects in the future. The idea is as simple as it is profound, and it can be seen as a generalization of the so-called 'permanent income hypothesis' presented by Milton Friedman more than seventy years later.

It is curious that it does not seem to occur to Böhm-Bawerk that insurance companies, as a routine, must calculate the value of contingent claims. He discusses, for instance, the value we should assign to our right to recover goods stolen from us, if the thief is caught. Even in Böhm-Bawerk's days such rights were evaluated by insurance companies, and entered in the balance sheet under the heading 'Claims reported but not settled'.

3. I cannot discuss in detail how the symmetry between Time and Uncertainty was developed, forgotten, and rediscovered in the Austrian School. Instead I shall make a long leap forward to 1934. In that year we find in the *Zeitschrift für Nationalökonomie* two articles by Morgenstern and the younger Menger, with practically the same titles as the two paragraphs in the revised edition of *Grundsätze* (Morgenstern (1934)). Much had happened since 1871. The theory of value was well established, and no longer a uniquely Austrian theory. The theory was far from satisfactory on all points, and it was not surprising that two inquisitive men in their early thirties should find that the two weakest points were the treatment of the Time and Uncertainty elements. This could have happened in any country, but the idea of discussing the two elements in parallel articles was unmistakably Austrian.

We find traces of the same idea in the work by Friedrich Hayek. He considers the distribution over time of the output following from an investment, and illustrates his discussion with cumulative distributions and frequency curves (Hayek (1941)). I cannot see that he gains much by this use of the language of probability theory, and I do not think Hayek himself claims more than that it will facilitate understanding. This way of presenting the problem would hardly have appeared as natural to anybody not reared in the Austrian School, with its vague, but strong feeling that time and uncertainty should be treated in a symmetric manner.

The idea also turned up — if my interpretation is correct — in the inaugural lecture of Erich Streissler, the present holder of the Chair once occupied by Carl Menger (Streissler (1966)). Streissler introduces the concept 'structural thought', which he considers as a unifying element in both the older and the younger Austrian schools. By structural analysis he means essentially decomposition of aggregates. As an illustration let P stand for price, and X for quantity. The total value involved in a series of transactions will then be $\sum_{t=0}^{n} P_t X_t$. In aggregate analysis one may often replace this product-sum with a simple product of the form $1/n\,(\sum_{t=0}^{n} P_t)\,(\sum_{t=0}^{n} P_t)$. For both expressions we can write PX and interpret this symbol either as a vector product, or as a simple product of two scalar index numbers, as the case may be. Structural analysis will then consist in replacing scalars with vectors, in order to obtain models with more explanatory power. This idea is not new, but Streissler's suggestion that $P(z) = (\sum_{t=0}^{n} P_t)\,(\sum_{t=0}^{n} X_t)^{-1}$ should be treated as a cumulative probability distribution, is both new and in good Austrian tradition.

4. In the *Grundsätze* Menger has little to say about the Time element, beyond observing that production usually takes time.

Menger is also very brief in his discussion of the Uncertainty element, but the point he makes is both important and interesting. Menger observes that there will always be an Uncertainty element inherent in the production process, i.e. in the transformation of goods of higher order into goods of lower order. He argues that output of goods is determined by the input of factors, and that uncertainty occurs when some factors are not goods. This may sound quaint today, but by a slight modification we can turn it into a modern definition, simply by saying that output depends on factor input and stochastic variables.

In economic theory it is natural to distinguish between two kinds of uncertainty. Both can be illustrated by considering a producer who must select a factor input $(x_1, x_2 \ldots x_n)$ for the next period. In this decision problem there are two kinds of uncertainty:

(i) There is uncertainty about the output which will be obtained for the chosen factor input.

(ii) There is uncertainty about the price which the output will fetch when sold in the market.

5. Menger was concerned only with uncertainty of the first kind, and he was one of the very few economists who considered it important. Menger concludes his discussion of the Uncertainty element by saying that it will be shown in the following that this element is of great practical importance in economics. I cannot see that he really fulfils this promise in the *Grundsätze*, which originally was planned as the 'First General Part' of a work in four volumes. In a Foreword to the 1923 edition of *Grundsätze* the younger Menger gives an outline of the plan for the three other volumes, and I think it is fairly safe to assume that it was here that the elder Menger intended to demonstrate the practical importance of Uncertainty.

Uncertainty of the first kind can be said to be caused by 'nature'. Most economists in the nineteenth century — and later — seem to have ignored, or assumed away this kind of uncertainty. The most explicit in this respect was probably Walras, who pointed out that an entrepreneur could buy insurance against losses caused by nature (Walras (1902)). These economists obviously knew that there might be uncertainty in the production process, but they believed, or hoped, that it would not be important. This is in itself rather strange, since the theory of production has been developed in close contact with agriculture, and any farmer can tell the economist that deterministic production functions do not exist. It is a sign of Menger's realism that right at the beginning of his book he found it necessary to reject the production process as a deterministic relation.

If mathematics had been Menger's natural language, he would have suggested that the production function

$$y = f(x_1, x_2 \dots x_n)$$

should be replaced by a stochastic relation, for instance the conditional probability distribution

$$\Pr(\text{Output } = y) = f(y \,|\, x_1 \dots x_n)\,.$$

It is surprising that seventy years should pass before this simple idea of Menger's was presented in mathematical form. When this was done, it was done by an Austrian, Gerhard Tintner (1941), who also brought the analysis one step further ahead. If the output corresponding to a certain input vector $\{x_1 \dots x_n\}$ is a stochastic variable, the profit resulting from an input decision must also be a stochastic variable. Tintner finds the distribution of this variable, and discusses the choice of the input vector in the resulting situation — a situation in which ordinary profit maximization obviously does not make sense. Tintner does not take the easy way followed by most economists. He does not assume that the producer's objective simply is to maximize expected profits. He argues that the producer will consider not only the expectation — i.e. the first moment of the profit distribution — but also other properties of this distribution, for example higher moments, the standard deviation or a measure of skewness. Today, thirty years later, this conclusion may seem obvious, almost trivial, but it represents the final clarification of a problem that had been the subject of confused discussion in two generations of economists.

6. Uncertainty of the second kind is essentially due to uncertainty about how other people, or 'the market', will react. This is clearly the kind of uncertainty that businessmen will consider as most important. A businessman may not be very concerned about the possibly stochastic nature of the input-output relation, but he will certainly worry about the price he will obtain for his product, or about how much he can sell at the price he chooses.

Menger did not discuss the second kind of uncertainty, and this is fairly natural. In *Grundsätze* he gives a rather rudimentary theory of price formation, with some emphasis on the bargaining process. This approach should lead to uncertainty over prices, but it seems clear that such refinements of the theory would have their natural place in the volumes which were to have followed *Grundsätze.* The Austrian discussion of uncertainty of the second kind began in earnest at a later stage, when the concept of economic equilibrium had moved to a central place in the theory.

In the first theories of general equilibrium one had to assume 'complete information', or 'perfect foresight'. These assumptions cause difficulties. They are obviously unrealistic, but hardly more so than other assumptions connected with the concept of static equilibrium. More important are the logical difficulties involved. If the theory assumes complete information, can there then be room for any uncertainty? The obvious answer seems to be 'No', and most of the Austrians seemed to want to retain the Uncertainty element in the theory.

I shall not try to give even a brief account of the long Austrian discussion about 'perfect foresight'. The most relevant parts of the discussion is summarized in some publications of Morgenstern (1935), which also point out the direction in which the solution was found later. As a paradox Morgenstern discusses the problem of Sherlock Holmes who tries to escape his enemy Moriarty. Holmes has the choice of taking the train to Dover, or to leave the train at the only stop on the way. In 1928 Morgenstern concluded that the problem had no solution in the conventional sense of the word. Today any undergraduate will recognize the problem as a two-person zero-sum game, and he will know that it has a solution only in 'mixed strategies'. Holmes's problem is to keep his enemy guessing, and the only certain way of achieving this is to remain guessing himself. Hence the solution is that Holmes should toss a coin, and let the outcome decide if he should stay on the train to Dover, or leave at the intermediary stop.

Uncertainty of the first kind is essentially due to our imperfect knowledge of, for instance, the production process. In theory we could eliminate such uncertainty completely, if we had full information about the state of nature, and could process this information fast enough. If we know exactly how much force the croupier applies when he spins the roulette wheel and releases the ball, we should in principle be able to predict with certainty the number at which the ball will come to rest. Uncertainty is then in a sense due to *errors* that we make, and it is quite natural that Menger should use the word *Irrthum* in the *Grundsätze*, and in his notes for a second edition change it to *Unsicherheit.*

Many economists who have given serious consideration to the question, seem to have believed that uncertainty of the second kind was of the same nature. With full knowledge of consumers' preferences and producers' cost, it should in principle be possible to make infallible economic predictions. The only reservation generally made in this context, seems to be that people occasionally make errors, and deviate from rational behaviour. The conclusion should then be that, given full information and perfectly rational behaviour, uncertainty of the second kind can be completely eliminated.

Morgenstern's argument shows that in a situation of conflict — or competition — rational behaviour will consist in creating uncertainty, just to make prediction impossible. His simple paradox has implications which are as far-reaching as those of Bernoulli's 'St. Petersburg Paradox'. These implications may not yet have had their full impact on economic thinking, and we can only hope that it will not be delayed as long as the impact from Bernoulli's idea.

This is not the place for a full discussion of the theory of games, created by von Neumann and Morgenstern in 1944. It is, however, appropriate to point out that the theory in a sense grew out of the discussions about Uncertainty in the Austrian School. It is also worth mentioning that the main mathematical theorems behind game theory had been established by von Neumann as early as 1928 (Neumann (1928)), and that he himself pointed out their obvious relevance to central problems in economics. This is one of many examples of mathematical tools being offered to economists, who were slow in accepting the offer. The Austrians who understood the value of the offer, and made use of it, should get the credit they deserve.

7. At this point I shall make a rather long digression, which I hope will not be judged as completely irrelevant. At the turn of the century Vienna was an important centre for insurance mathematics. The leading names were Ernst Blaschke and Emanuel Czuber, professors at the Technische Hochschule. They both made important contributions to the special branch of insurance mathematics that actuaries call *risk theory*. This theory has found most of its applications in reinsurance, and I shall take an illustrating example from this field.

Let us assume that an insurance company has underwritten a contract — say in fire insurance, and that the maximum loss can be $M = \$10$ millions. Let x be the amount which the company will have to pay to settle insurance claims made under the contract, and let the corresponding probability distribution be $F(x)$, $0 \leq x \leq M$. At the underwriting the company has collected a premium P. Usually $P > E\{x\}$, so that the contract is favourable to the company. Few companies will retain the whole of this contract on their own account. Usually most of the contracts will be reinsured. The two classical procedures are then:

(i) *Quota reinsurance.* The company retains only a fraction, say 10 per cent of the contract. In this case 90 per cent of the premium will be paid to the reinsurers, who in return undertake to pay 90 per cent of the claim. If the claim is x, the company's profit will be $0.1P - 0.1x$.

(ii) *Excess reinsurance.* The company can seek an arrangement so that it at most will have to pay a certain fraction, say 10 per cent of the maximum loss M. If the claim is x, the company's profit will be

$$P - Q - x \quad \text{for } x < 0.1M$$

$$P - Q - 0.1M \quad \text{for } x > 0.1M$$

Here Q is the premium that the company has to pay to the reinsurers. The determination of this premium for different types of reinsurance is the central problem in risk theory. The problem is obviously related to the questions discussed in Böhm-Bawerk's first book (Böhm-Bawerk (1881)), but no actuary seems to have been aware of this.

The Austrian School of insurance mathematics probably had its finest hours during the International Congress of Actuaries which took place in Vienna in 1909. Czuber was the President of the Congress, Blaschke was the leading member of the Scientific Committee, and Austrian actuaries presented a series of fundamental papers on risk theory.

The practical problem that the actuaries discussed, was how a company should best arrange its reinsurance, i.e. how much risk should the company retain, how much should be passed on to the reinsurers, and how much should be paid for the transaction. It is obvious that this problem must lead to a study of price formation in the reinsurance market. The actuaries almost realized this, but not quite. The one who came closest was probably Alfred Tauber of the insurance company Anker in Vienna (Tauber (1909)). He discusses the buying and selling of a conditional claim (*Anspruch*), that is almost the same problem as Böhm-Bawerk studied in his first book. Tauber's discussion is very brief, and it is obvious that his real interest lies in mathematical manipulations.

The Congress of 1909 gives a demonstration of how watertight compartments can exist in related fields of science. At the Congress eminent mathematicians were discussing an essentially economic problem, without any reference to — and probably without any knowledge of — economic theory. At the same time, and in the same city, leading economists were discussing risk and uncertainty, without ever trying to use the mathematical tools that the actuaries had developed. It is not very useful to speculate over what would have happened in history if events had taken a different turn. It is, however, interesting to think of how the economics of Uncertainty would have developed if the Congress had taken place five years earlier. It would then have been the task of Böhm-Bawerk, as Minister of Finance, to deliver the opening address.

Another illustration of scientific insulation is provided by a remarkable paper on the economics of insurance by J. Lindenbaum, published in the *Zeitschrift für Nationalökonomie* in 1932 (Lindenbaum (1931)). The author wants to mark a twenty-fifth anniversary, not of the actuarial Congress, but of the publication of the first edition of the *Handbook of Insurance* by Alfred Manes. Lindenbaum argues that a theory of insurance must be based on the 'Supply of Security' (*Sicherheitsangebot*) and the 'Demand for Risk' (*Risikennachfrage*). He also argues that it should be a natural task for the Austrian School to create a theory of this kind. The paper is long — twenty-five pages of small print, and one gets the impression that it was accepted with some reluctance by the editor. The paper, which is worth reading even today, has, as far as I know, had no influence on later economic or actuarial literature, and Lindenbaum does not show any knowledge of the actuaries 'Risk Theory'.

8. The basic problem in the Austrian School was to assign utility to collections of goods — which we informally refer to as 'market baskets'. If there was a choice, one would choose the basket with the highest utility.

In a situation with uncertainty, the choice is not between different market baskets, but between different probability distributions over sets of market baskets. These probability distributions can be interpreted as lotteries, so the problem is to assign utilities to lotteries of different kinds. This may sound fairly simple, but the amount of difficulty the problem has caused in economic theory, is really surprising, particularly when we realize that the solution was suggested by Daniel Bernoulli as early as 1732.

To illustrate the suggestion of Bernoulli it is sufficient to consider lotteries in which all prizes are amounts of money. A lottery of this kind can be described by a one-dimensional probability distribution $F(x)$. The classical rule, which goes back to Pascal, was to choose the lottery with the greatest expected gain, or 'mathematical expectation'. This meant that the lottery $F(x)$ could be assigned the utility:

$$\int_0^\infty x\,dF(x)$$

It soon became obvious that people — gamblers and others — did not do this. The famous counter-example is the so-called 'St. Petersburg Paradox'. This observation led Bernoulli to suggest that the utility of a lottery should be not the mathematical expectation, but the 'moral expectation' given by the expression

$$\int_0^\infty u(c+x)\,dF(x)$$

Here the function $u(x)$ represents the 'moral value', or utility associated with the amount x of money. It is convenient to refer to this suggestion as the 'Bernoulli Principle'. Bernoulli also argued that it was reasonable to assume that $u(x) = \log x$, and this suggestion is often referred to as the 'Bernoulli Hypothesis'.

9. The Bernoulli Hypothesis became popular for some time among mathematicians and philosophers, but it had little impact on economic theory. In the second half of the nineteenth century the hypothesis got some experimental support from psychology, and was often referred to as the Weber-Fechner law. The economists were obviously right in ignoring or rejecting the hypothesis. A logarithmic utility function will place strong restrictions on demand functions, and even a casual observer could see that these restrictions were unrealistic. It is, however, surprising that economists should be so slow in realizing the relevance and usefulness of the more general principle.

At the end of his *Exkurs X* Böhm-Bawerk refers to Fechner's law, and dismisses it as irrelevant. It is, however, not clear if it is the principle or the more special hypothesis that he rejects. This indirect reference seems to be all that the early Austrians had to say about Bernoulli's work. In this respect Marshall is different. His Principles shows that he accepts the relevance of Bernoulli's suggestion, without being aware of its full significance. In Note VIII Marshall gives a clear presentation of the Bernoulli Principle, and he observes that 'the guess which has attracted most attention after Bernoulli's is Cramer's suggestion that the pleasure afforded by wealth may be taken to vary as the square root of its amount'. In Note IX Marshall goes one step further, and observes that a sufficient condition that 'fair gambling is an economic blunder' is that $u''(x) < 0$. This is indeed a result which has been overlooked and rediscovered many times, right up to our days.

10. Gradually Bernoulli's theory of choice under uncertainty became known within the Austrian School, and to some extent accepted. The process was slow, and I cannot even try to follow it in detail. Bernoulli's *Specimen theoriae novae* was translated into German by A. Pringsheim in 1896, and published with an introduction by L. Fick in a series with the general title *Die Grundlage der modernen Wertlehre.* This should indicate that at least mathematicians in Germany could see a clear connection between Bernoulli's theory and the Austrian theory of marginal utility. Emanuel Czuber, who was Professor of Statistics at the Technische Hochschule in Vienna, stated flatly in 1902 that the Bernoulli Principle was the 'foundation of the modern theory of value, created by Menger, Jevons and Walras' (Czuber (1902)).

In 1934 the younger Menger, in his article on Uncertainty (Menger (1934)), took it for granted that the Bernoulli Principle is the natural starting-point for an analysis of the Uncertainty element in economics. He seems, however, to have had some doubts about the general validity of the principle, and tried to formulate alternative rules for decisions under uncertainty.

Economists realized what a powerful tool the Bernoulli Principle really is only after the axiomatic treatment given by von Neumann and Morgenstern (1947). These two showed that a few simple axioms of consistency implied that the utility of the lottery $F(x)$ must be of the form

$$U(F) = \int u(x)\, dF(x)$$

Here the function $u(x)$ represents the subjective evaluation which formed the basis of the Austrian School. This interpretation follows naturally if the Principle is applied to a degenerate lottery, that is to a lottery with only one prize, which is 'gained' with certainty.

The result of von Neumann and Morgenstern led to long discussions, and a number of equivalent formulations of the axioms have been given. I shall not go into this question here, since the relevant literature cannot be said to belong to the Austrian School. The result also seems to have opened the door to systematic study of the Uncertainty element. The sheer volume of the literature indicates that Uncertainty is one of the most fashionable topics in today's economic theory.

In retrospect I cannot help expressing a mild surprise that a pure mathematical proof should have had such an impact on economic theory. The Bernoulli Principle was available when the elder Menger wrote his notes about the Uncertainty element. Marshall indicated how the Principle could be used in economic analysis, Czuber spelt out the details for his Viennese colleagues, and the younger Menger gave more details and a number of illustrations. Still it was only when von Neumann and Morgenstern had proved the consistency of the Principle, that economists began to exploit its possibilities.

Usually economists seem to have little concern about the finer points of consistency in their models. I believe that few economists would have any qualms about working with demand functions that do not satisfy the integrability conditions, if this for some reasons should be convenient, although such functions imply inconsistent preferences. Econometricians regularly work with demand functions that are not even homogeneous in prices, and thus obviously valid only as approximations.

Considering the influence of Marshall, it is indeed odd that no economist followed the hint given, and added his own 'guess' about the shape of the utility function to the guesses of Bernoulli and Cramer. To work out the implications of a new guess would have been of interest not only as a classroom exercise, or as a thesis subject. Nobody did this, and it appears that it was the momentum of game theory that pulled the Bernoulli Principle from the fringes to the centre of economic theory.

11. I have several times mentioned the idea of a symmetry between Time and Uncertainty, which has existed in the Austrian School from the very beginning. I should like to end by pointing out that we have now reached the stage where it seems natural to seek a method for simultaneous treatment of the two elements.

The Austrian School found a way to assign utilities to goods distributed over time. It also struggled with the problem of assigning utilities to goods distributed over different 'states of the world', that is to lotteries described by simple probability distributions. This struggle eventually led to a satisfactory theory for the Uncertainty element in economics. The task ahead is obviously to combine the two elements and find ways of assigning utilities to stochastic time series. I think this is the message which today's students of Time and Uncertainty in economics can find in Menger's *Grundsätze*.

References for Section 4

Böhm-Bawerk von E. (1881): *Rechte und Verhältnisse vom Standpunkte der Volkswirtschaftlichen Güterlehre* (Innsbruck, 1881), reprinted in *Gesammelte Schriften* (Vienna, 1924).[1]

Czuber E. (1902): *Wahrscheinlichkeitsrechnung*, Vienna.

Hayek FA. (1941): *The Pure Theory of Capital*, London, chapter 8.

Lindenbaum J. (1931): "Ein Vierteljahrhundert der Bedarfstheorie der Versicherung", *Zeitschrift für Nationalökonomie 2*, 75–99.

Menger K. (1934): "Das Unsicherheitsmoment in der Wertlehre", *Zeitschrift für Nationalökonomie 5*, 459–85.

Morgenstern O. (1934): "Das Zeitmoment in der Wertlehre", *Zeitschrift für Nationalökonomie 5*, 433–58.

Morgenstern O. (1935): *Wirtschaftsprognose* (Vienna, 1928), and "Vollkommene Voraussicht und wirtschaftliches Gleichgewicht", *Zeitschrift für Nationalökonomie 6*, 337–357.

Neumann von J. (1928): "Zur Theorie der Gesellschaftsspiele" *Mathematische Annalen 295–320.*

Neumann von J., and Morgenstern O. (1947): *Theory of Games and Economic Behavior*, 2nd edn, Princeton.

Oxford University Press. (1951): "Quotation from J.A. Schumpeter", *Ten Great Economists*, p. 176.

Streissler E.W. (1966): "Structural Economic Thought — On the Significance of the Austrian School Today", *Zeitschrift für Nationalökonomie 29*, 237–66.

Tauber A. (1909): "Über Risiko und Sicherheitszuschlag", *Transactions of the Sixth International Congress of Actuaries I*, 781–842, Vienna.

Tintner G. (1941): "The Theory of Choice under Subjective Risk and Uncertainty", *Econometrica 9*, 298–304.

Walras L. (1902): *Éléments d 'économie politique pure* (Édition définitive, Lausanne), Leçon 23.

[1] I am grateful to Professor Erich Streissler, who drew my attention to this book, which has been unduly neglected.

CHAPTER 2

INSURANCE AND UTILITY THEORY

1. The Ordering of Insurance Risks

1.1 When we say that a person is exposed to a risk, we mean that he may suffer a loss which is uncertain, and must be represented by a random variable X. This variable can be described by a probability distribution

$$F(x) = \Pr\{X \leq x\}$$

If the person covers a part or the whole of the risk by insurance, he pays something — a premium P — to change the probability distribution which represents the risk. If he is not forced to buy insurance, he will do so only if he finds that the transaction brings him into a risk situation which he prefers to the original one. This observation implies that in order to make rational decisions about insurance, the person must have a preference ordering over the set of attainable probability distributions, i.e. he must know what he wants. This means that for any two distributions F_1 and F_2 he can decide whether one is preferred to the other, or if the two are equivalent. We shall write $F_1 \succ F_2$ when F_1 is preferred to F_2, and $F_1 \sim F_2$ when they are equivalent.

1.2 It is of course not trivial to assume that a buyer of insurance has a complete preference ordering over the set of all probability distributions. In the present context it is in addition necessary to assume that the ordering is "consistent" when applied probability distributions. Loosely the consistency assumption can be formulated as follows.

For any two distributions such that $F_1(x) \prec F_2(x)$, *and any scalar* $0 < \alpha < 1$ *it follows that*

$$F_1(x) \prec \alpha F_1(x) + (1-\alpha)F_2(x) \prec F_2(x)$$

This assumption makes it possible to describe the ordering in a simple way, known as *the expected utility theorem*, which says:

Under the consistency assumption, and assumptions of completeness and continuity

(i) *There exists a function $u(x)$ such that $F_1(x) \prec F_2(x)$ implies $\int u(x)\, dF_1(x) < \int u(x)\, dF_2(x)$.*

(ii) *The function $u(x)$ is unique up to a positive affine transformation, i.e. the functions $u(x)$ and $v(x) = Au(x) + B$, where $A > 0$, represent the same preference ordering.*

Von Neumann and Morgenstern (1947) gave a rigorous axiomatic proof of the theorem. Since then a number of authors have given different formulations of the axioms, and discussed the application of the result in decision making under uncertainty. It is not possible here to review this voluminous literature. Some early references are Herstein and Milnor (1953), Savage (1954), Luce and Raiffa (1957) and Borch (1968).

This axiomatics is not of particular interest in the present context. The Bernoulli principle was applied to insurance — although hesitantly — before there was any rigorous proof that it was the only decision rule that satisfied a set of consistency axioms.

1.3 The function $u(x)$ gives a very convenient description of a preference ordering over a set of probability distributions, and this provides the key which opens the door to mathematical analysis of insurance — and more generally to the economics of uncertainty.

The function $u(x)$ must be interpreted as the utility of the amount of money x. It is natural to assume that more money is preferred to less, i.e. that $u'(x) > 0$. In most applications it is also natural to assume that the utility function is concave, i.e. $u''(x) < 0$. The following examples illustrate how the expected utility theorem is used to analyze insurance problems.

Consider a person with preferences which can be represented by the utility function $u(x)$, and assume that his initial wealth is W. Assume further that he is exposed to a risk which can cause a loss, a random variable with the density $f(x)$. The expected utility associated with this situation is

$$\int_0^\infty u(W - x) f(x)\, dx$$

If the person can be completely relieved of the risk by paying an insurance premium P, his utility becomes $u(W - P)$. As the person chooses the risk situation with the highest expected utility, he will buy insurance only if

$$u(W-P) \geq \int_0^\infty u(W-x)f(x)\,dx \tag{1}$$

There is clearly an upper limit to the premium, say $\bar{P}$, at which the insurance contract is acceptable. For $P = \bar{P}$ the equality sign will hold in (1). From Jensen's inequality it follows that, if $u''(x) < 0$

$$E\{u(x)\} < u(E\{x\})$$

or

$$\int_0^\infty u(W-x)\,f(x)\,dx < u\big(W - E\{x\}\big)$$

Hence the equality sign will hold for some $\bar{P} > E\{x\}$, i.e. the buyer is willing to pay more than the expected loss to have the risk covered by insurance.

Consider now an insurer, the seller of the insurance contract, let his utility function be $u_1(\cdot)$ and his initial wealth W_1, and assume that he is not exposed to any risk. The insurer will agree to cover the risk against a premium P only if

$$u_1(W_1) \leq \int_0^\infty u_1(W_1 + P - x)f(x)\,dx \tag{2}$$

If there are values of P which satisfy both (1) and (2), the buyer and the seller can make an insurance contract which will increase the expected utility of both.

This example was discussed by Bernoulli, who explained the existence of insurance by assuming that the insurer was richer than the buyer.

1.4 To arrive at more interesting problems, assume that the person can pay a premium qP, and receive a compensation qx, if the loss amounts to x. This arrangement will give the person an expected utility:

$$U(q) = \int_0^\infty u(W - x - qP + qx)\,f(x)\,dx$$

The decision problem of the person is to find the value of q which maximizes his expected utility. The first order condition for a maximum is

$$U'(q) = \int_0^\infty (x-P)u'(w - x - qP + qx)\,f(x)\,dx = 0 \tag{3}$$

For full insurance, i.e. for $q = 1$ one finds

$$U'(1) = \int_0^\infty (x - P)u'(W - P)\, f(x)\, dx = u'(W - P)\, (E\{x\} - P)$$

If $E\{x\} < P$, $U'(1)$ will be negative, and hence it appear that it will never be optimal to buy full insurance. This result is usually accredited to Mossin (1968).

The second order condition is always satisfied, as

$$U''(q) = \int_0^\infty (x - P)^2 u''(W - x - qp + qx) f(x)\, dx < 0$$

provided that $u''(x) < 0$. Hence the solution of (3) gives a maximum.

Mossin's result depends on special assumptions about the premium formula. If the premium is computed as $P = qE\{x\} + c$, where c is a fixed amount which the insurer adds to expected claims, to cover his expenses, the first order condition takes the form

$$U'(q) = \int_0^\infty (x - E\{x\})\, u'\, (W - x - qE\{x\} - c + qx)\, f(x)\, dx = 0\,.$$

This condition is clearly satisfied for $q = 1$, so that full insurance becomes optimal. If c is too high, the only alternative of the prospective buyer is to go without insurance altogether. This seems to be in accordance with some observed behaviour. We would indeed be surprised if a traveller deliberately insured his baggage for less than its full value, but we would understand him if he found that insurance cost too much.

There is a discontinuity at $q = 0$ in this model. The prospective buyer will take full insurance only if he gains something by it, i.e. if

$$\int_0^\infty u(W - x) f(x)\, dx \leq u\big(W - E\{x\} - c\big)\,.$$

If c is too large the person will clearly prefer to go without insurance altogether, otherwise he will take full insurance. The fractional cover in Mossin's model will never be optimal if the premium is calculated by the formula $P = E\{x\} + c$.

1.5 In the example above the buyer had a very limited choice of insurance contracts. A general insurance contract will specify the amount of compensation $y(x)$ which the insured will receive if the loss is equal to x. Write $P\{y\}$ for the premium he pays for this contract, where $P\{y\}$ is some functional of the arbitrary function: $y(x)$. The problem of the buyer is then

$$\max_{y(x)\in Y} \int_0^\infty u\big(W - x - P\{y\} + y(x)\big) f(x)\,dx \tag{4}$$

where Y is some set of admissible functions.

This model was first studied by Arrow (1963), under the assumptions that

$$P\{y\} = (1+\lambda)E\{y(x)\} \quad \text{with} \quad \lambda > 0$$
$$0 \le y(x) \le x$$

The problem is essentially one in calculus of variation, and it is easy to show that the solution is an insurance contract of the form:

$$y(x) = x - D \quad \text{for} \quad x > D$$
$$y(x) = 0 \quad \text{for} \quad x \le D$$

Under this contract the insured himself will pay losses under the deductible D, and the insurer will pay any excess above the deductible.

As an example assume that the premium for an insurance contract with a deductible D is $P(D)$. If the buyer believes that the optimal form of insurance is full cover above a deductible, he will seek the value of D which maximizes:

$$U(D) = \int_0^D u\big(W - P(D) - x\big) f(x)\,dx + u\big(W - P(D) - D\big)\int_D^\infty f(x)\,dx$$

The first order condition for a maximum reduces to

$$U'(D) = -P'(D)\int_0^D u'(W - P - x)\, f(x)\,dx$$
$$- \big(1 + P'(D)\big)u'(W - P - D)\int_D^\infty f(x)\,dx = 0$$

an equation which can be solved when $P(D)$ is given. Expected claim payment under this insurance contract is

$$E\big\{\max(0, x - D)\big\} = \int_D^\infty (x - D) f(x)\,dx$$

If as in 1.4 the premium is equal to expected claim payments plus a flat fee c,

$$P'(D) = -\int_D^\infty f(x)\,dx$$

the first order condition reduces to

$$\int_0^D u'(W-P-x)f(x)\,dx = \left(1 - \int_D^\infty f(x)\,dx\right) u'(W-P-D)$$

which is satisfied for $D = 0$. Hence we again find that the optimal choice is either full cover, or no insurance at all, depending on the size of the charge c.

1.6 The two examples discussed in the preceding paragraphs seem to have led many authors to believe that it is never optimal to buy full insurance. The papers on optimal deductibles are too numerous to list, and most of them depend on *ad hoc* assumptions about how premiums are calculated. It is however tempting to mention one paper by Drèze (1981) since it combines advanced theory with a down-to-earth practical application. In Belgium fire insurance apparently has to be written on the assessed replacement value of a home, without any deductible. To avoid buying full cover Drèze "took a deductible" indirectly by insuring his furniture below replacement cost. He also remarks that after writing the note cited, he revised downward the insurance cover on the furniture.

There is no point in discussing whether he was right or not, but it may be useful to recall the premium formula of Adam Smith from Chapter 1. If the sum insured is small, the risk premium can be ignored, and one can reasonably assume that insurers will quote a premium equal to expected claims plus a fixed amount to cover expenses. When the sums insured are important the risk premium cannot be ignored, but as will be shown in the next section, it is not likely that it will be proportional to expected claim payments.

There is of course an extensive actuarial literature on insurance premiums, most of which is covered in the recent book by Goovaerts et. al. (1984) and in the references given in the book. There is however little economic reasoning in this literature, and it is not very helpful when we seek to determine the premium $P\{y\}$ necessary to solve problem (4).

2. The Development of Reinsurance

2.1 When an insurer is invited to cover a large risk, he may decide that he cannot, or does not want to accept the whole risk. He may then offer to cover a fraction of the risk, against the corresponding fraction of the premium. This leaves the buyer to seek other insurers in the market who are willing to accept the rest of the risk. From the 1680's he knew that he could find these other insurers in the coffee house of Edward Lloyd in London.

Lloyd's of London does still operate in this way. To buy insurance at Lloyd's one has to contact a broker who is accredited to Lloyd's. The broker takes a "slip", which contains all relevant information about the risk, to an underwriter who specializes in risks of this type. The underwriter will set a rate and accept to cover a certain fraction of the risk. The broker will then contact other underwriters until the slip is filled. Usually these underwriters will follow the rate set by the "leading underwriter".

2.2 The procedure described above may seem cumbersome, and it can be costly. To simplify matters most major insurance companies have built up a set of reinsurance treaties, so that larger risks are almost automatically reinsured in part with other insurers. Whether an insurance contract is reinsured or not is of no concern to the buyer of the contract, and will usually be unknown to him. The seller of the contract, the "prime insurer" is alone responsible for the settlement of any claims that the buyer makes under the contract. Under his reinsurance treaties the prime insurer (or the direct insurer) will however claim reimbursement from his reinsurers. Reinsurance can be said to be the insurance bought by insurers, and is also called "indirect" insurance.

Reinsurance treaties are often made on a reciprocal basis, between companies engaged in the selling of direct insurance. The effect of such treaties is to spread the risk, and this is obviously advantageous for risk averse insurers.

2.3 When a reinsurer is asked to cover a part of a risk, he will naturally require full information about the nature of the risk. In a reciprocal reinsurance treaty both parties are also direct insurers, and may be competing against each other in the market for direct insurance. In a situation of this kind insurers may be reluctant to give a competitor full information about the risks they have covered. This reluctance is the historical reason for the

Table 2.1: The 5 largest professional reinsurers in 1983.

Company	Country	Premiums Million dollars
Munich Reinsurers	W. Germany	3239
Swiss Reinsurers	Switzerland	2701
General Reinsurers	U.S.A.	1416
Gerling Group	W. Germany	648
Mercantile & General	Great Britain	632

Source: *Sigma*, October 1985.

emergence, about the turn of the century of the "professional" reinsurers, i.e. of insurance companies which are engaged exclusively in reinsurance.

Reinsurance and professional reinsurance companies play a particularly important role in Europe. The total amount of reinsurance premiums received by insurers in Western Europe is about 25 per cent of direct insurance premiums in the region. The corresponding percentage is 6 for the U.S. A substantial part of the premiums received by European reinsurers has its origin in direct insurance written overseas, so the figures do not necessarily mean that European insurance companies reinsure more than their American counterparts.

Table 2.1 gives the premium receipts in 1983 for the five largest professional reinsurers in the world. The amounts are converted into dollars at the exchange rates at the end of 1983.

2.4 Reinsurance treaties can be proportional, i.e. each reinsurer pays a fixed proportion of every claim. This means that reinsurers participate even in small claims which the direct insurer could easily pay himself, and could lead to much unnecessary paper work. Usually a treaty will therefore be of the "excess of loss" form — often in several layers. The following example may be typical of a two-layer reinsurance treaty.

Let x be the claim against the direct insurer under the contract:

If $x \leq D$, the whole claim is paid by the direct insurer.

If $D < x \leq M$, the amount D is paid by the direct insurer, and the excess $x - D$ is paid under the first layer of the reinsurance treaty.

If $M < x$, the direct insurer pays D, the amount $M - D$ is paid under the first layer, and $x - M$ under the second layer.

Let $f(x)$ be the probability density of claims.

The expected claim payments of the three parties to this reinsurance treaty are then:

(i) The direct insurer:

$$E_0 = \int_0^D x\, f(x)\, dx + D \int_D^\infty f(x)\, dx \tag{1}$$

(ii) The reinsurer of the first layer:

$$E_1 = \int_D^M (x - D) f(x)\, dx + (M - D) \int_M^\infty f(x)\, dx \tag{2}$$

(iii) The reinsurer of the second layer:

$$E_2 = \int_M^\infty (x - M) f(x)\, dx \tag{3}$$

It is easy to verify that

$$E_0 + E_1 + E_2 = E\{x\} = \int_0^\infty x f(x)\, dx$$

2.5 In Chapter 1 it was shown that Adam Smith's observations implied that the premium for an insurance contract can be decomposed into three elements:

$$P = E\{x\} + A + R \tag{4}$$

This premium must be divided between the three parties to the reinsurance treaty.

The first term in (8) represents the expected claim payments under the insurance contract, and the division is given by formulae (5)–(7). To apply these formulae presents no problems, if all parties agree on the shape of the probability density $f(x)$, but it may at first sight seem unrealistic to assume that such an agreement exists. The direct insurer must make all relevant information about the risk available to his reinsurers, and these may supply him with information about similar risks. Intuitively it seems reasonable to assume that this exchange of information will lead to a consensus about the shape of the probability density. In this case intuition is correct. It has been proved by several authors, i.a. by Blackwell and Dubins (1962) and by Aumann (1976) that under reasonable conditions a complete exchange of information will lead to a merging of opinions. If two parties "agree to disagree", it may be because it is too expensive to exchange and process all the information required to reach an agreement. It may be useful to stress that agreement does not mean that the parties agree on the "true distribution", a term which in any case has a doubtful meaning.

2.6 The second term in (8), A represents the administrative expenses. Most of these are naturally incurred by the direct insurer. He has negotiated with the buyer, and has drawn up an acceptable contract. He also bears the cost of verifying and settling claims, and it may seem reasonable that he keeps all or a substantial part of A.

Reinsurers like to stress that their transactions are carried out under conditions of "utmost good faith" — *uberrima fides*. This means that the reinsurers usually accept, without question, the direct insurer's estimate of the risk and his settlement of claims. In such cases the reinsurers' administrative expenses will be negligible, but it is still possible that a reinsurer — in spite of his strong faith — may find it necessary to incur some expenses in order to check the information supplied by the direct insurer, and his procedures for settlement of claims. Such checking costs must be seen as expenses necessary to conclude the reinsurance treaty. The direct insurer must estimate these expenses, and add them to his own administrative expenses. To the buyer of the insurance contract this additional charge will usually be indistinguishable from a risk premium.

2.7 The last term in (8), R is the expected reward to the risk-bearer, or the "risk premium". Evidently the top layer of the treaty is the most risky one. For large M expected claim payments given by (7) may be just a few dollars, but it is still possible that this layer can oblige the reinsurer to pay millions. It is reasonable to assume that a reinsurer will require a substantial premium in order to accept to cover this part of the risk.

In practice it is not possible for a reinsurer to distinguish between a risk premium and a payment of a part of the administrative expenses of the direct insurer. In the negotiations over a reinsurance treaty the two are discussed together. Usually the whole premium P for the direct insurance is taken as the starting point, and is divided between the parties to the treaties according to formulae similar to (5)–(7). The reinsurers pay the direct insurer a percentage of P as commission, and this must cover his administrative expenses, but also leave the reinsurers acceptable risk premiums.

It may be useful to illustrate these points by a numerical example. In (5)–(7) assume that $f(x) = e^{-x}$, and take $D = 2$ and $M = 5$. The expectation and variance of payments under the three layers of the treaty are:

$$E_0 = 0.865 \qquad V_0 = 0.441$$

$$E_1 = 0.128 \qquad V_1 = 0.213$$

$$E_2 = 0.007 \qquad V_2 = 0.013$$

It is not likely that the reinsurer holding the top layer of the treaty will accept that the risk premium should be proportional to expected claim payment — some times called the "net premium". The variance is widely used as a measure of risk, and a risk premium, often referred to as a "loading" of the net premium, proportional to the variance is frequently applied in insurance. This may be acceptable, even if the claim density is a skew as in the example. The holder of the last layer faces unlimited liability, but there is a probability of 0.993 that there shall be no claim, so that the premium received will be pure profit.

2.8 It is convenient to take reinsurance as the starting point for a general study of insurance and insurance premiums. A reinsurance contract brings professional insurers together, and forces them to reach an agreement on how to divide the premium and possible claim payments for a direct insurance contract. This must lead to some kind of consensus, and agreement on some general principles as to how risks shall be rated. A direct insurer who covers a large risk, must have some idea of the conditions under which he can reinsure parts of the risk, and this knowledge will influence the premium he quotes to the insurance buyer.

3. The Reinsurance Market

3.1 The starting point of this section is the classical model of a market of pure exchange, as generalized by Arrow (1953) to include uncertainty. Arrow interpreted his model as a stock market, and he determined the prices of the different securities when the market was in equilibrium. When the model is interpreted as a reinsurance market, an approach slightly different from his is natural.

The given elements in the model are:

(i) A set of n insurance companies.

(ii) The risk attitude of company r, represented by the Bernoulli utility function $u_r(\cdot)$, with the properties $u_r' > 0$ and $u_r'' < 0$.

(iii) The initial portfolio of company r, represented by the stochastic variable x_r, $r = 1, 2, \ldots, n$.

In the market the n companies can exchange parts of their initial portfolios among themselves. Through such exchanges company r obtains a final portfolio, represented by the stochastic variable y_r. $r = 1, 2, \ldots, n$.

Exchanges with outsiders is not possible, so the following condition must hold

$$\sum_{r=1}^{n} y_r = \sum_{r=1}^{n} x_n = x \tag{1}$$

where x is the sum of the stochastic variables representing the given initial portfolios.

If there are no restrictions on the kind of exchanges the companies can make, any n-tuple $y_1, \ldots, y_n$ which satisfies (9) will be a possible or "feasible" set of final portfolios.

3.2 Assume now that the companies engage in exchanges in order to increase the expected utility of their portfolios. This leads to problems which are difficult to handle unless we assume homogeneous beliefs, i.e. assume that all companies hold the same opinion on the joint probability density $f(x_1, \ldots, x_n)$ and hence also on the density $f(x)$. The assumption does not appear unreasonable, since as mentioned in the preceding section, reinsurance transactions are supposed to take place under conditions of *uberrima fides.*

If the companies behave rationally in any sense of the word, one must assume that they will end up with a set of Pareto optimal final portfolios. A set of final portfolios is Pareto optimal if there exists no other feasible portfolio which can increase the expected utility of any company, without reducing it for some other companies. Let $k_1, \ldots, k_n$ be arbitrary positive constants. It is then easy to see that an n-tuple $y_1, \ldots, y_n$ which maximizes the expression

$$\sum_{r=1}^{n} k_r E\{u_r(y_r)\}$$

subject to

$$\sum_{r=1}^{n} y_r = x \tag{2}$$

will represent a Pareto optimal set of final portfolios. If the stochastic variable x can take only a finite number of values, the maximizing problem can be solved by the classical method of Lagrange, i.e. for each value of x one solves the problem

$$\max \left[k_r \sum_{r=1}^{n} u_r(y_r) + \lambda\left(x - \sum_{r=1}^{n} y_r \right)\right]$$

The solution is given by (10) and the condition $k_r u_r'(y_r) = \lambda$, which will be written

$$k_r u_r'(y_r) = u'(x) \qquad r = 1, 2, \ldots, n \tag{3}$$

The conditions (10) and (11) determine the Pareto optimal final portfolios as n functions $y_1(x)$, ..., $y_n(x)$ of x. These functions will contain the arbitrary constants k_1, ..., k_n as parameters. Intuitively this means that the real problem of the n companies is to reach an *ex ante* agreement as to how total payoff from their portfolios shall be divided. The right hand side of (11), $u'(x)$ can be interpreted as aggregate marginal utility of the market as a whole, and it depends also on the arbitrary parameters.

The generalization of this result to continuous stochastic variables is not trivial, but straight forward. The result has been proved explicitly by Borch (1962), but is really contained in earlier work by Arrow (1953). More rigorous proofs have been given by others, i.a. Du Mouchel (1968).

3.3 Differentiation of (11) gives

$$k_r u_r''(y_r) y_r'(x) = u''(x)$$

If this equation is divided by (11), one obtains:

$$\frac{u_r''\big(y_r(x)\big) y_r'(x)}{u_r'\big(y_r(x)\big)} = \frac{u''(x)}{u'(x)} \qquad r = 1, 2, \ldots, n$$

The Pareto optimal portfolios can be found as the solution of these differential equations, with arbitrary constants of integration.

In economics "risk aversion" is usually defined as $R(x) = -u''(x)/u'(x)$. With this notation the equation above can be written as

$$R_r(y_r)y'_r(x) = R(x)$$

or

$$\frac{y'_r(x)}{R(x)} = \frac{1}{R_r(y_r)} \tag{4}$$

As $\sum y_r(x) = x$, it follows that $\sum y'_r(x) = 1$. Summing (12) over all r then gives

$$\frac{1}{R(x)} = \sum_{r=1}^{n} \frac{1}{R_r(y_r)}$$

$T(x) = 1/R(x)$ is some times called "risk tolerance". The equation above says that with any Pareto optimal exchange arrangement, the risk tolerance of the market as a whole is equal to the sum of the risk tolerances of the participants. As an illustration assume that company s is risk neutral, i.e. $u''_s(x) = 0$, so that its risk tolerance becomes infinite. Then the risk tolerance of the market will also be infinite, and the Pareto optimal arrangement is obviously that all risk should be carried by the risk neutral company.

3.4 The expected utility company r obtains from its initial portfolio is

$$E\{u_r(x_r)\} = \int u_r(x)f_r(x)\,dx$$

where $f_r(x)$ is the marginal density of x_r, obtained from the joint density $f(x_1, \ldots, x_n)$.

A Pareto optimal exchange arrangement will give the company the expected utility

$$E\{u_r(y_r)\} = \int u_r\big(y_r(x)\big)f(x)\,dx$$

Since the company will not take part in an exchange which reduces its expected utility, we must have:

$$\int u_r(x)\,f_r(x)\,dx \leq \int u_r\,(y_r(x))\,f(x)\,dx \tag{5}$$

The integrals are written without lower and upper limits, since it is convenient to present the argument in terms of portfolios. The portfolio of company r consists of assets R_r, which may be risk free, and liabilities under the insurance contracts. The liabilities are represented by the non-negative stochastic variable z_r, and $x_r = R_r - z_r$. Hence the upper limit in the left-hand integral is R_r, and the lower limit may be infinity.

The conditions (10), (11) and (13) define the set which in game theory is called the set of imputations. The conditions place some restrictions on the admissible values of the parameters $k_1, \ldots, k_n$. The game theoretical approach which seemed the natural one when these models were first studied, suggested that one should seek additional conditions which would place further restrictions on the parameters, and possibly enable us to determine them completely. These conditions must be derived from behavioral assumptions about how the participants bargain or negotiate their way to a set of final portfolios.

3.5 Game theory was created to generalize the behavioral assumptions usually made in neo-classical economic theory. Some of these assumptions are clearly unrealistic, for instance in theory of competitive equilibrium it is assumed that every participant in the market behaves as a "pricetaker". This means that he takes the quoted market prices as given, and just figures out how much he will buy or sell at these prices. As discussion and bargaining over prices can be observed daily this is obviously a heroic assumption. Its justification is usually that there is a very large number of participants in the market, and that none of them acting alone can influence prices. In the following we shall give a brief and oversimplified presentation of the essential elements in the game-theoretical approach.

Assume that the game has n players, and write N for the set of all players. Let S be an arbitrary subset of N.

The *characteristic function* of the game, $v(S)$ is a real-valued function defined for any $S \subset N$. The function $v(S)$ gives the total payoff which the players in S — belonging to the "coalition" S — can obtain by cooperating.

The characteristic function is superadditive, i.e. $v(S \cup T) \geq v(S) + v(T)$, where S and T are disjunct subsets of N. This means that the players cannot lose by cooperation.

3.6 Let z_r be the payoff to player r in the outcome of the game. The relevant behavioral assumptions in terms of game theory are:

$$\sum_{r=1}^{n} z_r = v(N)$$

This represents "collective rationality", and implies the players will co-operate so that they obtain the maximum total payoff. The assumption corresponds to (10) and (11).

$$z_r \geq v(\{r\})$$

This represents "individual rationality", and implies that no player will participate in the game if this should lead to a loss. The assumption corresponds to (13), and the two assumptions define the set of payoff vectors which constitute the "imputations" of the game.

It is natural to assume that corresponding rationality assumptions hold for all coalitions, not just for the one-player coalition, and for the coalition of all players. This suggests the following assumption

$$\sum_{r \in S} z_r \geq v(S) \tag{6}$$

for all $S \subset N$.

The set of payoff vectors which satisfies (14) is called the "Core" of the game, a concept introduced by Gillies (1959). The core appears as a very attractive solution concept for a general game, but it has the unpleasant property of being empty for large classes of games. For a three-person game one can make a transformation of the origin so that $v(\{r\}) = 0$ for $r = 1, 2$, and 3. The core is then defined by the conditions

$$z_1 + z_2 \geq v(\{1,2\})$$
$$z_1 + z_3 \geq v(\{1,3\})$$
$$z_2 + z_3 \geq v(\{2,3\})$$
$$z_1 + z_2 + z_3 = v(\{1,2,3\})$$

It is easy to see that this system has a solution only if

$$2v(\{1,2,3\}) \geq v(\{1,2\}) + v(\{1,3\}) + v(\{2,3\})$$

The fact that the core often does not exist may limit its usefulness in general game theory, but the concept has proved very useful in economic applications of game theory.

The presentation of some elements of game theory assumes side-payments, and inter-person comparability of utility. These assumptions are very strong, but they can be relaxed at the cost of a more cumbersome notation.

3.7 A market of pure exchange can be interpreted as a game. The players enter the game with an initial allocation of goods, exchange these goods in the market, and end up with a final allocation which has a higher utility. One of the original objectives of game theory was to analyze markets with so few participants that the assumptions behind the neo-classical competitive equilibrium appear unreasonable.

Debreu and Scarf (1963) have proved that the core of a market game is non-empty, and that it contains the allocation corresponding to the competitive equilibrium in the market.

They further proved that as the number of players increases to infinity, the core will, under certain assumptions, shrink to the competitive equilibrium. This means that the undesirable neo-classical behavioral assumptions used to determine the competitive equilibrium in an economy may not be necessary. The result can be reached from the assumptions of rational behavior behind game theory, i.e. it is not necessary to assume that players are "price takers." This really offers us two ways to the market equilibrium, the conventional one, and the way via the limit of the core in a market game.

Baton and Lemaire (1981a) have determined the core for a special case of a reinsurance market, essentially with the methods outlined in the beginning of this section. Their result is interesting, and may turn out to be important. It is however argued in the next chapter that the more classical approach to the competitive equilibrium seems more convenient. The number of insurance companies which participate in a particular reinsurance treaty may be relatively small, but the potential number of participants is very large.

3.8 Another solution concept which may be useful in the analysis of reinsurance is the Bargaining Sets introduced by Auman and Maschler (1964). The bargaining set contains the core, if it is not empty, and a number of other allocations, which may occur if the players for some reason fail to form the all-player coalition.

The starting point of the different bargaining sets is a "payoff configuration," which consists of a partition $N_1, N_2, \ldots, N_m$ of the set N of all players, and a payoff vector $(z_1, z_2, \ldots, z_n)$. A payoff configuration is individually rational if

$$\sum_{r \in N_s} z_r = v(N_s) \qquad s = 1, 2, \ldots, m$$

$$z_r \geq v(\{r\})$$

The simplest bargaining set consists of all stable individually rational payoff configurations.

Baton and Lemaire (1981b) have determined the bargaining set for some special cases of a reinsurance market. Their paper seems to be the first to apply the theory of bargaining sets to insurance, and the approach may be promising, for instance if there is some segmentation of the market.

References for Sections 1–3

Arrow K.J. (1963): "Uncertainty and the Welfare Economics of Medical Care," *American Economic Review 53*, 941–73.

Aumann R. and M. Maschler (1964): "The Bargaining Set for Cooperative Games," *Annals of Mathematical Studies 52*, 443–76.

Aumann R. (1976): "Agreeing to Disagree," *Annals of Statistics 4*, 1236–9.

Baton B. and J. Lemaire (1981a): "The Core of a Reinsurance Market," *The ASTIN Bulletin 12*, 57–71.

Baton B. and J. Lemaire (1981b): "The Bargaining Set of a Reinsurance Market," *The ASTIN Bulletin 12*, 101–14.

Blackwell D. and L. Dubins (1962): "Merging of Opinions with Increasing Information," *Annals of Mathematical Statistics 33*, 882–6.

Borch K. (1962): "Equilibrium in a Reinsurance Market," *Econometrica 30*, 424–44.

Borch K. (1968): *The Economics of Uncertainty*, Princeton University Press.

Debreu G. and H. Scarf (1963): "A Limit Theorem on the Core of an Economy," *International Economic Review 4*, 235–46.

Drèze J. (1981): "Inferring Risk Tolerance from Deductibles in Insurance Contracts," *The Geneva Papers on Risk and Insurance 20*, 48–52.

Dumouchel W.H. (1968): "The Pareto Optimality of an n-Company Reinsurance Treaty," *Skandinavisk Aktuartidsskrift*, 165–70.

Gillies D.B. (1959): "Solutions to General Non-Zero-Sum Games," *Annals of Mathematical Studies 40*, 47–85.

Goovaerts M.J, F. de Vylder and J. Haezendonck (1984): *Insurance Premiums*, North-Holland.

Herstein I.N, and J. Milnor (1953): "An Axiomatic Approach to Measurable Utility," *Econometrica 21*, 291–7.

Luce R.D. and H. Raiffa (1957): *Games and Decisions*, Wiley.

Mossin J. (1968): "Aspects of Rational Insurance Purchasing," *Journal of Political Economy 76*, 553–68.

Neumann J. von and O. Morgenstern (1947): *Theory of Games and Economic Behavior*, 2nd Edition, Princeton University. Press.

Savage L.J. (1954): *The Foundation of Statistics*, Wiley.

4. Some Elements of a Theory of Reinsurance*

This paper will attempt to show that the so-called mathematical theory of risk is inadequate for proper analysis of the reinsurance companies have to deal with in practice. It will indicate how a more complete and possibly more useful theory can be developed by bringing in some elements of modern decision theory.

The theory of risk, which has been the pride of actuarial mathematics for almost a century, looks very impressive. In developing this theory, actuaries have overcome formidable mathematical problems and they have made important contributions to theoretical statistics. These byproducts are probably of greater value than the theory itself, which has found few applications in practice. Most of the insurance world seems, with some justification, to consider the theory of risk as a harmless hobby cultivated by actuaries in Continental Europe and particularly in the Scandinavian countries. In a review article in a recent number of this *journal*, Houston (1960) concludes that the contemporary theory of risk, in spite of its many attractions, can hardly be considered as "practical".

The purpose of developing a theory of risk was to obtain a scientific basis for determining the correct safety-loading of premiums and the optimum amount of self-retention in life insurance, two eminently practical problems. In this paper, the question of safety-loading will not be discussed. A full analysis of this problem will require some assumptions about the demand for insurance and its price elasticity. This in itself is a very difficult subject which cannot be taken up here without being diverted from the main purpose of this paper.

When an insurance company reinsures a part of its portfolio, it buys security and pays for it. The company will forego a part of its expected profits in order to reduce the possibility of inconvenient losses. The management of the company has to weigh expected profit against possible loss. To reach the right decision in such situations is the main problem in reinsurance, and on this point the theory of risk is of little help.

The present theory of risk

A practical example from a paper by Hultman (1942) will illustrate the problem. Examining the records of the Swedish life insurance company

---

* Reprinted from *The Journal of Insurance*, September 1961, volume 28:3, 35–43, copyright (c) The American Risk and Insurance Association.

Table 1:

Maximum retention on one life	Probability of ruin
2 M	0.000 051
3 M	0.000 21
5 M	0.001 61
10 M	0.011 8
20 M	0.048 5
50 M	0.190
80 M	0.350
∞	0.387

Table 2:

Maximum Retention	Expected Profits	Probability of Ruin
8000	114000	0.000 051
12000	150000	0.000 21
20000	184000	0.001 61
40000	225000	0.011 8
80000	258000	0.048 5
200000	266000	0.190
320000	290000	0.350
∞	300000	0.387

THULE over the years 1929–1931, Hultman found that the *probability of ruin* for the company would be 0.387 if the company had made no arrangements for reinsurance. Usually it is extremely difficult to calculate this probability of ruin, which plays a leading part in the modern, so-called "collective" theory of risk, and Hultman's figure is an approximation, deliberately overestimated to be on the "safe side".

Hultman found that the average amount under risk on the insurance contracts in the company's portfolio was $M =$ Swedish Kronor 4061. Hultman investigated what the probability of ruin would be under various reinsurance arrangements. Some of his results are given in Table 1.

Hultman and most other writers on the theory of risk, conclude their papers with a table of this kind. However, in spite of all the elegant mathematics which usually is displayed to calculate the probability of ruin, this is a rather sterile result. It is hard to imagine how a board of directors will use such a table when deciding what should be the maximum retention of their company. It is only in Finland that results of this kind seem to have found any important applications in practice. The Finnish law of Insurance Companies of 1952 (§46) obliges the companies to keep an "adjustment reserve" calculated by the methods of the theory of risk.

In practice this means that the Government Inspector can order an insurance company to maintain adjustment reserves which are sufficient to keep the probability of ruin below a certain acceptable figure. So far no hard and fast rules have been laid down as to what ruin probability the Government Inspector will consider permissible for various types of companies. The principal reason appears to be that the probability can only be calculated approximately, and usually one knows little about how close the approximation may be. Another reason is that the practical significance of the probability of ruin is hard to grasp. By definition, the probability of ruin is the probability that the company shall be insolvent at least once, some time in the future, if there are changes neither in premium income nor in the basic probabilities underlying the claims, a very drastic *ceteris paribus* assumption.

In the example used by Hultman, the total amount of risk premium received by the company is Kronor 3 million. He assumes the safety-loading to be 10 per cent, so that the expected profit will be Kronor 300000 if the company retains all risks for its own account. If the company reinsures a part of the larger risks, it is obvious that a part of expected profits will have to be passed on to the reinsurer, and Hultman assumes that the reinsurer requires a safety-loading of 15 per cent. On the basis of these assumptions, Table 2 has been constructed as perhaps having a bearing on the real problem of reinsurance as it appears to a board of directors.

This table illustrates how the management of an insurance company has to weigh expected profits against risks, measured by probability of ruin, and decide on a maximum retention. Decisions of this kind have to be taken by managers in any kind of business, although they will hardly ever appear as clear cut as in the case of an insurance company.

Table 2 brings out the fact that the model considered in the theory of risk is very simple and quite arbitrary. The theory assumes that management considers only two *decisions parameters*, the probability of ruin, and another which usually is left unspecified, although tacitly assumed to be expected profits.

A more general theory

It is easy to generalize the model described in the preceding paragraphs. Any portfolio of insurance contracts will define a probability distribution $F(x)$, where $F(x)$ is the probability that the total profits on the portfolio shall not exceed x. The function $F(x)$ can be determined in two ways:

(i) As in that classical theory of risk, by building up $F(x)$ from the probability distributions defined by the individual contracts in the portfolio. (See Cramér (1930).)

(ii) As in the collective theory of risk, by estimating the probability that a claim shall occur in a unit interval of time, and by determining the probability distribution of the size of the claims will occur. (See Cramér (1955).)

For practical purposes, the latter method is obviously the easiest to apply. The data required can be obtained without difficulty from the records kept by any insurance company.

The two decisions parameters of Table 2 are easily expressed by $F(x)$:

$$\text{Expected profits} = \int_{-\infty}^{+\infty} x \, dF(x)$$

$$\text{Probability of ruin} = \int_{-\infty}^{-S} dF(x)$$

where S is the total assets of the company. If profits are smaller than $-S$, the company will obviously be ruined.[1]

Assume now that a company considers a proposed reinsurance arrangement which will change the probability distribution of its portfolio from $F(x)$ to $G(x)$. It is obvious that the company will accept this arrangement only if in some way $G(x)$ is considered as "better" than $F(x)$. To select the best among a number of possible reinsurance arrangements is therefore the same problem as that of selecting the best in a set of probability distributions. The basic assumption of the theory of risk so far has been that when selecting the best probability distribution, it is sufficient to consider only the two parameters referred to above, and that all other properties of the probability distribution can be ignored. This assumption can, at best, be only a first approximation to a realistic analysis of reinsurance problems.

---

[1] The ruin probability in Hultman's table is defined in a different way. It is however not necessary to discuss the point for the purpose of this paper.

To give some meaning to the term "the best probability distribution", it is necessary to assume that an insurance company has some rule or standard which enables it to rank probability distributions according to their "goodness". In principle it is sufficient to assume that the set of all probability distributions is *completely ordered* with regard to the company's preference. This assumption implies the following:

(i) When confronted with two probability distributions $F(x)$ and $G(x)$, the company is able to decide either that one of the distributions is better than the other, or that the two distributions are equally good.

(ii) If a company considers $F(x)$ as better than $G(x)$, and $G(x)$ as better $H(x)$, it will also consider $F(x)$ as better than $H(x)$.

It seems almost self-evident that these assumptions must hold for any rationally managed insurance company. Now let $U\,(F(x))$ be a function defined for any probability distribution, such that

$$U\big(F(x)\big) < U\big(G(x)\big)$$

if, and only if $G(x)$ is better than $F(x)$. $U\big(F(x)\big)$ will be referred to as the *utility* function of $F(x)$.

Consider now the degenerate probability distribution $\varepsilon(x - R)$ defined by

$$\varepsilon(x - R) = 0 \quad \text{for } x < R$$

$$\varepsilon(x - R) = 1 \quad \text{for } x \geq R$$

The utility of this distribution, $U\big(\epsilon(x-R)\big)$ will then be the utility attached to the certainty of a profit R, and it is convenient to write $U\big(\varepsilon(x - R)\big) = u(R)$.

If in addition to the assumptions made in the preceding paragraph, an assumption of continuity is also made, it follows that $u(R)$ is determined up to a linear transformation, and that

$$U\big(F(x)\big) = \int_{-\infty}^{+\infty} u(x)\, dF(x)$$

This result is usually referred to as the Bernoullian hypothesis. It gives the utility of a probability distribution expressed by the utility of events which are certain, or colloquially it states the utility of a lottery ticket equals the weighed sum of the utilities of the prizes, and that the weights are the probabilities of gaining the various prizes. The assumptions leading to this result can be given in different forms. The most elegant derivation of the result is probably the one given by Herstein and Milnor (1953).

The function $u(x)$ is usually referred to as the *utility of money*. It should be seen as an operator establishing an ordering over the set of all possible probability distributions, unless one is prepared to attach a meaning to statements such as: A profit of 2 million dollars is 10 per cent better than a profit of 1 million dollars.

At this stage it is convenient to make a slight change of notation:

Let $F(x)$ stand for the probability that the amount of *claims paid* under the contracts in the portfolio shall not exceed x. In order to assume responsibility for this portfolio, the company has received a net premium

$$P = \int_0^\infty x\, dF(x)$$

In addition to the funds P, which the company must have in order to be solvent, it is assumed that the company has funds amounting to R. R will be referred to as the company's "free reserves".

The *risk situation* of the company is then completely determined by the following three elements:

(i) Its underwriting responsibility, represented by the function $F(x)$, referred to as the *risk distribution.*

(ii) Its technical reserves P.

(iii) Its free reserves R.

The utility which the company attaches to this situation will be:

$$\int_0^\infty u(R + P - x)\, dF(x)$$

Assume now that the company makes a insurance arrangement such that if a claim amounting to x occurs, the company will itself only pay the amount $y(x)$. The difference $x - y(x)$ will be paid by the reinsurer. It is easy to see that this arrangement will change the utility of the company to

$$\int_0^\infty u\big(R + P - y(x)\big)\, dF(x)$$

$Y(0)$, the amount to be paid if no claim occurs, can obviously be interpreted as the *price* which the company pays for reinsurance coverage. If there exists a reinsurance market where a company can obtain any kind of reinsurance coverage at a uniquely determined price, the company's problem would be to maximize its utility in the same way as consumers do in classical economic theory. However, it is by no means obvious that such a market exists, and this general problem will not be tackled in all its complexity. Instead, the simplest possible case will be analyzed in detail, that of two companies which seek to negotiate an agreement for exchange of risks, to the benefit of both parties. In insurance terminology, this is the case of two companies which negotiate a reciprocal reinsurance treaty. In the "Theory of Games" (Neumann (1944)), the situation is referred to as a "Two-person Co-operative Game".

Now let the risk situation of Company 1 be determined by the elements

$$F_1(x_1)\,,R_1 \text{ and } P_1$$

where

$$P_1 = \int_0^\infty x_1\,dF_1(x_1)$$

Assume further that the utility which the company attaches to an amount x of money is $u_1(x)$

For Company 2 we have in the same way:

$$F_2(x_2)\,,R_2\,,P_2 \text{ and } u_2(x)$$

Assume that x_1 and x_2 are stochastically independent. The purpose of the negotiations between the two companies is to agree on a function $y(x_1, x_2)$. If the claims occurring in the two portfolios amount to x_1 and x_2 respectively, Company 1 will pay the amount $y(x_1, x_2)$, and Company 2 the remainder of the claims, i.e. $x_1 + x_2 - y(x_1, x_2)$.

It is clear that Company 1 will seek agreement on a function $y(x_1, x_2)$ which makes the expression:

$$\int_0^\infty \int_0^\infty u_1\big(R_1 + P_1 - y(x_1\,,x_2)\big)\,dF_1(x_1)\,dF_2(x_2) = U_1(y)$$

as great as possible. On the other hand, Company 2 will seek to maximize the expression:

$$\int_0^\infty \int_0^\infty u_2\big(R_2 + P_2 - x_1 - x_2 + y(x_1, x_2)\big)\,dF_1(x_1)\,dF_2(x_2) = U_2(y)$$

It is evident that the interest of the two companies, to some extent, are opposed, and that they will have to negotiate their way to a compromise.

If the two companies proceed in a rational manner, their first step will be to discard all functions which can be considered as *non-efficient* solutions to their problem. It can be said that a function $\bar{y}(x_1, x_2)$ is non-efficient if there exists another function $y(x_1, x_2)$ which gives both companies a higher utility. If no such function exists, it can be concluded that $\bar{y}(x_1, x_2)$ is an efficient solution to the bargaining problem.

It has been shown in a previous paper (2) that a necessary and sufficient condition that $y(x_1, x_2)$ is an efficient solution, is that it satisfies the condition

$$u_1'\big(R_1 + P_1 - y(x_1\,, x_2)\big) = ku_2'\big(R_2 + P_2 - x_1 - x_2 + y(x_1\,, x_2)\big)$$

where k is a positive constant. This general equation will not be discussed. Instead, the principles will be illustrated by analysis of a special case.

A special case

Let it be assumed that the utility of money to the two companies is given by:

$$u_1(x) = -a_1x^2 + x$$

$$u_2(x) = -a_2x^2 + x$$

Utility functions of this form have been studied in a previous paper (Borch (1960)), and they seem to give satisfactory results.

In this case the condition for an efficient solution becomes:

$$2a_1\big(R_1 + P_1 - y(x_1\,, x_2)\big) - 1 = 2a_2k\big(R_2 + P_2 - x_1 - x_2 + y(x_1\,, x_2)\big) - k$$

which gives:

$$\begin{aligned} y(x_1\,, x_2) &= \frac{2a_1(R_1 + P_1) - 2a_2k(R_2 + P_2) + 2a_2k(x_1 + x_2) + k - 1}{2(a_2 + a_2k)} \\ &= \frac{a_2k}{a_1 + a_2k}(x_1 + x_2) + \frac{a_1}{a_1 + a_2k}P_1 - \frac{a_2k}{a_1 + a_2k}P_2 \\ &\quad + \frac{2a_1R_1 - 2a_2kR_2 + k - 1}{2(a_1 + a_2k)} \end{aligned}$$

To simplify this expression the following symbols are introduced:

$$h = \frac{a_1}{a_1 + a_2 k}, \qquad 1 - h = \frac{a_2 k}{a_1 + a_2 k}$$

$$\begin{aligned} Q &= \frac{2a_1 R_2 1 - 2a_2 k R_2 + k - 1}{2(a_1 + a_2 k)} \\ &= (1-h)\left(\frac{1}{2a_2} - R_2\right) - h\left(\frac{1}{2a_1} - R_1\right) \end{aligned}$$

One can then write:

$$y(x_1, x_2) = (1-h)(x_1 + x_2) + hP_1 - 1(1-h)P_2 + Q$$

It is easy to see that the reciprocal reinsurance treaty defined by this function, is an exchange of quota shares, where the quotas which are ceded add up to unity. Company 1 cedes to Company 2 a quota of $100h$ per cent of its net premium P_1. If claims amounting to x_1 occur in the portfolio of Company 1, a corresponding quota will be paid by Company 2. Company 1 itself will pay only the remainder $(1-h)x_1$. In the same way, Company 2 will cede a quota of $100(1-h)$ per cent to Company 1.

The last term Q, which may be positive or negative, represents a net transfer of free reserves from Company 1 to Company 2.

When the utility function has the special form introduced in the first paragraph of this section, the initial utility of Company 1 is:

$$\begin{aligned} U_1(0) &= \int_0^\infty u_1(R_1 + P_1 - x_1)\, dF_1(x_1) \\ &= \int_0^\infty \left[-a_1(R_1 + P_1 - x_1)^2 + (R_1 - P_1 - x_1)\right] dF_1(x_1) \\ &= -a_1 \int_0^\infty \left[R_1^2 + 2R_1(P_1 - x_1) + (P_1 - x_1)^2\right] dF_1(x_1) \\ &\quad + \int_0^\infty (R_1 + P_1 - x_1)\, dF_1(x_1) \\ &= -a_1 R_1^2 - a_1 \int_0^\infty (P_1 - x_1)^2\, dF_1(x_1) + R_1 \end{aligned}$$

which by some rearrangement can be written:

$$U_1(0) = \frac{1}{4a_1} - a_1\left(\frac{1}{2a_1} - R_1\right)^2 - a_1V_1$$

where

$$V_1 = \int_0^\infty (x - P_1)^2\, dF_1(x)$$

is the variance of the company's risk distribution. It is easy to verify that the reinsurance treaty defined by $y(x_1, x_2)$ will give the company a utility:

$$U_1(y) = \frac{1}{4a_1} - a_1(1-h)^2\left[\left(\frac{1}{2a_1} + \frac{1}{2a_2} - R_1 - R_2\right)^2 + V_1 + V_2\right]$$

For Company 2, the same procedure shows:

$$U_2(0) = \frac{1}{4a_2} - a_2\left(\frac{1}{2a_2} - R_2\right)^2 - a_2V_2$$

and

$$U_2(y) = \frac{1}{4a_2} - a_2h^2\left[\left(\frac{1}{2a_1} + \frac{1}{2a_2} - R_1 - R_2\right)^2 + V_1 + V_2\right]$$

The subject of the negotiations between the companies is reduced to reaching agreement on a value of h. It is evident that Company 1 will try to get agreement on the largest possible value of $h \leq 1$, and that Company 2 will hold out for a value of h as small as possible.

If the companies act rationally, neither of them will accept a treaty which gives a lower utility than the company has in the initial situation, i.e. before any treaty is concluded. Hence we must have

$$U_1(0) \leq U_1(y)$$
$$U_2(0) \leq U_2(y)$$

These inequalities will define an interval for the values of h which are acceptable to both companies.

However, which value of h within the interval, which the companies finally will agree upon cannot be determined without making some assumptions about the manner in which the negotiations are carried out.

Nash (1950) has given an elegant proof that under some general and very acceptable assumptions rational bargainers will agree upon the value of h which maximizes the product

$$\left[U_1(y) - u_1(0)\right]\left[U_2(y) - u_2(0)\right]$$

This solution will not be discussed further. Its meaning will become clear in the following paragraphs.

It may be useful to discuss a simple numerical example to illustrate the results.

$$\text{Let } R_1 = 1\,, R_2 = 3 \quad \text{and} \quad V_1 = 1\,, V_2 = 3$$

Assume that the two companies have the same attitude to risk, and let

$$a_1 = a_2 = 1/8$$

It is evident that Company 2 is considerably better off than Company 1. If the initial utilities are calculated by the formulae given earlier, they are found to be respectively 3/4 and 3/2. To avoid unnecessary fractions, multiply all utilities by 8, (a change of unit measurement) so that the situation can be written:

$$U_1(0) = 6 \quad \text{and} \quad U_2(0) = 12$$

If the companies conclude an efficient reinsurance treaty, the utilities will become:

$$U_1(y) = 16 - 20(1 - h)^2$$

$$U_2(y) = 16 - 20h^2$$

where h must lie in the interval

$$0.29 \leq h \leq 0.49$$

We find further $Q = 1 - 4h$

The Nash solution is the value of h which maximizes the product

$$\left[10 - 20(1 - h)^2\right]\left[4 - 20h^2\right]$$

This value will be determined by a third-degree equation which has only one root between 0 and 1. This root is found to be approximately $h = 3/8$. The corresponding transfer of free reserves is $Q = -0.5$.

Assume now that the two companies have realized that the efficient arrangement is to exchange quota shares which add up to unity. This really

Table 3: Utilities of the two companies by various reinsurance arrangements.

h/Q	-1.0	-0.75	-0.5	-0.25	0	+ 0.25
1/8	8.96	7.90	6.71	5.39	3.96	2.40
	11.94	12.88	13.69	14.40	14.96	15.90
1/4	9.75	8.69	7.50	6.18	*4.75*	3.19
	11.75	12.69	13.50	14.19	*14.75*	15.69
3/8	10.44	9.38	*8.19*	6.87	5.44	3.88
	11.44	12.38	*13.19*	13.88	14.44	15.38
1/2	*11.00*	9.94	8.75	7.43	6.00	4.44
	11.00	11.96	12.75	13.44	14.00	14.94
5/8	11.44	10.38	9.19	7.87	6.44	4.88
	10.44	11.38	12.19	12.88	13.44	14.38
3/4	11.75	10.69	9.50	8.18	6.75	5.19
	9.75	10.69	11.50	12.19	12.75	13.69
7/8	11.94	10.88	9.69	8.37	6.94	5.38
	8.96	9.90	10.71	11.40	11.96	12.90

means that the companies pool their portfolios and divide claims against the pool between themselves, in a fixed proportion, and it is fairly easy to realize that this arrangement will give the best spread of risk. It is not so obvious how Q, the transfer of free reserves should be determined. For this purpose, simply assume that the companies make some arrangement. They can for instance agree that only net premiums should be paid for reinsurance cover, i.e. that $Q = 0$, or they can agree to calculate Q by adding a proportional loading to the net premiums ceded.

Table 3 gives the utilities of the two companies for some selected values of h and Q. The upper figure in each box gives the utility of Company 1 and the lower figure the utility of Company 2. The figures representing efficient solutions are set in italics. The Nash solution, corresponding to $h = 3/8$ and $Q = -0.5$ gives utilities 8.19 and 13.19. It clearly represents a deal which two rational bargainers might settle for.

This table shows a whole range of possible agreements. However, only the agreements corresponding to the figures within the contour will have practical interest, since they alone will give *both* companies a higher utility than they have in the initial situation. The table brings out clearly that some preconceived idea, for instance that only net premiums should be paid to the reinsurer, can lead to non-efficient solutions. The column corresponding to $Q = 0$ is clearly non-efficient, since the columns to its left contain pairs which give both companies higher utility.

It has been assumed that each company has full knowledge of its own risk situation, as well as of the other party's. This is a reasonable assumption. It is not usual in reinsurance negotiations to hide information from the other party. There may be uncertainty about how one should evaluate some of the probabilities which enter into the risk distribution. However, it is still reasonable to assume that, having considered all the available information, the two companies arrive at the same evaluation of these probabilities.

It has also been assumed that both companies know the shape of the utility function which the other party seeks to maximize. This may be a dangerous assumption. There is nothing to prevent a company, during some reinsurance negotiation, from hiding its real motives from the opponent, and this may bring substantial advantages. This can be illustrated by an example.

If the utility function has the form $-ax^2 + x$, it is clear that the smaller a is, the less worried will the company be about risk. In the limiting case $a = 0$, the company will not be concerned with risk at all. Its sole objective will be to maximize expected profits.

Assume now that in reality the two companies' attitude to risk is such that $a_1 = a_2 = 1/8$ as in our example, but that Company 1 is able to give the impression that in its utility function $a_1 = 1/6$. This means essentially that Company 1 pretends to be more worried over risk than it really is, and exacts a higher compensation for the reinsurance cover it gives to Company 2. If the bluff succeeds, and if the two companies, through some rational bargaining procedure, arrive at a Nash solution as a best possible deal, this will be the solution corresponding to $a_1 = 1/6$ and $a_2 = 1/8$. From the general formulae already given, the solution is found to be approximately

$$h = 0.5 \quad \text{and} \quad Q = -0.5$$

Table 3 shows that this solution will give Company 1 a higher utility than $h = 3/8$ and $Q = -0.5$, the solution corresponding to the true situation $a_1 = a_2 = 1/8$. In other words, Company 1 has made a gain at the expense of Company 2, by hiding its real objectives.

This problem does not need to be discussed in more detail. It is obvious that possibilities of deceiving the opponent exist in most bargaining situations in real life, and a realistic theory of reinsurance should take account of such possibilities.

Conclusion

One who studies the theory of risk, inevitably becomes impressed by the brilliant mathematical analysis so may actuaries have produced in order to calculate the probability of ruin. However, one is also a little surprised that they hardly ever take time to explain why and how this probability is relevant to the decisions which are made by the management in an insurance company. This trivial question is pushed aside for the fascination of mathematical display.

A paper by Tauber (1909) at the Sixth International Congress of Actuaries is typical in this respect. Tauber presented his paper in Vienna in 1909 when the Austrian school of economics had its heyday. It was therefore natural that he should begin with some introductory words to the effect that a reinsurance contract is a purchase of security, and that security like all other commodities must have its price. This price must be determined by supply and demand, i.e. by cost and utility. If Tauber had followed up this idea, the "theory of games and economic behaviour" might have begun in Vienna in 1909 and not at Princeton in 1944. However, he dropped the subject, and after his two-page introduction, Tauber presents 60 pages of mathematics which has not bearing on the general problem which he formulated in a surprisingly modern manner.

The mathematical tools which Tauber needed to solve his problems have since been developed outside that insurance world. The purpose of this paper has been to show that these tools can be applied to the problems of reinsurance, and that they may help in gaining a deeper understanding of the mechanism of insurance markets.

References for Section 4

Borch K. (1960): "Reciprocal Reinsurance Treaties seen as a Two-Person Cooperative Game". *Skandinavisk Aktuarietidsskrift.*

Borch K. (1960): "Reciprocal Reinsurance Treaties", *The ASTIN Bulletin I*, 170–191.

Cramér H. (1930): "On the Mathematical Theory of Risk", *Skandia Jubilee, Volume 7–84.*

Cramér H. (1955): "Collective Risk Theory", *Skandia Jubilee Volume ???.*
Herstein I.N. and Milnor J. (1953): "An Axiomatic Approach to Measurable Utility", *Econometrica*, 291–297.
Houston D.B. (1960): "Risk Theory", *The Journal of Insurance, 27*, 77–82.
Hultman K. (1942): "Einige Numerische Untersuchungen auf Grund der kollektiven Risikotheorie", *Skandinavisk Aktuarietidsskrift*, 84–119 and 169–199.
Nash J. (1950): "The Bargaining Problem", *Econometrica*, 155–162.
Neumann J. von and Morgenstern O. (1944): "Theory of Games and Economic Behavior", Princeton.
Tauber A. (1909): " Über Risiko und Sicherheitszuschlag", *Report of the Sixth International Congress of Actuaries*, 781–842.

5. The Safety Loading of Reinsurance Premiums*

1. Introduction

1.1 In the older forms of reinsurance, often referred to as "proportional" reinsurance, there is no real problem involved in determining the correct safety loading of premiums. It seems natural, in fact almost obvious, that reinsurance should take place on "original terms", and that any departure from this procedure would need special justification. The only problem which may be troublesome is to determine the three components of the gross premium, i.e. net premium, safety loading and loading for expenses. The last of these components is calculated to cover costs connected with the direct underwriting, such as agent's commission, and does not, in principle concern the reinsurer.

1.2 In non-proportional reinsurance it is obviously not possible to attach any meaning to "original terms". It is therefore necessary to find some other rule for determining the safety loading. The easiest solution is clearly to make the loading proportional to the net premium. However, this may be inconvenient, particularly for extremely skew forms of reinsurance, such as Stop Loss contracts and various kinds of catastrophe cover. For reinsurance contracts of this kind the net premiums may become practically negligible, so that the safety loading may amount to several thousand per cent if the contract is to be acceptable to a reinsurer.

1.3 A more convenient rule may be to make safety loading proportional to the *standard deviation* of the probability distribution of the claims which may be made under the contract.

---

* Reprinted from *Skandinavisk Aktuarietidskrift*, 1960; 163–184, copyright (c) Almqvist & Wiksell International, Stockholm.

This has been proposed by a number of authors, right through the alphabet from Ammeter (1955) to Wold (1936). The justifications given for this procedure vary a great deal, but they are all rather similar to the arguments which a manufacturer might put forward to justify what he considers a "fair" price for his product. However, the price which the manufacturer actually gets will be determined by what the market is willing to pay and not by considerations of fairness. It therefore seems necessary to investigate the mechanism of the reinsurance market in order to find a general solution to the problem of safety loading.

1.4 In a previous paper (Borch (1960)) we have studied the case of two insurance companies negotiating with the purpose of concluding a reciprocal reinsurance treaty. We found that under certain assumptions there existed a unique treaty which was optimal in the sense that both companies would consider it the best bargain they could make in the given circumstances. We also found that if the companies had some preconceived idea as to what constitutes a "fair" or "proper" price for reinsurance cover, they might be led to conclude a non-optimal treaty. In the present paper we shall generalize these results to an arbitrary number of companies.

2. A model of the Reinsurance Market

2.1 Consider n insurance companies, each holding a portfolio of insurance contracts. The *risk situation* of company i ($i = 1, 2, \ldots, n$) is defined by the following two elements:

(i) The *risk distribution*, $F_i(x_i)$, which is the probability that the total amount of claims occurring under the contracts in the company's portfolio shall not exceed x_i.

(ii) The *funds*, S_i which the company has available to pay claims.

We will assume that $x_1 \ldots x_i \ldots x_n$ are stochastically independent.

To this risk situation that company attaches a utility $U_i\big(S_i F_i(x)i\big)$. From the axioms of von Neumann and Morgenstern (1944), often referred to as the Bernoullian hypothesis, it follows that

$$U_i\big(S_i\,, F_i(x)\big) = \int_0^\infty u_i(S_i - x_i)\, dF_i(x_i)\,,$$

where $u_i(x)$ is the "utility of money" to company i. In the following it will be assumed that $u(x)$ is a continuous non-decreasing function of x, and that its two first derivatives exist. The assumptions necessary to prove the Bernoullian hypothesis as a theorem are discussed in some detail in a previous paper (Borch (1960)).

2.2 In this initial situation company i is committed to pay an amount x_i if the claims which occur under the contracts in portfolio i amount to x_i. In the reinsurance market the companies can conclude treaties which change their initial commitments. For instance, a reciprocal treaty between company i and company j can be defined by two functions $y_i(x_i, x_j)$ and $y_j(x_i, x_j)$, where $y_i(x_i, x_j)$ is the amount company i has to pay if claims in the two portfolios amount to be paid by company j. Since all claims must be paid, it follows that

$$y_i(x_i\,, x_j) + y_j(x_i\,, x_j) = x_i + x_j$$

2.3 The obvious generalization of these considerations, is to introduce a set of functions:

$$y_i(x_1\,, x_2\,, \dots\,, x_n) \quad i = 1\,, 2\,, \dots\,, n$$

such that $y_i(x_1, x_2, \dots, x_n)$ is the amount company i has to pay if claims in the respective portfolios amount to x_1, x_2, $\dots$, x_n. These functions must clearly satisfy the condition:

$$\sum_{i=1}^{n} y_i(x_1\,, x_2\,, \dots\,, x_n) = \sum_{i=1}^{n} x_i$$

This set of functions will define a unique set of treaties concluded by the n companies in the reinsurance market. These treaties will change the utility of company i from

$$\int_0^\infty u_i(S_i - x_i)\, dF_i(x)$$

to

$$\int_0^\infty \cdots \int_0^\infty u_i\big(S_i - y_i(x_i \dots, x_n)\big)\, dF_1(x_1) \dots\, dF_n(x_n)$$

For simplicity we will write x for the vector $\{x_1 \dots, x_n\}$, so that the utility of the company after concluding the treaties can be written:

$$U_i(y) = \int_R u_i\big(S_i - y_i(x)\big)\, dF(x)\,,$$

where $F(x)$ is the joint probability distribution of $x_1 \ldots x_n$, and R stands for the positive orthant in the n-dimensional x-space. Further we will write y for the vector $\{y_1(x), \ldots, y_n(x)\}$.

2.4 If the companies act rationally, they will not conclude a set of treaties represented by a vector y, if there exists another set of treaties with a corresponding vector $\bar{y}$, such that

$$U_i(y) \leq U_i(\bar{y}) \quad \text{for all } i$$

y will in this case clearly be inferior to $\bar{y}$. If there exists no vector $\bar{y}$ satisfying the above condition, the set of treaties represented by y will be referred to as *Pareto optimal.*

A pareto optimal set of treaties will represent a stable equilibrium situation in the reinsurance market. Additional treaties concluded in this situation cannot increase the utility of any company without decreasing the utility of at least one other company.

2.5 We now assume that $y(x)$ is Pareto optimal, and consider the vector $\bar{y}(x)$ whose elements are given by

$$\bar{y}_i(x) = y_i(x) + \varepsilon_i(x)$$

We find

$$U_i(\bar{y}) - U_i(y) = -\int_R \Big[u_i\big(S_i - y_i(x) - \varepsilon_i(x)\big) - u_i\big(S_i - y_i(x)\big) \Big] \, dF(x)$$

If $\varepsilon_i(x)$ is small in absolute value, this can be written

$$U_i(\bar{y}) - U_i(y) = -\int_R u_i'\left(S_i - y_i(x)\right) \varepsilon_i(x) d\,F(x)$$

As we assumed that $y(x)$ is Pareto optimal, this difference cannot be non-negative for all i.

2.6 It is easy to see that a *sufficient* condition that $y(x)$ is Pareto optimal, is that there exist $n-1$ positive constants $k_2 \ldots k_n$ such that

$$u_i'\big(S_i - y_i(x)\big) = k_i u_i'\big(S_1 - y_1(x)\big)$$

If this condition is fulfilled, we have

$$U_i(\bar{y}) - U_i(y) = -k_i \int_R u_1'\big(S_1 - y_1(x)\big)\varepsilon_i(x)\, dF(x)$$

Since we obviously must have

$$\sum_{i=1}^{n} \bar{y}_i(x) = \sum_{i=1}^{n} y_i(x) = \sum_{i=1}^{n} x_i\,,$$

it follows that:

$$\sum_{i=1}^{n} \varepsilon_i(x) = 0 \quad \text{for all } x$$

If we divide by k_i and sum over all i, we obtain;

$$\sum_{i=1}^{n} \frac{1}{k_i}\big(U_i(\bar{y}) - U_i(y)\big) = -\int_R u_1'\big(S_1 - y_1(x)\big) \sum_{i=1}^{n} \varepsilon_i(x)\, dF(x) = 0\,,$$

where $k_1 = 1$. Since $k_i > 0$ for all i, all terms in the sum on the left can be non-negative only if $U_i(\bar{y}) - U_i(y) = 0$ for all i. This will, however, imply $\varepsilon_i(x) \equiv 0$ for all i. Hence we must have $\bar{y}(x) = y(x)$ which proves our statement.

2.7 To prove that the condition is *necessary*, we shall show that if it is not fulfilled, it will be possible to find a set of functions $\varepsilon_1(x) \ldots \varepsilon_n(x)$ not identically zero so that

$$U_i(\bar{y}) - U_i(y) \geq 0$$

for all i, the inequality being strict for at least one value of i.

Let

$$\varepsilon_1(x) = \begin{cases} a' \text{ over a set } A'\,, \text{ where } u_1'\big(S_1 - y_1(x)\big) > u_2'\big(S_2 - y_2(x)\big)\,, \\ a'' \text{ over a set } A''\,, \text{ where } u_1'\big(S_1 - y_1(x)\big) < u_2'\big(S_2 - y_2(x)\big)\,, \\ 0 \text{ for all points belonging neither to } A' \text{ nor } A''\,, \end{cases}$$

$$\varepsilon_2(x) = -\varepsilon_1(x)\,,$$

$$\varepsilon_1(x) = 0 \quad \text{for } i = 3\,, 4 \ldots n$$

We find:

$$U_1(\bar{y}) - U_1(y) = -\,a' \int_{A'} u_1'(S_1 - y_1(x))\,dF(x)$$

$$-\,a'' \int_{A''} u_1'(S_1 - y_1(x))\,dF(x)$$

and

$$U_2(\bar{y}) - U_2(y) = -\,a' \int_{A'} u_2'(S_2 - y_2(x))\,dF(x)$$

$$-\,a'' \int_{A''} u_2'(S_2 - y_2(x))\,dF(x)$$

It is easily seen that, if a' and a'' are chosen so that

$$\frac{\int_{A''} u_1'(S_1 - y_1(x))\,dF(x)}{\int_{A'} u_1'(S_1 - y_1(x))\,dF(x)} < \frac{a'}{a''} < \frac{\int_{A''} u_2'(S_2 - y_2(x))\,dF(x)}{\int_{A'} u_2'(S_2 - y_2(x))\,dF(x)}\,,$$

both $U_1(\bar{y})-U_1(y)$ and $U_2(\bar{y})-U_2(y)$ will be positive. Since $U_i(\bar{y})-U_i(y) = 0$ for $i = 3, 4 \ldots$ n, $y(x)$ is not Pareto optimal, provided that neither of the two sets A' and A'' are empty. Assume now that A' is empty, i.e. that

$$u_1'(S_1 - y_1(x)) < u_2'(S_2 - y_2(x)) \quad \text{for all } x$$

Since the utility function is determined only up to a linear transformation, any relation between $u_i'(x)$ is multiplied by an arbitrary constant c. However, unless $u_2'(S_2 - y_2(x)) = k_2 u_1'(S_1 - y_1(x))$, it will be possible to find a c, such that

$$cu_1'(S_1 - y_1(x)) < u_2'(S_2 - y_2(x)) \quad \text{for a set } A''$$

and

$$cu_1'(S_1 - y_1(x)) > u_2'(S_2 - y_2(x)) \quad \text{for a non-empty set } A'$$

This completes the proof.

2.8 We have thus found that the functions $y_1(x) \ldots y_n(x)$, which satisfy the conditions:

$$\left.\begin{array}{ll} (1) & u_i'(S_i - y_i(x)) = k_i(S_1 - y_1(x))\,, \\[2ex] (2) & \sum_{i=1}^{n} y_i(x) = \sum_{i=1}^{n} x_i\,, \end{array}\right\} k_i > 0\,, \quad i = 2, 3 \ldots n\,,$$

define a Pareto optimal set of reinsurance treaties.

If we differentiate both equalities with respect to x_j, we obtain

$$\frac{\partial y_i(x)}{\partial x_j} u_i''\big(S_i - y_i(x)\big) = k_i \frac{\partial y_1(x)}{\partial x_j} u_1''\big(S_1 - y_1(x)\big)$$

and

$$\sum_{i=1}^{n} \frac{\partial y_i(x)}{\partial x_j} = 1$$

If we divide the first equation by $u_i''\big(S_i - y_i(x)\big)$ and sum over all i, we obtain;

$$1 = u_i''\big(S_1 - y_1(x)\big) \frac{\partial y_1}{\partial x_j} \sum_{i=1}^{n} \frac{k_i}{u_i''\big(S_i - y_i(x)\big)}$$

It is easy to see that in general we have

$$\frac{\partial y_i(x)}{\partial x_j} = \frac{\dfrac{k_i}{u_i''\big(S_i - y_i(x)\big)}}{\displaystyle\sum_{i=1}^{n} \frac{k_i}{u_i''\big(S_i - y_i(x)\big)}},$$

where $k_1 = 1$. The right-hand side does not depend on j. Hence

$$\sum_{j=1}^{n} \frac{\partial y_i}{\partial x_j} d\,x_j = \sum_{j=1}^{n} \frac{\partial y_i}{\partial x_k} d\,x_j = \frac{\partial y_i}{\partial x_k} d\,z$$

for any value of k. It then follows that the vector function $y_i(x)$ must be a scalar function $y_i(z)$ of one single variable

$$z = \sum_{i=1}^{n} x_i\,,$$

so that we have

$$\frac{d\,y_i(z)}{d\,z} = \frac{\dfrac{k_i}{u_i''\big(S_i - y_i(x)\big)}}{\displaystyle\sum_{i=1}^{n} \frac{k_i}{u_i''\big(S_i - y_i(x)\big)}}$$

2.9 The fact that $y_i(x)$ is a function of z alone means that the only Pareto optimal arrangement is that the companies should cede their entire portfolio to a pool, and then agree on some rule as to how payment of claims against the pool should be divided among the companies. There may be an infinity of such rules, since the positive constants $k_2 \dots k_n$ can be chosen arbitrarily.

If the companies conduct their reinsurance negotiations in a rational manner we will expect them, in some way, to end by concluding a Pareto optimal set of treaties. However, this assumption of rationality is not sufficient to determine which of the Pareto optimal sets the companies will arrive at. To make the problem determinate, i.e. to determine $k_2 \dots k_n$, it is necessary to make some *additional assumptions* about the manner in which the companies negotiate their way to a final of treaties.

We shall not take up this general problem, which really is that of finding a unique solution to an n-person game (Neumann(1944)). The problem is extremely complex, particularly if there is no restriction on how companies can form coalitions to strengthen their bargaining position versus those outside the coalition.

3. Equilibrium Price in a Market

3.1 In para 2.8 we used the notation $y_i(z)$ for the amount which company i had to pay if claims against the pool were z. $y_i(0)$, i.e. payment if there are no claims, can then obviously be interpreted as the company's net outlay of reinsurance premiums.

If there is a market price for reinsurance, i.e. a price which has to be applied in all treaties, $y_i(0)$ will obviously be determined for all i, and this may enable us to determine the constants $k_2 \dots k_n$.

3.2 We shall first illustrate the part played by price in an ordinary commodity market. Assume that x units of a certain good can be sold for a amount of money $p(x)$. If the market is perfectly competitive, and if $p(x)$ is an equilibrium price, the x units must bring in the same amount of money regardless of whether they are sold in several lots, or in one single transaction. Hence if $x = x_1 + x_2$, we must have

$$p(x) = p(x_1 + x_2) = p(x_1) + p(x_2)$$

Apart from the trivial $p(x) = 0$, the only function which satisfies this equation is $p(x) = px$. Hence there exists a unit price which does not depend on the number of units included in any transaction.

3.3 In the reinsurance market the commodity traded is probability distributions. The price concept we need should make it possible to associate a number $P(F(x))$ to any probability distribution $F(x)$, so that $P(F(x))$ is the amount of money an insurance company can obtain by accepting to pay a claim which is a random variable with probability distribution $F(x)$.

As a natural extension of the concepts from commodity markets, we require that

$$P(F(x)) = P(F_1(x_1)) + P(F_2(x_2)),$$

where $F(x)$ is the convolution of the two independent probability distributions $F_1(x_1)$ and $F_2(x_2)$.

There is clearly an infinity of functionals which satisfy this additivity condition. It is, for instance, satisfied by the cumulant generating function

$$\psi(t) = \log \phi(t),$$

where $\phi(t)$ is the characteristic function

$$\phi(t) = \int_0^\infty e^{itx}\, dF(x)$$

It is convenient to work with a complex-valued function, so in the following we will use the corresponding real functions

$$\phi(t) = \int_0^\infty e^{-tx}\, dF(x)$$

and

$$\psi(t) = \log \phi(t),$$

which exist for any non-negative value of t. The cumulants are given by the expansion

$$\psi(t) = \sum_{n=1}^{\infty} (-1)^n \frac{\kappa_n}{n!} t^n$$

3.4 It follows that for any non-negative value of t, $\psi(t)$ can be interpreted as a price which satisfies the condition in the preceding paragraph. The same will hold for any linear combination of the form:

$$c_1\psi(t_1) + c_2\psi(t_2) + \cdots,$$

where c_1, c_2 ... are constants. Similar expressions containing derivatives of $\psi(t)$ of any order will also satisfy the condition.

However, any such expression will be a linear combination of cumulants, so that we can write

$$P\big(F(x)\big) = \sum_{n=1}^{\infty} p_n \kappa_n = \sum_{n=1}^{\infty} b_n \psi^{(n)}(0),$$

where κ_n is the nth cumulant of the distribution $F(x)$. Here we must clearly place some restrictions on the coefficients p_n and b_n to ensure that the series converge. If these restrictions are met, the series will be the most general price concept which satisfies the additivity condition of §3.3. We shall not prove this, but we note that a safety loading proportional to the standard deviation is a price concept which does not satisfy the condition.

We shall require, as a continuity condition that $p_1 = 1$. If $F(x)$ is degenerate, so that all cumulants except the first vanish, we must have

$$F(x) = 0 \quad \text{for } x < \kappa_1$$

and

$$F(x) = 1 \quad \text{for } \kappa \leq x$$

Hence p_1 is the price of one monetary unit, to be claimed with certainty, and it is reasonable to require that this shall be unity.

3.5 In §3.3 we assumed that x_1 and x_2 were stochastically independent. If we drop this assumption and require that the condition

$$P\big(F(x_1 + x_2)\big) = P\big(F_1(x_1)\big) + P\big(F_2(x_2)\big)$$

shall hold also when x_1 and x_2 are dependent, it is obvious that the only price concept which satisfies the condition is

$$P\big(F(x)\big) = \int_0^{\infty} x\, dF(x) = \kappa_1$$

This means that the risk situations are traded against cache payment equal to the expected amount of claims, or in insurance terminology that all reinsurance is done on a net premium basis.

3.6 The price concept we have introduced appears forbiddingly complicated, but it becomes fairly simple for some special distributions.

For the normal distribution

$$N(x) = \frac{1}{\sigma\sqrt{2\pi}} e - \frac{(x-m)^2}{2\sigma^2}$$

we have

$$P\big(N(x)\big) = m + p_2\sigma^2 ,$$

since all cumulants of higher order are zero.

For the Poisson distribution

$$P(x) = \frac{m^x}{x!} e^{-m}$$

we have

$$P\big(P(x)\big) = m \sum_{i=1}^{\infty} p_i = \alpha m$$

since for this distribution, all cumulants are equal to m. This provides some justification for making the loading proportional to the net premium.

We shall not pursue our discussion of the general case. In the following we shall analyze in some detail a very simple special case.

4. Discussion of a Special Case

4.1 From the formula at the end of para 2.8 we see that the expressions for $y_i(z)$ will become particularly simple if all utility functions are polynomials of second degree. We shall therefore study the case where;

$$u_i(x) = -a_i x^2 + x \quad \text{for all } i$$

This utility function gives acceptable results, provided that a_i is positive and sufficiently small. This has been demonstrated in a previous paper (Borch (1960)).

If $a_i < 1/2S_i$, $u_i(x)$ will be increasing over the whole range from $-\infty$ to S_i. This is obviously a reasonable requirement, since it means that "no claim" is considered as the best possible result company i can get from its direct underwriting.

If $a_i \leq 1/2 \sum S_j$ for all i, the regions where there is decreasing utility of money will be completely excluded from consideration. However, this condition may be too strong if the number of companies is great.

It is clear that a_i can be interpreted as a measure of the company's "risk aversion". If $a_i = 0$, the company will be indifferent to risk. Its sole objective will then be to maximize expected profits, ignoring all risk of deviations from the expected value.

4.2 From the formulae in para 2.8 we find

$$y_i(z) = k_i \frac{z + \sum_{j=1}^{n} \dfrac{\frac{1}{2} - a_j S_j}{a_j}}{a_i \sum_{j=1}^{n} \dfrac{k_j}{a_j} - \dfrac{\frac{1}{2} - a_i S_i}{a_i}}$$

Hence the optimum arrangement is that company i shall pay a fixed quota

$$\frac{\dfrac{k_i}{a_i}}{\sum \dfrac{k_j}{a_j}} = q_i$$

of the amount of claims made against the pool. For $z = 0$ we find:

$$y_i(0) = q_i \sum_{j=1}^{n} \left(\frac{1}{2a_j} - S_j \right) - \left(\frac{1}{2a_j} - S_i \right)$$

4.3 The utility of company i in the initial situation is

$$U_i(x_i) = \int_0^\infty \{-a_i(S_i - x_i)^2 + S_i - x_i\}\, dF_i(x_i)$$

or

$$U_i(x_i) = -a_i(S_i - P_i)^2 + S_i - P_i - a_i V_i\,,$$

where

$$P_i = \int_0^\infty x_i \, dF_i(x_i)$$

and

$$V_i = \int_0^\infty (x_i - P_i)^2 \, dF_i(x_i)$$

4.4 We introduce the symbols

$$P = \int_0^\infty z dF(z) = \sum_{i=1}^n P_i$$

and

$$V = \int_0^\infty (z - P)^2 \, dF(z)$$

Since $x_1, x_2 \ldots x_n$ are stochastically independent, we have $V = \sum_{i=1}^n V_i$, and that $F(z)$ is then the convolution of $F_1(x_1) \ldots F_n(x)$.

It is convenient to write $R_i = S_i - P_i$. R_i can be interpreted as the "free reserves" of company i.

The dealings in the reinsurance market will then change the utility of company i from

$$U_i(x_i) = -a_i R_i^2 + R_i - a_i V_i = \frac{1}{4a_i} - a_i \left[\left(\frac{1}{2a_i} - R_i \right) + V_i \right]$$

to

$$U_i(y) = \frac{1}{4a_i} - a_i q_i^2 \left[\left(\sum_{j=1}^n \left(\frac{1}{2a_j} - R_j \right) \right)^2 + \sum_{j=1}^n V_j \right]$$

4.5 If company i acts rationally, it will take part in these transactions only it they increase the company's utility, i.e. only if

$$U_i(x_i) < U_i(y)$$

From this condition we obtain the following inequality which must be satisfied for all i:

$$q_i^2 < \frac{\left(\frac{1}{2a_i} - R_i \right)^2 + V_i}{\left(\sum_{j=1}^n \left(\frac{1}{2a_j} - R_j \right) \right)^2 + \sum_{j=1}^n V_j}$$

The condition $\sum_{j=1}^n q_j = 1$ will give a lower limit for q_i.

It is easy to see that these conditions in general will give an interval for the constants $k_2 \dots k_n$. We see that $U_i(y)$ will decrease when q_i increases. Hence the smaller q_i is, the more favorable will the corresponding set of reinsurance treaties be to company i.

4.6 The assumption that the utility of money is of the form $u(x) = -ax^2 + x$ implies that the companies will be indifferent to any change in the cumulants of the risk distribution, κ_n for $n > 2$. This means that no company is willing pay anything to obtain a change which only affects the cumulants of higher order. It then follows that in the general expression for the price

$$P\big(F(x)\big) = \sum_{n=1}^{\infty} p_n \kappa_n$$

we must have $p_n = 0$ for $n > 2$. Hence the most general price in the special case we consider will be

$$P\big(F(x)\big) = P + pV\,,$$

where P and V are respectively the mean and variance of $F(x)$.

4.7 The Pareto optimal arrangement described in para 4.2 can obviously be brought about by a series of reciprocal treaties between two companies.

If we consider company i and j, we see the Pareto optimality will be reached if company i cedes a quota q_j of its portfolio to company j, and in return accepts a quota q_i from company j. In the notation of para 4.2, this means that company i should pay to company j the amount

$$q_j P_i + p q_j^2 V_i - q_i P_j - p q_i^2 V_j\,,$$

where p is the market price applicable to all reinsurance transactions. Summing this for all $j \neq i$, we obtain

$$P_i \sum q_j - q_i \sum P_j + p_2 \left(V_i \sum q_j^2 - q_i^2 \sum V_j \right),$$

which is equal to

$$P_i - q_i \sum_{j=1}^{n} P_j + p \left(V_i \sum_{j=1}^{n} q_j^2 - q_i^2 \sum_{j=1}^{n} V_j \right),$$

since $\sum_{j=1}^{n} q_j = 1$. However, this expression must be equal to the total net payment of company i, which, according to §4.2, is

$$y_i(0) = q_i \sum_{j=1}^{n} \left(\frac{1}{2a_j} - S_j \right) - \left(\frac{1}{2a_i} - S_i \right)$$

Hence we must have

$$p\left(V_i \sum_{j=1}^{n} q_j^2 - q_i^2 \sum_{j=1}^{n} V_j \right) = q_i \sum_{j=1}^{n} A_j - A_i$$

where

$$A_j = \frac{1}{2a_j} - R_j \qquad \text{and} \qquad R_j = S_j - P_j$$

This expression for $i-1, 2 \ldots n$, together with $\sum_{j=1}^{n} q_j = 1$, gives a system of $n+1$ equations for the determination of the $n+1$ unknowns $q_1 \ldots q_n$ and p_2. However, this system has no meaningful solution.

4.8 If we substitute

$$t_i = \frac{q_i}{\sum_{j=1}^{n} q_j},$$

the equation corresponding to $i = 1$ becomes;

$$p\left(V_1 \sum_{j=1}^{n} t_j^2 - t_1^2 \sum_{j=1}^{n} V_j \right) = t_1 \sum_{j=1}^{n} t_j \sum_{j=1}^{n} A_j - A_1 \left(\sum_{j=1}^{n} t_j \right)^2$$

This is a quadratic form in $t_1 \ldots t_n$ with a determinant

$$\begin{vmatrix} \alpha & \beta & \beta & \beta & \cdots \\ \beta & pV_1 + A_1 & A_1 & A_1 & \cdots \\ \beta & A_1 & pV_1 + A_1 & A_1 & \cdots \\ \beta & A_1 & A_1 & pV_1 + A_1 & \cdots \\ \beta & A_1 & A_1 & A_1 & \cdots \\ \cdots & \cdots & \cdots & \cdots & \cdots \end{vmatrix}$$

where

$$\alpha = p\left(V_1 = \sum_{j=1}^{n} V_j \right) + A_1 - \sum_{j=1}^{n} A_j \quad \text{and} \quad \beta = A_1 = \tfrac{1}{2} \sum_{j=n}^{n} A_j$$

It is easy to see that this determinant is strictly negative for any $p > 0$. Hence the quadratic form is strictly negative for any $t_1 \dots t_n$, provided that $p > 0$. This obviously holds, also for $i = 2, \dots n$. For $p = 0$ we obtain the solution

$$q_i = \frac{A_1}{\sum\limits_{i=1}^{n}} = \frac{\frac{1}{2a_i} - R_j}{\sum\limits_{j=1}^{n}(\frac{1}{2a_j} - R_j)}$$

4.9 We have thus found that the only solution consistent with our conditions is $p = 0$, i.e. that all reinsurance is made on a net premium basis.

However, even this solution is not acceptable if it gives one of the companies a lower utility than it has in the initial situation. We must also require that q_i satisfies the inequalities in §4.5. That $p = 0$ actually can lead to values of q_i which do not satisfy the inequalities has been demonstrated by an example in a previous paper (Borch (1960)).

4.10 The practical implication of these results can be stated as follows. If the companies believe that there is a certain market price for reinsurance, and apply this price to all their transactions, they will inevitably end in a situation which is not Pareto optimal. If some of the companies realize this, they may find a way, for instance, a reciprocal treaty between two companies which will increase the utility of both, without changing the utility of any other company. However, a treaty of this kind will imply a price different from the one used in the first set of transactions. hence there exists n market price which will lead to a Pareto optimal arrangement, if applied to all transactions.

4.11 The result which we have reached is in a way completely negative. It shatters any illusions which we have held to the effect that reinsurance transactions are made in a perfectly competitive market, where competition brings about an equilibrium which also is an optimum.

It may be useful to examine ordinary commodity markets more closely, to see if we have any reason to be disappointed or surprised over our negative result. In the classical model an individual brings quantities x_0, y_0, z_0 ... of various goods to the market. Here he barters his goods with the other participants in the market. Classical economic theory has created order in this apparently confused situation by making two simple assumptions:

(1) Each participant acts as if the market price of the various goods is given, i.e. as if nothing which ha can do will change the price.

(2) Each participant seeks to maximize a utility function.

From these assumptions it follows that:

(1) Each participant will leave the market with quantities x, y, z ... which maximize his utility function $u(x, y, z)$ subject to the condition

$$p_1x_0 + p_2y_0 + p_3z_0 + \cdots = p_1x + p_2y + p_3z + \cdots ,$$

where p_1, p_2 ... are the prices which make supply of each good equal to demand.

(2) The distribution of goods resulting from these market transactions is Pareto optimal.

It is indeed surprising that it is possible to derive such a far-reaching result from some extremely simple assumptions. We have really no reason to expect that a few equally simple assumptions should create order in a reinsurance market, which is essentially different from the classical commodity market.

4.12 The different is brought out clearly by the following point. In a commodity market, the "market value" of the goods an individual holds, does not change. The so-called budget equation

$$p_1x_0 + p_2y_0 + \cdots = p_1x + p_2y + \cdots$$

must hold regardless of what transactions the individuals does at the market price. In §4.4 we found that the variance of company i from V_i to $q_i^2 \sum_{j=1}^n V_j$. Since obviously

$$\sum_{j=1}^n V_j > \left(\sum_{j=1}^n q_i^2\right)\left(\sum_{j=1}^n V_j\right),$$

there is nothing corresponding to the budget equation in a reinsurance market.

4.13 Reinsurance brokers should rejoice over our result. If there is no simple price mechanism which more or less automatically brings about an optimal situation, it seems that brokers must perform an essential function in reconciling different interests and desires, and possibly steering the market into an optimal situation.

5. Market Equilibrium under Uncertainty

5.1 The problem we have studied in this paper is really that of extending the classical Walras-Cassel model of market equilibrium to include risk. This is obviously a problem of fundamental importance to economic theory, and it is surprising that so few economists have taken it up for systematic study.

It appears that only Allais (1953) and Arrow (1953) have made any serious attempts to tackle the problem. Their results have recently been generalized by Debreu (1959), but his treatment of the matter is too abstract to have any real bearing on our problem.

5.2 Allais (1953) has proved that there exists an equilibrium price, which also as Pareto optimal, in a market for lottery tickets. However, his proof rests on the assumption that lottery tickets can be bought and sold only in integral numbers, i.e. one can buy one ticket, but not a 50% interest in two tickets. This is a rather serious limitation if one wants to interpret his model as a reinsurance market.

5.3 Arrow (1953) has proved that a price mechanism will bring about a Pareto optimal equilibrium in a model which is considerably more general than required for our purpose. Firstly he deals with n different commodities, and secondly he allows himself the luxury of considering subjective probabilities. This may be necessary for a theory of stock exchanges, which apparently is what Arrow has in mind. However, in a reinsurance market such refinements are not essential.

Stripped of these refinements and presented in insurance terms, Arrow's model can be described as follows.

(i) Company i has a utility of money $u_i(x)$, $i = 1, 2 \ldots I$.

(ii) As a result of its direct underwriting company i is committed to pay an amount x_{is} if "state of the world" s occurs $s = 1, 2 \ldots S$.

(iii) The company has funds amounting to S_i available for meeting these commitments.

(iv) The probability that state of the world s will occur is p_s.

The utility of company i in the initial situation is then

$$U_i(0) = \sum_{s=1}^{S} p_s u_i(S_i - x_{is})$$

5.4 It is then assumed that the company pays an amount $g_s y_{is}$ in order to be assured of receiving the amount y_{is} if state of the world s occurs. This means that should this state of the world occur, the company will have to make a net payment of $x_{is} - y_{is}$.

The utility of the company after having made a series of such contracts will be:

$$U_i(y) = \sum_{s=1}^{S} p_s u_i \left[\left(S_i - \sum_{s=1}^{S} g_s y_{is} \right) - (x_{is} + y_{is}) \right]$$

If we maximize this function in a straightforward manner, we find:

$$\frac{\partial U_i(y)}{\partial y_{it}} = -g_t \sum_{s=1}^{S} p_s u_i' \left[\left(S_i - \sum_{s=1}^{S} g_s y_{is} \right) - x_{js} + y_{is} \right]$$

$$+ p_t u_i' \left[\left(S_i - \sum_{s=1}^{S} g_s y_{is} \right) - x_{it} + y_{it} \right]$$

The first order conditions for maximum are:

$$g_t \sum_{s=1}^{S} p_s u_i'(R_i - x_{is} + y_{is}) = p_t u_i'(R_i - x_{it} + y_{it}), \quad t = 1, 2 \ldots S,$$

where we have put

$$S_i - \sum_{s=1}^{S} g_s y_{is} = R_i$$

If the utility function fulfills some reasonable conditions, these equations will lead to a solution of the form

$$y_{it} = g_i \left(\frac{p_t}{g_t}, x_{it} \right)$$

If $u_i'(x)$ is monotonically decreasing, y_{it} will decrease with increasing g_t, and increase with increasing p_t and x_{it}. Since we obviously must have

$$\sum_{i=1}^{I} y_{is} = 0 \qquad \text{for all } s,$$

we obtain S equations to determine the S prices $g_1 \ldots g_s$. That these equations, under certain conditions have a non-trivial solution follows from Arrow's paper.

5.5 Arrow's price g_s depends on the probability p_s that state of the world s shall occur, *and* on the initial distribution among the companies of the amounts x_{is} which become payable if this state of the world should occur. The latter element is not include in our model, which assumes that the market price depends exclusively on the probability that a claim will occur. This is obviously the reason why we found that no equilibrium price exists.

We shall illustrate this by a practical example. Assume that the probability of total loss of an ocean liner worth \$100 million is the same as the probability that a house worth \$10000 will be totally destroyed by fire. According to ordinary actuarial theory, an insurance company should demand the same premium for covering the house against total destruction by fire, as for paying out \$10000 if the ocean liner should be lost.

According to Arrow's theory, the company will demand different premiums for the two coverages. It is easy to show that under fairly reasonable assumptions, the company will — or can — ask a higher premium for covering a part of the ocean liner. The reason being that other companies in the market will feel uneasy about the large amounts they have to pay if the liner should be lost. Hence there will be a great demand for reinsurance cover of this particular risk, so that an uncommitted company can exact a high premium for such coverage.

5.6 Arrow's paper shows that it is possible to construct a model of a reinsurance market in which unrestricted competition will lead to an equilibrium which is Pareto optimal. In order to reach this result, he has to sacrifice the *principle of equivalence* which has been sacrosanct ever since the beginning of rational insurance.

This may perhaps have been expected. The principle of equivalence may have its proper place in ethics, rather than in a business world where everything depends on supply and demand. Whether insurance essentially is a business aiming at making money or a benevolent social service is a point which probably will never be finally settled. If we press the analogy with business to the utmost, as we have done in this paper, we should not be surprised that we either run into inconsistencies or have to sacrifice a principle deemed essential to insurance.

References for Section 5

Allais M. (1953): "L'extension des théories de l'équilibre économique général et du rendement social au cas du risque", *Econometrica*, 269–290.

Ammetter H. (1955): "The calculation of premium rates for excess of Loss and Stop Loss reinsurance treaties", S. Vajda, ed. *Non-proportional Reinsurance*, Brussels, 79–110.

Arrow K.J. (1953): "Le rôle de valeurs boursièrs pour la répartition la meilleure des risques", *Collques Internationaux du Centre National de la Recherche Scientifique, XL*, Paris, 41–48.

Borch K. (1960): "Reciprocal reinsurance treaties seen as a two-person co-operative game", *Skand. Aktuarietidskr*, 29–58.

Debreu G. (1959): *Theory of value*, New York: John Wiley & Sons.

von Neumann J. and Morgenstern O. (1944): *Theory of Games and Economic Behavior*, Princeton.

Wold H. (1936): *Landsbygdens Brandförsäkringsbolags Maximaler och Återfösäkring*, Stockholm.

6. Equilibrium in a Reinsurance Market*

1. Introduction

1.1 The Walras-Cassel system of equations which determines a static equilibrium in a competitive economy is certainly one of the most beautiful constructions in mathematical economics. The mathematical rigor which was lacking when the system was first presented has since been provided by Wald (1936) and Arrow and Debreu (1954). For more than a generation one of the favorite occupations of economists has been to generalize the system to dynamic economies. The mere volume of the literature dealing with this subject gives ample evidence of its popularity.

1.2 The present paper investigates the possibilities of generalizing the Walras-Cassel model in another direction. The model as presented by its authors assumes complete certainty, in the sense that all consumers and producers know exactly what will be the outcome of their actions. It will obviously be of interest to extend the model to markets where decisions are made under uncertainty as to what the outcome will be. This problem seems to have been studied systematically only by Allais (1953) and Arrow (1953) and to some extent by Debreu (1959) who includes uncertainty in the last chapter of his recent book. It is surprising that a problem of such obvious and fundamental importance to economic theory has not received more attention. Allais ascribes this neglect of the subject to *son extrême difficulté.*

---

* Reprinted from *Econometrica*, July 1962, Volume 30:3, 424–444, copyright (c) The Econometric Society.

1.3 The subject does not appear inherently difficult, however, at least not when presented in Allais' elegant manner. What seems to be forbiddingly difficult is to extend his relatively simple model to situations in the real world where uncertainty and attitude toward risk play a decisive part, for instance in the determination of interest rates, share prices, and supply and demand for risk capital. Debreu's abstract treatment also seems very remote from such familiar problems. There are further difficulties of which Allais, particularly, seems acutely aware, such as the psychological problems connected with the elusive concepts of "subjective probabilities" and "rational behaviour". In the present paper we shall put these latter difficulties aside. It then appears fairly simple to construct a model of a competitive market which seems reasonably close to the situations in real life where rational beings exchange risk and cash among themselves. The problem still remains difficult, but it seems that the difficulty is the familiar one of laying down assumptions which lead to a determinate solution of an n-person game.

1.4 The reason why neither Allais nor Arrow has followed up his preliminary study of the problem is probably that their relatively simple models appear too remote from any really interesting practical economic situation. However, the model they consider gives a fairly accurate description of a *reinsurance market.* The participants in this market are insurance companies, and the commodity they trade is risk. The purpose of the deals which the companies make in this market is to redistribute the risk which each company has accepted by its direct underwriting for the public. The companies which gain from this redistribution of risk are ready to pay compensation in cash to the other companies. This is a real life example of just the situation which Allais and Arrow have studied in rather artificial models.

It seems indeed that the reinsurance market offers promising possibilities of studying how attitudes toward risk influence decision making and the interaction between the decisions made by the various participants. This problem has so far been studied mainly in the theory of investment and capital markets where one must expect that a large number of "disturbing factors" are at play. It is really surprising that economists have overlooked the fact that the problem can be studied, almost under laboratory conditions, in the reinsurance market.

2. A Model of the Reinsurance Market

2.1 Consider n insurance companies, each holding a portfolio of insurance contracts.

The *risk situation* of company i ($i = 1, 2, \ldots, n$) is defined by the following two elements:

(i) The *risk distribution*, $F_i(x_i)$, which is the probability that the total amount of claims to be paid under the contracts in the company's portfolio shall not exceed x_1.

(ii) The *funds*, S_i, which the company has available to pay claims.

We shall assume that $x_1, \ldots, x_n$ are stochastically independent. To this risk situation the company attaches a utility $U_i\big(S_i, F_i(x_i)\big)$. From the so-called "Bernoulli hypothesis" it follows that

$$U_i\big(S_i, F_i(x_i)\big) = \int_0^\infty u_i(S_i - x_i)\, dF_i(x_i)$$

Here $u_i(S) = U_i\big(S\,, \varepsilon)\big)$, where $\varepsilon(x)$ is the degenerate probability distribution defined by

$$\varepsilon(x) = 0 \quad \text{for } x < 0\,,$$

$$\varepsilon(x) = 1 \quad \text{for } 0 \leq x$$

Hence $u_i(S)$ is the utility attached to a risk situation with funds S and probability of 1 that claims shall be zero. In the following we shall refer to the function $u_i(S)$ as the "utility of money to company i". We shall assume that $u_i(S)$ is continuous and that its first derivative is positive and decreases with increasing S.

2.2 Von Neumann and Morgenstern (1944) proved the Bernoulli hypothesis as a theorem, derived from a few simple axioms. Since then there has been considerable controversy over the plausibility of the various formulations which can be given to these axioms. There is no need to take up this question here, since it is almost trivial that the Bernoulli hypothesis must hold for accompany in the insurance business.

2.3 In the initial situation company i is committed to pay x_i, the total amount of claims which occur in its own portfolio. The commitments of company i do not depend on the claims which occur in the portfolios of the other companies. In the reinsurance market the companies can conclude agreements, usually referred to as *treaties* which redistribute the commitments that the companies had in the initial situation.

In general these treaties can be represented by a set of functions:

$$y_i(x_1, x_2, \ldots, x_n) \quad (i = 1, 2, \ldots, n)$$

where $y_i(x_1, x_2, \ldots, x_n)$ is the amount company i has to pay if claims in the respective portfolios amount to $x_1, x_2, \ldots, x_n$. Since all claims have to be paid, we must obviously have

$$\sum_{i=1}^{n} y_i(x_1, \ldots, x_n) = \sum_{i=1}^{n} x_i$$

These treaties will change the utility of company i from

$$U_i(x) = \int_0^\infty u_i(S_i - x_i)\, dF_i(x_i)$$

to

$$U_i(y) = \int_R u_i\big(S_i - y_i(x)\big)\, dF(x)\,,$$

where $F(x)$ is the joint probability distribution of $x_1, \ldots, x_n$, and where R stands for the positive orthant in the n-dimensional x-space.

For simplicity we have written x and y respectively for the vectors $\{x_1, \ldots, x_n\}$ and $\{y_1(x), \ldots, y_n(x)\}$

2.4 If the companies act rationally, they will not conclude a set of treaties represented by a vector y if there exists another set of treaties with a corresponding vector $\bar{y}$, such that

$$U_i(y) \leq U_i(\bar{y}) \quad \text{for all } i\,,$$

with at least one strict inequality. y will in this case clearly be inferior to $\bar{y}$. If there exists no vector $\bar{y}$ satisfying the above condition, the set of treaties represented by y will be referred to as *Pareto optimal.* If the companies act rationally, the treaties they conclude must obviously constitute a Pareto optimal set.

2.5 It has been proved in a previous paper (Borch (1960)) that a necessary and sufficient condition that a vector y is Pareto optimal is that its elements, the functions $y_1(x)$, ..., $y_n(x)$ satisfy the relations:

$$u_i'\big(S_i - y_i(x)\big) = k_i u_i'\big(S_1 - y_1(x)\big)\,, \tag{1}$$

$$\sum_{i=1}^{n} y_i(x) = \sum_{i=1}^{n} x_i\,, \tag{2}$$

where k_2, k_3, ..., k_n are positive constants which can be chosen arbitrarily.

The proof is elementary. It will not be repeated here since a rigorous statement is lengthy and rather tedious. Heuristically it is almost self-evident that if the condition is fulfilled, a change in y cannot increase the utility of all the companies, i.e., that the condition is sufficient. The proof that it is necessary is slightly less transparent.

2.6 Differentiation of the equations in the preceding paragraph with respect to x_j gives

$$u_i''\big(S_i - y_i(x)\big)\frac{\partial y_i}{\partial x_j} = k_i u_1''\big(S_1 - y_1(x)\big)\frac{\partial y_1}{\partial x_j}$$

and

$$\sum_{i=1}^{n} \frac{\partial y_i}{\partial x_j} = 1$$

Dividing the first equation by $u_1''\big(S_i - y_i(x)\big)$ and summing over all i, we obtain

$$u_1''\big(S_1 - y_1(x)\big)\frac{\partial y_1}{\partial x_j}\sum_{i=1}^{n}\frac{k_i}{u_i''\big(S_i - y_i(x)\big)} = 1$$

where $k_1 = 1$. It then follows that for any i and j we must have

$$\frac{\partial y_1}{\partial x_i} = \frac{\partial y_1}{\partial x_j}$$

This implies that the vector function $y_1(x)$ is a scalar function of one single variable

$$z = \sum_{i=1}^{n} x_i$$

It is easy to verify that in general we have

$$\frac{dy_i(z)}{dz} = \frac{\dfrac{k_i}{u_i''(S_i - y_i(z))}}{\displaystyle\sum_{j=1}^{n} \frac{k_j}{u_j''(S_j - y_j(z))}}$$

This means that the amount $y_i(z)$ which company i has to pay will depend only on $z = x_1 + \cdots + x_n$, i.e., on the total amount of claims made against the insurance industry. Hence any Pareto optimal set of treaties is equivalent to a pool arrangement, i.e., all companies hand their portfolios over to a pool, and agree on some rule as to how payment of claims against the pool shall be divided among the companies. In general there will be an infinity of such rules, since the $n-1$ positive constants $k_2, k_3, \ldots, k_n$ can be chosen arbitrarily. In general the utility of company i will decrease with increasing k_i $(i \neq 1)$. Since the company will not be party to a set of treaties unless $U_i(y) \geq U_i(x)$ there must be an upper limit to k_i. We shall return to this question in Section 4.

2.7 The results reached in the preceding paragraphs correspond very well to what one could expect on more intuitive grounds. If all companies are averse to risk, it was to be expected that the best arrangement would be to spread the risks as widely as possible. It was also to be expected that the solution should be indeterminate, since no assumptions were made as to how the companies should divide the gain resulting from the greater spread of risks.

In the Walras-Cassel model there is a determinate equilibrium, i.e., unique Pareto optimal distribution of the goods in the market. The basic assumption required to reach this result is that each participant considers the market price as given, and then buys or sells quantities of the various goods so that his utility is maximized. In the following section we shall investigate the possibility of finding some equally simple assumptions which will bring a reinsurance market into an equilibrium.

3. The Price Concept in a Reinsurance Market

3.1 In insurance circles it is generally assumed that there exists a well defined market price, at least for some particular forms of reinsurance. It is also generally believed that Lloyd's in London is willing to quote a price for any kind of reinsurance cover.

If a market price exists, it must mean that it is possible to associate a number $P(F)$ to any probability distribution $F(x)$, so that an insurance company can receive the amount $P(F)$ from the market by undertaking to pay the claims which occur in a portfolio with risk distribution $F(x)$. It must also be possible for the company to be relieved of the responsibility for paying such claims by paying the amount $P(F)$ to the market.

3.2 Assume now that a company accepts responsibility for two portfolios with risk distributions $F_1(x_1)$ and $F_2(x_2)$. Assume further that x_1 and x_2 are stochastically independent and that $x = x_1 + x_2$ has the probability distribution $F(x)$. It is natural to require that the company shall receive the same amount whether it accepts the two portfolios separately or in one single transaction. This means that we must have

$$P(F) = P(F_1) + P(F_2)$$

This additivity condition is clearly a parallel to the assumption in the classical model that the price per unit is independent of the number of units included in a transaction.

3.3 The additivity condition is obviously satisfied by a number of functionals. It is for instance satisfied by the cumulant generating function

$$\psi(t) = \log \varphi(t)$$

where $\varphi(t)$ is the characteristic function

$$\varphi(t) = \int_0^\infty e^{itx}\, dF(x)$$

As it is inconvenient to work with a complex valued function, we shall in the following use the corresponding real functions

$$\varphi(t) = \int_0^\infty e^{-tx}\, dF(x)$$

and

$$\omega(t) = \log \varphi(t)$$

which exist for any nonnegative value of t. The cumulants are then given by the expansion

$$\psi(t) = \sum_{n=1}^{\infty} (-1)^{n-1} \frac{\kappa_n}{n!} t^n$$

3.4 It follows that for any nonnegative value of t, $\psi(t)$ can be interpreted as a price which satisfies the additivity condition. The same will hold for any linear combination of the form:

$$c_1\psi(t_1) + c_2\psi(t_2) + \cdots$$

where c_1, c_2, ... are constants. Similar expressions containing derivatives of $\psi(t)$ of any order will also satisfy the condition.

It is obvious that any expression of this kind can be written as a sum of cumulants. Hence we can write

$$P(F) = \sum_{n=1}^{\infty} p_n \kappa_n$$

where p_1, ..., p_n are constants.

It follows from a theorem by Lukacs (1952) that this is the most general expression which satisfies the additivity condition.

3.5 Let now $\varepsilon(x)$ be the degenerate probability distribution defined in paragraph 2.1.

$\varepsilon(x-m)$ can then be interpreted as a risk distribution according to which the amount m will be claimed with probability 1. The price associated with this distribution will be

$$P\big(\varepsilon(x-m)\big) = p_1 m$$

since $\kappa_n = 0$ for $1 < n$. We shall therefore require as a continuity condition that $p_1 = 1$.

3.6 We now assume that a market price of this form is given, and we consider a company in the risk situation $\big(S, F(x)\big)$. The utility of the company in this situation is

$$U\big(S, F(x)\big) = \int_0^{\infty} u(S-x)\, dF(x)$$

If the company undertakes to pay a claim y with probability distribution $G(y)$, it will receive an amount $P(G)$. If x and y are stochastically independent this transaction will change the company's utility to

$$U\big(S+P(G)\,,H(x)\big) = \int_0^\infty u\big(S+P(G)-x\big)\,d\left(\int_0^\infty F(x-y)\,dG(y)\right)$$
$$= \int_0^\infty u\big(S+P(G)-x\big)\,dH(x)$$

where $H(x)$ is the convolution of $F(x)$ and $G(y)$.

If the company acts rationally, it will select among the portfolios available in the market one with a risk distribution $G_0(y)$ which maximizes $U\big(S+P(G)\,,H(x)\big)$. This function $G_0(y)$ can be considered as the amount of reinsurance cover which the company will supply at the given price.

3.7 The nature of the maximization problem appears more clearly if we introduce the cumulants explicitly in the formula of the preceding paragraph.

Let $f(t)$ and $g(t)$ be the characteristic functions of $F(x)$ and $G(y)$ respectively. The characteristic function of $H(x)$ is then $f(t)\,g(t)$, and if $H(x)$ has a derivative, we have

$$\frac{dH(x)}{dx} = \frac{1}{2\pi}\int_{-\infty}^{+\infty} e^{-itx} f(t)\,g(t)\,dt = \frac{1}{2\pi}\int_{-\infty}^{+\infty} e^{-itx} e^{\log f(t)+\log g(t)}\,dt$$
$$= \frac{1}{2\pi}\int_{-\infty}^{+\infty} \exp\left(-itx + \sum_{n=1}^{\infty}\frac{(it)^n}{n!}(k_n+\kappa_n)\right)dt$$

where k_n and κ_n are the n-th cumulants of $F(x)$ and $G(y)$, respectively. Hence the problem becomes that of determining the values of $\kappa_1, \kappa_2, \ldots, \kappa_n$ which maximize the expression

$$\int_0^\infty u\Big(S-x+\sum_{n=1}^{\infty} p_n\kappa_n\Big)\int_{-\infty}^{+\infty}\exp\left(-itx+\sum_{n=1}^{\infty}\frac{(it)^n}{n!}(k_n+\kappa_n)\right)dt\,dx$$

It is interesting to note that the cumulants of different order appear as different commodities, each with its particular price. The "quantities" κ_1, $\ldots$, κ_n however, must satisfy certain restraints in order to be the cumulants of a probability distribution. These restraints will be of a complicated nature. A sufficient set of restraints can be derived from the Liapunoff inequalities

$$\frac{1}{n}\log m_n \leq \frac{1}{n+1}\log m_{n+1}$$

where m_n is the nth absolute moment about an arbitrary point. Since $G(y) = 0$ for $y < 0$, the inequalities must hold for the moments about zero of $G(y)$. It is easy to see that the sign of equality will hold only in the degenerate case when $G(y) = \varepsilon(y - m)$.

The problem on the *supply* side of a reinsurance market thus appears to be similar to the problems of maximization under restraints which occur in some production models. It is clear that the problem will have a solution, at least under certain conditions.

3.8 The problems on the demand side are more complicated. Assume that with a given price a company demands reinsurance cover corresponding to a probability distribution $G(y)$. This means that in order to be relieved of an obligation to pay a claim with a probability distribution $G(y)$, the company is willing to pay an amount

$$P\big(G(y)\big) = \sum_{n=1}^{\infty} p_n \kappa_n$$

where $\kappa_1, \ldots, \kappa_n \ldots$ are the cumulants of $G(y)$.

Assume now that the company can buy its reinsurance cover in two transactions, for instance by placing two portfolios with risk distribution $G(\frac{1}{2}y)$ with two different reinsurers. If the market price is applied to both transactions, the company will have to pay

$$2P\left(G\left(\tfrac{1}{2}y\right)\right) = \sum_{n=1}^{\infty} \frac{p_n}{2^{n-1}}\kappa_n$$

for the reinsurance cover. $2P\big(G(\frac{1}{2}y)\big)$ will generally be different from $P\big(G(y)\big)$. Hence the reinsurance arrangement which maximizes the company's utility will depend not only on the given price, but also on the number of reinsurers who are willing to deal at this price. This makes it doubtful if any meaning can be given to the term "market price" in a reinsurance market. We shall not at present discuss this problem in further detail. We shall, however, consider it again for a special case in Section 4.

4. Existence of an Equilibrium Price

4.1 In the preceding section we studied separately the demand and supply of reinsurance cover. It is fairly obvious, however, that if the companies shall reach the Pareto optimum which we found in Section 2.5, each company must act both as seller and buyer of reinsurance cover. In a previous paper (Borch (1960b)) it was proved by a more direct approach that it will in general be to the advantage of a company to act in both capacities at the same time.

In this section we shall study whether a price mechanism can bring supply and demand into an equilibrium which also represents a Pareto optimal distribution of the risks.

4.2 Since the problem is rather complex, we shall analyze only a special case. We assume that the utility of money to all companies can be represented by a function of the form:

$$u_i(x) = -a_i x^2 + x \,, \qquad \text{for } i = 1, 2, \ldots, n$$

We assume that a_i is positive and so small that $u_i(x)$ is an increasing function over the whole range which enters into consideration.

a_i can evidently be interpreted as a measure of the company's "risk aversion". If $a_i = 0$, the company will be indifferent to risk. Its sole objective will then be to maximize expected profits, ignoring all risk of deviations from the expected value. The greater a_i is, the more concerned will the company be about the possibility of suffering great losses.

From the formulae in Section 2.6 we find

$$\frac{dy_i(z)}{dz} = \frac{k_i/a_i}{\sum k_j/a_j} = q_i$$

Hence the optimum arrangement is that company i shall pay a fixed quota q_i of the amount of claims z made against the pool. It is easily verified that

$$y_i(z) = q_i z + q_i \sum j = 1^n \left(\frac{1}{2a_j} - S_j\right) - \left(\frac{1}{2a_i} - S_i\right) = q_i z + q_i \sum_{j=1}^{n} A_j - A_i$$

For $z = 0$ we find

$$y_i(0) = q_i \sum_{j=1}^{n} A_j - A_i$$

$y_i(0)$ is the amount (positive or negative) that company i has to pay if there are no claims. Hence $y_i(0)$ must be the difference between the amount the company pays for the reinsurance cover it buys and the amount the company receives for the reinsurance cover it sells.

4.3 If $u(x) = -ax^2 + x$, the utility of the company in the initial situation is

$$U(0) = \int_0^\infty u(S-x)\,dF(x) = \int_0^\infty \{-a(S-x)^2 + (S-x)\}\,dF(x)$$
$$= -a(S-\kappa_1)^2 + (S-\kappa_1) - a\kappa_2$$

where κ_1 and κ_2 are the two first cumulants, i.e., the mean and the variance of $F(x)$. We see that in this case the utility which the company attaches to a risk situation will depend only on the two first cumulants of the risk distribution. If the utility function $u(x)$ is of the form $-ax^2 + x$ for all companies, the cumulants of higher order can have no effect of the optimal arrangement. They will appear as "free goods" in the market, i.e., with price zero. Hence, in the expression for price we must have $p_n = 0$ for all $n > 2$. The amount paid for reinsurance cover of a risk distribution $F(x)$ will then be

$$P(F) = \kappa_1 + p_2\kappa_2 = m + pV$$

if we drop the index of p_2, and write m and V for the mean and variance of $F(x)$, respectively.

4.4 We now consider two companies, i and j, with risk distributions $F_i(x_i)$ and $F_j(x_j)$ where x_i and x_j are stochastically independent. In a Pareto optimal set of reinsurance treaties the two companies will have to pay fixed quotas, q_i and q_j, of the claims made against the pool $z = \sum_{j=1}^n x_j$.

It is evident that a Pareto optimal arrangement will result if every pair of companies concludes a reciprocal treaty, according to which company i undertakes to pay $q_i x_j$ if claims against company j amount to x_j, and company j in return pays $q_j x_i$ if claims x_i are made against company i (i.e., q_i is the same for every j).

If m_i and V_i are the mean and variance of $F_i(x_i)$, company i will receive an amount $q_i m_j + pq_i^2 V_j$ for the reinsurance cover it gives company j. Similarly company i will have to pay out $q_j m_i + pq_j^2 V_i$ for the cover it receives from company j.

Hence the net payment from company i to company j will be

$$q_j m_i + p q_j^2 V_i - q_i m_j - p q_i^2 V_j$$

Summing this for all $j \neq i$, we obtain

$$m_i \sum q_j - q_i \sum m_j = p\left\{V_i \sum q_j^2 - q_i^2 \sum V_j\right\}$$

which is equal to

$$m_i - q_i \sum_{j=1}^{n} m_j + p\left(V_i \sum_{j=1}^{n} q_i^2 - q_i^2 \sum j = 1^n V_j\right)$$

This expression, however, must be equal to the total net payment of company i, which according to Section 4.2 is

$$y_i(0) = q_i \sum_{j=1}^{n} A_j - A_i$$

Hence we must have

$$p\left(V_i \sum_{j=1}^{n} q_j^2 - q_i^2 \sum_{j=1}^{n} V_j\right) - q_i \sum_{j=1}^{n}(A_j + m_j) + (A_i + m_i) = 0$$

This expression for $i = 1, 2, \ldots, n$, together with $\sum_{j=1}^{n} q_j = 1$ gives a system of $n+1$ equations for the determination of the $n+1$ unknowns q_1, $\ldots$, q_n and p.

These equations are not independent, however, since the last one can be obtained by adding together the first n. Hence the system will give q_1, $\ldots$, q_n as functions of p. For $p = 0$ we find

$$q_i(0) = \frac{A_j + m_j}{\sum_{j=1}^{n}(A_j + m_j)}$$

Differentiating the equations with respect to p, we find

$$\left[\frac{dq_i(p)}{dp}\right]_{p=0} \sum_{j=1}^{n}(A_j + m_j) = V_i \sum j = 1^n q_j^2 - q_i^2 \sum_{j=1}^{n} V_j$$

Hence it follows from considerations of continuity that $q_i(p)$ will be real and positive when p lies in some interval containing zero.

4.5 We shall now assume that a price p is given, and study how company 1 can increase its utility by dealing in the market at this price.

(i) The company can sell reinsurance cover, i.e., it can accept responsibility for paying a claim with mean m_0 and variance W_1. For giving this cover the company will receive the amount $m_0 + pW_1$.
According to the formulae in Section 4.3, this transaction will change the utility of the company from

$$-a_1(S_1 - m_1)^2 + (S_1 - m_1) - a_1V_1 = U_1(S_1 - m_1, V_1) = U_1(R_1, V_1)$$

to

$$\begin{aligned} &- a_1(S_1 - m_1 + pW_1)^2 + (S_1 - m_1 + pW_1) - a_1(V_1 + W_1) \\ &= U_1(R_1 + pW_1, V_1 + W_1) \end{aligned}$$

Here $R_1 = S_1 - m_1$, which in insurance terminology is called the "free reserves" of the company, i.e., funds in excess of expected amount of claims. We see that the utility does not depend on m_0, but only on free reserves and variance.

(ii) The company can *buy* reinsurance cover from the $n-1$ other companies, i.e. by paying the amounts $pv_2, \ldots, pv_n$ of its free reserves to the other companies, it can "get rid of" variances $v_2, \ldots, v_n$.
These transactions will leave the company with a variance

$$v_1 = V_1 - \sum_{i=2}^{n} v_i - 2\sum_{i \neq j} C_{ij}$$

where C_{ij} is the covariance between claims in the portfolios taken by companies i and j.

Since the utility of company 1 will increase with decreasing v_1, the company will seek to arrange its purchases so that C_{ij} is as great as possible, i.e., so that

$$C_{ij} = (v_i v_j)^{1/2}$$

This clearly means that there must be perfect positive correlation between claims in the part of the original portfolio which the company retains and the parts which are reinsured. Hence we must have $v_i = q_i^2 V_1$ and

$\sum_{j=1}^{n} q_i = 1$. This is the same as the result which we in Section 4.2 derived from the general condition for Pareto optimality of Section 2.5.

4.6 If the company buys and sells reinsurance cover in this way, its utility will become

$$U_1\left[\left(R_1 + p\left(W_1 - \sum_{1=2}^{n} v_i\right)\right),\ \left(W_1 + \left(V_1^{\frac{1}{2}} - \sum_{i=2}^{n} v_i^{\frac{1}{2}}\right)^2 - V_1\right)\right]$$

The company will then seek to determine W_1, and $v_2, \ldots, v_n$ so that this expression is maximized.

The first order conditions for a maximum are

$$\frac{\partial U_1}{\partial W_1} = -p\left[2a_1\left(R_1 + p\left(W_1 - \sum_{j=2}^{n} v_j\right)\right) - 1\right] - a_1 = 0\,,$$

$$\frac{\partial U_1}{\partial v_i} = p\left[2a_1\left(R_1 + p\left(W_1 - \sum_{j=2}^{n} v_j\right)\right) - 1\right]$$

$$+\, a_1\frac{V_1^{\frac{1}{2}} - \sum_{j=2}^{n} v_j^{\frac{1}{2}}}{v_i^{\frac{1}{2}}} = 0 \qquad (i = 2, 3 \ldots n)$$

Adding the first of these equations to the one obtained by differentiating with respect to v_i, we obtain

$$V_1^{\frac{1}{2}} - \sum_{j=2}^{n} v_j^{\frac{1}{2}} = v_i^{\frac{1}{2}}$$

Since this must hold for all i, we must have

$$v_i = \frac{1}{n^2}V_1 \qquad \text{for all } n$$

This means that regardless of what the price is, the company will seek to divide its portfolio into n identical parts, and reinsure $n-1$ of these with the other companies.

Inserting the values of v_i, in the first equation, we find

$$W_1 = \frac{n-1}{n^2}V_1 + \frac{2p\left(\frac{1}{2a_1} - R_1\right) - 1}{2p^2}$$

4.7 In general we find that for a given price p, company i is willing to supply reinsurance cover for a variance

$$W_1 = \frac{n-1}{n^2}V_i + \frac{2p\left(\frac{1}{2a_1} - R_1\right) - 1}{2p^2}$$

The company will demand cover for a variance

$$W_i' = \frac{n-1}{n^2}V_i$$

regardless of what the price is, provided that this variance can be divided equally between the $n-1$ other companies.

It is obvious that in this case we cannot determine p by simply requiring that total supply shall be equal to total demand, i.e., from the "market equation"

$$\sum_{i=1}^{n} W_i = \sum_{i=1}^{n} W_i'$$

Instead we have the conditions that supply from company i must equal the sum of $1/(n-1)$ of the demand from the other $n-1$ companies, i.e.,

$$W_i = \frac{1}{n-1}\sum_{j \neq i} W_i' = \frac{1}{n^2}\sum_{j \neq i} V_j$$

Hence p must satisfy the n equations

$$\frac{1}{n^2}\sum_{j=1}^{n} V_j - \frac{1}{n}V_i = \frac{2p\left(\frac{1}{2a_i} - R_i\right) - 1}{2p^2} \qquad (i = 2, 3 \ldots n)$$

This is clearly impossible, except for special values of a_i, R_i and V_i.

4.8 It is obvious from the preceding paragraph that unrestricted utility maximization with a given price has little meaning in our model. The procedure may, however, have some meaning if we introduce restrictions so that it necessarily leads to a Pareto optimal arrangement.

These restrictions can be formulated as follows. For all i and j, $j \neq i$, company i can satisfy its demand for reinsurance cover only by placing a part $q_j^2 V_i$, of its variance with company j.

Company i will then be willing to supply reinsurance cover for a variance

$$W_i = V_i \sum_{j \neq i}^{n} q_j^2 + \frac{2p\left(\frac{1}{2a_i} - R_i\right) - 1}{2p^2}$$

The n market equations from Section 4.7 will then take the form

$$q_i^2 \sum_{j=1}^{n} V_j - V_i \sum_{j=1}^{n} q_j^2 = \frac{2p\left(\frac{1}{2a_i} - R_i\right) - 1}{2p^2} \qquad (i = 1, 2, \ldots, n)$$

It is easy to see that these n equations, which are linear in q_i^2, have a determinant of rank $n-1$. Hence the equations have a solution only if the sum of the right hand sides is zero. This condition is satisfied:

(i) if the right hand sides all vanish, i.e., if p tends to infinity. The corresponding values of q_i are then

$$q_i = \frac{V_i^{\frac{1}{2}}}{\sum_{j=1}^{n} V_j^{\frac{1}{2}}};$$

(ii) if

$$p = \frac{n}{2\sum_{j=1}^{n}\left(\frac{1}{2a_j} - R_j\right)}$$

This appears to be all that we can get, even from a diluted principle of utility maximization.

The result is not very satisfactory. The general assumptions which lead to these "equilibrium prices" are rather artificial, and it is easy to construct numerical examples where the result becomes meaningless.

From the formulae in Section 4.2 we see that the utility of company i will decrease with increasing q_i. The price we have found may lead to values of q_i which will give some companies a lower utility than they have in the initial situation. These companies will obviously refuse to trade at such a price.

The conditions which q_i must satisfy in order to give a meaningful solution are discussed in the paper (Borch (1960b)) already referred to, and we shall not pursue the point further in the present paper.

5. The Models of Allais and Arrow

5.1 Both Allais (1953a) and Arrow (1953) have proved that in models very similar to ours, there exists a price such that utility maximization, when this price is considered as given, will lead to a Pareto optimal situation. To explain the apparent contradiction with our result, we shall examine their models in some detail.

5.2 Allais (1953) studied a model which essentially is a market for lottery tickets. The prize of the tickets is a normally distributed random variable with mean equal to one unit of money, and a given standard deviation. Allais proves that in this model there exists a market price for lottery tickets which will lead to a uniquely determined, optimal distribution of the risks.

The crucial assumption which Allais makes in order to reach this result is that lottery tickets can be bought and sold only in integral numbers, i.e., one can buy one ticket, but not a 50 per cent interest in two tickets. It is obvious that when this assumption is given up, the Pareto optimum is no longer unique. The situation will be similar to the one we found in Section 2.7, which is an example of the familiar problem that an n-person game has an indeterminate solution. To make it determined, one will have to make some assumptions about how the participants form coalitions to buy packages of lottery tickets.

5.3 In the model of Allais there is only one kind of lottery ticket. If tickets are indivisible as Allais assumes, it is almost trivial that there must exist a price which leads to a Pareto optimal situation. The problem will change completely, however, if the model is generalized by the introduction of several kinds of tickets, i.e., tickets where the prize is drawn from different probability distributions. The problem can be handled as we did in the preceding sections if one accepts the Bernoulli hypothesis. Allais (1953b) has emphatically rejected this hypothesis, however, and thus barred the most obvious, and probably the only way to generalize his model.

5.4 The model studied by Arrow (1953) is far more general. He considers n different commodities, and he assumes that each participant in the market may have his own subjective probabilities. In this paper we shall disregard both these refinements. The generalization to n commodities appears inessential when our main objective is to study the interplay of different attitudes toward risk and uncertainty. The subjective probabilities play a key part in Arrow's model, but it seems unnecessary to introduce them in a study of a reinsurance market. When a reinsurance treaty is concluded, both parties will survey all information relevant to the risks concerned. To hide information from the other party is plain fraud. Whether two rational persons on the basis of the same information can arrive at different evaluations of the probability of a specific event, is a question of semantics. That they may act differently on the same information is well known, but this can usually be explained assuming that the two persons attach different utilities to the event. In some situations, for instance in stock markets, it may be useful to resort both to subjective probabilities and different utility functions to explain observed behaviour. This seems, however, to be an unnecessary complication in a first study of reinsurance markets.

5.5 When simplified as indicated in the preceding paragraph, Arrow's model can be described as follows:

(i) Company i has a utility of money $u_i(x)$, $i = 1, 2, \ldots, I$.

(ii) As a result of its direct underwriting the company is committed to pay an amount x_{is} if "state of the world" s occurs, $s = 1, 2, \ldots, S$.

(iii) The company has funds amounting to S_i available for meeting the commitments.

(iv) The probability that state of the world s shall occur is $p_s \left(\sum_{s=1}^{S} p_s = 1 \right)$.

The utility of company i in the initial situation is then

$$U_i(0) = \sum_{s=1}^{S} p_s u_i(S_i - x_i s)$$

where x_{is} may be zero for some s.

5.6 It is then assumed that there exists a price vector $g_1, \ldots, g_s, \ldots, g_S$ so that the company can pay an amount $g_s y_{is}$, and then be assured of receiving the amount y_{is} if state of the world s occurs. This means that should this state occur, the company will have to make a net payment of

$x_{is} - y_{is}$. If the company makes a series of such contracts, its utility will change to

$$U_1(y) = \sum_{s=1}^{S} p_s u_i \left[\left(S_i - \sum_{s=1}^{S} g_s y_{is} \right) - (x_{is} - y_{is}) \right]$$

where y_{is} may be positive or negative.

Differentiating with respect to y_{it} we find:

$$\frac{\partial U_i(y)}{\partial y_{it}} = -g_t \sum_{s=1}^{S} p_s u_i' \left[\left(S_i - \sum_{s=1}^{S} g_s y_{is} \right) - x_{is} + y_{is} \right] + p_t u_i' \left[\left(S_i - \sum_{s=1}^{S} g_s y_{is} \right) - x_{it} + y_{it} \right]$$

Since we have placed n restrictions on y_{it}, the first order conditions for a maximum will be

$$g_t \sum_{s=1}^{S} p_s u_i' \left(S_i - \sum_{s=1}^{S} g_s y_{is} - x_{is} + y_{is} \right) = p_t u_i' \left(S_i - \sum_{s=1}^{S} g_s y_{is} - x_{it} + y_{it} \right) \qquad (t = 1, 2, \ldots, S)$$

5.7 We now assume that the utility function is of the same simple form as in Section 4, i.e., that

$$u_i(x) = -a_i x^2 + x \qquad (i = 1, 2, \ldots, I)$$

The first order conditions for a maximum will then become

$$2a_i g_t \sum_{s=1}^{S} p_s \left(S_i - \sum_{s=1}^{S} g_s y_{is} - x_{is} + y_{is} \right) - g_t = 2a_i p_t \left(S_i - \sum_{s=1}^{S} g_s y_{is} - x_{it} + y_{it} \right) - p_t$$

By some rearrangement this system of equations can be written

$$(g_t - p_t)\left(\frac{1}{2a_i} - S_i\right) g_t \sum_{s=1}^{S} p_s x_{is} - p_t x_{it}$$

$$= g_t \sum_{s=1}^{S} p_s y_{is} - p_t y_{it} - (g_t - p_t) \sum_{s=1}^{S} g_s y_{is}$$

$$(t = 1, 2, \ldots, S \quad \text{and } i = 1, 2, \ldots, I)$$

y_{is} is the amount (positive or negative) which company i will receive if state of the world s occurs. Since this amount necessarily must be paid out by the other companies, we must have

$$\sum_{i=1}^{I} y_{is} = 0 \qquad \text{for all } s$$

Hence if we sum the equations over all i, the right hand side will disappear, so that we get the system

$$(g_t - p_t) \sum_i = 1^I \left(\frac{1}{2a_i} - S_i\right) + g_t \sum_{s=1}^{S} p_s \sum_{i=1}^{I} x_{is} - p_t \sum_{i=1}^{I} x_{it} = 0$$

$$(t = 1, 2, \ldots, S)$$

From this we obtain

$$g_t = p_t \frac{X_t + A}{X + A}$$

where

$$A = \sum_{i=1}^{I} A_i = \sum_{i=1}^{I} \left(\frac{1}{2a_i} - S_i\right),$$

$$X_s = \sum_{i=1}^{I} x_{is} \quad \text{and} \quad X = \sum_{s=1}^{S} p_s X_s$$

The complete solution of the system is given by

$$x_{it} - y_{it} = q_i X_t$$

and

$$q_i = \frac{A_i + \sum_{s=1}^{S} g_s x_{is}}{A + \sum_{s=1}^{S} g_s X_s}$$

where

$$\sum_{i=1}^{I} q_i = 1$$

5.8 This solution implies that company $i (i = 1, 2, \ldots, I)$ shall pay a fixed quota q_i of the total claim payment, regardless of which state of the world may occur, hence the solution belongs to the set of Pareto optimal arrangements that we found in Section 4.2.

Since

$$\sum_{s=1}^{S} g_s x_{is} = \sum_{s=1}^{S} p_s \frac{X_s + A}{X + A} x_{is} = \frac{1}{X + A} \sum_{s=1}^{s} p_s (A x_{is} + X_s x_{is})$$

$$= \frac{1}{X + A} \left(A m_i + X m_i + \sum_{s=1}^{S} p_s (X_s - X)(x_{is} - m_i) \right)$$

$$= m_i + \frac{\sum_{s=1}^{S} p_s (X_s - X)(x_{is} - m_i)}{X + A} = m_i + \frac{C_i}{X + A}$$

where $m_i = \sum_{s=1}^{S} p_s x_{is}$, and since $X = \sum_{i=1}^{I} m_i$, we have

$$q_i = \frac{A_i + m_i + \dfrac{C_i}{X + A}}{\sum_{j=1}^{I} (A_j + m_j) + \dfrac{\operatorname{var} X_s}{X + A}}$$

It is interesting to compare this with the expression which we found in Section 4.4 for the case $p = 0$.

5.9 The difference between Arrow's model and ours obviously lies in the price concept. In Arrow's model there is a price associated with every state of the world. The price will be the same for all states which lead to the same amount of total claim payment.

Our model is essentially a drastic simplification. Instead of the really infinite number of prices considered by Arrow, we have introduced one single price, a specific price of risk. We found that this price would have to be a vector with an infinite number of elements. If the utility function has the simple form studied in Section 4, the number of elements is reduced to two. However, in this case a competitive equilibrium cannot in general be a Pareto optimal distribution of risks.

5.10 The price in Arrow's model increases with the probability of a particular state of the world, and with the total amount to be paid if this state occurs. In insurance this means that a reinsurer who is asked to cover a modest amount if a certain person dies, will quote a price increasing with the total amount which is payable on the death of this person.

Such considerations are not unknown in insurance practice. It is well known that it can be difficult, i.e., expensive to arrange satisfactory reinsurance of particularly large risks. Practice seems here to be ahead of insurance theory, however, which still is firmly based on the *principle of equivalence*, i.e., that "net premiums" should be equal to the expected value of claim payments.

To apply Arrow's theory to stock market speculation we just have to reverse the signs of the formulae in this section.

We then find that the price of a certain share will depend not only on its "intrinsic value", but also on the number of such shares in the market. This may seem reasonable, although it implies that one pays more for a chance of getting rich alone, than for an identical chance of getting equally rich together with a lot of other speculators. The implication is that even in a model using essentially classical assumptions, there is a positive price attached to "getting ahead of the Joneses", and this may be a little unexpected.

6. The Problem seen as an n-person Game

6.1 We noted in Section 2.6 that a Pareto optimal set of reinsurance treaties was equivalent to a pool arrangement. Once the pool was established, the companies had to agree on some rule as to how each company should contribute to the payment of claims against the pool. In the special case which we considered in Section 4, this rule was that each company should pay a fixed proportion of these claims, regardless of its size. The quotas which each company should pay remained to be fixed, however.

When the problem is presented in this way, it seems natural to consider it as a problem of bargaining and negotiation which logically should be analyzed in the terms of the theory of games. A priori it appears unlikely that there should exist some price mechanism which automatically will lead the companies to such a rather special arrangement as a Pareto optimal set of treaties.

6.2 In general an n-person game has an indeterminate solution. To get a determinate solution we must make *additional assumptions* about how the companies negotiate their way to an agreement.

The point is brought out clearly by the special case studied in Section 4. The usual assumptions of game theory leave the quotas $q_1, \ldots, q_n$ undetermined, except for the restriction $\sum q_i = 1$. The solution has, so to speak, $n-1$ "degrees of freedom". During the negotiations each company will try to get the smallest possible quota for itself.

We then lay down the additional rule that the same price must be applied to all the reciprocal treaties which constitute a Pareto optimal set. This amounts really to a ban on "price discrimination" or a partial ban on coalitions. The rule leaves only the price p to be determined by negotiation, so that the number of degrees of freedom is reduced to one.

6.3 From the expressions in Section 4.4 we can conjecture that a given price p will divide the companies in two groups or coalitions. One group will benefit from a higher price, the other from a lower one. The higher the price, the more companies will be in the latter group. The "equilibrium price" must then be determined so that it divides the companies in two groups, which in some unspecified manner are equal in strength. There are obviously a number of possible ways in which the concept "strength" can be defined, and hence a number of possible determinate solutions. We shall, however, not explore these possibilities in the present paper.

6.4 In real life reinsurance treaties are concluded after lengthy negotiations, often with brokers acting as intermediaries. The concept of prevailing market prices plays a part in the background of these negotiations, but the whole situation is more similar to an n-person game than to a classical market with utility maximization when the price is considered as given.

Little is known about the laws and customs ruling such negotiations in the reinsurance market. It seems, however, that further studies of this subject should be a promising, if not the most promising, way of gaining deeper knowledge of attitudes toward risk and the decisions which rational people make under uncertainty.

References for Section 6

Allais, Maurice. (1953a): "L'Extension des Théories de I'Équilibre Économique General et du Rendement Social au Cas du Risque", *Econometrica*, 269–290.

Allais, Maurice. (1953b): "Le Comportement de l'Homme Rationnel devant le Risque: Critique des Postulates et Axiomes de I'École Americaine, *Econometrica*, 503–546.

Arrow, Kenneth J. (1953): "Le Rôle de Valeurs boursières pour la Repartition la meilleure des Risques", *Colloques Internationaux du Centre National de la Recherche Scientifique, Paris, XL*, 41–48.

Arrow, Kenneth J, and Gerard Debreu (1954): "Existence of an Equilibrium for a Competitive Economy", *Econometrica*, 265–290.

Borch, Karl. (1960a): "An Attempt to Determine the Optimum Amount of Stop Loss Reinsurance", *Transactions of the XVI International Congress of Actuaries II*, 597–610.

Borch, Karl. (1960b): "The Safety Loading of Reinsurance Premiums", *Skandinavisk Aktuarietidskrift*, 163–184.

Debreu Gerard (1959): *Theory of Value*, New York: John Wiley & Sons.

Lukacs E. (1952): "An Essential Property of the Fourier Transforms of Distribution Functions", *Proceedings of the American Mathematical Society*, 508-510.

Neumann J. Von, and O. Morgenstern (1944): *Theory of Games and Economic Behavior*, Princeton: Princeton University Press.

Wald, Abraham (1936): "Über einige Gleichungssysteme der mathematischen Ökonomie", *Zeitschrift für Nalionalökonomie*, 637–670. English translation, *Econometrica 1951*, 368–403.

7. The Theory of Risk*

1. Historical Note

The word "risk" is used colloquially in many different senses, but has also been defined as a precise technical term in a number of different contexts.

Economists will generally recall Frank Knight's (1921) sharp distinction between the concepts of "risk" and "uncertainty". In Knight's terminology risk is present in a situation where an action can lead to several different, mutually exclusive outcomes each of known probability. If these

* Reprinted from *The Journal of the Royal Statistical Society, Series B*, 1967, Volume 29:3, 432–467, copyright 9c) Royal Statistical Society, London.

probabilities are unknown, the situation will in Knight's language contain *uncertainty.* The development of the Bayesian approach to statistics and decision theory seems to have made Knight's distinction between the concepts obsolete, or at least to indicate that the distinction is not essential to a systematic study of the subject.

Statisticians will probably associate risk with Wald's (1950) theory of statistical decision functions. Wald defines risk as the sum of expected cost of experimentation and expected loss due to wrong terminal decisions, when a particular decision function is used. This is a concept which appears to be essential in a theory of rational decisions, but the technical term chosen by Wald may have been unfortunate. In recent years authors have preferred words such as "pay-off", which do not have so many colloquial connotations as risk.

In insurance the word "risk" has a long tradition, and has been used in many different senses. It is generally assumed that it was first used as a precisely defined mathematical concept by Tetens (1786) in a work on life annuities. In this, Tetens proposed to attach the name risk to what we today would describe as "one half of the mean deviation". This terminology, now obsolete, persisted in actuarial circles at least up to the Second World War, and led to the development of risk theory, a term which still has a well-defined meaning to most actuaries. It is this theory which we shall discuss in the following sections.

It will become apparent that actuarial risk theory has, to a large extent, developed outside the mainstream of probability theory and mathematical statistics. It is difficult now to explain why this should have happened. One reason may be that for a long time insurance — together with gambling — was the only practical application of probability theory. Actuaries had the field to themselves, and tended to formulate their results as solutions to insurance problems, without taking the trouble of explaining their general nature. As probability theory found other applications, it was apparently easier to rediscover the results than to trace them in existing literature, where they were hidden behind clouds of insurance jargon.

2. The Classical Theory of Risk

To present the actuarial theory of risk in its proper setting, it is necessary to restate some of the elements in the theory of insurance. The basic concept in insurance is the *insurance contract.* In its simplest form an insurance contract will give a person — the insured — the right to claim an amount of money, S, from the company, if certain events should occur. To be entitled to this right, the insured pays the company a premium P.

If the probability of events leading to a claim is p, the premium is determined so that

$$P = pS \tag{1}$$

This equation illustrates the *principle of equivalence*, which constitutes the very foundation of insurance theory. In its general form, this principle states that the expected value of claim payments under a contract should be equal to the expected value of premiums received.

Strictly speaking the equation determines the so-called *net premium*. In practice one must add to this premium a "loading" to cover the expected administrative costs of the company. We shall, however, ignore these costs, since they do not raise any new questions of principle; such costs can be brought into our formulae at any stage, if it should be desirable.

A more general insurance contract is defined by a probability distribution $F(x)$, where $F(x)$ is the probability that claim payments under the contract shall not exceed x. The net premium for this contract is, by the principle of equivalence,

$$P = \int_0^\infty x\, dF(x) \tag{2}$$

As a more complicated example, let us consider a contract according to which a person undertakes to pay a premium P at the beginning of each year as long as he lives. In return the insurance company undertakes to pay an amount S at the end of the year in which he dies.

Let q_t be the probability that the person considered shall die in year t. As obviously

$$q_1 + q_2 + \cdots q_t + \cdots = 1\,,$$

the expected claim payment will be S. Expected premium receipts will be:

$$P(q_1 + 2q_2 + \cdots + tq_t + \cdots)$$

We could use these two observations to determine the premium by the principle of equivalence. For a contract of long duration, we should, however, take into account the interest earned by accumulated funds. This leads us to determine the premium from the equation

$$P\{q_1 + (1+v)q_2 + (1+v+v^2)q_3 + \cdots\} = S\{vq_1 + v^2q_2 + v^3q_3 + \cdots\}\,,$$

where $v = (1+i)^{-1}$, and i is the rate of interest. This illustrates the general principle of equivalence: *The expected discounted values* (or the "present values") of premium receipts and claim payments must be equal.

Classical actuarial mathematics consists of estimating probabilities and computing expected discounted values. These problems are not always easy, since it is possible to draw up very complicated insurance contracts. The problems are, however, by no means unique to insurance. The development of operational research has shown that mathematical problems of this kind may occur in any industry, and that the real difficulty is to discover the problems and to give them a suitable formulation.

Let us now consider two insurance contracts. Under the first the only possible claim is $S_1 = 100$, and the probability that it shall be paid is $p_1 = 0.1$. The second contract is of the same form, but with $S_2 = 1000$ and $p_2 = 0.01$.

The principle of equivalence will lead to the same premium, $P = 10$, for both these contracts. Most people will, however, feel that the second contract is more dangerous, or "riskier" than the first, and that this ought to be reflected in the premium. In some cases it may be possible to dismiss this argument with an appeal to the Law of Large Numbers, which is, after all, the real basis of insurance.

In order to obtain a measure of the risk of a contract, Tetens (1786) defined risk as expected loss to the company, if the contract leads to a loss. Applied to the first example of the preceding paragraph, this gives the risk as:

$$R = \int_P^\infty (x - P)\, dF(x) = \tfrac{1}{2} \int_0^\infty |x - P|\, dF(x) \tag{3}$$

For the two examples above, we find the risks:

$$R_1 = \tfrac{1}{2}\{0.9 \times 10 + 0.1 \times 90\} = 9\,,$$

$$R_2 = \tfrac{1}{2}\{0.99 \times 10 + 0.01 \times 990\} = 9.9$$

It is usually more convenient to work with the standard deviation than with the mean deviation, so the idea of Tetens naturally led to suggestions that risk should be defined as M, where M is determined by the equation

$$M^2 = \int_0^\infty (x - P)^2\, dF(x) \tag{4}$$

This concept was discussed in considerable detail by Hausdorff (1897), and is usually associated with his name, although it has been studied earlier by other authors. For the examples above we find $M_1 = 30$ and $M_2 = 99$.

The pioneers of the theory of risk are not very clear when it comes to explaining the practical use which should be made of the different measures of risk. There seems to have been a vague feeling that some amount, proportional to the risk, should be added to the net premium as a "safety loading", but this was first explicitly suggested by Wold (1936).

It is interesting to note that few actuaries seem to have recognized the significance of the work by Daniel Bernoulli (1738) on the problem we now refer to as the "St. Petersburg Paradox". Bernoulli suggested that mathematical expectation should be replaced by "moral expectation", a concept which we today know as *expected utility.*

In modern terms Bernoulli's idea can be expressed as follows: The company has a *preference ordering* over the set of all insurance contracts. This ordering can be represented by a utility function $u(x)$, in the sense that the expected utility

$$\int_0^\infty u(P - x)\, dF(x) \tag{5}$$

is greater, the higher the contract is placed in the preference ordering.

The company will then accept an insurance contract only if it is preferred to a degenerate contract, which is certain to give neither loss nor gain. This means that the premium Q must be determined so that

$$u(0) \leq \int_0^\infty u(Q - x)\, dF(x)$$

The function $u(x)$ can be interpreted as the *utility of money*, and it is usually assumed that $u'(x) > 0$ and $u''(x) < 0$, i.e. the marginal utility of money is decreasing. From these assumptions it follows that $Q \geq P$, so that we obtain the "safety loading" which was mentioned above.

The ideas of Bernoulli were taken up by Barrois (1834), who used them to develop a fairly complete and surprisingly modern theory of fire insurance. To illustrate this, let us assume that the wealth of a person is S, and that he may suffer a loss from fire x, where x is a variety with the distribution $F(x)$. If the utility function for money of this person is $w(x)$, he is willing to pay a premium Q to be insured against the loss, provided that

$$\int_0^\infty w(S - x)\, dF(x) \leq w(S - Q)$$

A premium which satisfies this inequality, as well as the inequality in the preceding paragraph, should be acceptable to both the person to be insured and the insurance company. The insurance contract will then increase the expected utility of both parties.

The work of Barrois seems to have been ignored by following generations of actuaries. The ideas of Bernoulli reappeared in insurance literature only when the game theory of von Neumann and Morgenstern (1944) had made utility fashionable, and demonstrated that this concept must occupy a central position in any theory of decisions under risk and uncertainty. The first who applied modern utility theory to insurance was Nolfi (1957), and his results have been developed by a number of other authors, including Borch (1961).

The ideas of Bernoulli and Barrois indicate that the logical approach to the subject should be to consider insurance cover as a commodity, which is bought and sold. The premium must then be considered as a price, which is determined by supply and demand in the market. This should, as demonstrated in another paper (Borch, 1962), lead to an economic theory of insurance, and to ideas which in general may be rather unfamiliar to actuaries and statisticians.

It is in some ways surprising that the development of mathematical economics during the last 80 to 100 years has had next to no influence on the theory of risk developed by actuaries. One explanation may be the reputation for integrity and high moral standards which the insurance industry seeks to maintain. These standards led actuaries to seek general rules for determining "correct loadings" and "fair premiums". They may have been well aware that some people might be prepared to pay more than a "fair premium" for insurance cover, but the idea of exploitation in order to make profits seems not to have commended itself to the traditional thinking in the insurance world. This is directly opposed to the thinking in economics, where it is assumed — usually without question — that a "rational" person will charge the price which the market is willing to pay.

After this digression, we return to the theory of risk. There are no real difficulties involved in computing the risk, R or M, for insurance contracts far more complicated than those considered earlier. The expressions may, however, be exceedingly complex, and in life insurance they will have to be recalculated for each year in which the contract runs, since the probability of dying will vary with a person's age. The relevant formulae can be found in older actuarial literature. We shall, however, neither reproduce nor discuss these formulae, since they seem to have found little application in practice.

Let us consider instead a portfolio of n independent insurance contracts, with premiums $P_1, P_2, \ldots, P_n$ and risks $M_1, M_2, \ldots, M_n$. We can then define the risk of the portfolio, M, by the equation

$$M^2 = M_1^2 + M_2^2 + \cdots + M_n^2 \tag{6}$$

Let the company's gain on this portfolio be a variety z. If the premiums are determined by the principle of equivalence, the expected value of this variety will evidently be zero, i.e. $E\{z\} = 0$. If n is large, z will under certain conditions be approximately normally distributed, with standard deviation M.

If the company holds a reserve fund S, in addition to the premiums collected for contracts in force, the expression

$$\begin{aligned} \alpha = \Pr\{z < -S\} &= \frac{1}{M\sqrt{(2\pi)}} \int_{-\infty}^{-S} \exp\left[-\frac{1}{2}\left(\frac{x}{M}\right)^2\right] dx \\ &= \Phi\left(-\frac{S}{M}\right) \end{aligned} \tag{7}$$

will give the probability that the company shall not be able to fulfil its commitments under the contracts in the portfolio. This probability, which is referred to as the *probability of ruin*, has become the central concept in the theory of risk.

The ideas outlined in the preceding paragraph make it possible to give the theory of risk some operational content.

The starting-point is usually an assumption that the probability of ruin must be kept below a certain level, which represents the acceptable maximum. If S is so great that the ruin probability is smaller than this maximum, the company can pay a part of its reserve fund out as dividends — to share holders or policy holders, as the case may be. If S is so small that the ruin probability exceeds the acceptable level, the company may obtain additional guarantee capital, or it may seek a reinsurance arrangement, which will reduce the risk, and hence the probability of ruin. Usually the latter alternative is chosen, and as a result the theory of risk became almost identical with the theory of reinsurance in actuarial literature.

The argument above implies that the company must obtain additional reserve funds as its volume of business grows. Theoretically the company could obtain these funds by calling upon share holders to put up more equity capital. In practice, these funds will usually be obtained from the company's customers by a loading of the premium. One usually assumes that the loading is proportional to the net premium, so that the premium actually paid under contract i is $(1+\lambda)P_i$. The expected gain on the company's portfolio will then be

$$E\{z\} = \lambda P\,, \tag{8}$$

where $P = P_1 + P_2 + \cdots + P_n$.

The probability of ruin will then be

$$\Pr\{z < -S\} = \Phi\left(-\frac{S+\lambda P}{M}\right) \tag{9}$$

In actuarial literature it is usually assumed that the maximum acceptable probability of ruin is decided outside the insurance industry, for instance, that it is imposed by the government as a solvency condition which the companies must satisfy.

An insurance company will then take α as given. It is natural to assume that the reserve fund S also is given and unchangeable, at least in the short run. The problem of the company will then be to determine the optimal loading factor λ. In order to make this a well-defined problem, we will have to specify the objectives of the company, and the conditions at which reinsurance can be obtained. If we do this, we will have a problem typical of operational research.

The actuaries who created the classical theory of risk, could not be expected to formulate their problem with the precision required by modern operational analysis. They probably came nearest to it when they sought to determine the value of λ which would leave the reinsured proportion of the portfolio constant when the volume of business increases. However, even this problem is without meaning, unless the nature of the insurance contracts and the conditions or reinsurance are specified.

The loading factor λ may, however, also have to be taken as given — it may be determined by competition in the market, or by government control of insurance premiums. The only decision left to the company will then be to choose the most favorable reinsurance arrangement. This means, as we have observed earlier, that the theory of risk is reduced to a theory of reinsurance, and as pointed out in Borch (1962), already referred to, that the whole problem should be analysed in term of economic theory.

The foundation of insurance is the Law of Large Numbers. It turns out, however, that the number of insurance contracts in the portfolio of a company is not usually "large enough", i.e. one cannot apply the law and ignore deviations from expected values. The theory of risk was developed to analyse these deviations, and the classical theory fell back on the central limit theorem, and assumed that the deviations were normally distributed. It seems, however, that the number of contracts is also usually too small to justify this assumption, as has been pointed out by a number of actuaries, *inter alios* by Cramér (1930), who suggests that this is the main reason why the theory has found so little application in practice.

Cramér's criticism certainly contains a good deal of truth, but one may think of other explanations. It seems likely that the amount of computation required to apply the theory has played a part in its neglect. With electronic computers it may, however, be feasible to apply the theory in practice. Insurance companies are required to compute their reserves, i.e. the expected value of claims to be paid under the contracts in hand at the end of an accounting period. It should not be impossible to do some additional calculations and provide an estimate of the probability that total claim payments will be below the assets of the company. The practical usefulness of an estimate of this kind seems, however, to be very doubtful. The estimate is bound to be a fairly rough approximation, and it may obviously be very misleading. It should further be evident that one single number — the probability of ruin — cannot give a complete description of the real situation of the company.

The probability of ruin gives us the probability that the company shall be unable to meet the commitments under the contracts it holds at a certain moment. But this is a static measure; before these contracts have expired, it is likely that the company will have underwritten a large number of new contracts, and this may substantially change the company's ability to pay claims made under contracts in the original portfolio.

These considerations indicate that we need a dynamic theory of risk, in order to come to grips realistically with the problems of insurance companies. The fact that the classical theory of risk is essentially static is probably the main reason why it has found little application in the real, dynamic world. Arguments of this kind form the starting-point of the theory of Lundberg, which we shall discuss in the following section.

3. The Collective Risk Theory

The collective theory of risk was created by Lundberg (1909), and has been developed by a relatively small group of actuaries, mainly Scandinavians. The theory seems to have found even less practical application than the classical theory discussed earlier, which Lundberg's followers usually refer to as the "individual theory of risk". The reason is, as we shall see, that Lundberg's theory does not, according to practising actuaries, come to grips with the problems of insurance companies.

Lundberg's papers contain exceptionally penetrating analysis, and a very high degree of mathematical originality, and they have certainly not received the attention which they deserve. It is natural to compare Lundberg with Bachelier. Both studied problems connected with stochastic processes in continuous time about 30 years before this concept had been rigorously defined (Bachelier, 1900), and the work of both was ignored and practically forgotten.

It is not easy to explain why the significance of Bachelier's work should have been overlooked. In the case of Lundberg it is, however, easy to see that part of the explanation lies in his style.

Lundberg's mathematical arguments were — and probably still are — too advanced for most actuaries and practical insurance people. His results are, however, almost invariably presented in actuarial terms, so that it is very hard for a mathematician without knowledge of insurance to see that some of the results are mathematical theorems of quite general validity.

Lundberg's theory has been developed in a number of papers, but most of these are written in a style which appeals neither to the mathematician nor to the practical insurance man. It may be quite natural for some members of a small group, working on a very special set of problems, to write mainly for the other initiated members of the group. It is, however, surprising that so few of the group have tried to write survey articles to inform the outsider. Cramér has written two good survey articles (Cramér, 1930, 1955), but they appear in publications which are not easily accessible. There is also a comprehensive survey by Segerdahl (1959), which is of a rather limited value, since it does not contain any references to original papers.

Lundberg considered an insurance company as a container, or as a dam, to use the more popular current statistical term. Into this dam flows a continuous stream of premiums, and out of the dam goes a sequence of claim payments.

He then considered a model consisting of the following three elements:

(i) The stream of premiums, $P(t)$ = the total value of premiums received in the period $(0,\ t)$.

(ii) $q(n, t)$ = the probability that n claims occur in the period $(0, t)$.

(iii) The probability distribution of individual claims, $G(x)$ = the probability that if a claim should occur, the amount payable will not exceed x.

This is a very general model. The most important restriction is the assumption that $G(x)$ does not depend on t and n. The restriction may be lifted, but few authors seem to have studied such generalizations. The reason is probably that it is not quite clear what kind of dependence one should assume in insurance problems.

From the three elements it follows that the probability that claim payments in the period $(0, t)$ shall not exceed x is given by the formula:

$$F(x,t) = \sum_{n=0}^{\infty} q(n,t) G^{(n)}(x) \,, \tag{10}$$

where $G^{(n)}(x)$ for $n > 0$ is the nth convolution of $G(x)$ with itself, and $G^{(0)}(x) = H(x)$, where $H(x)$ is the Heaviside function defined by

$$H(x) = \begin{cases} 1 & \text{for } x \geq 0 \,, \\ 0 & \text{for } x < 0 \end{cases}$$

$F(x, t)$ can obviously be considered as the claim distribution for a portfolio of insurance contracts, which all expire in the period $(0, t)$. If claim payments under different contracts are stochastically independent, $F(x, t)$ can be obtained as the convolution of all the claim distributions, defined by the contracts in the portfolio. Hence the second moment about the mean of $F(x, t)$ will be the square of the risk M^2, by analogy with (4).

These observations illustrate the elegance and power of Lundberg's method. With his approach it is no longer necessary to consider each contract in the portfolio in order to determine the probability distribution of the total amount of claim payments. Instead this distribution is built up from the two elements $q(n, t)$ and $G(x)$, from two distributions which it should be possible to estimate from the records of the company. From this point of view it seems natural to refer to Lundberg's theory as the collective theory of risk. It is, however, clear that the real innovation of the theory lies in its *dynamic* aspects, and it would have been preferable to use this word to distinguish Lundberg's theory from the essentially static, classical risk theory.

The discrete distribution $q(n, t)$ can be interpreted as the mechanism which generates claims. One can make assumptions about this mechanism, and deduce some of the properties of the distribution. This question has been studied by many actuaries, and, as one would expect, the assumptions which appear most natural differ from one branch of insurance to another.

Lundberg himself worked with the stationary and time-independence assumptions which lead to the Poisson process

$$q(n,t) = e^{-\alpha t}\frac{(\alpha t)^n}{n!}$$

The claim distribution then becomes the compound Poisson process

$$F(x,t) = e^{-\alpha t}\sum_{n=0}^{\infty}\frac{(\alpha t)^n}{n!}G^{(n)}(x) \tag{11}$$

The expected value of the claim payments x_t during the period $(0,t)$ is then

$$E\{x_t\} = \int_0^{\infty} x\,dF(x,t) = \alpha t\bar{x}\,, \tag{12}$$

where

$$\bar{x} = \int_0^{\infty} x\,dG(x)$$

It is convenient to choose the unit of time such that

$$E\{x_t\} = t$$

There is, however, more than just convenience involved. It will clearly always be possible to make a transformation of the time scale, so that expected claim payments in any period are equal to the length of the period. This means that the stationary assumptions, which lead to the Poisson process, are unnecessary if we work with this transformed "operational time".

Operational time is one of Lundberg's most ingenious concepts. It is closely related to the "entropy time" used in theoretical physics, and it makes it possible both to simplify the theory and to extend its validity. It seems, however, that this concept has also been the main obstacle to practical application of the theory.

The principle of equivalence implies that the net premium received by the company during a period of length t in operational time must be equal to t, the expected claim payments during the period. If there is a loading λ, the amount of premium received by the company during the period will be

$$P(t) = (1+\lambda)t$$

Let us now assume that the company has an initial capital S_0. At time t, the capital will then be:

$$S_t = S_0 + (1 + \lambda)t - x_t \tag{13}$$

This means that the development of the company's capital is described by a stochastic process with independent increments. It was a remarkable achievement of Lundberg to penetrate to the very core of the risk problem, and arrive at this formulation, which at his time could not be given with full mathematical rigor.

If the capital S_t is negative at time t, the company is insolvent or ruined. As a natural generalization of the classical probability of ruin, we are then led to study:

$$\Pr\{\min S_t \geq 0\}$$

for t belonging to a suitable subset of the positive real line. If we select a subset consisting of one single point, we are back in the classical theory.

A practical insurance man may suggest a subset consisting of a sequence $t_1, t_2, \ldots, t_n$ corresponding to the dates of the n next valuations, or to the ends of the n next accounting years. He will then be interested in the probability that the company shall be solvent at all these dates, and presumably take some action if this probability falls below the acceptable minimum. It is, however, not easy to answer such practical questions, because the theory works with operational time. In order to obtain a simple and elegant theory, one has paid a heavy cost in the form of difficulties in practical applications.

If we take a subset consisting of an interval $(0, T)$, we are led to study the probability

$$\Pr\left\{\min_{0 \leq t \leq T} S_t \geq 0\right\} = R(S_0, T) \tag{14}$$

that the company shall be solvent during the whole period $(0, T)$. It is probably fair to say that most of the work in the collective risk theory has been concerned with deriving approximate expressions for $R(S, T)$ for large T. These expressions may be extremely complicated, but there are no serious mathematical problems involved. As we would expect, the expressions become simpler if we go to the limit, so let us write

$$\lim_{T \to \infty} R(S, T) = R(S), \tag{15}$$

where we have omitted the subscript on S. $R(S)$ is the probability that a company with initial capital S shall never become insolvent. We shall sketch a derivation of the integral equation satisfied by $R(S)$.

The probability that the first claim shall occur at time t is $e^{-t}dt$. The probability that this claim shall amount to x is $g(x)\,dx$, where $g(x) = G'(x)$. Provided that $x < S+(1+\lambda)t$, the company will not be ruined by the first claim, and the probability that it shall remain solvent in the future will be $R\big(S+(1+\lambda)t - x\big)$. By integrating over the relevant domains of t and x we obtain the integral equation

$$R(S) = \int_0^{\infty} e^{-t} \left(\int_0^{S+(1+\lambda)t} R\big(S+(1+\lambda)t - x\big) g(x) dx \right) dt \tag{16}$$

To simplify the expression we substitute $y = S + (1+\lambda)t$, and write the equation

$$R(S) = \frac{1}{1+\lambda} \int_S^{\infty} \exp\left(-\frac{y-S}{1+\lambda}\right) \left(\int_0^y R(y-x)\, g(x)\, dx \right) dy$$

The easiest way of solving this equation seems to be to differentiate and take Laplace transforms. Differentiation with respect to S gives

$$(1+\lambda)R'(S) = R(S) - \int_0^S R(S-x)\, g(x)\, dx \tag{17}$$

Multiplying this equation by e^{-sS} (Re $s > 0$) and integrating over S from 0 to ∞, we obtain

$$(1+\lambda)\big(s\psi(s) - R(0)\big) = \psi(s) - \psi(s)\,\phi(s)$$

or

$$\psi(s) = \frac{(1+\lambda)R(0)}{(1+\lambda)s - 1 + \phi(s)} \tag{18}$$

Here $\phi(s)$ is the Laplace transform of $R(S)$, i.e.

$$\psi(s) = \int_0^{\infty} e^{-sS} R(S)\, dS\,,$$

and $\phi(s)$ is the Laplace transform of $g(x)$.

From the expression found for $\psi(s)$, we can find $R(S)$ itself by taking the inverse Laplace transform. It is easy to see that $\psi(s)$ under certain conditions can be represented by a convergent series of powers of $\phi(s)$, so that $R(S)$ can be expressed as an infinite series of convolutions of $g(x)$ with itself. The constant $R(0)$ can be determined, for instance by Tauberian methods, and one finds

$$R(0) = \frac{\lambda}{1+\lambda}$$

In the preceding paragraphs we have solved our problem in a purely formal manner. We have done this in order to gain some insight into the nature of the problem. The results can be derived in a rigorous manner, by methods which by now are fairly standard, and which can easily be found in the literature, for instance in the textbook by Feller (1966). It is, however, remarkable that these results were achieved — admittedly in a heuristic manner — by Lundberg in the first decade of this century.

The methods we have outlined can be applied also for finite values of T, to determine $R(S,T)$. This will not lead to any essentially new difficulties, but it is clear that the explicit expressions will be even more complicated than in the limiting case.

The collective risk theory was created when few actuaries had even an electric desk calculator. It is therefore natural that the early development of the theory should have concentrated on deriving simple approximate expressions for $R(S)$ and $R(S,T)$. This has led to results which in many ways are impressive, but which are of little theoretical or practical interest today. The arrival of electronic computers has shifted the focus of interest to algorithms for computing the convolutions of high order, which enter in the series in the preceding paragraph. Some recent papers in this field (inter alios by Bohman and Esscher, 1963) seem to have a considerable general interest. The fact remains, however, that — in spite of these developments — collective risk theory has found virtually no application in practice.

To illustrate the point, let us assume that an insurance company has to make a decision with regard to, say, loading and reinsurance. The company will then need a criterion for comparing the merits of the different possible decisions. The collective risk theory suggests that one should compute the probability that the company will never be ruined, provided that the decision, once it is made, can never be changed. One should then make the decision which gives the highest value to this "probability of survival". It does not seem very likely that insurance companies should wish to make their decisions in this manner, and there is certainly no reason why experts should advise companies to do so.

These considerations indicate that there is a need for a radical reformulation of the basic model behind Lundberg's theory. In the following section we shall discuss this question, which so far has received little attention.

4. The Modern Risk Theory

It is doubtful if one should talk about modern risk theory as a continuation of the theories discussed in the two preceding sections. All results in these older theories can today be considered as special cases of more general results in pure or applied mathematics created without any reference to insurance. It is clear that these general results can be applied to the problems of insurance, and it is likely that the future development of "risk theory" in our sense will consist of finding such applications. Actuaries no longer have the whole field of probability theory to themselves, nor do they have to create their own tools as they proceed from one problem to the next.

The task of a modern actuary is above all to analyse and find the right formulation of his problem. The mathematical tools he needs to solve it are almost certain to be available.

As an illustration, we shall first discuss a model due to de Finetti (1957), which has been generalized and studied in more detail by Borch (1966, 1967a, b).

The capital of our company at time t was given in equation (13), and the expected value of the capital is

$$E\{S_t\} = S_0 + (1+\lambda)t - E\{x_t\} = S_0 + \lambda t \qquad (19)$$

This means that the capital can be expected to grow to infinity with t. De Finetti observed that this is a most unrealistic model, and assumed that there must be an upper limit, say Z, to the amount of capital which an insurance company would want — or be allowed — to accumulate. This assumption implies, however, that the company is certain to be ruined some time in the future, i.e. $R(S_0) = 0$, so that all the results of the collective risk theory become irrelevant.

The model suggested by de Finetti can be described as follows:

(i) The company has an initial capital S.

(ii) In each operating period the company underwrites a portfolio of insurance contracts with a claim distribution $F(x)$. We shall assume $F(x) = 0$ for $x \leq 0$.

(iii) In each operating period the company collects an amount of premium P.

(iv) If at the end of an operating period the company's capital exceeds Z, the excess is paid out — as dividend or taxes, as the case may be.

(v) If at the end of an operating period the capital is negative, the company is ruined, and has to go out of business.

In this model the company's capital performs a *random walk*, and there is an absorbing barrier at $S = 0$, and a reflecting barrier at $S = Z$. If we let Z go to infinity, we obtain the model of Lundberg. The introduction of a finite reflecting barrier makes the model far more interesting, and makes it possible to ask a number of new questions.

As a first example we shall find the expected number of periods during which the company will operate, i.e. the "expected life" of the company. Since this number obviously will depend on the initial capital S, and on the upper limit Z, we shall denote it by $D(S,Z)$.

From the definition of the process it follows that

$$\begin{aligned} D(S,Z) &= 0 && \text{for} \quad S < 0\,, \\ D(S,Z) &= D(Z,Z) && \text{for} \quad S > Z \end{aligned}$$

For $0 \le S \le Z$, $D(S,Z)$ must satisfy the integral equation

$$D(S,Z) = 1 + \int_0^{S+P} D(S+P-x,Z)\,dF(x) \tag{20}$$

This is easily verified by using an argument similar to that used in setting up equation (16). The equation can be solved by standard methods, which we shall discuss below. De Finetti considered only the special case where $P = 1$, and where x can take only the values 0 and 2. The integral equation then reduces to the difference equation,

$$D(S,Z) = 1 + pD(S+1,Z) + qD(S-1,Z)\,,$$

where

$$\begin{aligned} \Pr\{x = 0\} &= p\,, \\ \Pr\{x = 2\} &= q = 1 - p \end{aligned}$$

If $p > q$, the solution of the difference equation is

$$D(S,Z) = \frac{p}{(p-q)^2}\left[\left(\frac{p}{q}\right)^{Z+1} - \left(\frac{p}{q}\right)^{Z-S}\right] - \frac{S+1}{p-q} \qquad (21)$$

It is obvious that $D(S, Z)$ will go to infinity with Z, and that the probability of ruin may then become smaller than one. It is a well-known classical result that the probability of ruin in the limit is

$$1 - R(S) = \left(\frac{q}{p}\right)^{s}$$

By some elementary manipulations we find that

$$D(S+1,Z) - D(S,Z) = \frac{1}{p-q}\left[\left(\frac{p}{q}\right)^{Z-S} - 1\right]$$

from which it follows that $D(S, Z)$ increases with S.

As a second example, let us assume that excess capital is paid out as dividends, and let $V(S, Z)$ be the expected discounted value of the dividend payments, which the company will make during its lifetime. As in the preceding paragraph we have

$$V(S,Z) = 0 \qquad \text{for } S < 0$$

$$V(S,Z) = S - Z + V(Z,Z) \quad \text{for } S > Z$$

For $0 \leq S \leq Z$ we see that $V(S, Z)$ must satisfy the integral equation

$$V(S,Z) = v\int_0^{S+P} V(S+P-x,Z)\,dF(x)\,, \qquad (22)$$

where v is a discount factor.

In the special case considered by de Finetti, the integral equation reduces to the difference equation

$$V(S,Z) = vpV(S+1,Z) + vqV(S-1,Z)\,,$$

whose solution is

$$V(S,Z) = \frac{r_1^{S+1} - r_2^{S+1}}{r_1^{Z+2} - r_2^{Z+2} - r_1^{Z+1} + r_2^{Z+2}}\,, \qquad (23)$$

where r_1 and r_2 are the roots of the characteristic equation

$$r = vpr^2 + vq$$

It is easy to verify that both roots are positive, and that $r_1 > 1$, $r_2 < 1$. It then follows that $V(S, Z)$ will increase with S, as we would expect. It follows also that $V(S, Z)$ will go to zero as Z goes to infinity — i.e. if dividend payments are postponed indefinitely. There may, however, be a value of $Z > 0$, which maximizes $V(S, Z)$ and may in a sense be considered as the "optimal" reserve capital for the company. This observation has been made by Shubik and Thompson (1959) in a study of economic problems not having any formal connection with insurance.

The special case, studied by de Finetti, clearly gives some information about the general shape of the functions $D(S, Z)$ and $V(S, Z)$. To investigate this question in more detail, we shall study the continuous case, assuming that a density function $f(x) = F'(x)$ exists. Omitting the argument Z, we can write the integral equation (20) as follows:

$$D(S) = 1 + \int_0^{S+P} D(S + P - x)\, f(x)\, dx$$

or

$$D(S) = 1 + D(Z)\, F(S + P - Z) + \int_0^Z f(S + P - x)\, D(x)\, dx \tag{24}$$

This is an equation of Fredholm's type. To solve it, we form the iterated kernels

$$f^{(0)}(S + P - x) = \delta(S - x)\,,$$

where δ is the Dirac δ-function,

$$f^{(n)}(S + P - x) = \int_0^Z f(S + P - t) f^{(n-1)}(t + P - x)\, dt \quad (n = 2, 3, \ldots)$$

The solution is then given by the Neumann expansion

$$D(S) = 1 + D(Z) \sum_{n=0}^{\infty} \int_0^Z f^{(n)}(S + P - x)\, F(x + P - Z)\, dx \\ + \sum_{n=1}^{\infty} \int_0^Z f^{(n)}(S + P - x)\, dx \tag{25}$$

The terms in the expansion are integrals over a finite range of products of density functions — or "truncated convolutions". It is therefore obvious that the series converges, and gives a solution of the integral equation. The unknown $D(Z)$ is determined by requiring the solution to be continuous to the right at $S = Z$. This gives

$$D(Z) = 1 + D(Z)\sum_{n=0}^{\infty}\int_0^Z f^{(n)}(Z+P-x)\,F(x+P-Z)\,dx + \sum_{n=1}^{\infty}\int_0^Z f^{(n)}(Z+P-x)\,dx$$

or

$$D(Z) = \frac{1+\sum_{n=1}^{\infty}\int_0^Z f^{(n)}(Z+P-x)\,dx}{1-\sum_{n=0}^{\infty}\int_0^Z f^{(n)}(Z+P-x)\,F(x+P-Z)\,dx}$$

The continuous solution is obviously unique.

The series will usually converge fairly rapidly for small values of Z, so it is possible to compute $D(Z)$ and $D(S)$ with only a reasonable amount of labour. In general it is, however, impossible to find an explicit and simple expression for the function $D(S)$, and study its properties by elementary means. It may therefore be useful to discuss a special case, which gives a fairly simple expression. The basic idea is to reduce Fredholm's integral equation to an equation of a simpler kind.

Let us assume

$$f(x) = e^{-x} \quad (x \geq 0)$$

The integral equation will then become

$$D(S) = 1 + e^{-S-P}\int_0^{S+P} D(x)\,e^x\,dx \tag{26}$$

Differentiating with respect to S we find

$$D'(S) = -e^{-S-P}\int_0^{S+P} D(x)\,e^x\,dx + D(S+P),$$

adding this to the original equation, we obtain

$$D(S) + D'(S) = 1 + D(S + P) \tag{27}$$

This is a differential-difference equation, valid for $0 \leq S \leq Z$.

We shall now solve this equation, following a procedure developed by Bellman and Cooke (1963). It is, however, convenient first to make a change in the notation, which will give the results in a more familiar form. We shall write

$$t = Z - S$$

and

$$u(t) = D(S)$$

The equation then becomes

$$u(t) - u'(t) - u(t - P) = 1\,, \tag{28}$$

which is valid for $0 \leq t \leq Z$. In the following we shall assume that the equation also holds for $Z < t$, although the solution in this domain is irrelevant to our concrete problem. For $t \leq 0$ we have the boundary condition $u(t) = D(Z) = c$.

Taking the Laplace transform we obtain (when Re $s > 0$)

$$\int_0^\infty u(t)e^{-st}dt - \int_0^\infty u'(t)e^{-st}dt - \int_0^\infty u(t - P)e^{-st}dt = \frac{1}{s}\,,$$

which reduces to

$$\left(1 - s - e^{-sP}\right)\int_0^\infty u(t)e^{-st}dt = \frac{1}{s}\left(1 + c - cs - ce^{-sP}\right)$$

provided that s is sufficiently large. For the Laplace transform of $u(t)$ we therefore find

$$u^*(s) = \int_0^\infty u(t)e^{-st}dt = \frac{c}{s} + \frac{1}{s(1 - s - e^{-sP})} \tag{29}$$

The inversion of the expression $(1+s-e^{-sP})^{-1}$ is discussed in another context by Feller (1948). Since a factor s^{-1} in the transform corresponds to an indefinite integration with respect to t in the original, easy manipulations of Feller's result yield

$$u(t) = c + \sum_{n=0}^{\infty} \left(1 - e^{t-nP} \sum_{j=0}^{n} \frac{(-1)^j}{j!}(t-nP)^j\right) H(t-nP) \tag{30}$$

In the interval, $NP \leq t \leq (N+1)P$, this may be written

$$u(t) = c + N + 1 - \sum_{n=0}^{N} e^{t-nP}\left(1 - (t-nP) + \cdots + (-1)^n \frac{(t-nP)^n}{n!}\right),$$

or

$$u(t) = c + 1 + \left[\frac{t}{P}\right] - A(t),$$

where $\left[\frac{t}{P}\right]$ is the greatest integer not exceeding t/P, and $A(t)$ stands for the sum on the right-hand side. It is easy to verify that this function is continuous for $0 < t$.

To determine the constant c, we return to the integral equation (26) and note that

$$D(-P, Z) = u(Z+P) = 1$$

It then follows that

$$c = A(Z+P) - 1 - \left[\frac{Z}{P}\right]$$

and

$$u(t) = A(Z+P) - \left[\frac{Z}{P}\right] - A(t) + \left[\frac{t}{P}\right] \tag{31}$$

Returning to our original notation, we find the following expression for the solution:

$$\begin{aligned} D(S,Z) = & \sum_{n=0}^{\left[\frac{Z}{P}\right]+1} e^{Z-(n-1)P}\left[1 + \cdots \frac{(-1)^n}{n!}(Z-(n-1)P)^n\right] \\ & - \sum_{n=0}^{\left[\frac{Z-S}{P}\right]} e^{Z-S-nP}\left[1 + \cdots \frac{(-1)^n}{n!}(Z-S-nP)^n\right] \\ & - \left[\frac{Z}{P}\right] + \left[\frac{Z-S}{P}\right] \end{aligned} \tag{32}$$

The function $V(S, Z)$ can be found by similar methods, as shown in another paper (Borch, 1965). The expression will, however, be even more complicated than the one we have found for $D(S, Z)$ — essentially because the boundary conditions are more complicated for the differential-difference equation satisfied by $V(S, Z)$.

To obtain really simple expressions for the two functions, we can assume that the gain of the company has the density function

$$\begin{aligned} f(x) &= k\alpha e^{-\alpha x} && \text{for } x > 0\,, \\ f(x) &= (1-k)\alpha e^{\alpha x} && \text{for } x < 0 \end{aligned}$$

In this case there is no upper limit to the company's gain, so the example may not be quite appropriate to an insurance company. It may, however, be accepted as a reasonable approximation, and the example may provide an adequate model for companies in other lines of business, as has been shown in another paper (Borch, 1967b).

With this assumption, the integral equation (20) becomes

$$\begin{aligned} D(S) = 1 + (1-k)\alpha e^{-\alpha s} \int_0^S D(x) e^{\alpha x}\, dx \\ + k\alpha e^{\alpha S} \int_S^Z D(x) e^{-\alpha x}\, dx + k e^{\alpha(S-Z)} D(Z) \end{aligned} \tag{32}$$

Differentiating twice we find that the integral equation can be reduced to the differential equation

$$(2k-1)\alpha D'(S) + D''(S) + \alpha^2 = 0\,,$$

and the general solution of this equation is

$$D(S) = C_1 e^{-(2k-1)\alpha S} - \frac{\alpha}{2k-1} S + C_2\,, \tag{33}$$

where C_1 and C_2 are constants, which must be determined so that the solution also satisfies the integral equation.

Similarly we find that the integral equation (22) can be written as

$$V(S) = v(1-k)\alpha e^{-\alpha s} \int_0^S V(x)e^{\alpha x}\,dx + vk\alpha e^{\alpha S} \int_S^Z V(x)e^{-\alpha x}\,dx + vkV(Z)e^{\alpha(S-Z)} + \frac{vk}{\alpha} e^{\alpha(S-Z)} \quad (34)$$

Differentiating this twice, we find that the integral equation can be reduced to the differential equation

$$(1-v)\alpha^2 V(S) + v(1-2k)\alpha V'(S) - V''(S) = 0,$$

which has the general solution

$$V(S) = C_1 \exp(r_1 S) + C_2 \exp(r_2 S) \quad (35)$$

Here r_1 and r_2 are the roots of the characteristic equation

$$r^2 - v(1-2k)\alpha r - (1-v)\alpha^2 = 0,$$

and the constants C_1 and C_2 must be determined so that the general solution of the differential equation also is a solution of the integral equation.

To get some idea of the shape of the two functions, we shall take a numerical example in which $\alpha = 1$, $v = 0.97$ and $k = 0.603$. We then find:

$$V(S, Z) = \frac{143e^{0.1S} - 91e^{-0.3S}}{16e^{0.1Z} + 21e^{-0.3Z}}$$

and

$$D(S, Z) = 37.5e^{0.2Z} - 5(1+S) - 30e^{0.2(Z-S)}$$

Tables 1 and 2 give the value of $D(S, Z)$ and $V(S, Z)$ for some selected values of S and Z.

The two functions $D(S, Z)$ and $V(S, Z)$ obviously have some relevance to practical problems. If the objective of an insurance company is to maximize the expected discounted value of the dividends it will be able to pay before ruin, it will clearly set its "reserve requirements" at the level Z which maximizes $V(S, Z)$. This level, which the company will consider its optimal reserve, may not give the insured an adequate security. The company may therefore — on its own initiative, or following instructions from the

Table 1: $D(S, Z)$ = Expected life of the company.

S \ Z	0	1	2	3	4	5	6
0	2.5	4.2	6.2	8.7	11.7	15.4	19.1
1	2.5	5.8	9.6	13.3	19.0	25.1	33.0
2	2.5	5.8	11.2	16.7	23.6	32.4	42.7
3	2.5	5.8	11.2	18.3	27.0	37.0	49.8
4	2.5	5.8	11.2	18.3	28.6	40.4	54.6
5	2.5	5.8	11.2	18.3	28.6	42.0	57.9
6	2.5	5.8	11.2	18.3	28.6	42.0	59.5

Table 2: $V(S, Z)$ = Expected discounted value of dividend payments.

S \ Z	0	1	2	3	4	5	6
0	1.41	1.57	1.68	1.74	1.73	1.68	1.60
1	2.41	2.74	2.93	3.02	.302	2.94	2.70
2	3.41	3.74	4.03	4.16	4.16	4.04	3.84
3	4.41	4.74	5.03	5.21	5.20	8.14	4.88
4	5.41	5.74	6.03	6.21	6.19	6.02	5.70
5	6.41	6.74	.03	7.21	7.19	6.98	6.60
6	7.41	7.74	8.03	8.21	8.19	7.98	7.53

government — set the reserves at a higher level, for instance a level such that $D(S, Z)$ is above a certain acceptable minimum. The objective of the company can then be expressed as

$$\max V(S, Z)$$

subject to the condition

$$D(S, Z) > D_0 \, ,$$

where D_0 is the acceptable minimum expected life.

It does not make sense to assume that the company's objective is to maximize $D(S, Z)$, since this implies that the company will never pay any dividend. It is, however, possible to assume that its objective can be expressed as

$$\max\left[\alpha \log V(S,Z) + (1-\alpha)\log D(S,Z)\right]$$

Here α and $1-\alpha$ can be interpreted as the relative weights given to the company's objectives as a profit-making business concern, and the objectives which spring from its obligation to provide adequate security to the public. A high weight on the second group of objectives may be imposed by the government, or it may be due to a desire of the directors and the employees of the company to secure their own position by giving the company a long expected life.

The two objectives suggested in the preceding paragraph show that the modern theory makes it possible to give an operational formulation of the basic problems in insurance. If, for instance, the objective of the company is to maximize a function of the type suggested, one can determine the optimal value of Z, i.e. the optimal dividend policy. One can, however, also select the best of the available reinsurance arrangements, and the best underwriting policy — provided of course that these concepts can be defined precisely.

This seems to open a vast field for further generalizations, a field which so far has not been explored at all. To illustrate the possibilities, let us return to the stochastic process S_t of (13).

Let us assume that the company reinsures a quota k of its portfolio, against a premium $(1+\pi)k$ per unit of time. This means that the reinsurer will pay a proportion k of all claims, and that the company itself will pay the remainder $(1-k)$. The reinsurance arrangement will change the stochastic process to

$$S_t(k) = S_0 + (1-k+\lambda-\pi k)t - (1-k)x_t \tag{36}$$

It is natural to assume $\pi > \lambda$, i.e. that the loading on reinsurance is higher than on the direct underwriting, since we cannot neglect the cost of the reinsurance arrangement.

The real problem of the company now is to find the value of k which gives the "best" of the stochastic processes in the set we have defined. The problem can obviously be generalized by assuming that other types of reinsurance are available.

However, there is no sense in talking about the "best stochastic process", unless one has some rule or criterion for deciding when one process should be preferred to another, i.e. a *preference ordering* over a set of stochastic processes. This points to the need for a generalization of the Bernoulli principle, which was shown in Section 2 to give a very convenient representation of preference ordering over a set of probability distributions. So far there does not seem to have been any attempt to extend this principle to sets of stochastic processes. It is, however, evident that such a generalization will present some very intricate mathematical problems.*

A preference ordering over the elements of a set is essentially a mapping from the set to the real line. The two functions $D(S, Z)$ and $V(S, Z)$ give such mappings from a set of stochastic processes, and will therefore represent preference ordering; so also will any combination of them. These ordering will, however, be of a special kind, and it is clearly desirable to study preference ordering of a more general nature. An insurance company may, for instance, be interested, not only in the expected discounted value of its dividend payments, but also in avoiding large variations in these payments from one year to another. Such a desire for stability seems to be important in practice, but it is not taken into account in the preference ordering represented by $V(S, Z)$, and seems very difficult to formulate mathematically.

These considerations indicate that the real difficulty is to formulate the insurance problem, i.e. to describe with sufficient precision what the company really wants to achieve. Once this is done, it may not be so difficult to discover how the objective should be reached: to determine the decision which selects the best of the attainable stochastic processes.

The most unrealistic assumptions in the models we have discussed seem to be:

(i) The stationary assumptions, which imply that the nature of the company's business will never change. These assumptions become less drastic than they may seem at first sight, if we introduce operational time.

(ii) The assumption that the probability laws governing the process are completely known.

(iii) The implicit assumption that a decision once it has been made cannot be changed.

The real life situations, which these models should represent, are rather different. The reserve capital of an insurance company can obviously be considered as a stochastic process, but the laws governing the process will

* Added in proof: Such an extension to stochastic processes has now been carried out by Aase K.K. (1989).

usually be known only partially. As time passes, the company may acquire more knowledge about these laws, for instance by statistical analysis of the current claim payments. The company will then have to decide if, in view of the new knowledge, existing reinsurance arrangements or plans for future dividend payments should be changed. In general the problem of the company will be to devise:

(i) *An information system*: a system for observing the stochastic process as it develops.

(ii) *A decision function*: a set of rules for translating the observations into action.

The optimal solution to this problem should enable the company to control the process so that it develops in the way which is considered best, according to some preference ordering over sets of stochastic processes.

The possible generalizations of the risk theory, which we have outlined in the preceding paragraph, should lead to models which contain all the essential elements of the real problems in insurance companies. The models are, however, so general that they can be given a number of other interpretations, and applied to a wide range of practical problems in different fields.

We have now reached the point where the actuarial theory of risk again joins the mainstream of theoretical statistics and applied mathematics. Our general formulation of the actuary's problem leads directly to the general theory of *optimal control processes or adaptive control processes*, a theory which it is natural to associate with the names of Bellman (1961) and Pontryagin (1962). This theory has grown out of problems in engineering, and it is appropriate, as suggested by Bellman, to place its origin in the paper which Maxwell read to the Royal Society of London (Maxwell, 1868).

The theory of control processes seems to be "tailor-made" for the problems which actuaries have struggled to formulate for more than a century. It may be interesting and useful to meditate a little over how the theory would have developed, if actuaries and engineers had realized that they were studying the same problems and joined forces fifty years ago. A little reflection should teach us that a "highly specialized" problem may, when given the proper mathematical formulation, be identical to a series of other, seemingly unrelated problems.

References for Section 7

Aase K.K. (1989); *Dynamic equilibrium and the structure of premiums in a reinsurance market.* Technical report, Norwegian school of Economics and Business Administration.

Bachelier L. (1900): *Théorie de la speculation.* Thesis, Paris.

Barrois T. (1834): Essai sur l'application du calcul des probabilités aux assurances contre l'incendie. *Mém Soc Sci Lille*, 85–282.

Bellman R. (1961): *Adaptive Control Processes — A Guided Tour.* Princeton University Press.

Bellman R, and Cooke K. (1963): *Differential-Difference Equations.* New York: Academic Press.

Bernoulli D. (1738): Specimen theoriae novae de mensura sortis. *Commentarii academiae scientarum imperialis Petropolitanae.* (English translation: *Econometrica 22*, 23–36.)

Bohman H, and Esscher F. (1963): Studies in risk theory with numerical illustrations. I. *Skand. Aktuar*, 173–225.

Borch K. (1961): The utility concept applied to the theory of insurance. *ASTIN Bull 1*, 245–255.

Borch K. (1962): Equilibrium in a reinsurance market. *Econometrica 30*, 424–444.

Borch K. (1965): Una generalización de la teoria del riesgo colectivo. *An Inst Actuar Españoles 5(2)*, 13–30.

Borch K. (1966): Control of a portfolio of insurance contracts. *ASTIN Bull 4*, 59–71.

Borch K. (1967a): Dynamic decision problems in an insurance company. *ASTIN Bull.* (to appear).

Borch K. (1967b): Die optimale Dividendenpolitik der Unternehmen. *Unternehmensforschung* (to appear).

Cramér H. (1930): On the mathematical theory of risk. *Skandia Jubilee Volume.* Stockholm.

Cramér H. (1955): Collectiverisktheory. *Skandia Jubilee Volume.* Stockholm.

Feller W. (1948): A problem in the theory of counters. *Papers presented to Richard Courant.* New York.

Feller W. (1966): *An Introduction to Probability Theory and its Applications*, Volume II. New York and London: Wiley.

Finetti B. DE (1957): Su una impostazione alternativa della theoria collettiva del rischio. *Trans XV Int Congr Actuaries*, Volume II, 433–443.

Hausdorff F. (1897): Das Risico bei Zufallsspielen. *Leipziger Berichte 49*, 497–548.

Knight F. (1921): *Risk, Uncertainty and Profits.* Houghton, Mifflin & Co.

Lundberg F. (1909): Über die Theorie der Rückversicherung. *Trans VI Int Congr Actuaries*, Volume I, 877–955.

Maxwell JC. (1868): On governors. *Proc Roy Soc Lond 16*, 270–283.

Neumann J. VON and Morgenstern O. (1944): *Theory of Games and Economic Behavior.* Princeton University Press.

Nolfi P. (1957): Zur mathematischen Darstellung des Nutzens in der Versicherung. *Bull. Actuaires Suisses 57*, 395–407.

Pontryagin LS, Boltyanskii VG, Gamkrelidze RV, Mischenko EF. (1962): *Mathematical Theory of Optimal Processes.* New York: Wiley.

Segerdahl CO. (1959): A survey of results in the collective theory of risk. *Studies in Probability and Statistics — The Harald Cramér Volume*, 276–299. New York: Wiley.

Shubik M, and Thompson G. (1959): Games of economic survival. *Naval Res Logist Quart 6*, 111–124.

Tetens JN. (1786): *Einleitung zur Berechnung der Leibrenten und Anwartschaften.* Leipzig.
Wald A. (1950): *Statistical Decision Functions.* New York: Wiley.
Wold H. (1936): *Landsbygdens Brandförsäkringsbolags Maximaler och Återförsäkring.* Stockholm.

8. The Utility Concept Applied to the Theory of Insurance*

1. Introduction

1.1 In some recent papers (Borch, (1960a)), (Borch, (1960b)) and (Borch, (1960c)) about reinsurance problems I have made extensive use of utility concepts. It has been shown that if a company follows well defined objectives in its reinsurance policy, these objectives can be represented by a utility function which the company seeks to maximize. This formulation of the problem will in general make it possible to determine a unique reinsurance arrangement which is optimal when the company's objectives and external situation are given.

1.2 More than 50 years ago Guldberg (1909) wrote (about the probability of ruin): "Wie hoch diese Wahrscheinlichkeit gegriffen werden soll, muss dem subjektiven Ermessen oder von Aussen kommenden Bedingungen überlassen bleiben". This is the traditional approach to reinsurance problems. It does obviously not lead to a determinate solution. Most authors taking this approach conclude their studies by giving a mathematical relation between some measure of "stability", such as the probability of ruin, and some parameter, for instance maximum retention, to which the company can give any value within a certain range. Such studies do usually not state which particular value the company should select for this parameter, i.e. what degree of stability it should settle for. This question is apparently considered as being outside the field of actuarial mathematics.

1.3 The traditional approach implies that the actuary should play a rather modest part in the management of his company. He should provide facts and figures for the use of his superiors, who would make the final decisions on behalf of the company. How these decisions were reached should in principle be no concern of the actuary. This may have been correct in theory 50 years ago, when the famous "hunch" of the born manager was

* Reprinted from *The ASTIN Bulletin*, July 1961, Volume I:V, 245–255.

the best available guide for top-level decisions in business. However, the last decades have seen the development of mathematical theories for decision making under uncertainty, and in the light of these theories it appears that the actuary should take a broader view of his duties.

1.4 These mathematical theories can obviously not eliminate the subjective element referred to by Guldberg. However, if one assumes that there is, or at least that there should be some consistency in the various subjective judgements made by an insurance company, fairly extensive mathematical treatment becomes possible. To introduce a utility function which the company seeks to maximize, means only that such consistency requirements are put into mathematical form.

2. *The Theory of Risk*

2.1 To illustrate our point, we shall begin by studying a very simple model. We shall consider an insurance company which holds a portfolio of insurance contracts, all of which will expire before the end of a certain period. We assume that the premium for all contracts has been paid to the company in advance.

The *risk situation* of the company is then determined by the following two elements:

(i) $F(x)$ = the probability that the total amount of claims being made under the contracts in the portfolio shall not exceed x.

(ii) S = the funds which the company holds, and which it can draw upon to pay claims.

At the end of the period the company will hold the amount $y = S-x$, where y is a variety with the probability distribution $G(y) = I - F(S-y)$ where $-\infty \leq y \leq S$. It is convenient to refer to $G(y)$ as the *profit distribution* associated with the risk situation $(S, F(x))$.

2.2 In this simple model we can assume that the only thing which matters to the company, is the situation when all contracts have expired. This means that the contract period must be so short that we can ignore the interest earned by the premiums paid in advance into the company's funds. In this case all relevant properties of the risk situation are contained in the profit distribution. In the classical theory of risk attention is focussed on the probability that profit shall be negative at the end of the period, i.e. that the company shall be ruined. This probability is obviously given by:

$$\int_S^\infty dF(x) = p(S, F) = 1 - F(S)$$

2.3 The classical theory seems to assume, usually tacitly, that a company should reinsure as little as possible. The reasoning behind this appears to be that reinsurance invariably means a reduction of expected profit. Taking this as a starting point, we can formulate the objectives of the classical theory in an operational manner as follows:

If there are n possible reinsurance arrangements, which will change the risk situation of the company from the initial $\big(S, F(x)\big)$ to $\big(S_1, F_1(x)\big)$ $\ldots \big(S_n, F_n(x)\big)$, the company should select the arrangement i which maximizes expected profit

$$S_i - \int_0^\infty x\, dF_i(x)$$

subject to the condition

$$p(S_i, F_i) \leq \alpha$$

where α is the probability which Guldberg considered had to be given from outside.

2.4 This formulation leads to the familiar mathematical problem of maximizing a given function when the solution is restrained by an inequality. When α is given, the solution of the problem is straight forward, although the computation involved can present considerable difficulties.

It is, however, evident that this formulation of the reinsurance problem is not very satisfactory. We have taken into account only *two* properties of the profit distribution, namely its mean, and the part to the left of the origin. It seems unreasonable to assume that an insurance company is completely disinterested in any other property of this distribution, so it is desirable to develop a more general theory. For such a theory it appears that a utility concept, or something equivalent is indispensable.

2.5 The modern, so-called "collective" theory of risk considers a more general model than the one we have discussed. However, the generalization is not along the lines indicated in the preceding paragraph. This theory drops the assumption we made in §2.1 that all premiums have been paid in advance. Instead it is assumed that premiums are paid continuously into the company's funds. This will in general make it necessary to take into account the probability of ruin *within* the period considered. It is well known that this leads to a family of ruin probabilities, far more complicated than the simple $p(S, F)$ which we have introduced above. Whether this generalization is worth the heavy mathematics involved is an open question. Personally I think it of more interest to generalize the classical model to take into account all properties of the profit distribution.

3. Measurable Utility

3.1 The utility concept was the very corner stone of the economic theory developed in the last decades of the nineteenth century. However, many economists found it difficult to accept this concept which was impossible to measure, and difficult even to define in a precise manner. It was therefore considered as a major advance when Pareto showed that one could do without utility, and derive all the results of classical economics from the theory of indifference curves.

However, classical theory was not very successful when it came to analyzing the uncertainty element in economics. When the first real breakthrough was made in this field by Von Neumann and Morgenstern (1944), it appeared that utility was indispensable after all.

3.2 The authors of "Theory of Games" showed that utility could be defined in a rigorous manner, and that this utility concept was "measurable" in the sense that it was determined up to a linear transformation. They derived this result from a few axioms which essentially are topological in nature. The necessary axioms have later been given in several different forms, in order to make the basic assumptions clearer and more acceptable. However, the way to a desired theorem will in general become longer and more complicated when one takes simpler and more basic axioms as starting point. The reformulation of the axioms has therefore not encouraged many economists — or actuaries — to make full use of the possibilities of mathematical manipulations which are open, once utility is assumed measurable.

3.3 The few economists who have tried to apply this utility concept to "practical" problems, have approached their task with extreme suspicion. They usually have, like for instance Markowitz (1959), gone through the axioms, one by one, in order to satisfy themselves that the axioms can be justified in the particular economic situation which they want to study. I have taken this approach myself in a previous paper (Borch, 1960), where incidentally, axiom 4 is given in a meaningless form. However, such an elaborate procedure can usually be avoided. All economic analysis is based on a number of assumptions, and in most cases we will find that these assumptions either imply, or are closely related to the axioms which lead to measurable utility.

3.4 In insurance a basic assumption is that there will always exist a unique amount of money which is the lowest premium at which a company will undertake to pay a claim with a known probability distribution. This assumption establishes an equivalence between certain and uncertain events. The crucial, and most debated point in the utility theory of Von Neumann and Morgenstern is the existence of an equivalence of this kind. Once it is taken for granted, as it seems natural to do in insurance, the measurable utility follows as an almost trivial consequence.

3.5 The basic assumption referred to can be formulated as:

Axiom 1 An insurance company has a complete preference ordering over the set of all probability distributions so that:

(i) To any probability distribution $F(x)$ there corresponds one, and only one number R, so that the two probability distributions $F(x)$ and $\varepsilon(x-R)$ are equivalent.

(ii) $\varepsilon(X-R_1)$ is preferred to $\varepsilon(x-R_2)$ if, and only if $R_1 > R_2$.

Here $\varepsilon(x)$ is the degenerate probability distribution defined by

$$\varepsilon(x) = 0 \quad \text{for } x < 0$$

$$\varepsilon(x) = 1 \quad \text{for } 0 \leq x$$

To each probability distribution $F(x)$ we can now associate a utility indicator, i.e. a number $U\big(F(x)\big)$, such that:

(i) $U\big(F(x)\big) = U\big(G(x)\big)$ if $F(x)$ and $G(x)$ are equivalent.

(ii) $U\big(F(x)\big) > U\big(G(x)\big)$ if $F(x)$ is preferred to $G(x)$.

3.6 The utility indicator $U\big(F(x)\big)$ is indeterminate in the sense that $\phi(U)$, where $\phi(y)$ is an arbitrary increasing function of y, can serve as utility indicator for the preference ordering. To get a more determinate indicator, one must make some assumptions that the company is "rational" or "consistent" in its preferences. We will express this as:

Axiom 2 If the probability distributions $F_1(x)$ and $F_2(x)$ are equivalent, the probability distributions $\alpha F_1(x)+(1-\alpha)G(x)$ and $\alpha F_2(x)+(1-\alpha)G(x)$ will also be equivalent.

Here $G(x)$ is an arbitrary probability distribution, and α is a real number $0 < \alpha < 1$.

3.7 From Axiom 2 it follows that

$$U\big(\alpha F_1(x) + (1-\alpha)G(x)\big) = U\big(\alpha F_2(x) + (1-\alpha)G(x)\big)$$

or if we take $G(x) = F_2(x)$

$$U\big(\alpha F_1(x) + (1-\alpha)F_2(x)\big) = U\big(F_2(x)\big)$$

Since the left-hand side must be independent of α, it follows that the utility indicator must be of the form

$$U\big(\alpha F_1(x) + (1-\alpha)F_2(x)\big) = \alpha U\big(\alpha F_1(x)\big) + (1-\alpha)U\big(\alpha F_2(x)\big)$$

For an arbitrary probability distribution we can write

$$F(x) = \int_{-\infty}^{+\infty} \varepsilon(x-y)\, dF(y)$$

Hence we have in general

$$U\big(F(x)\big) = \int_{-\infty}^{+\infty} U\big(\varepsilon(x-y)\big)\, dF(y)$$

This is the Bernoullian hypothesis, which gives the utility of a probability distribution (or a risk situation) as a weighed sum of the utilities attached to degenerate distributions, i.e. certain events.

3.8 It is convenient to write

$$u(y) = U\big(\varepsilon(x-y)\big)$$

$u(y)$ is then the utility attached to an amount of money y, payable with probability 1, i.e. $u(y)$ can be interpreted as the "utility of money", which plays an important part in classical economic theory.

We can then write

$$U\big(F(x)\big) = \int_{-\infty}^{+\infty} u(x)\,dF(x)$$

It is easily verified that the preference ordering determines $u(x)$ only up to a linear transformation, i.e. $u(x)$ and $Au(x) + B$, where A and B are constants, will represent the same preference ordering.

3.9 The "utility of money" can best be considered as an operator which establishes an ordering over the set of profit distributions. To give it a more direct interpretation implies that we attach a meaning to statements such as: "An increase in profits from \$0.5 million to \$1 million is 50% better than an increase from \$2 millions to \$3 millions". This is not an attractive starting point for a rational theory of insurance, although something of this nature obviously is implied in the two axioms.

4. Application to Reinsurance

4.1 We will now consider an insurance company which has a preference ordering over the set of all profit distributions. We will assume that this preference ordering satisfies the two axioms in section 3, and that it can be represented by a "utility of money" $u(x)$.

The utility which the company attaches to the risk situation $\big(S, F(x)\big)$ is then given by

$$U\big(S, F(x)\big) = \int_{0}^{\infty} u(S - x)\,dF(x)$$

The reinsurance problem formulated in §2.3 can now be generalized to that of maximizing this expression over the set of risk situations which the company can reach by reinsurance arrangements. This procedure will obviously take into account all properties of $F(x)$ as we required in §2.5.

4.2 The previous papers (Borch, (1960a)), (Borch, (1960b)) and (Borch, (1960c)) already referred to, contain several examples of such maximizing problems. We shall therefore in the present paper only consider one simple example.

We assume that a company in the risk situation $\big(S, F(x)\big)$ wants to reinsure a quota k of its portfolio. For this reinsurance cover the company has to pay the net premium kP of the ceded quota, plus a loading λkP.

The optimal quota will then evidently be the value of k which maximizes the expression

$$\int_0^\infty u\big(S - (1+\lambda)kP - (1-k)x\big)\, dF(x)$$

where P is the net premium of the whole portfolio, i.e.

$$P = \int_0^\infty x\, dF(x)$$

It is obvious that this maximizing problem can be solved when $F(x)$ and $u(x)$ are given.

4.3 We will now assume that

$$F(x) = 1 - e^{-x}$$

and

$$u(x) = -ax^2 + x + b$$

This form of $u(x)$ has been studied in some detail in previous papers. It seems to give acceptable results, provided that a is positive, and so small that $u(x)$ is increasing over the whole range considered, i.e. $2aS < 1$. a can obviously be taken as a measure of the company's "risk aversion". If $a = 0$, the company will be indifferent to risk. The utility attached to any risk situation will then be proportional to expected profit.

It is easy to verify that the value of k which maximizes the company's utility, is given by

$$k = \frac{2a(1-\lambda) - \lambda(1-2aS)}{2a(1+\lambda^2)}$$

4.4 To give a numerical illustration, we will take

$$a = \tfrac{1}{3}, \qquad b = 0.135$$

$$S = 1.2, \qquad \lambda = 0.1$$

We find that in this case the company's utility is maximized for $k = 0.86$. The table below gives the utility for different values of k. That utility is zero in the initial situation, i.e. for $k = 0$, has of course no significance, since the origin and the unit of measurement for the utility scale can be

Quota Share Reinsurance

k	Utility	Expected Profit	Probability of ruin
0	0.0	0.20	0.3012
0.1	0.056	0.19	0.2982
0.2	0.101	0.18	0.2923
0.3	0.142	0.17	0.2865
0.4	0.174	0.16	0.2808
0.5	0.195	0.18	0.2725
0.6	0.216	0.14	0.2645
0.7	0.230	0.13	0.2393
0.8	0.237	0.12	0.2019
0.86	0.240	0.115	0.1791
0.9	0.238	0.11	0.1225
1.0	0.231	0.10	0.0

chosen arbitrarily. The last two columns of the table give expected profit and the probability of ruin, i.e. the probability that the company shall be insolvent at the end of the period considered.

5. Conclusion

5.1 The example in section 4 shows that it is relatively simple to determine the optimal reinsurance arrangement if we assume that the utility of money to an insurance company can be represented by a continuous, increasing function. However, the existence of such a function follows from the innocent looking axioms in section 3, and it seems difficult to argue that well managed insurance companies should violate these axioms.

5.2 The validity of the axioms leading to the Bernoullian theorem has been questioned by several authors, on different grounds. The most important criticism has been directed against the substitution principle implicit in the axioms. It is easy to show by examples that this principle does not seem to be generally applicable. It is doubtful, to say the least, that there exist certain public honors (or disgrace) which are equivalent to a fifty-fifty chance of either being hanged or receiving one million dollars. One of Walter Scott's heros ("Waverly") is willing to make a toss for a coronet or a coffin, but we cannot assume, as the axioms imply, that any person would be willing to play such a game if the probabilities were suitably adjusted. It seems, however, that this general criticism does not concern the applicability of the Bernoullian hypothesis to insurance where the only events considered are payment of different amounts of money.

5.3 Another group of critics has contested the relevance of probabilities to economic decisions made under uncertainty. The most eloquent member of this group is probably Shackle (1949). Shackle maintains that a businessman will not consider all possible outcomes which may follow a decision he is about to make. Instead he will pay attention only to two *focal values.* These values are the worst and the best outcome which the businessman considers so likely that they must be taken into account. Other outcomes, which are "out of focus" are ignored.

It seems almost preposterous to maintain that companies ignore probabilities when they take decisions concerning reinsurance. It should, however, be noted that Shackle does not consider his theory as *normative* in the sense that it states how rational]businessmen *should* take decisions. All he claims is that his theory describes, or explains how businessmen actually reach their decisions. This might apply to insurance companies, since as we have seen, the theory of reinsurance has almost exclusively considered the two "focal values", ruin and expected profit.

5.4 Shackle's views are well expressed by Giraudoux's Belle Hélène ("La guerre de Troie n'aura pas lieu"):

Hélène: Ne me brusquez pas. Je choisis les événements comme je choisis les objects et les hommes. Je choisis ceux qui ne sont pas pour moi des ombres. Je choisis ceux que je vois.

Hector: Voici ta concurrante, Cassandre. Celle-là aussi lit l'avenir.

Hélène: Je ne lis pas l'avenir. Mais dans cet avenir, je vois des scènes colorées, d'autres ternes. Jusqu'ici ce sont toujours les scènes colorées qui ont eu lieu.

If Cassandra should look for a job, any insurance company could profitably employ her. As she presumably is not available, companies seem to have engaged, as a substitute, la belle Hélène, who can only see the dreadful possibility of ruin and the rosy situation where everything goes according to mathematical expectation. She may have her attractions, but one may ask if she is the right person to take charge of the reinsurance arrangements.

References for Section 8

Borch K. (1960a): "An Attempt to Determine the Optimum Amount of Stop Loss Reinsurance", *Transactions of the XVIth International Congress of Actuaries 2*, 597–610.

Borch K. (1960b): "Reciprocal Reinsurance Treaties", *The Astin Bulletin 1*, 170–191.

Borch K. (1960c): "Reciprocal Reinsurance Treaties seen as a two-person Co-operative Game", *Skandinavisk Aktuarietidskrift*, 29–58.

Guldberg, Alf: "Zur Theorie des Risikos", *Reports of the Sixth International Congress of Actuaries 1*, 753–764.

Markowitz, Harry. (1959): *Portfolio Selection*, John Wiley & Sons.

Neumann, J. von and Morgenstern O. (1944): *Theory of Games and Economic Behavior*, Princeton.

Shackle, GLS. (1949): *Expectation in Economics*, Cambridge.

9. Optimal Insurance Arrangements*

1. In a recent paper on the theory of demand for insurance Arrow (1974) has proved that the optimal policy for an insurance buyer is one which gives complete coverage, beyond a fixed deductible. The result is proved under very general assumptions, but its content can be illustrated by the following simple example.

Assume that a person is exposed to a risk which can cause him a loss x, represented by a stochastic variable with the distribution $F(x)$. Assume further that he by paying the premium $P(y)$ can obtain an insurance contract which will guarantee him a compensation $y(x)$, if his loss amounts to x. The problem of our person is to find the optimal insurance contract, i.e. the optimal function $y(x)$, when the price is given by the functional $P(y)$.

2. In order to give an operational formulation to the problem we have outlined, we shall assume that the person's attitude to risk can be represented by a Bernoulli utility function $u(x)$, and we shall write S for his "initial wealth". His problem will then be to maximize

$$\int_0^\infty u\big(S - P(y) - x + y(x)\big)\, dF(x)\,,$$

when the functional $P(y)$ is given, and $y(x) \in Y$. The set Y can be interpreted as the set of insurance policies available in the market. It is

---

* Reprinted from *The ASTIN Bulletin*, September 1975, Volume VIII:3, 284–290.

natural to assume that $0 \leq y(x) \leq x$, but beyond this there is no need for assuming additional restrictions on the set Y.

Arrow makes the assumption that

$$P(y) = (1+\lambda) \int_0^\infty y(x)\, dF(x) \tag{1}$$

i.e. that the premium is proportional to the net premium, with a loading λ. With this assumption he proves that the optimal policy is of the form

$$y(x) = 0 \qquad \text{for } x < M$$
$$y(x) = x - M \qquad \text{for } x \geq M$$

The problem of determining the optimal insurance contract is then reduced to finding the optimal deductible M, i.e. to the problem:

$$\max_{0 \leq M} \left[\int_0^M u(S-P-x)\, dF(x) + u(S-P-M) \int_M^\infty dF(x) \right]$$

subject to

$$P = (1+\lambda) \int_M^\infty (x-M)\, dF(x) \tag{2}$$

3. Writing

$$U = \int_0^M u(S-P-x)\, dF(x) + u(S-P-M) \int_M^\infty dF(x)$$

we obtain

$$\frac{dU}{dM} = -\frac{dP}{dM} \int_0^M u'(S-P-x)\, dF(x)$$
$$- \left(1 + \frac{dP}{dM}\right) u'(S-P-M)\{1 - F(M)\}$$

From (2) it follows that

$$\frac{dP}{dM} = -(1+\lambda)\big(1 - F(M)\big)$$

Hence we obtain the following equation for the determination of the optimal deductible M:

$$(1+\lambda)\int_0^M u'(S-P-x)\,dF(x) = \big((1+\lambda)F(M)-\lambda\big)u'(S-P-M)$$

From this equation we can prove that the optimal M will increase with the loading λ, provided that $u''(x) < 0$. This result is a special case of Arrow's Theorem 6, and it means that as insurance becomes more expensive, the consumer buys less of it.

4. It should be easy to recognize Arrow's results as generalizations of results familiar from the theory of reinsurance. Several authors have shown, i.a. in (Borch, (1960a)), (Kahn, (1957)) and (Ohlin, (1966)), that a stop loss treaty is the optimal reinsurance arrangement, from the ceding company's point of view. These authors have proved their result under more restrictive assumptions than Arrow, but it is clearly equivalent to his. When a private person buys full insurance with a deductible, he does in reality conclude a stop loss contract.

A reinsurance treaty is generally a contract negotiated on equal terms between two insurance companies. It is not usual that the reinsurer states his price-system, for instance in the form of condition (1), and then lets the ceding company select the function $y(x)$ which it considers as most advantageous. This means that it makes little sense to study arrangements which are optimal for only one of the parties to the negotiations. Both parties have to be considered and this has been pointed out in several papers, i.a. in (Borch, (1966)) and (Vajda, (1962)).

5. The considerations above suggest that the situation could be formulated as a problem in game theory. Assume that the claim distribution $F(x)$ of the ceding company is given. The game would then be played in two moves:

(i) The reinsurer selects a mapping $P(y)$ from the set of functions $y(x)$, such that $\{y(x) | 0 \leq y(x) \leq x\}$ to the real line. $P(y)$ will be the premium he demands for a contract obliging him to pay an amount $y(x)$, if claims against the ceding company amount to x.

(ii) The ceding company selects a function $y(x)$.

This problem may have some mathematical interest, but its relevance to reinsurance in real life seems doubtful. There is little evidence that insurance companies behave in this way during reinsurance negotiations. The game-theoretical formulation outlined may, however, be appropriate in direct insurance.

6. Arrow's results indicate that much of the insurance currently sold may be sub-optimal from the consumer's point of view. This would, for instance, apply to all kinds of liability policies, which place an upper limit on the company's obligations. Such policies may give the insured inadequate protection if extremely unlikely catastrophic events should occur. In most cases there is no reason why the company should not provide full cover, but it seems natural that the company should be unwilling to provide such catastrophe cover against an infinitesimal net premium with a "normal" proportional loading. Hence it appears that assumption (1) is the critical element behind Arrow's results.

It is easy to construct examples which show that an insurance company cannot in general operate with premium rates as assumed by (1).

We can, for instance, assume that there are some fixed costs c associated with issuing and handling the insurance contract. With a deductible M, the net premium is

$$\bar{P}(M) = \int_M^\infty (x - M)\, dF(x)$$

The minimum premium which the company can quote to customers will then be

$$P(M) = \bar{P}(M) + c = \left(1 + \frac{c}{\bar{P}(M)}\right) \bar{P}(M)$$

Hence the loading will be

$$\lambda = \frac{c}{\bar{P}(M)}$$

which must increase with the deductible M.

7. We can reach a similar result by a simple risk theory argument. Assume that

$$P(M) = (1 + \lambda)\bar{P}(M)$$

so that the company's expected profit from the contract is $\lambda\bar{P}(M)$. The variance of the profit is

$$V(M) = \int_M^\infty (x - M)^2\, dF(x) - \left(\bar{P}(M)\right)^2$$

It is natural to require that

$$\lambda^2 \left(\bar{P}(M)\right)^2 = k^2 V(M) \tag{3}$$

This condition can be written

$$\lambda^2 = k^2 \left[\left(\int_M^\infty (x - M)\, dF(x) \right)^2 \int_M^\infty (x - m)^2\, dF(x) - 1 \right]$$

With L'Hôpital's rule it is easy to show that the first term on the right-hand side goes to infinity with M.

The condition (3) can be justified by an appeal to the Hattendorff rule in classical risk theory. Assume that the company holds a large number of insurance contracts, so that the claim distribution of its portfolio is approximately normal. The probability of negative profit (or of ruin) may then be considered as satisfactorily low if the loading is at least equal to k times the standard deviation. If now one person wants a larger deductible in order to reduce his premium, the company must quote him a premium, so that (3) remains satisfied.

8. Our two simple examples open some unpleasant perspectives. Assume that an insurance company for some reason must increase the loading on its premiums. If the company uses formula (1), i.e. retains a proportional loading, this will induce the customers to take higher deductibles. This will again force the company to increase the loading — to cover costs, or to satisfy solvency requirements. It is a sobering thought to ask if a process of this kind can occur in real life, and if the process, once started, will ever stop.

9. In the discussion above we have in a sense taken existing institutions and current insurance practice as given. It may be useful for a time to forget about these, and study general arrangements for risk sharing, which can be considered optimal. We can then ask ourselves if there are institutional or other aspects which make it impossible to make such arrangements in practice.

We shall consider a group of n persons, and assume:

(i) Person i is exposed to a risk which can cause him a loss, represented by a stochastic variable x_i.

(ii) The attitude to risk of person i can be represented by a utility function $u_i(x)$.

The most general insurance arrangement these persons can make will be defined by a set of functions $y_i(x_1 \ldots x_n)$ $(i = 1, 2, \ldots, n)$ stating the loss which will be carried by person i if all losses are given by the vector $(x_1 \ldots x_n)$. An arrangement defined by a set of y-functions which satisfies the following conditions, will be Pareto optimal:

$$k_i u_i'\big(y_i(x)\big) = k_j u_j'\big(-y_j(x)\big) \tag{4}$$

Here $k_1 \ldots k_n$ are arbitrary positive constants,

$$x = \sum_{i=1}^{n} x_i \qquad \text{and} \qquad \sum_{i=1}^{n} y_i(x) = x$$

This result was first proved in Borch (1960). More stream-lined proofs have been given in a number of later publications, i.a. in Bühlmann (1970).

10. In real life we do not often find insurance arrangements which meet the conditions of Pareto optimality, but there are cases in which these conditions may be approximately satisfied.

(i) The mutual fire-insurance schemes which still can be found in some rural communities, may come close to satisfying (4).

(ii) Some large liability risks in business are currently insured by mutual arrangements. Shipowners have formed their P & I Clubs, and off shore oil operators have devised their own insurance schemes, which may approximately satisfy (4).

It is, however, clear that such insurance arrangements made by relatively small groups can be improved by cooperation with other groups.

11. Arrow's results demonstrate that the normal risk-averse person wants an insurance which places an upper limit on the loss he can suffer, i.e. he wants an arrangement which satisfies a condition of the form

$$P_i \geq y_i(x_1 \ldots x_n) \tag{5}$$

With strict equality this becomes a conventional insurance contract with premium P_i. Condition (5) may satisfy (4) for some i, provided that there are other persons which are willing to carry unlimited liability. This argument indicates that an institution as Lloyds of London is essential to bring about an optimal insurance arrangement.

In practice most insurance is sold by companies with limited liability. This means that condition (5) cannot be satisfied in an absolute manner.

There will always be a non-zero probability that the insured may suffer a loss beyond the premium he has paid. The task of the government supervision is to see that this probably is sufficiently low, preferably infinitesimal. This is usually achieved by requiring that the company must hold large reserves, and these reserves must as a rule be obtained as equity capital.

12. The general picture emerging from these considerations consists of two groups. One group seeks to get rid of risk by buying insurance, the other group is willing to accept risk by holding shares in insurance companies. The real problem should then be to find an optimal arrangement for sharing the risks between the members of these two groups.

References for Section 9

Arrow KJ. (1974): "Optimal Insurance and Generalized Deductibles", *Skandinavian Actuarial Journal*, 1–42.

Borch K. (1960a): "An Attempt to Determine the Optimum Amount of Stop Loss Reinsurance", *Transactions of the 16th International Congress of Actuaries 2*, 579–610.

Borch K. (1960b): "The Safety Loading of Reinsurance Premiums", *Skandinavish Aktuarietidskrift*, 163–184.

Borch, K. (1966): "The Optimal Reinsurance Treaty", *The ASTIN Bulletin 5*, 293–297.

Bühlmann H. (1970): *Mathematical Methods in Risk Theory*, Springer Verlag.

Kahn PM. (1957): "Some Remarks on a Recent Paper by Borch", *The ASTIN Bulletin 1*, 265–272.

Ohlin J. (1966): "On a Class of Measures of Dispersion with Application to Optimal Reinsurance", *The ASTIN Bulletin 5*, 249–266.

Vajda S. (1962): "Minimum Variance Reinsurance", *The ASTIN Bulletin 2*, 257–260.

10. Objectives and Optimal Decisions in Insurance*

1. Introduction

1.1 In this paper we shall examine some of the decision problems which occur in the management of an insurance company. We shall approach the subject by constructing a mathematical model of the environment in which the company operates, and of the objectives which the company wants to achieve. In any situation the best, or optimal decision will then be the decision which brings the company closest to its objectives.

---

* Reprinted from *Transactions of the 20th International Congress of Actuaries*, Tokyo 1976, Volume 3, 433–441.

A mathematical model will usually be an enormous oversimplification of real life, but often even a simple model may seem to capture most of the essential elements in the situation we want to study. In such cases we can use the model to compute the optimal decision and recommend it to the management. It may however happen that the recommendation is rejected by a manager, who prefers a decision which, according to the model, is far from optimal. We can then conclude that the manager makes a mistake, but a more likely explanation is that the model is too simple to be applied in practice.

1.2 In the following we shall study some models which at first sight seem reasonable and acceptable. We shall show that these models lead to decisions, which as far as we can judge from observations, are not considered as optimal by managers in real life. We shall then generalize the models, so that they lead to decisions more in accordance with those which we can observe in practice, and we shall note that the models lose some of their intuitive appeal in this process.

2. Some Simple Formulations of the Objectives

2.1 As our starting point we shall take a simple model which Bruno de Finetti (1957) presented to the International Congress of Actuaries in 1957. The model which represents a substantial generalization of the older theories of risk, can be described by the following elements:

(i) $F_t(x)$ = the claim distribution of the portfolio of insurance contracts underwritten by the company in operating period t.

(ii) P_t = the total amount of premiums received by the company in period t.

(iii) S_t = the company's free reserves at the beginning of period t, before any dividend payment.

(iv) s_t = the dividend paid by the company at the beginning of period t, i.e., when the results of operating period $t-1$ have become known.

These give us what a physicist would call the "law of motion":

$$S_{t+1} = S_t - s_t + P_t - x_t$$

With this formulation, the only decision problem of the company consists in determining s_t, the amount which should be paid out as dividend before the new operating period begins.

A reasonable "rule of the game" is:

(v) If for some t, $S_t < 0$, the company is ruined, and is not allowed to operate in the following periods.

One of the objectives suggested by De Finetti is that the company should find the dividend policy which maximizes the expected discounted sum of the dividend payments which the company will make before ruin occurs.

The problem is then to maximize the sum $\sum_{t=0}^{\infty} v^t E\{s_t\}$.

2.2 In order to solve the problem we have outlined we must have full information about the future underwriting of the company, i.e. we must know the sequences $F_0(x)$, $F_1(x)$, ... and P_0, P_1, ..., P_t. It may not be too difficult to make reasonable forecasts for these two sequences. We may for instance assume that the volume of business will grow, partly because the number of contracts will increase, and partly because the sums insured under each contract increase with inflation. We shall not make any forecasts of this kind in the present paper. Our purpose is to present the essential features of the model. We shall just assume that $F_t(x) = F(x)$ and $P_t = P$ for all t, i.e. we assume that the company will underwrite identical portfolios in all future operating periods.

This simplified model has been studied by many authors, and we shall give only a brief outline of how the problem can be solved. Extensive discussions can be found in the books (Borch, 1974) and (Bühlmann, 1970) which also contain fairly complete bibliographies.

2.3 Let us now assume that for $t = 0$, the free reserves of the company amount to S, and write

$$V(S) = \max \sum_{t=0}^{\infty} v^t E\{S_t\}$$

The function $V(S)$ will then stand for the expected discounted sum of the dividend payments, provided that the company follows an optimal dividend policy. The existence of an optimal policy is not trivial, but the following heuristic considerations should make it plausible:

If the company is very conservative with its dividend, payments will come late, and the sum will be small, due to the discounting. If on the other hand the company follows a liberal policy, and pays substantial dividends early in the game, ruin can be expected to come soon, so that the sum will contain few terms and be small. It is reasonable to assume that there will be an optimal policy somewhere in the middle.

2.4 It is easy to see that the function $V(S)$ must satisfy the functional equation

$$V(S) = \max \left[s + v \int_0^{S+P-s} V(S - s + P - x)\, dF(x) \right]$$

where $0 \leq s < S$. The argument leading to this equation is known as the "Principle of Optimality". It says that with an optimal policy the first payment plus the expected discounted value of future payments must be maximized.

It is convenient to assume that a density $f(x) = F'(x)$ exists, and to write $Y = S - s$, so that the functional equation takes the form

$$V(S) = \max_{0 \leq Y \leq S} \left[S - Y + v \int_0^{Y+P} V(Y + P - x)\, f(x)\, dx \right]$$

Here Y stands for the free reserves which the company, under an optimal dividend policy, will keep for the next underwriting period.

If an interior maximum exists, the derivative of the expression in braces must be zero, i.e.

$$-1 + vV(0)\, f(Y + P) + v \int_0^{Y+P} V'(Y + P - x)\, f(x)\, dx = 0 \qquad (1)$$

In the "normal" case this equation will have just one positive solution. The optimal dividend policy will then be

$$s = S - Y \qquad \text{for } S > Y$$

$$s = 0 \qquad \text{for } S \leq Y$$

This means that the company will pay no dividend if its free reserves are below the optimal level y determined by (1). If at the end of an operating period the reserves exceed this level, the whole excess will be paid out as dividend immediately.

2.5 The dividend policy we have found above can clearly lead to violent fluctuations in the company's dividend payments, and this does not correspond very well with what we can observe in real life. In practice most insurance companies seem anxious to avoid such fluctuations, and this desire for stability is not included in our assumptions about the objectives. Before we seek to revise our assumptions, it is worth noting that three pathological cases can occur, in addition to the case termed "normal" above.

(i) The left-hand side of equation (1) may be negative for all values of $Y \geq 0$. The optimal reserve is then $Y = 0$, corresponding to the case in which the game is so unfavorable that the optimal policy is to get the money out of the company as soon as possible.

(ii) The left-hand side of the equation is positive for all Y. This will occur i.a. if the discount factor $v = 1$, and corresponds to the objective of maximizing the expected life of the company. The objective has been suggested by de Finetti (1957) and is discussed in Borch (1974).

(iii) Equation (1) has more than one positive solution. This case was discovered by Miyasawa (1962), and was applied to insurance by Morrill (1966). The optimal dividend policy in this case has the form which Morrill called a "band strategy". Examples in which a policy of this form is optimal appear to be known only for discrete claim distributions.

2.6 There is no room for reinsurance in the model which we have outlined. To introduce reinsurance in a simple way, we shall assume that only proportional reinsurance on original terms is available. This means that the company can pay an amount $(1-k)P$ to the reinsurer, who in return undertakes to pay a quota $1-k$ of the claims. This assumption leads us to consider the following situation:

At the end of an operating period, the company's free reserves are S. The company then has to make two decisions; i.e. to select values for the two parameters

(i) $s =$ the amount which should be paid as dividend.

(ii) $k =$ the quota to be retained in the next underwriting period.

If the company's objective is to maximize the expected discounted sum of the dividend payments, we arrive at the functional equation:

$$V(S) = \max \left[s + v \int_0^{(S-s)/k+P} V\big(S - s + k(P-x)\big)\, f(x)\, d(x) \right]$$

or substituting $s = S - kY$:

$$V(S) = \max \left[S - kY + v \int_0^{Y+P} V\big(k\{Y + P - x\}\big)\, f(x)\, dx \right]$$

Here the maximizing problem has to be solved under the constraints

$$0 \leq k \leq 1, \qquad Y \geq 0 \quad \text{and} \quad S - kY \geq 0$$

2.7 The Kuhn-Tucker conditions for a maximum in the problem above are:

$$k\left\{-Y + v\int_0^{Y+P} (Y+P-x)V'\big(k\{Y+P-x\}\big)\, f(x)\, dx - \lambda_1 Y - \lambda_2\right\} = 0$$

$$Y\left\{-k + vV(0)\, f(Y+P) + vk\int_0^{Y+P} V'\big(k\{Y+P-x\}\big)\, f(x)\, dx - \lambda_1 k\right\} = 0$$

$$\lambda_1(kY - S) = 0 \tag{i}$$

$$\lambda_2(k-1) = 0 \tag{ii}$$

and λ_1, $\lambda_2 \geq 0$.

The two first conditions can be rewritten as follows:

$$kY\left[-1 + v\int_0^{Y+P} V' f(x)\, dx - \lambda_1\right] + k\left\{v\int_0^{Y+P} (P-x)V' f(x)\, dx - \lambda_2\right\} = 0 \tag{2}$$

$$kY\left[-1 + v\int_0^{Y+P} V' f(x)\, dx - \lambda_1\right] + vYV(0)\, f(Y+P) = 0 \tag{3}$$

If the common term in (2) and (3) is nonnegative, the equations can be satisfied only for $Y = 0$. This corresponds to case (i) in para 2.5, where the game is so unfavorable that the optimal decision is to pull the reserves out of the company.

If the underwriting is sufficiently favorable, i.e. if the premium P is sufficiently high, we will have

$$\int_0^{Y+P} (P-x)V'\big(k(Y+P-x)\big)\, f(x)\, dx > V(0)\, f(Y+P)$$

This means that (2) and (3) can be satisfied only if $\lambda_2 > 0$, i.e. that the constraint (ii) must be binding, so that $k = 1$. This again means that the company will never take any reinsurance, so that we are back with the model introduced in para 2.1, and with the dividend policy which we rejected in para 2.5 as contradicting observations from real life.

2.8 It is in itself not surprising that we should find that a company engaged in a sufficiently favorable business, never will consider it optimal to give a part of its portfolio away to a reinsurer. We did however reach this conclusion under the very unrealistic assumption that the company was allowed to operate — on any scale — regardless of how small the free reserves were, as long as they remained positive.

If the free reserves amount to S, the probability that the company shall be able to meet claim payments is:

$$\Pr\{x \leq S + P\} = F(S + P)$$

It is natural to assume that the government supervisor will not allow the company to operate unless this probability is close to unity, say at least equal to α. Let $F(Z + P) = \alpha$, so that Z becomes the minimum reserve which the company must hold if it shall be allowed to operate without reinsurance. If $S < Z$, the company can then retain only a quota k, so that the following inequality is satisfied:

$$\Pr\{kx \leq S + kP\} = \Pr\left\{x \leq \frac{S}{k} + P\right\} = F\left(\frac{S}{k} + P\right) \geq \alpha$$

2.9 If we introduce the government's solvency requirement into our model in the manner indicated above, we are led back to the problem considered in para 2.6 and 2.7, with the additional constraint $Y \geq Z$. It is easy to show that in this model the optimal policy will be:

(i) For $S > Z$: Pay dividend $S - Z$, and retain the whole portfolio.

(ii) For $S \leq Z$: Pay no dividend and retain a quota $k = \frac{S}{Z}$ of the portfolio.

This gives us the same kind of fluctuations in dividend payments as before, so that the introduction of reinsurance and solvency requirements has not removed the main undesirable feature of our model.

3. A More Realistic Model

3.1 The unsatisfactory implications of our model seem to spring from the essentially linear assumptions about the company's objectives. An alternative assumption would be to assume that the company seeks the dividend-reinsurance policy which maximizes the sum

$$\sum_{t=0}^{\infty} v^t E\{u(s_t)\}$$

Here $u(s)$ is a utility function, and it is natural to assume concavity, i.e. that $u'(s) > 0$ and $u''(s) < 0$.

This generalization implies that the company's objective is to maximize the expected discounted sum of the utility of the dividend payments. The basic functional equation now becomes

$$V(S) = \max \left[u(s) + v \int_0^{(S-s)/k+P} V\big(S - s + k(P - x)\big)\, f(x)\, dx \right]$$

or

$$V(S) = \max \left[u(S - kY) + v \int_0^{Y+P} V\big(k\{Y + P - x\}\big)\, f(x)\, dx \right]$$

Here the maximizing has to be carried out under the constraints

$$0 \le k \le 1\,, \qquad S - kY \ge 0 \quad \text{and} \quad Y \ge 0$$

If the company must satisfy some governmental solvency conditions, the last constraint has to be replaced by $Y \ge Z$.

Models of this kind, which were first studied by Phelps (1962), and later by Hakansson (1970) have become very popular in the theory of investment and portfolio management.

In general little is known about the shape of the optimal dividend policy in such models. It is however clear that the sequence of dividend payments will have more stability than in the models studied in Section 2.

3.2 We obtain fairly simple, explicit results if we assume that the utility function is of the form

$$u(s) = s^{\beta}\,, \quad \text{with } 0 < \beta < 1$$

The Kuhn-Tucker conditions for a maximum will now take the form

$$k\left[-\beta Y(S-kY)^{\beta-1} + v\int_0^{Y+P}(Y+P-x)V'f(x)\,dx - \lambda_1 Y - \lambda_2\right] = 0 \tag{4}$$

$$Y\left[-\beta k(S-kY)^{\beta-1} + vV(0)\,f(Y+P) + vk\int_0^{Y+P}V'f(x)\,dx - \lambda_1 k + \lambda_3\right\} = 0 \tag{5}$$

$$\lambda_1(kY-S)=0 \tag{i}$$

$$\lambda_2(k-1)=0 \tag{ii}$$

$$\lambda_3(Z-Y)=0 \tag{iii}$$

If we can find k and Y, as functions of S, which satisfy these conditions, our basic functional equation can be written as an integral equation

$$V(S) = (S-kY)^\beta + v\int_0^{Y+P} V\big(k(Y+P-x)\big)\,f(x)\,dx \tag{6}$$

This is an equation of Fredholm's type, and it is known that it has a unique continuous solution — for given functions k and Y.

3.3 The equations (4), (5) and (6) can be solved by a frontal attack. The form of the solution is however well known, and also fairly easy to guess, so we shall just verify that the equations are satisfied by:

$$V(S) = KS^\beta \tag{7}$$

$$s = (S-kZ) = DS \tag{8}$$

Here D and K are constants to be determined, and Z is given by the supervisor's solvency condition. Substituting the suspected solution in (6) we obtain

$$KS^\beta = D^\beta S^\beta + K(1-D)^\beta S^\beta M$$

or

$$K = D^\beta + (1 - D)^\beta M \tag{9}$$

where

$$M = \frac{v}{Z^\beta} \int_0^{Z+P} (Z + P - x)^\beta f(x)\, dx$$

is an expression which contains only given elements.

In the same way substitution in (4) gives

$$D^{\beta-1} = K(1 - D)^{\beta-1} M \tag{10}$$

if we assume $\lambda_1 = \lambda_2 = 0$, i.e. that the constraints (i) and (ii) are not binding. The solution of the equations (9) and (10) is found to be

$$D = 1 - M^{1/(1-\beta)}$$

$$K = D^{\beta-1} = \{1 - M^{1/(1-\beta)}\}^{\beta-1}$$

We can then verify that this solution also satisfies (5) with $\lambda_3 > 0$, so that the constraint (iii) is binding, i.e. $Y = Z$.

3.4 From the results above we see that — under certain conditions — the optimal policy can be described as follows:

For $S > ZM^{-1/(1-\beta)}$: Pay a dividend DS and retain the whole portfolio.

For $S < ZM^{-1/(1-\beta)}$: Pay a dividend DS, and retain a quota $SM^{1/(1-\beta)}/Z$.

With this policy the company will, at the end of each operating period, pay out a fixed proportion D of its free reserves as dividend. In the following period the company will reinsure if this is necessary to satisfy the government's solvency condition. If the company holds large free reserves, it will operate with a higher degree of solvency than required by the government. Casual observations suggest that companies in the real world may well follow a policy of this kind.

Our mathematical argument is far from rigorous, and the space available does not allow us to tie up all the loose ends. We should however note that the results have no meaning unless

$$M = v \int_0^{Z+P} \left(1 + \frac{P - x}{Z}\right)^\beta f(x)\,dx < 1$$

It can be shown that M will decrease with increasing Z, and tend to v as Z tends to infinity. This means that our results may be valid only if the solvency requirements are fairly strict. It is not very difficult? but tedious to determine the optimal policy under weak solvency conditions.

4. Conclusion

4.1 Our purpose in this paper was to find assumptions about the objectives and operating conditions of insurance companies, which would give optimal decisions not contradicting the decisions that companies seem to choose in real life. To some extent we have achieved this purpose. It is however not easy to justify the assumptions we made in para 4.1 and para 4.2. They do in a sense run counter to the conventional thinking in financial mathematics. It is usually assumed that it is preferred to receive a payment as early as possible. The objectives we have introduced imply a preference for having payments spread out over time.

4.2 To illustrate the point, let us assume that an amount C is available for dividend payments. The problem is then

$$\max \sum_{t=0}^{\infty} v^t x_t^\beta$$

subject to

$$\sum_{t=0}^{\infty} x_t = C \qquad x_t \geq 0$$

For $\beta = 1$, the solution will clearly be $x_0 = C$.
For $0 < \beta < 1$ the solution is:

$$x_t = v^{t/(1-\beta)}\left(1 - v^{1/(1-\beta)}\right)C = \left(1 - v^{1/(1-\beta)}\right)^2 \sum_{i=t}^{\infty} x_i$$

i.e. each payment is a fixed proportion of the amount which is left.

This solution may be relevant to a consumer who makes a plan for consuming his capital, and the model was first applied by Phelps to such problems. There are no a priori reasons for assuming the same model can be applied to insurance companies, but it seems to give a better explanation of observed behavior than any other model which has been studied.

References for Section 10

Borch K. (1974): *The Mathematical Theory of Insurance* D.C. Heath and Company.

Bühlmann H. (1970): *Mathematical Methods in Risk Theory* Springer Verlag.

Finetti B. de (1957): "Su una Impostazione Alternativa della Teoria Collettiva del Risclio", *Transactions of the XV International Congress of Actuaries 2*, 433–443.

Hakansson N. (1970): "Optimal Investment and Consumption Strategies under Risk for a Class of Utility Functions", *Econometrica*, 587–607.

Miyasawa K. (1962): "An Economic Survival Game", *Journal of the Operations Research Society of Japan.*

Morrill J. (1966): "One Person Games of Economic Survival", *Naval Research Logistics Quarterly*, 49–69.

Phelps E. (1962): "The Accumulation of Risk Capital: A Sequential Utility Analysis", *Econometrica*, 729–743.

CHAPTER 3

INSURANCE AND COMPETITIVE EQUILIBRIUM

1. Principles of Premium Calculation

1.1 A risk is described by a random variable, and a premium calculation principle is a rule that assigns a real number (the premium) to the given risk. We shall write $P\{x\}$ for the premium assigned to the random variable x. Usually one has $P\{x\} > E\{x\}$, and the difference between the two is called the "loading" of the net premium $E\{x\}$. If administrative expenses are not brought explicitly into the calculations, the difference $P\{x\} - E\{x\}$ will be the risk premium, i.e. the insurer's expected reward for risk-bearing. This reward will be determined by market forces.

Administrative expenses cannot be ignored, but they are often of random nature, and their expectation can be added to the net premium. This means that the random variable x is taken to represent the total cost to the insurer of a contract, and we will give a method for charging proper premiums, for instance for insurance contracts which can lead to costly litigation.

1.2 In Chapter 1.1 we mentioned two premium calculation principles

$$P\{x\} = E\{x\} + c\,, \tag{i}$$

and

$$P\{x\} = \alpha E\{x\} \qquad \text{with} \quad \alpha > 1 \tag{ii}$$

A third principle which is widely used in practice is the "variance principle"

$$P\{x\} = \alpha E\{x\} + \beta \operatorname{var} x \tag{iii}$$

Occasionally one also uses a "standard deviation principle", which is (iii) with var x replaced by $\sigma = \sqrt{\operatorname{var} x}$.

The book by Goovaerts et al. (1984) presents eleven different principles, and most of these, and some others are used in insurance practice. The book begins by laying down a number of properties which are desirable in a premium calculation principle.

1.3 A very desirable property which a good premium calculation principle should have is *additivity*, i.e. that the following relation should hold:

$$P\{x_1 + x_2\} = P\{x_1\} + P\{x_2\} \tag{1}$$

Of the principles mentioned above, (ii) is additive, and so is (iii) when applied to risks which are stochastically independent. The standard deviation principle is not additive, and neither is (i).

Condition (1) implies that one cannot make risk-free profits by arbitrage operations in the market. It is not possible to buy risks, reshuffle them and resell the contracts at a risk-free profit. More informally this "axiom" is expressed as: "There ain't no free lunch".

If administrative expenses are ignored, it seems essential that (1) should hold. If these expenses are included, it is reasonable to expect that there will be some cost savings if several risks are covered under one single insurance contract. Hence the study of sub-additive premium principles is of practical interest, but it will lead to problems in accounting and office organization. These problems are not very relevant in a study of risk premiums.

1.4 Consider the two random variables x_1 and x_2, and assume that they are independent with the probability densities f_1 and f_2. The density of $x = x_1 + x_2$ is

$$f(x) = \int_0^x f_1(x-y) f_2(y)\, dy \tag{2}$$

The integral in (2) is known as the convolution of the two densities $f_1(x)$ and $f_2(x)$.

The Laplace transform of a density f(x) is defined as

$$\phi(t) = \int_0^\infty e^{-tx} f(x)\, dx$$

Taking the Laplace transform of both sides of (2) one finds:

$$\phi(t) = \phi_1(t)\, \phi_2(t) \tag{3}$$

This is the important result that the Laplace transform of the sum of two independent random variables is the product of their Laplace transforms.

Differentiation of (3) gives:

$$\phi'(t) = \phi_1'(t)\,\phi_2(t) + \phi_1(t)\,\phi_2'(t)$$

Dividing this by (3) one finds

$$\frac{\phi'(t)}{\phi(t)} = \frac{\phi_1'(t)}{\phi_1(t)} + \frac{\phi_2'(t)}{\phi_2(t)} \tag{4}$$

It is often convenient to write $\psi'(t) = d\bigl(\log\phi(t)\bigr)/dt$, so that (4) takes the form

$$\psi'(t) = \psi_1'(t) + \psi_2'(t) \tag{5}$$

It is easy to see that the formulae (4) or (5) lead to an additive premium assignment. This means that the premium calculation principle

$$P\{x\} = \frac{\phi'(t)}{\phi(t)} = \frac{d\,\log\phi(t)}{dt} = \frac{\int_0^\infty xe^{-tx} f(x)\,dx}{\int_0^\infty e^{-tx} f(x)\,dx} \tag{6}$$

will for any value of t have the additivity property, when applied to independent random variables.

The formula (6) has been extensively used in actuarial work, i.a. by Borch (1962). It is some times called the "Esscher principle" because Esscher (1932) used this transformation in a different context.

1.5 The premium principle expressed by (6) is practically the most general one which has the additivity property. This follows from a theorem by Lukacs (1952) and (1964), which has been generalized to multivariable distributions by Cuppens (1975). This theorem can be formulated loosely as follows:

Let $K(t,x)$ be an arbitrary kernel and

$$f(x) = \int_0^x f_1(x-y)\,f_2(y)\,dy$$

then

$$\int_0^\infty K(t,x)\,f(x)\,dx = \int_0^\infty K(t,x)\,f_1(x)\,dx \int_0^\infty K(t,x)\,f_2(x)\,dx$$

if and only if

$$K(t,x) = e^{xA(t)}$$

where $A(t)$ is a function which assumes all values on a half-line.

Comparison with (6) shows that the only generalization brought in by $A(t)$ is to multiply the last term by a scale factor. Hence it seems that all premium calculation principles which are additive when applied to independent risks are of the form

$$P\{x\} = \frac{c\int_0^\infty xe^{-tx}f(x)\,dx}{\int_0^\infty e^{-tx}f(x)\,dx} = c\psi'(t) \tag{7}$$

This is however not quite correct, since there are a number of approximations to $\psi(t)$ which also leads to additive premium principles.

1.6 The function $\phi(t)$ is a "moment-generating" function. Its Taylor expansion is

$$\phi(t) = \sum_{n=0}^{\infty} \frac{(-t)^n}{n!} m_n$$

Here the coefficient m_n is the n-th moment of the density $f(x)$, i.e.

$$m_n = \int_0^\infty x^n f(x)\,dx$$

From (3) it easy to see that there are not two independent variables with moments m_n' and m_n'' ($n = 1, 2, \ldots$) such that

$$m_n = m_n' + m_n''$$

except for $n = 1$, i.e. for the first moment, which is equal to the expectation.

The function $\psi(t)$ is called the "cumulant-generating" function. Its expansion is

$$\psi(t) = \sum_{n=1}^{\infty} \frac{(-t)^n}{n!} \kappa_n$$

and the coefficient κ_n is called the n-th cumulant. From (5) it is easy to see that if the random variables x' and x'' are independent, and $x' + x'' = x$, we have for all n

$$\kappa_n = \kappa_n' + \kappa_n''$$

Hence a premium calculation principle which is the sum of a finite number cumulants, say

$$P\{x\} = a_1\kappa_1 + a_2\kappa_2 + a_3\kappa_3$$

will be additive. This is an approximation, since the order of premiums assigned to different risks may change if more cumulants are brought into the formula.

The only exception is the normal distribution, for which all cumulants of order higher than two are zero.

The remarkable properties of the cumulants has made them very important in theoretical and applied work. The property has been applied to insurance i.a. by Borch (1982) and (1983), and by Aase (1985).

1.7 In Chapter 2, section 3.2 we studied functions $y_1(y)$, $y_2(x)$, ... of a random variable x, which could be interpreted as total claim payments in the market. The function $y_r(x)$ represents the amount which will be charged to company r. We need to assign a premium to the Company's obligations under the reinsurance arrangement considered.

We have, if y_1 and y_2 are stochastically independent, that

$$\phi(t) = \int_0^\infty e^{tx} f(x)\,dx = \int_0^\infty e^{t\left(y_1(x)+y_2(x)\right)} f(x)\,dx$$

$$= \int_0^\infty e^{ty_1} f(x)\,dx \int_0^\infty e^{ty_2(x)} f(x)\,dx$$

Here we have dropped the minus sign of t, to simplify the notation, it being assumed that t is negative, to secure that the integrals exist. As a further simplification the equation will be written as:

$$E\{e^{tx}\} = E\{e^{ty_1}\}E\{e^{ty_2}\} \tag{8}$$

Differentiation with respect to t gives:

$$E\{xe^{tx}\} = E\{y_1e^{ty_1}\}E\{e^{ty_2}\} + E\{e^{ty_1}\}E\{y_2e^{ty_2}\}$$

Division by (8) gives

$$\frac{E\{xe^{tx}\}}{E\{e^{tx}\}} = \frac{E\{y_1e^{ty_1}\}}{E\{e^{ty_1}\}} + \frac{E\{y_2e^{ty_2}\}}{E\{y_2e^{ty_1}\}} \tag{9}$$

Since all expectations are over x, no misunderstanding should be possible.

It is easy to see that (4) can be written in the same form as

$$\frac{E\{xe^{tx}\}}{E\{e^{tx}\}} = \frac{E\{x_1e^{tx_1}\}}{E\{e^{tx_1}\}} + \frac{E\{x_2e^{tx_2}\}}{E\{e^{tx_2}\}} \tag{10}$$

The formula was derived under the assumption that x_1 and x_2 were independent random variables, but it can be proved that (10) holds also when the two are stochastically dependent.

1.8 In formula (9) y_1 and y_2 are functionally dependent. In this case the additive formula can be expressed more simply.

If

$$x = y_1(x) + y_2(x)$$

the following holds for any function $w(x)$

$$\int_0^\infty xw(x)\,dx = \int_0^\infty y_1(x)\,w(x)\,dx + \int_0^\infty y_2(x)\,w(x)\,dx \tag{11}$$

provided only that the integral exist. In fact any additive functional of $y(x)$ can be expressed in this form, with a suitable generalization of the definition of integrals. This is one of the classical results in analysis, and is known as the Riesz Representation Theorem. In this special case it can be formulated as

$$\int_0^\infty x\,dw(x) = \int_0^\infty y_1(x)\,dw(x) + \int_0^\infty y_2(x)\,dw(x)$$

where the integrals must be interpreted in the Lebesgue — Stieltjes sense. If $w(x)$ is differentiable, $dw(x) = w'(x)\,dx = w(x)\,dx$, and the integrals become the ordinary Riemann integrals. If $w(x)$ is a step function, the integrals have to be replaced by sums.

2. Insurance Premiums in the Market

2.1 In the preceding section $P\{x\}$ was interpreted as an insurance premium, i.e. the amount of money one has to pay in the market to be relieved of a potential liability. The buyer of the insurance contract will probably consider that he buys an asset, the insurance policy. The seller, the insurer, may also consider that he acquires an asset, which can be expected to yield a profit, but which also carries the risk of incurring heavy losses. This indicates that the theory of insurance premiums and the theory of asset prices are special cases of a more general theory. The point will be discussed in more detail in the next section.

In Chapter 2 we considered all participants in the transactions which take place in the insurance market. We assumed that these participants would behave rationally, and somehow would negotiate or bargain their way to a Pareto optimal allocation of the risks. This is the natural first step in a game theoretical approach, and it does essentially consist in not using some of the behavioral assumptions used to determine the neo-classical equilibrium in a competitive market. We also outlined some of the second steps suggested by game theory.

It is however of interest to examine in more detail the neo-classical equilibrium, if for no other reason because it appears as a limiting case of the core — one of the most attractive definitions of the "solution" of an n-person game.

2.2 In Chapter 2 it was assumed that company r entered the market with an initial portfolio described by a random variable x_r, and left with a final portfolio described by the variable y_r. No assumptions were made about premiums or prices, and hence the final portfolios were not unique, but depended on n parameters that could be chosen arbitrarily. To determine these parameters we assumed:

$$P\{x_r\} = P\{y_r\} \qquad r = 1, 2, \ldots, n \tag{1}$$

The meaning of (12) is that the market values of the initial and the final portfolio must be equal for any company. This will be the case if all exchanges are settled at market prices, or more generally, if it is impossible to make risk-free profits by arbitrage transactions in the market.

2.3 In the conventional approach to the competitive equilibrium it is assumed that the problem of company r is to maximize the expected utility of its final portfolio $E\{u_r(y_r)\}$ subject to the resource constraint $P\{x_r\} = P\{y_r\}$.

From (11) it follows that

$$P\{y_r\} = \int_0^\infty y_r(x)\, w(x)\, f(x)\, dx \tag{2}$$

In (11) $w(x)$ is an arbitrary function, and there is no loss of generality in writing it as $w(x)\, f(x)$. The problem then takes the form

$$\max \int_0^\infty u_r(y_r)\, f(x)\, dx$$

Subject to

$$P\{x_r\} = \int_0^\infty y_r(x)\, w(x)\, f(x)\, dx$$

The maximization is over the set of all functions $y(x)$ in a certain set Y, which may be unrestricted. The problem is equivalent to

$$\max_{y_r \in Y} \int_0^\infty \Big[u_r(y_r) + \lambda\big(P\{x_r\} - y_r(x) w(x)\big) \Big] f(x)\, dx$$

2.4 This is a problem in the classical calculus of variation, which is most familiar in a more general form: Determine the function of $y(t)$ which maximizes the integral

$$\int_0^a F(t, y, y')\, dt$$

A necessary condition that $y(t)$ is a solution is given by the Euler equation

$$\frac{\partial F}{\partial y} = \frac{d}{dt}\left(\frac{\partial F}{\partial y'}\right)$$

The derivative of $y(x)$ does not occur in the problem of the company, so the right-hand side of the Euler equation disappears. Hence we obtain

$$u'_r\big(y_r(x)\big) = \lambda w(x)$$

From (2.11) it follows that $k_r u'\big(y_r(x)\big) = u'(x)$ and hence that

$$u'(x) = \lambda k_r^{-1} w(x)$$

The constants λ and k_r can be chosen arbitrarily, so there is no loss of generality if we write $u'(x) = w(x)$. Substitution in (13) then gives

$$P\{y_r\} = \int_0^\infty y_r(x)\, u'(x)\, f(x)\, dx \tag{3}$$

The problem we have considered is so simple that there is no real need to use calculus of variation. The result can be reached by the methods used in Chapter 2, section 3.2 for solving a similar problem. There it was assumed that the random variable could take only a finite number of different values, so that the Lagrange method could be used. Both these classical procedures break down if the problem only has corner solutions. In such cases one must resort to the more recent Kuhn-Tucker methods, and control theory. The book by Hestenes (1966) gives a broad and rigorous method for handling mathematical problems of this kind.

2.5 It is easy to see that (14) also can be written as $P\{y_r\} = E\{y_r(x)\, u'(x)\}$, and it can be shown that the left-hand side of (12) can be written as $P\{x_r\} = E\{x_r u'(x)\}$. The conditions (12) then take the form:

$$E\{x_r u'(x)\} = E\{y_r u'(x)\} \qquad r = 1, 2, \ldots, n \tag{4}$$

In (15) the expectation on the left-hand side is taken over the two variables x_r and x. It can be expressed as an integral with a joint density of the form $f(x_r, x)$.

The conditions (15) give n equations, which are not independent, since they add up to the identity $E\{xu'(x)\} = E\{xu'(x)\}$. Under some regularity assumptions (15) will however determine the parameters k_1, k_2, ..., k_n, up to a scale factor. It is tedious, and not easy to spell out the assumptions necessary to secure the existence of a unique competitive equilibrium, and we shall not try to do so here. Instead we shall present a number of examples which should give some insight into how the model works, and indicate the kind of complications which can arise.

2.6 *Example 1.* Let $u_r'(x) = (c_r - x)^\alpha$ for $r = 1, 2, \ldots, n$. This marginal utility function has the properties $u' > 0$ and $u'' < 0$ only when α is an odd integer and $x < c_r$. For fractional values of α the function is not even uniquely defined. Some of these complications can be overcome by writing $u'(x) = \operatorname{sgn}(c_r - x)\,|(c_r - x)^\alpha|$. This is however cumbersome, and the notation will not be used in the rest of the example, but it must be kept in mind, and if necessary corrections made in results obtained for particular values of α and c_r.

In the example (2.11) takes the form

$$k_r(c_r - y_r)^\alpha = u'(x) \tag{5}$$

From this we obtain

$$c_r - y_r = \left(k_r^{-1} u'(x)\right)^{1/\alpha}$$

Summation of these equations over all r, and the use of (2.10) gives

$$\sum_{r=1}^{n} c_r - x = \left(u'(x)\right)^{1/\alpha} \sum_{r=1}^{n} k_r^{-1/\alpha}$$

Substituting $\sum_{r=1}^{n} c_r = c$ and $\sum_{r=1}^{n} k_r^{-1/\alpha} = K^{-1/\alpha}$ one obtains

$$u'(x) = K(c - x)^\alpha$$

Substitution into (16) gives

$$k_r(c_r - y_r)^\alpha = K(c - x)^\alpha$$

and the explicit expression for $y_r(x)$:

$$y_r(x) = c_r - (c - x)(Kk_r^{-1})^{1/\alpha}$$

or

$$y_r(x) = k_r x + c_r - h_r c$$

where $h_r = (Kk_r^{-1})^{1/\alpha}$. It is easily verified that $\sum_r h_r = 1$.

It then follows that the right-hand side of (15) is

$$\begin{aligned} P\{y_r\} &= E\{y_r(x)u'(x)\} = E\{(h_r x + c_r - h_r c)(c - x)^\alpha\} \\ &= h_r E\{x(c - x)^\alpha\} + (c_r - h_r \cdot c)E\{(c - x)^\alpha\} \end{aligned}$$

As the left-hand side of (15) is $P\{x_r\} = E\{x_r(c - x)^\alpha\}$, one finds:

$$h_r = \frac{E\{(c_r - x_r)(c - x)^\alpha\}}{E\{(c - x)^{\alpha+1}\}}$$

In this example it is thus possible to determine the arbitrary parameters in the Pareto optimum from the market clearing equation (15). For this equation we find

$$P\{x_r\} = P\{y_r\} = E\{(c_r - x_r)(c - x)^\alpha\} \tag{6}$$

Here the last term gives the market value of the company's initial portfolio, expressed by the marginal utility in the market, and the stochastic relationship between the company's portfolio and the market as a whole.

The market value of a portfolio cannot change when exchanges are settled at market prices. The expected utility of the portfolio can however be increased by such exchanges, and this is the very purpose of reinsurance transactions.

2.7 *Example 2.* Assume that $u'(x_r) = \exp\left(-\frac{x_r}{\alpha_r}\right)$, $r = 1, 2, \ldots, n$. Condition (2.11) then takes the form $k_r \exp(-y_r\alpha_r^{-1}) = u'(x)$. Here we take the logarithm of both sides, multiply by α_r, and as in the example above sum over all r. This gives:

$$\sum \alpha_r \log k_r - x = \sum \alpha_r \log u'(x)$$

Writing $\sum \alpha_r \log k_r = K$ and $\sum \alpha_r = A$, one can transform the equation into the form

$$K - x = A \log u'(x)$$

or

$$u'(x) = \exp\left(\frac{K - x}{A}\right)$$

For the payoff function one finds

$$y_r(x) = \frac{\alpha_r x}{A} + \alpha_r \log k_r - \frac{\alpha_r K}{A}$$

As in the first example it is possible to determine the arbitrary parameter k_r. Elementary manipulations show that

$$\alpha_r E\left\{\exp\left(\frac{K-x}{A}\right)\right\} \log k_r = E\left\{\left(x_r - \frac{\alpha_r}{A}x\right)\exp\left(\frac{K-x}{A}\right)\right\} + \frac{\alpha_r K}{A} E\left\{\exp\left(\frac{K-x}{A}\right)\right\}$$

and for the market value of the portfolios

$$P\{x_r\} = P\{y_r\} = E\left\{x_r \exp\left(\frac{K-x}{A}\right)\right\}$$

2.8 These two examples were relatively easy to handle because the payoff functions (or the sharing rules) were linear, i.e. $y_r(x) = q_r x + c_r$, when $\sum q_r = 1$ and $\sum c_r = 0$.

The sharing rules have this simple form only if all utility functions belong to one of the following two classes:

$$u_r'(x) = (x + c)^\alpha \,, \tag{i}$$

or

$$u_r'(x) = e^{\alpha_r x} \tag{ii}$$

This is well known, and the two classes are sometimes referred to as the HARA class (Harmonic Absolute Risk Aversion). The risk aversion associated with a utility function in class (i) is $\alpha(x + c)$, and in class (ii) the risk aversion is α_r. The "risk tolerance" is the inverse of the absolute risk aversion (see Chapter 2, section 3.2). These classes of utility functions can therefore also be characterized by linear risk tolerance.

When the sharing rules are linear, it is possible to reach a Pareto optimum by an exchange of fractions of the initial portfolios.

In a reinsurance market this means that there should be no need for any other contract than the standard proportional reinsurance contract. Applied to a stock market, the assumption that the optimal sharing rules are linear implies that there should be no need for trading any other securities than ordinary shares (common stock). Non-proportional reinsurance and securities such as preference shares and options both exist and are important, so we must conclude that the preferences of decision makers are at least so diverse that they cannot be represented by one, and one only, of the two classes of utility functions above.

For some reason many economists refer to a market in which it is impossible to reach a Pareto optimum through an exchange of proportions of the initial portfolios as an "incomplete market". The term seems to have been made fashionable by Hirshleifer (1970), although such markets were discussed a few years earlier by Baudier (1968).

3. Insurance Premiums and Asset Prices

3.1 It should be evident from the preceding sections that there is a considerable formal similarity between the calculation of insurance premiums, and estimating the values of security prices in a stock market. Usually a mere change of some signs will make it possible to interpret a model developed in one of the fields as applicable to the other. There are however important differences between insurance and investment in the stock market, and some of these will be discussed in this section.

In insurance the relevant probabilities are reasonably well known. This is particularly the case in life insurance, where analysis of mortality statistics over more than 300 years makes it possible to predict mortality in the near future fairly accurately. In general insurance claim records from the past seem to have a considerable predictive power when it comes to make forecasts of claims in the next year. Further, and this is important, there is a high degree of consensus among insurers over these forecasts.

There are theories about how behaviour of stock prices in the past influence prices in the near future. There is no general agreement about these theories, and few of them are even considered as respectable. Hence it is not likely that there is much of a consensus behind transactions in the stock market. This only to be expected. In any transaction there is a buyer and a seller, and the natural explanation is that at present prices the seller believes it is the time to sell a certain share, and the buyer believes that the time has come to buy. It seems that the assumption of "homogeneous beliefs" regularly made in theoretical studies of the stock market is more "heroic" than in most other studies. In insurance the assumption appears quite reasonable, as has been argued earlier.

3.2 There is an abundance of statistical information about stock markets. Practically every transaction is recorded and the price published. The quoted price is not exactly the price at which one can buy a share in the market, since the broker will add his commission. Similarly when one sells a commission is deducted from the quoted market price. There is however nothing secret about commission scales, they are often published, and in any case easily obtainable.

The availability of statistics has led to a number of empirical studies of the stock market. Practically any theoretical model of the stock market has been tested against different sets of data and with different methods.

Things are very different in insurance. Information about premiums is available mainly from the advertising material of the insurance companies. These are however gross premiums, which include a loading to cover administrative expenses, a risk premium and possibly commission to a broker. Information about the premium calculation principle actually used by a company is difficult to obtain, although in some countries this information is in principle available from the department supervising, or regulating private insurance. This will however be the case only for insurance offered to the public. Insurance contracts between insurance companies, i.e. reinsurance is treated as strictly confidential by practically all insurers.

This paucity of statistics seems to be the main reason that insurance has not developed the fruitful cross fertilization between theoretical and empirical research which is usually found in finance.

3.3 The premium calculation principles discussed at the beginning of this chapter are very similar to the first steps in the approach of Markowitz (1952) and (1959) to the problem of portfolio selection. The obvious difference is that the premium of an insurance contract is greater than expected claim payments, and that the value of a risky security on the other hand is less than the expected payoff.

Markowitz proceeds beyond these first steps, and shows how one can determine the optimal portfolio of securities when prices are given. He examines several "pricing principles", and settles for the one which was called the variance principle in the beginning of this chapter.

These ideas could obviously be applied to insurance companies, and it should be possible to determine the optimal portfolio of insurance contracts, under a given premium calculation principle. The models of Markowitz were applied in the study of insurance, only after they had become a part of the conventional wisdom in financial economics, and even then only half-heartily.

One reason for the reluctance of actuaries about applying portfolio models may have been that they believed that the probability distributions in insurance were so skew that the variance was an inadequate measure of risk. They found some support for this belief in an automotive statement by Cramér (1930) who wrote: "... in many cases the approximation obtained by using the normal function is not sufficiently good to justify the conclusions that have been drawn in this way".

3.4 The portfolio model has turned out to be one of the most fertile ideas in applied economics. These ideas have had a profound influence, not only on the analysis of optimal combinations of risky investments.

Still the model is unsatisfactory on at least one point. For given prices it may turn out that no investor — no matter what his risk aversion is — will hold certain securities. This does not make sense, and one must conclude that the prices taken as given cannot exist in a market in equilibrium. Market forces must adjust prices such that some investors are willing to hold all the securities in the market. This leads to a problem which was solved independently, and virtually simultaneously by Sharpe (1964), Lintner (1965) and Mossin (1966). Their solution has become known as the "Capital Asset Price Model", or CAPM, and has found wide applications in the practical analysis of investments.

CAPM is a special case of the models developed in this chapter. If in (17) one takes $\alpha = 1$, one obtains:

$$P\{x_r\} = E\{x_r(c+x)\} = cE\{x_r\} + E\{xx_r\}$$
$$= cE\{x_r\} + E\{x_r\}E\{x\} + \text{cov } xx_r$$

This can be written as

$$P\{x_r\} = (c+\bar{x})\bar{x}_r + \text{cov } xx_r$$

The minus sign of x has been omitted. This involves no loss of generality, since the interval of integration is left unspecified.

For $x_r = x$ this takes the form

$$P\{x\} = (c+\bar{x})\bar{x} + \text{var } x$$

From these two equations one obtains

$$P\{x_r\} = (c+\bar{x})\bar{x}_r + \big(P(x) - (x+\bar{x})\bar{x}\big)\frac{\text{cov } xx_r}{\text{var } x} \tag{18}$$

3.5 Formula (18) gives CAPM in what one could call the "original form". It gives the market value of an arbitrary portfolio expressed in terms of expected payoff from the portfolio itself, the covariance with total payoff in the market, and the expectation and variance of total payoff.

When the model is interpreted as an insurance market, no particular complications arise. The probability distribution of total claim payments in an insurance market is not exactly known, but its expectation and variance can be estimated with reasonable accuracy.

The corresponding concept when the model is interpreted as a stock market is total payoff from all assets in the market, and this seems to be an elusive concept, and the same holds for the value of all assets in the market. For these reasons it has become customary to consider the rate of return on an asset, instead of its value. This is done by a simple transformation of the variables.

3.6 In (18) we substitute

$$x_r = P\{x_r\}(1 + R_r) \qquad \text{and} \qquad x = P\{x\}(1 + R)$$

where R_r and R are random variable.

The expression

$$\frac{x_r - P\{x_r\}}{P\{x_r\}} = R_r \tag{19}$$

will then be the random rate of return on portfolio r, and a corresponding expression is found for the rate of return in the "market portfolio".

The substitution further gives

$$\text{cov } xx_r = P\{x\}P\{x_r\}\,\text{cov}RR_r \quad \text{and} \quad \text{var } x = (P\{x\})^2\,\text{var}R$$

Hence (18) can be written

$$(c + \bar{x})\bar{x}_r - P\{x_r\} = \big((c + \bar{x})\bar{x} - P\{x\}\big)\frac{P\{x_r\}\,P\{x\}\,\text{cov}RR_r}{\big(P\{x\}\big)^2\text{var}R}$$

or

$$\frac{(c + \bar{x})\bar{x}_r - P\{x_r\}}{P\{x_r\}} = \frac{(c + \bar{x})\bar{x} - P\{x\}}{P\{x\}}\,\frac{\text{cov}RR_r}{\text{var}R} \tag{20}$$

Adding the subscript m (for market) to R, this can be written

$$\bar{R}_r = R_m\frac{\text{cov}R_mR_r}{\text{var}R_m}$$

Consider now a degenerate portfolio x_e, where the "random" variable takes the value e with probability one.

From (18) it follows that the value of this portfolio is

$$P\{x_e\} = (c + \bar{x})e$$

Substituting this into (19) we get

$$\frac{e - (c + \bar{x})e}{(c + \bar{x})e} = \frac{1}{c + \bar{x}} - 1 = R_f$$

or

$$c + \bar{x} = \frac{1}{1 + R}$$

where R_f is the risk-free rate of interest in the market.

Substitution of the expression for $c + \bar{x}$ into (20) gives

$$\frac{\bar{x}_r - P\{x_r\}(1 + R_f)}{P\{x_r\}} = \frac{\bar{x} - P\{x\}(1 + R_f)}{P\{x\}} \frac{\mathrm{cov} R_m R_r}{\mathrm{var} R_m}$$

or

$$\bar{R}_r = R_f + (\bar{R}_m - R_f) \frac{\mathrm{cov} R_m R_r}{\mathrm{var} R_m} \tag{21}$$

This is the usual form of CAPM. Formula (21) gives the expected rate of return on an arbitrary security (or a portfolio) in terms the risk-free rate of interest, the expected rate of return on the market portfolio, and the covariance between the return on the particular security, and return in the market as a whole.

3.7 The CAPM has gained an almost incredible popularity. It is widely applied in practical investment analysis, and virtually every assumption behind the model and every implication of it has been tested empirically — often with conflicting conclusions. An excellent survey of some of these tests has been given by Roll (1977).

No matter what the outcome of this testing is, simple observation of the market should lead one to suspect the model. We have derived CAPM as a special case of Example 1 in Section 2. The example assumed that all traders in the market had linear risk tolerance. It was shown that in this case it was possible to reach a Pareto optimum by exchanging fractions of the initial portfolios, or in other words that only the markets for common stock were needed. A glance at the market will show that there is a brisk trade in other securities, such as preference shares and options. One may well ask why these securities have been created, and why they find buyers.

3.8 A model which has gained a popularity almost comparable to CAPM is the Black-Scholes (1973) model of option prices. We shall give a brief outline of the model.

Let $f(x)$ be the probability density of the price of a share at some future date. The expected value of an option callable at that date, with an exercise price D is

$$E\{D\} = \int_D^\infty (x - D) f(x)\, dx$$

Black and Scholes found an expression for the premium when $f(x)$ is the lognormal density, i.e.

$$f(x) = \frac{1}{x\sigma\sqrt{2\pi}} \exp\left(-\frac{(\log x - m)^2}{2\sigma^2}\right)$$

This result is extensively applied in practice.

The price in the Black-Scholes model is an expected present value but under a "risk-adjusted" probability distribution. Equivalently this result can be derived along our lines by determining the market's marginal utility function. This turns out to be a Radon Nikodym derivative (see Aase (1988), (1989)).

References for Sections 1–3

Aase K.K. (1985): "Accumulated Claims and Collective Risk in Insurance: Higher Order Asymptotic Approximations", *Scand. Actuarial J.* 65–85.

Aase K.K. (1988): "Contingent claims analysis when the security price is a combination of an Ito process and a random point process", *Stochastic processes and their applications* 28:185–220.

Aase K.K. (1989): *Dynamic equilibrium and the structure of premiums in a reinsurance market.* Techn. Report, Norwegian School of Economics and Business Administration.

Baudier, E. (1968): "Minimax Behaviour and Price Prediction" in K. Borch and J. Mossin (Eds.): *Risk and Uncertainty*, London: MacMillan.

Black, F. and M. Scholes (1973): "The Pricing of Options and Corporative Liabilities," *Journal of Political Economy*, 637–654.

Borch, K. (1982): "Additive Insurance Premiums," *The Journal of Finance 37*, 1295–1298.

Borch, K. (1983): "Insurance Premiums in Competitive Markets," *Geld, Banken und Versicherungen*, Göppl and Henn (Eds.), Karlsruhe.

Cramér, H. (1930): "On the Mathematical Theory of Risk," *Skandia Jubilee Volume*, 7–84.

Cuppens, R. (1975): *Decomposition of Multivariate Probability*, Academic Press.

Esscher, F. (1932): "On the Probability Function in the Collective Theory of Risk," *Skandinavisk Aktuarietidskrift*, 175–195.

Hestenes, M.R. (1966): *Calculus of Variation and optimal Control Theory*, Wiley & Sons.

Hirshleifer, J. (1970): *Investment, Interest and Capital*, Prentice-Hall.

Lintner, J. (1965): "The Evaluation of Risky Assets and the Selection of Risky Investments in Stock Portfolios," *Review of Economics and Statistics 47*, 13–37.

Lukacs, E. (1952): "An Essential Property of the Fourier Transform of Distribution Functions," *Proceedings of the American Mathematical Society 3*, 508–510.

Lukacs, E. (1964): "A Linear Mapping of the Space of Distribution Functions onto a Set of Bounded Continuous Functions," *Zeitschrift für Wahrscheinlichkeitstheorie und Verwandte Gebiete 3*, 1–6.

Markowitz, H. (1952): "Portfolio Selection," *The Journal of Finance 7*, 77–91.

Morkowitz, H. (1959): *Portfolio Selection: Efficient Diversification of Investments*, John Wiley & Sons.
Mossin, J. (1966): "Equilibrium in Capital Asset Market," *Econometrica 34*, 768–783.
Roll, R. (1977): "A Critique of the Asset Pricing Theory's Tests," *Journal of Financial Economics*, 129–176.
Sharpe, W. (1964): "Capital Asset Prices," *The Journal of Finance 19*, 425–442.

4. Insurance and the Theory of Financial Markets*

1. Introduction

1.1 A market is a place where buyers and sellers meet. A financial market is the meeting place for investors who have capital to offer, and for entrepreneurs who want to obtain capital for different purposes. An insurance company will usually have substantial funds available for investment, and will generally come to the market as an investor. The company will then buy a portfolio in the market, and the problem is to find the portfolio which best suits the company's particular investment objectives.

In general insurance companies do not seem to have investment objectives which differ significantly from those of some other investors, such as conservative mutual funds, and little has been done to develop a special theory for the investments of insurance companies. The reason may be that the company's investment activity usually is carried out independently of its underwriting operations. If the two activities are seen together and coordinated, it may be desirable to develop a specific theory of investment for insurance companies. The first step towards a theory of this kind is made in the work by Redington (1952) on the "matching" of assets and liabilities. These problems have been taken up in a few other studies, i.a. Borch (1968) and Wehrle (1961), but have hardly received the attention they deserve. In this paper we shall, however, not discuss the insurance company's role as an investor in the capital market. We shall instead study the company as an entrepreneur.

1.2 It may be an unfamiliar idea to consider an insurance company as an entrepreneur coming to the market in search of capital to finance its operations. An insurance company does not need large amounts of capital for plant and equipment, and in most countries an insurance company is not allowed to borrow money to finance current operations. The main problem

---

* Reprinted from *Transactions of the 19th International Congress of Actuaries*, Oslo 1972; 3:193–201.

in business finance is to obtain the necessary capital from the market at the lowest possible cost.

For most firms this is a complicated problem, because the range of choices is wide. The firm may obtain capital by borrowing in the bank on short term, by selling long term bonds in the market, or by selling other kinds of securities, such as ordinary shares, preference shares, debentures and convertible bonds. Usually an insurance company will have no choice in this respect, and the problem is of little importance.

Some authors, i.a. Launie (1971) have argued that the concept "cost of capital", which plays a central part in the theory of business finance, can be adapted and applied in insurance. We shall, however, not find this concept useful in the following.

An insurance company does, however, need equity capital, and this capital must, in general, be obtained from the financial markets. In the following we shall study the conditions under which these markets are willing to supply such capital.

2. A Simple Model

2.1 In this section we shall discuss a simple model, which contains most of the essential elements in the situation from real life, which we want to study. Our basic concept is the *insurance contract* which is defined by the following two elements:

$p =$ the premium which the company receives under the contract.

$x =$ a stochastic variable which represents the amount the company pays to settle insurance claims made under the contract.

It is obviously possible to define a more general insurance contract, by bringing in the time-element explicitly, and by letting both p and x be stochastic processes. Such generalizations are, however, not necessary for our present purposes.

2.2 We shall now assume that the company has acquired a portfolio of insurance contracts.

Let $P = \sum p_i$ be the total amount of premiums received, and let the stochastic variable $X = \sum x_i$ represent the amount paid to settle claims. Let further $F(x)$ be the distribution of X. If claim payments exceed the premium received, i.e. $X > P$, the underwriting of the portfolio will bring the company a loss. The probability of this event is:

$$\Pr\{X > P\} = 1 - F(P)$$

If the company has no reserves, it will be unable to meet its obligations if an underwriting loss should occur. This means that if the probability above is significantly different from zero, the insurance contracts sold by the company will not give adequate protection. It is, therefore, usual to require that an insurance company must hold reserve funds, or equity capital, which can be drawn upon to cover underwriting losses. If these funds amount to S, the probability that the company shall be unable to meet its obligations will be:

$$\Pr\{X > S + P\} = 1 - F(S + P)$$

2.3 The concepts introduced above are familiar, and they lead us to ask how much equity capital the insurance company will need in order to operate. The obvious answer seems to be that the capital must be so large that the public has confidence in the company, and is willing to buy the insurance contracts which it offers to sell. In practice this answer is not very useful. The public complains, only too often, about difficulties in understanding and interpreting the fine print in the insurance contract. If in addition the public should be asked to read the company's balance sheet and evaluate the company's ability to fulfill the promises made in big print, the public may well revolt and ask for government protection. The revolt has not taken place, but in most countries the government has stepped in to protect the insurance-buying public. Often the government supervision has been established at the explicit request of the insurance companies, simply because they found it difficult to do business without some official stamp of approval. *Caveat emptor* is not a good foundation for a business which depends on a high degree of mutual confidence.

2.4 The general objective of government supervision of insurance has been formulated as follows: "To safeguard proposers, policy holders, beneficiaries and any other third party interested in the due performance of the contract" (OECD (1963) page 10). This leads straight to minimum requirements for the company's equity capital. The government wants to make sure that the company fulfills the insurance contract, and this means that it must see that the company is able to do so, which finally means that the government must make sure that the insurance company has a sufficient equity capital.

In most cases it will be impossible to set the capital requirement so high that it is absolutely certain that the insurance company will be able to fulfill the contracts. In real life one must settle for practical certainty, i.e. a probability very close to one. The objectives of the supervision can then be achieved by requiring that an inequality of the following form shall be satisfied:

$$\Pr\{X > S + P\} = 1 - F(S + P) \leq \alpha\,, \tag{1}$$

and take $1 - \alpha$ as a measure of the minimum *quality* of the insurance contracts which the government allows the company to offer to the public.

2.5 Let us now consider a new insurance company, which proposes to do underwriting that will give it a portfolio of insurance contracts described by P and $F(x)$. If the company shall be allowed to operate, it must obtain an equity capital S, so that the condition (1) is satisfied. This capital must be obtained from the financial market, and we must discuss how a potential investor will evaluate the proposed insurance company. If he provides the required capital S, his net profit will be the stochastic variable y, defined by

$$y = P - X \qquad \text{if } X < S + P$$

$$y = -S \qquad \text{if } X > S + P$$

It is easy to see that this investment will become more attractive with increasing P, and less attractive with increasing S. If $S + P = Z$ is determined by the condition $F(S + P) = 1 - \alpha$, imposed by the government, the problem is to determine the value of P which will make the investment acceptable to the investor, or to the market as a whole.

As a first step in our approach to this problem, we compute expected profit

$$E\{y\} = \int_0^{S+P} (P - x)\,dF(x) - S\int_{S+P}^{\infty} dF(x) = P + \int_0^Z (Z - x)\,dF(x) - Z\,,$$

and the second moment

$$E\{y^2\} = \int_0^{S+P} (P - x)^2\,dF(x) + S^2\int_{S+P}^{\infty} dF(x)$$

$$= (Z - P)^2 - \int_0^Z (Z^2 - x^2)\,dF(x) + 2P\int_0^Z (Z - x)\,dF(x)$$

The variance of the profit is

$$V(y) = E\{y^2\} - (E\{y\})^2 = \int_0^Z (Z-x)^2\, dF(x) - \left(\int_0^Z (Z-x)\, dF(x)\right)^2$$

We see that the variance depends on P only through $Z = S + P$.

These expressions bring out more clearly the observations made earlier:

(i) An increase in the premium P, with Z held constant, will increase the expected profit, and leave unchanged the risk, measured by the variance.

(ii) An increase in Z, i.e. in the government's quality requirements, will reduce the expected profit, and increase the risk.

2.6 The investor we have considered will naturally compare the proposed insurance company with investments offered by other entrepreneurs in the market. In order to make such comparisons, he must have some rule which enables him to decide when one investment should be preferred to another. If this rule is consistent, it can be represented by a utility function $u(x)$, in the sense that the investment which is most attractive, also has the greatest "expected utility".

Let us assume that the most attractive alternative to investing the amount S in the new insurance company, is to lend the money out, without risk, at a rate of interest r. The investment in the insurance company will then be preferred if:

$$\int_0^{S+P} u(P-x)\, dF(x) + u(-S) \int_0^{S+P} dF(x)\, u(rS)\,.$$

This inequality says that the expected utility of the profits obtained by investing in the insurance company, is greater than the utility of the certain profit rS.

Replacing the inequality sign by that of equality, we obtain the equation:

$$\int_0^Z u(P-x)\, dF(x) + (1-\alpha)u(-S) = u(rS) \tag{2}$$

where $\alpha = 1 - F(S+P) = 1 - F(Z)$.

This equation will determine the lowest premium P, which will make the new insurance company an acceptable investment. The two given elements are:

Table 1: Minimum Premium when the Interest Rate and the Acceptable Probability of Ruin are given.

Acceptable probability of ruin	Rate of Interest 0.04	0.05	0.06
10^{-3}	1.70	1.78	1.85
10^{-4}	1.82	1.92	2.03
10^{-5}	1.98	2.13	2.28
10^{-6}	2.13	2.38	2.53

(i) $r =$ the risk-free rate of interest in the market,

(ii) $1-\alpha =$ probability that the company will be able to meet its obligation, a standard set by the government.

In our model these two elements will determine the minimum premium. Should the government insist on a lower and "more reasonable" premium, the company cannot go to the market and obtain the equity capital necessary to satisfy the quality standard set by the government.

2.7 The model we have discussed is extremely simple, but it brings out an essential relationship between premium levels and conditions in the capital market. This relationship must have some significance for any insurance company which operates in a free economy, and it may be useful to give a simple numerical example as an illustration. Let

$$F(x) = 1 - e^{-x}$$

$$u(x) = x - cx^2$$

Equation (2) then becomes

$$\int_0^Z u\left(P - x - c(P-x)^2\right) e^{-x}\,dx + (S + cS^2)e^{-Z} = rS - cr^2S^2$$

From this we obtain a quadratic equation in P:

$$c(1-r^2)P^2 - \left\{1 + r - 2cr^2Z + 2c(1-e^{-Z})\right\} P$$
$$+ \{1 + 2c + rZ - cr^2Z^2\} - \{1 + 2c + 2cZ\}e^{-Z} = 0$$

Here we take $c = 0.1$ and solve for some selected values of r and Z. The results are given in Table 1.

As an illustration, let us assume that the highest probability of ruin which the government will allow, is $\alpha = 10^{-6}$. From $e^{-S-P} = 10^{-6}$ we find $S + P = 14$. If the rate of interest is 0.04, the premium can be set at $P = 2.13$. This will make the company so attractive as an investment opportunity, that it can obtain the necessary capital $S = 11.87$ from the market. Should the interest rate be 0.05, the premium must be set at $P = 2.38$ in order to attract an equity capital of $S = 11.62$.

If on the other hand the government allows a maximum premium of, say $P = 2.0$, the company will not be able to raise a sufficient equity capital. A simple calculation shows:

For an interest rate $r = 0.04$, the company will be able to obtain a capital $S = 10$, which will give a probability of ruin $\alpha = e^{-12} \approx 6.10^{-6}$.

For an interest rate $r = 0.05$, the company can obtain a capital $S = 8$, and the probability of ruin will be $\alpha = e^{-10} \approx 5.10^{-5}$.

3. Discussion of the Simple Model

3.1 Our model brings out a fact which should be well known. Supervision and legislation cannot alone provide insurance of good quality at low premiums. Substantial reserve capital is required, and unless the government itself is prepared to supply this capital, for instance in the form of guarantees of some kind, the capital must be obtained from the market. The amount of capital which can be raised in this way, will clearly depend on the profitability of the insurance business, compared to other investment opportunities in the market.

This argument appears almost self-evident, but it may be unfamiliar. In practice, in their day to day operations, insurance companies do not seem to be particularly concerned about the sufficiency of the equity capital. The reason is clearly that reinsurance arrangements can compensate a lack of equity capital.

3.2 To illustrate the last point, let us return to condition (1) in §2.4. An insurance company may be unable to satisfy the government requirement, either because some of the equity capital has been lost, or because the volume of its underwriting is greater than anticipated. The company can then reinsure a quota $1 - k$ of its portfolio, i.e. retain only a quota k. If the reinsurance is obtained on original terms, the company will retain only an amount kP of the premium, and pay only the amount kx if total claims are x. The probability of ruin then becomes

$$\Pr\{kx > S + kP\} = \Pr\left\{x > \frac{1}{k}S + P\right\} = 1 - F\left(\frac{1}{k}S + P\right).$$

By choosing k sufficiently small, the company can bring this probability under the maximum acceptable to the government.

The crucial assumption in this example is that reinsurance on original terms is available. The reinsurer will usually be an other insurance company, which may or may not, be subject to the same kind of government supervision as the first company. In any case the reinsurer will also have to watch his equity capital to remain able to meet his obligations with a sufficiently high probability. From these considerations a general picture emerges:

By reinsurance arrangements the companies reduce the probabilities that they shall be unable to meet their obligations. If the reductions which can be obtained in this way are unsatisfactory, there will be complaints that the reinsurance market has insufficient capacity. This can only mean that the insurance sector as a whole does not have enough equity capital. The obvious remedy is to increase the premiums, so that more capital can be attracted from other sectors of the economy. This is in fact the only remedy in a world with free competitive capital markets.

3.3 The function of the equity capital of an insurance company is to cover losses in the underwriting. If the premiums are adequate, such losses should not occur too often. The capital can, therefore, be invested in the market and yield a return. It must, however, be invested in assets which are fairly liquid, since the capital at any time can be called in to meet emergencies. The interest rate, r, in our simple model should, therefore, not be taken as the market rate for risk-free loans — of long or short duration. It should rather be taken as the additional return which the investor could obtain if the capital did not have to be kept in a liquid form. Often the government will lay down rules as to how the companies should invest their reserve funds. The stricter these rules are, the greater will the potential loss in earnings be, and hence the higher will be the premiums necessary to attract the capital.

3.4 Our model may throw some light on the discussion about how far an insurance company's investment income should be considered when premium rates are determined. The premiums are usually paid to the company in advance, and some time will pass before they are paid out to settle claims.

If the premiums earn some interest during the period they are kept by the company, this income should as every actuary knows, be brought into the calculations.

In the model P will represent the usual premium reserve at the beginning of the underwriting period, and the investment income derived from P should be included in the company's actuarial calculations. The S in the model represents the "free reserves", or the contingency funds of the company. This capital will, in general, have been supplied by investors, who expect a return comparable to that which they could have obtained from alternative investments in the market. In the company's hands the capital 5 must be kept in a fairly liquid form, and will presumably earn a lower return than if it could be invested without restrictions.

The investors who make capital available to insurance companies, run a risk of total loss, and their capital is likely to earn the modest return usually associated with conservative management. As compensation they will require a share of the company's underwriting profits, and they will not supply the capital unless premiums are set at a level which will give a positive expected profit on the underwriting.

The discussion of this question has on occasions been heated, and this is surprising, since the basic relations involved are clear and simple. The reason may be that the discussion originated in mutual insurance companies, where the questions of ownership may be confused. A mutual company can, when necessary, make an assessment on its members to cover underwriting losses, and does not really need large contingency reserves. It has been argued in another paper (Borch (1962)) that considerations of administrative convenience should determine the size of the reserve funds kept by such companies. To make an assessment is likely to be a costly operation, and reserves should be so high that the probability of this event is very small.

Things are clearer at the other end of the line of insurers. A member of Lloyd's must have a personal fortune, which he presumably has invested so that it gives a good return. It has never been suggested that a member with an unusually high investment income should do his underwriting cheaper than other members.

4. Generalization of the Simple Model

4.1 In this section we shall give some brief indications as to how the simple model of Section 2 can be generalized in different directions.

In para 2.6 we assumed that all relevant information about the situation in the capital market was contained in one single parameter r, which could be interpreted as the risk-free market rate of interest. This is an obvious oversimplification, and we shall sketch a more general model, often referred to as the *Sharpe-Mossin Asset Price Model* (Sharpe (1964)) and (Mossin (1966)).

The model consists of two groups of elements.

(i) m investors. Investor i has an initial capital w_i, and his preferences are represented by the utility function $x - a_i x^2$.

(ii) n assets or "firms". Form j will give a profit x_j, a stochastic variable, such that

$$E\{x_j\} = E_j$$

$$E\{(x_j - E_j)(x_k - E_k)\} = C_{jk}$$

To this model we add an insurance company, which will give a profit with expectation E and variance V. We shall assume that the profit of the insurance company is stochastically independent of the profits of all firms.

Let further p_j be the market value of firm j, and p the value of the insurance company.

4.2 We shall now assume that investor i buys ordinary shares in the n firms and the insurance company, so that he obtains a fraction z_{ij} of firm j, and a fraction z_i of the insurance company. This will give him a portfolio with expected profits:

$$E^{(i)} = z_i E + \sum_{j=1}^{n} z_{ij} E_j$$

the variance of the profit will be:

$$V^{(i)} = z_i^2 V + \sum_{j=i}^{n} \sum_{k=1}^{n} z_{ij} z_{ik} C_{jk}$$

To this portfolio the investor will assign the expected utility

$$U^{(i)} = E^{(i)} - a_i \left(E^{(i)}\right)^2 - a_i V^{(i)}$$

His problem is now to determine the portfolio which will maximize this expression, subject to the condition

$$pz_i + \sum_{j=1}^{n} p_i z_{ij} = w_i$$

i.e. that he cannot spend more than his initial capital. The problem is easy to solve, and the solution will give us the optimal portfolio $\{z_1, z_{i1} \dots z_{in}\}$. The elements of this vector will be functions of the — so far unknown — market values p, $p_1 \dots p_n$. These can be determined by requiring that the market shall be cleared, i.e. that all shares must be held by some investor. This gives the conditions:

$$\sum_{i=1}^{n} z_i = 1 \quad \text{and} \quad \sum_{i=1}^{m} z_{ij} = 1\,, \quad j = 1, 2 \dots n\,.$$

4.3 By making use of these conditions it can be shown that the value of the insurance company is

$$p = \frac{B_1}{B_1 + B_2} \sum_{i=1}^{m} w_i$$

where

$$B_1 = E\left\{A - \sum_{j=1}^{n} E_j\right\} - E^2 - V$$

$$B_2 = \sum_{j=1}^{n} E_j\left\{A - \sum_{j=1}^{n} E_j\right\} - \sum_{j=1}^{n}\sum_{k=1}^{n} C_{jk}$$

$$A = \sum_{i=1}^{m} \frac{1}{2a_i}$$

This formula shows how p, the amount which investors will pay for the insurance company, depends on:

(i) The capital available for investment: $\sum w_i$

(ii) Other investment opportunities in the market, represented by E_j and C_{jk}

(iii) The investors' attitude to risk, represented by a_i.

If we now require that $p = S =$ the amount of equity capital the insurance company must obtain in order to satisfy the government condition, we get an equation which will determine the premium P.

4.4 The Mossin-Sharpe model which we have outlined, obviously gives a grossly over-simplified representation of the financial markets in the real world. The model is static in the sense that an investment is assumed to be completely described by a single probability distribution. Further the model rests on the assumption that only the first two moments of this distribution are considered when alternative investments are compared.

In spite of such objections, the model seem to capture some of the essential elements in the real situations we want to study. The model brings out some of the aspects which have to be taken into account when an insurance company considers raising additional equity capital, for instance, to become less dependent on reinsurance.

References for Section 4

Borch, K. (1962): "The Objectives of an Insurance Company". *Skandinavisk Aktuarietidskrift*, 162–175.

Borch, K. (1968): "The optimal portfolio of assets in an insurance company". *Transactions of the 18th International Congress of Actuaries, Munich 2*, 21–31.

Launie, JJ. (1971): "The Cost of Capital of Insurance Companies". *The Journal of Risk and Insurance 38*, 263–268.

Mossin, J. (1966): "Equilibrium in a Capital Asset Market". *Econometrica 34*, 768–783.

OECD (1963): *Supervision of Private Insurance*, OECD, Paris.

Redington, FM. (1952): "Review of the Principles of Life-Office Valuation". *Journal of the Institute of Actuaries 78*, 14–73.

Sharpe, WF. (1964): "Capital Asset Prices: A Theory of Market Equilibrium under Conditions of Risk". *Journal of Finance 19*, 425–442.

Wehrle, LS. (1961): "Life Insurance Investment: The Experience of Four Companies". *Yale Economic Essays 1*, 70–136. A revised version is included in Cowles Foundation Monograph No. 20, John Wiley & Sons 1967.

5. Additive Insurance Premiums: A Note*

If a competitive market is in equilibrium, values must be additive in the sense that the value of a basket of goods must be equal to the sum of the values of the commodities it contains. Similarly, the value of a portfolio of

* Reprinted from *The Journal of Finance*, 1982; 37:1295–1298, copyright (c) American Finance Association.

securities must be equal to the sum of the values of the constituent securities. Applied to insurance, this principle means that the total premium should be the same whether a complex risk is insured under one single or several separate insurance contracts, provided, of course, that administrative expenses and transaction costs are ignored. One implication is that there must be some restrictions on the methods used to compute premiums if additivity and market equilibrium are to be preserved. With this starting point, we shall derive some well known results and indicate how they can be generalized.

Additive Premiums

Let the stochastic variable x represent claim payments under an insurance contract, and let $P\{x\}$ be the market premium for this contract.

In insurance, it is often natural to assume that x is stochastically independent of claim payments under an other insurance contracts. If one assumes further, as a first approximation, that the market premium depends only on the two first moments of x, it follows from the Capital Asset Pricing Model that

$$P\{x\} = \gamma_1 E\{x\} + \gamma_2 \mathrm{var}\, x \tag{1}$$

Traditionally, one will here take $\gamma_1 \geq 1$, so that the first term in (1) is sufficient to cover expected claim payments and the insurer's administrative expenses. It is then natural to interpret the second term, with $\gamma_2 \geq 0$, as a risk premium, determined by market forces. Formula (1) is additive, in the sense that if x_1 and x_2 are stochastically independent, we have

$$P\{x_1 + x_2\} = P\{x_1\} + P\{x_2\}$$

Many other formulae, based for instance on the standard deviation, have been used to compute insurance premiums. These will, however, not in general have the additivity property which seems essential in equilibrium.

The probability distributions of claim payments under insurance contracts can be very skew, and of very different shapes. A risk premium proportional to the variance may therefore be unsatisfactory. It is, however, easy to generalize (1) by adding a term $\gamma_3 E\left\{(x - \bar{x})^3\right\}$. By writing the expectation $\bar{x} = 0$ it is easy to see that $E\left\{(x_1 + x_2)^3\right\} = E\{x_1^3\} + E\{x_2^3\}$ if x_1 and x_2 are stochastically independent.

Things do not work quite so well for higher moments, since we have $E\left\{(x_1+x_2)^4\right\} = E\{x_1^4\} + 6E\{x_1^2\}E\{x_2^2\}$.

It is, however, easy to verify that the expression

$$\kappa_4 = E\left\{(x-\bar{x})^4\right\} - 3\Big(E\left\{(x-\bar{x})^2\right\}\Big)^2$$

has the desired additivity property.

In general, we can define κ_n as the coefficient of $(it)^n/n!$ in the expansion

$$\psi(t) = \sum_{n=1}^{\infty} \frac{(it)^n}{n!}\kappa_n$$

where

$$\psi(t) = \log \int_{-\infty}^{\infty} e^{itx}\, dF(x)$$

The coefficients κ_1, κ_2, ... are the cumulants of the stochastic variable x, introduced by Thiele (1889) and (1903), just because they are additive for independent variables. Hence, the generalization of (1) is

$$P\{x\} = \sum_{n=1}^{\infty} \gamma_n \kappa_n \tag{2}$$

The first cumulants are

$$\kappa_1 = \bar{x}\,, \qquad \kappa_2 = \operatorname{var} x\,, \qquad \kappa_3 = E\left\{(x-\bar{x})^3\right\}$$
$$\kappa_4 = E\left\{(x-\bar{x})^4\right\} - 3(\operatorname{var} x)^2$$
$$\kappa_5 = E\left\{(x-\bar{x})^5\right\} - 10E\left\{(x-\bar{x})^3\right\}(\operatorname{var} x)^2 \text{ etc.}$$

It is remarkable that any additive premium formula, for independent variables, can be written in Form (2). This follows from a theorem by Lukacs (1952) which says essentially:

If for an arbitrary bounded kernel $K(t,x)$ the transform

$$\varphi(t) = \int_{-\infty}^{+\infty} K(t,x)\, dF(x)$$

has the properties

$$\varphi_1(t) = \varphi_2(t) \quad \text{implies } F_1(x) = F_2(x) \tag{i}$$

$$F(x) = \int_{-\infty}^{+\infty} F_1(x-y)\,dF_2(y) \quad \text{implies } \varphi(t) = \varphi_1(t)\varphi_2(t) \tag{ii}$$

then

$$K(t,x) = e^{ixA(t)}$$

Stochastic Dependence

In order to generalize Formula (1) to the case of stochastic dependence, we shall write $x = x_1 + x_2$. We then have

$$\begin{aligned} \text{var}\, x &= \text{var}\, x_1 + 2\text{cov}\, x_1 x_2 + \text{var}\, x_2 \\ &= \text{cov}\, x x_1 + \text{cov}\, x x_2 \end{aligned}$$

Substitution in (1) will then give the additive premium formula

$$P\{x_i\} = \gamma_1 E\{x_i\} + \gamma_2 \text{cov}\, x x_i \qquad i = 1, 2 \tag{3}$$

Elimination of γ_2 between (1) and (3) gives

$$P\{x_i\} = \gamma_1 E\{x_i\} + \frac{\text{cov}\, x x_i}{\text{var}\, x}\big(P\{x\} - \gamma_1 E\{x\}\big) \tag{4}$$

This formula gives the premium for an arbitrary component of an insurance contract. In practice it can be used, for instance, if industrial fire, and loss of profit, are to be reinsured under separate arrangements.

Formula (4) will clearly give the Capital Asset Pricing Model, with a different interpretation of the terms.

As another example consider:

$$x_1 = \min(x, Q) \quad \text{and } x_2 = \max(x - Q, 0)$$

It is then easy to verify that

$$\bar{x}_1 = \int_0^Q x\,f(x)\,dx + Q\int_Q^\infty f(x)\,dx = Q + \int_0^Q (x-Q)\,f(x)\,dx$$

$$\bar{x}_2 = \int_Q^\infty (x-Q)\,f(x)\,dx$$

$$\operatorname{cov} xx_1 = \int_0^Q x(x-\bar{x})\,f(x)\,dx + Q\int_Q^\infty (x-\bar{x})\,f(x)\,dx$$

$$\operatorname{cov} xx_2 = \int_Q^\infty x(x-\bar{x})\,f(x)\,dx + Q\int_Q^\infty (x-\bar{x})\,f(x)\,dx$$

Substitution of these expressions into (3) will give the premiums required to cover the two components of the risk. The most obvious interpretations of this example are the following:

> If $P\{x\}$ is the premium for complete cover of a risk, $P\{x_1\}$ will be the reduction which the insured will get if he accepts a deductible Q.
>
> If $P\{x\}$ stands for the total premium paid to cover a portfolio of insurance contracts, $P\{x_2\}$ will be the premium for a stop loss treaty, under which the reinsurer pays the excess, if total claims should exceed the limit Q.

In the example, one can also take x as the price of a security at some future date. $P\{x-2\}$ can then be interpreted as the price of a European option with call price Q.

As a numerical example, we take $F(x) = 1 - e^{-1}$, so that $E\{x\} = 1$ and var $x = 1$. Further, let $\gamma_1 = \gamma_2 = 1$, so that $P = 2$. For the two components we find:

$$\text{Retained premium:}\quad P_1 = 2 - 2e^{-Q} - Qe^{-Q}$$

$$\text{Stop loss premium:}\quad P_2 = 2e^{-Q} + Qe^{-Q}$$

The table below gives the two premiums for some selected values of Q.

The last four columns in the table are really irrelevant. They do, however, indicate that one will run into difficulties if one tries to set premiums for both components with loadings proportional to expectation or variance.

Table 2:

Q	P_1	P_2	$\bar{x}_1$	$\bar{x}_2$	var x_1	var x_2
0.5	0.48	1.52	0.39	0.61	0.02	0.85
0.69	0.65	1.35	0.50	0.50	0.06	0.75
1.0	0.89	1.11	0.63	0.37	0.13	0.60
1.5	1.23	0.77	0.78	0.22	0.28	0.40
2.0	1.44	0.56	0.86	0.14	0.414	0.25
3.0	1.75	0.25	0.95	0.05	0.69	0.01

These examples illustrate how Formula (1) can be generalized to hold for dependent stochastic variables. To generalize (2) in a similar manner, it is sufficient to write

$$P\{x_i\} = \sum_{n=1}^{\infty} \gamma_n \kappa_{1,n-1}^{(i)} \qquad i = 1, 2 \tag{5}$$

where $\kappa_{1,n-1}^{(i)}$ is the cumulant corresponding to the bivariate moment $E\left\{(x_i - \bar{x}_i)(x - \bar{x}_1)^{n-1}\right\}$. Clearly (5) is a generalization of (3).

To apply (5) to the numerical example, we consider only the three first terms in the expansion; take $\gamma_1 = 1$, $\gamma_2 = 0.4$, $\gamma_3 = 0.3$ and find

$$\text{Retained premium:} \quad P_1 = 2 - 2e^{-Q} - Qe^{-Q} - 0.3\,Q^2 e^{-Q}$$

$$\text{Stop loss premium:} \quad P_2 = 2e^{-Q} + Qe^{-Q} + 0.3\,Q^2 e^{-Q}$$

As one would expect, consideration of the skewness will lead to a higher stop loss premium.

References for Section 5

Eugene Lukacs. (1952): "An Essential Property of the Fourier Transforms of Distribution Functions". *Proceedings of the American Mathematical Society*, 508–510.

Thorvald N. Thiele. (1889): *Forelaesninger over Almindelig Iagttagelseslaere.* Copenhagen: Reitzel.

Thorvald N. Thiele. (1903): *Theory of Observations.* London: Layton. Reprinted 1931 in *Annals of Mathematical Statistics 2*, 165–308.

6. Static Equilibrium under Uncertainty and Incomplete Markets*

1. Introduction

1.1 The first model of general economic equilibrium was presented by Walras (1875–1877) more than hundred years ago. As the model became generally known, it must have been clear that it was desirable to generalize it, and take uncertainty into account. The most visible markets at the end of the last century were probably the stock exchanges, where uncertainty obviously played an important part. Insurance was also well developed, and it was natural to assume that premiums were determined by market forces. It is possible that some economists attacked the problem, but apparently they were not successful. The literature from that period has little to say about economic risk, beyond general statements that there should be a price, so that supply of, and demand for risk-bearing services are equal.

One who may have missed the boat is Böhm-Bawerk. In his first book (Böhm-Bawerk (1881)) he discusses the value one should assign to conditional claims. He observed for instance that if some property is stolen, the owner has the right to get it back if the thief is caught. The question is which value should the owner assign to this right. Apparently it did not occur to Böhm-Bawerk that this right also might have a market value. Had he asked the question, it would have led straight to the market premium for burglary insurance, which had been introduced in England about twenty years earlier.

1.2 In retrospect it seems that it should have been quite possible to construct an equilibrium model explaining how insurance premiums are determined by market forces, at the turn of the century. The key to the problem is the Bernoulli Principle, today usually referred to as "the expected utility hypothesis", which was well known, and often discussed among mathematicians at the time. The paper Bernoulli (1954) presented in St. Petersburgh was translated into German in 1896, and Czuber (1902) in a much used textbook on probability, stated that Bernoulli Principle had become the "foundation of the modern theory of value". (Grundlage der Modernen Wertlehre). Most economists at the time seem however to have been unaware of this.

---

* Reprinted from *The Geneva Papers on Risk and Insurance*, 1983; 8:307–315,

Marshall (1890) seems to have been well aware of the Principle's possibilities. In his "Mathematical Appendix", he mentions Bernoulli's assumption, which we today would write $u(x) = \log x$, and refers to the other "interesting guess" by Bernoulli's contemporary Cramér, that $u(x) = \sqrt{x}$. Apparently it did not occur to Marshall that either guess, or any other concave function would open the way to get rid of the "evils of uncertainty", which Marshall discusses in connection with insurance.

1.3 It is surprising that no economists seem to have taken these hints and put the Bernoulli Principle to use. It was obviously possible to apply the principle before von Neumann and Morgenstern (1947) had proved that it could be derived as a theorem by a simple axiomatic method. Actually this result had been proved more than 15 years earlier by Ramsey (1931), but it did not seem to have made any stronger impact in Cambridge than Marshall's hints 40 years earlier. If one seeks an explanation of the late development of an economic theory of uncertainty, it may be that only the generation of economists who moved to the forefront of research after World War II mastered the mathematical tools which were required to solve the old problems. The fact that these tools had been available for a long time, may possibly have a message for future generations of economists.

1.4 When satisfactory models of economic equilibrium under uncertainty were presented, this was done independently by Allais (1953a) and Arrow (1953). That this should happen is almost normal, since the problem had been in the air for some time. It is however remarkable that both models were presented simultaneously, at a colloquium arranged by CNRS in Paris, May 1952.

The two authors took very different approaches to the problem. Allais is closest to the then conventional approach. He assumes that among the goods in the market there are some conditional claims of the kind studied by Böhm-Bawerk. These goods can only be described by probability distributions, and their equilibrium prices must be determined by their stochastic properties. He then gives a complete analysis of the special case in which all contingent claims are normally distributed. In a later version of the paper (Allais (1953b)) he remarks that the reader should have no difficulties in generalizing the model for himself. This may be true, but Allais certainly makes the task more difficult than necessary by explicitly rejecting the Bernoulli principle.

Arrow on the other hand accepts the principle, but does not really need it. His starting point is the, by now well-known model based on "states of the world". In this model a specific commodity available in two different states, is considered as two different commodities. This simple and ingenious idea makes it possible to reduce the case of uncertainty to the original model of Walras, but with a larger number of commodities. The consistency conditions behind the expected utility theorem are not necessary for this reduction, but they simplify the results.

2. Arrow's state Model

2.1 Arrow's model does of course represents an important generalization, but it can also be derived as a special case of the classical exchange model.

With the usual notation the Walras model can be described as follows:

x_r^j = the amount of good j held initially by agent r;

y_r^i = the amount of good j held by agent r in equilibrium;

p_j = the equilibrium price of good j;

u_r = the utility function which represents the preferences of agent r, and has the properties $u'(\cdot) > 0$, and $u''(\cdot) < 0$.

The problem of agent r is then

$$\max u_r(y_r^1, y_r^2, \ldots, y_r^i, \ldots)$$

subject to the budget condition

$$\sum_j p_j y_r^j = \sum_j p_j x_r^j \tag{1}$$

The familiar solution is given by (1) and the conditions

$$\frac{\partial u_r}{\partial y_r^j} = \lambda_r p_j \qquad \text{for all } r \text{ and } j\,. \tag{2}$$

The market clearing conditions are

$$\sum_r y_r^j = \sum_r x_r^j = x^j \qquad \text{for all } j\,. \tag{3}$$

These three sets of equations will under certain conditions determine the general equilibrium, i.e. the equilibrium prices p_j, and the final holdings y_r^j.

2.2 Let us now interpret x_r^j as the monetary payoff which agent r will receive from his initial portfolio, if state j occurs, and give a corresponding interpretation to y_r^j. This reduction to a one-good model is convenient, but by no means essential.

From the expected utility theorem it follows that the utility function of agent r is of the form

$$\sum_j f_j U_r(y_r^j)$$

where f_j is the probability that state j shall occur, and $\sum_j f_j = 1$. With the assumption of "homogeneous beliefs", i.e. that all agents agree on the probabilities assigned to the different states, the three sets of conditions can be written as follows:

$$\sum_j p_j y_r^j = \sum_j p_j x_r^j \tag{1'}$$

$$f_j u_r'(y_r^j) = \lambda_r p_j \tag{2'}$$

$$\sum_r y_r^j = \sum_r x_r^j = x^j \tag{3'}$$

2.3 From (3′) it follows that the superscript j really is redundant. A state is completely described by the value assumed by the stochastic variable x^j, i.e. the total payoff if state j occurs. Solving the equations (2′), subject to (3′), we obtain a solution which depends only on x^j, so that we can write $x^j = x$ and

$$p_j = p(x)\,, \quad f_j = F9x) \quad \text{and} \quad y_r^j = y_r(x)$$

The solution of (2′) and (3′) will give $y_r(x)$ as a function of x, and of the Lagrange multipliers $\lambda_1, \ldots, \lambda_r, \ldots$. It is easy to see that this solution will give the set of Pareto optimal portfolios. The equations (1) will then determine the Lagrange multipliers, and hence the point in the Pareto optimal set, which corresponds to the competitive equilibrium.

From (2′) it follows that $\lambda_r^{-1} u_r'\big(y_r(x)\big)$ depends only on the state, hence the expression must, in equilibrium be the same for all agents, so that we can write

$$\lambda_r^{-1} u_r'\big(y_r(x)\big) = U'(x)$$

Substitution then gives the three sets of conditions in the following form:

$$E\{p(x)y_r(x)\} = E\{p(x)x_r\} \tag{1''}$$

$$p(x) = U'(x)\,f(x) \tag{2''}$$

$$\sum_r y_r(x) = x \tag{3''}$$

Substitution of (2″) into (1″) gives

$$E\{U'(x)y_r(x)\} = E\,\{U'(x)x_r\} \tag{4}$$

These equations together with (3″), give a set of equations, which under reasonable assumptions will determine the competitive equilibrium.

2.4 The equations (1′) interpreted literally do of course imply that there must be one price for each state, i.e. the amount one has to pay for a claim to one monetary unit, payable if and only if a particular state occurs. This has led some authors to assume that the model implies that there must exist a competitive market for each state. In many applications the number of states is infinite, often a continuum, so the assumption seems unrealistic. This has led to the suggestion that it is necessary to develop a theory of "incomplete markets", a term often associated with Hirshleifer (1970), although the point had been made earlier by others, i.a. by Baudier (1968).

From the preceding derivation of Arrow's model it should be clear that the state concept is essentially a technical device to make the mathematical proof rigorous — for a finite number of states. There is no need to trade claims contingent on the occurrence of any single state. This is brought out by (4), which shows that only expectations over states are relevant.

2.5 The situation can be summed up as follows:

In the initial situation agent r holds a portfolio described by a stochastic variable x_r. The expected utility he assigns to this portfolio is $E\,\{u_r(x_r)\}$, and depends only on x_r.

The market value of the initial portfolio of agent r will depend on the stochastic relationship between $x_1, \ldots, x_r, \ldots$, not on the stochastic properties of x_r alone.

In the final situation agent r will hold a portfolio described by the stochastic variable $y_r(x)$, determined by (2″) and (3″). He will assign a higher utility to this portfolio than to his initial holding — except in trivial cases.

From (1″) it follows that the market values of the final and initial portfolio are equal. It also follows that the market value depends only on the stochastic variable x.

Hence there should be a need for only one market — a market for uncertain prospects, or portfolios described by stochastic variables. The essential assumption is that an agent can sell his initial portfolio in this market, and buy a Pareto optimal portfolio. The form of Pareto optimal portfolios is given by (2″) and (3″), and an agent's purchasing power is equal to the market value of his initial portfolio.

3. The Traditional Approach

3.1 Arrow's model has had an extraordinary impact, and has virtually pushed all earlier work into oblivion. In fact Allais seems to have been the last who has tried to reach general results by the older methods. It will be shown that this, once conventional approach can lead to the same results as Arrow's model.

As a starting point we note that the left-hand side of (4) can be interpreted as the marginal utility of a portfolio described by the stochastic variable $y_r(x)$. In equilibrium this marginal utility must be proportional to the market value $P\{y_r\}$, of the portfolio. Hence we write

$$P\{y_r\} = E\{U'(x)y_r(x)\}$$

Summing (4) over all r, we obtain on the right-hand side (from (3″)) $E\{xU'(x)\}$, which can be interpreted as the total value of all portfolios in the market. It is then natural to write:

$$P\{x\} = E\{x\,U'(x)\} = \int_0^\infty x\,U'(x)\,f(x)\,dx \tag{5}$$

for this value. It is worth noting that marginal utility and probability density enter (5) in a symmetrical manner.

3.2 It seems reasonable to assume that the total value is independent of how initial endowments are distributed among the agents. This implies that the following condition

$$P\{x\} = \sum_r P\{x_r\} \tag{6}$$

must hold for any partition of the stochastic variable x. Clearly (6) means that there are no arbitrate possibilities in the market, i.e. one cannot make a risk-free profit by buying a portfolio, splitting it up, and selling the parts separately.

The problem is now to find a mapping from a set of stochastic variables to the real line, which has the additivity property expressed by (6). To see that a mapping of this kind exists, it is sufficient to observe that

$$\sum_r E\{x_r e^{itx}\} = E\{xe^{itx}\} = \int_0^\infty e^{itx} x\, f(x)\, dx \quad \text{if } \sum_r x_r = x\,.$$

3.3 To obtain a convenient notation we shall write

$$\varphi(t_1, \ldots, t_r, \ldots) = E\Big\{\exp\Big(i \sum_r t_r x_r\Big)\Big\},$$

$$\left[\frac{\partial \varphi}{\partial t_r}\right]_{t_1 = \ldots t_r \ldots = t} = \varphi_r'(t)$$

and

$$cr\varphi(t, t, \ldots) = \varphi(t)$$

Setting

$$P\{x\} = \varphi'(t) \qquad \text{and} \qquad P\{x_r\} = \varphi_r'(t) \tag{7}$$

it is easy to verify that (6) is satisfied. With this notation φ is the Fourier transform of the density, which always exists, and can be interpreted as a moment generating function. If moments exist, this makes it possible to express the value assigned to a stochastic variable in terms of moments, an idea which was very popular at the pre-Arrow period in the economics of uncertainty.

3.4 The assignment of values which we have found is derived from the fundamental property of the Fourier transform. Addition of independent stochastic variables corresponds to multiplication of their Fourier transforms. As we have seen, this result, with minor modifications, carries over to the case of stochastic dependence.

Clearly any linear functional of the functions defined by (7) will satisfy (6). From the Riesz representation theorem it follows that for any continuous linear functional $T(g)$ there exists a function $V(t)$ such that

$$T(g) = \int_{-\infty}^{+\infty} g(t)\, dV(t)$$

Hence

$$P\{x\} = K \int_{-\infty}^{+\infty} \varphi'(t)\, V'(t)\, dt \tag{8}$$

where K is some constant, gives the most general continuous mapping which satisfies (6). In (8) we have written $V'(t)\,dt$ for $dV(t)$. If no derivative exists, we shall interpret $V'(t)$ as a "generalized function".

3.5 Substituting the expression for $P\{x\}$ given by (8) into (5), we obtain

$$K \int_{-\infty}^{+\infty} \varphi'(t)\, V'(t)\, dt = \int_0^{\infty} x\, U'(x)\, f(x)\, dx \tag{9}$$

From the definition of the Fourier transform it follows that

$$\varphi'(t) i \int_0^{\infty} x\, f(x) e^{itx}\, dx\,.$$

Taking the inverse transform, we find

$$x\, f(x) = \frac{1}{2\pi i} \int_{-\infty}^{+\infty} \varphi'(t) e^{-itx}\, dt$$

Substituting this expression for $xf(x)$ in the right-hand side of (9), and absorbing the constant factors into K, we obtain

$$K \int_{-\infty}^{+\infty} \varphi'(t)\, V'(t)\, dt = \int_0^{\infty} U'(x) \varphi'(t) e^{-itx}\, dt\, dx$$

If the order of integration can be reversed, i.e. under the conditions of Fubinis theorem, the equation can be written

$$\int_{-\infty}^{+\infty} \varphi'(t) \left\{ KV'(t) - \int_0^{\infty} U'(x) e^{-itx}\, dx \right\} dt = 0$$

A solution of this equation is

$$V'(t) = \frac{1}{K} \int_0^{\infty} U'(x) e^{-itx}\, dx \tag{10}$$

For the sake of symmetry we shall write $V'(t) = \omega'(-t)$, so that $\omega'(t)$ is the Fourier transform of $U'(x)$. Substitution into (9) then gives

$$\int_{-\infty}^{+\infty} \varphi'(t)\omega'(-t)\,dt = \int_0^{\infty} x\,f(x)\,U'(x)\,dx \tag{11}$$

3.6 This formula is just the classical Parseval's theorem (see i.a. Rudin (1970)), and could have been written down immediately, and (10) could have been found by using the uniqueness property. The right-hand side of (11) was derived simply and directly from Arrow's state model, which rests on assumptions which many economists have found difficult to accept. The left-hand side was derived after more complicated mathematical manipulations, but rests on the simple assumptions that any asset which can be described by a stochastic variable, will have a market value and that in equilibrium these values will be additive. Earlier generations of economists seem to have accepted these assumptions, almost without questioning. It is interesting — and comforting — that the two sets of assumptions lead to the same result.

From (4) and (7) it follows that the market value of the portfolio held initially by agent r is

$$P\{x_r\} = \int_{-\infty}^{+\infty} \varphi_r'(t)\omega'(-t)\,dt = \int_0^{\infty} x_r\,U'(x)\,f(x,x_r)\,dx\,dx_r \tag{12}$$

On the right-hand side $f(x,x_r)$ is the joint density of the stochastic variables representing the whole market, and the initial portfolio of agent r.

In (11) and (12) $\omega'(t)$ is the Fourier transform of the marginal utility $U'(x)$. In the more classical theory of Fourier analysis the transform does not always exist, but in the more general theory created by Schwartz (1957), it will exist as a "generalized function".

3.7 Formula (12) may give some insight into the formation of prices in a market. It may also be useful for computational purposes.

As an illustration we shall consider the special case in which the preferences of all agents can be represented by quadratic utility functions, i.e. when

$$u_r'(x) = 1 - \frac{x}{a_r} \qquad \text{for all } r$$

It is easy to show that in this case we have

$$U'(x) = A - x\,, \qquad \text{with } A = \sum_r a_r$$

Substitution in the right-hand term of (12) then gives

$$P\{x_r\} = E\{Ax_r - xx_r\} = \big(A - E\{x\}\big)E\{x_r\} - \operatorname{cov} xx_r$$

which is a familiar result from portfolio theory.

Considering the middle term in (12), we observe that, in the ordinary sense the Fourier transform of $U'(x) = A - x$ does not exist, but it exists as a generalized function, and we have

$$\omega(t)\; A\delta(t) + \delta'(t)$$

Here $\delta(t)$ is the Dirac function, which has the properties

$$\int_{-\infty}^{+\infty} g(x)\,\delta(x)\,dx = g(0) \quad \text{and} \quad \int_{-\infty}^{+\infty} g(x)\,\delta'(x)\,dx = g'(0)$$

As

$$\varphi'(0) = E\{x_r\} \quad \text{and} \quad \varphi''(0) = E\{xx_r\} = \operatorname{cov} xx_r$$

it follows immediately that the middle term is equal to the right-hand side.

4. Incomplete Markets

4.1 It is not easy to trace the origin and the increasing popularity of the concept "incomplete market". In the discussion following the paper by Baudier ((1968) pp. 305–310) it seems to have been agreed that Arrow's state model, in spite of its elegance, was too complex to be realistic. In the real world one would expect a group of agents to organize their exchanges of assets or liabilities in a simpler way — through the rules they lay down, and the institutions they set up. Such arrangements will in general lead to an equilibrium, which however may not necessarily be Pareto optimal.

Baudier argued that such sub-optimal arrangements are of considerable practical interest, and deserve further study. Others maintained that arrangements of this kind will in some sense be transient, since a group of rational agents must be expected, sooner or later, to find their way to a Pareto optimum — through bargaining or institutional changes.

4.2 A simple arrangement would be to set up markets where the agents could buy and sell fractions of the initial portfolios. If there are n agents in the market, it will be necessary to create n markets. A smaller number is required if the initial portfolios are made up of $m < n$ identifiable assets, such as stock in m different companies.

In general, markets of this kind will have an equilibrium, but this may not be a Pareto optimum. An exchange of fractions of portfolios — or of common stock — can lead to a Pareto optimum if the utility functions satisfy some rather restrictive conditions. If these conditions are not satisfied, the market is said to be "incomplete", because the equilibrium can be brought closer to a Pareto optimum, if markets are set up for new securities, such as preferred stock, bonds and options. It seems reasonable to assume that only transactions costs can prevent a Pareto optimum to be reached through the creation of additional markets. The question is however not simple, and we shall not discuss it in any detail in the present context.

4.3 The traditional approach, discussed in Section 3, assumes from the start that the market is complete. The approach has its origin, at least in part, in insurance. In this industry it seems quite natural to assume that the market can quote a premium for cover of any risk, described by a well defined probability distribution with finite expectation. It is also generally assumed that the risk can be split up, or merged with others, and reinsured in the market at the going rate.

The exceptions, the uninsurable risks, seem to occur only when some element of "moral hazard" is present. In these cases the probability distribution describing the risk depends on the insurance cover, and is not well defined.

4.4 Similar situations evidently exist, also outside the insurance industry. If both an entrepreneur and his workers are risk averse, a conventional wage contract will be sub-optimal, since it implies that all risk is carried by the entrepreneur. Clearly both parties could be made better off with some profit-sharing arrangement, but it is possible that the workers would not accept this unless they get some say in the management.

In this example the labor market may be said to be incomplete. The example does however indicate that the concept "incomplete market" is more closely connected with incentives and moral hazard than with the large number of states in Arrow's model. The owner of a well insured factory may not have the incentive to make desperate efforts to put out a fire. Things might be different if he had to fight for his economic survival.

It may be appropriate to close by noting that the possibilities in existing markets can be overlooked. No boutique will sell a woman a black dress with accessories, to be delivered only if she should become a widow within a year. Should however a woman want a conditional claim of this kind in her portfolio, any insurance salesman will be glad to arrange it for her.

References for Section 6

Allais M. (1953): "Généralisation des théories de l'équilibre économique général et du rendement social an cas du risque", *Colloques Internationaux du CNRS, XL. Paris*, 81–120.

Allais M. (1953): "L'extension des théories de l'équilibre économique général et du rendement social an cas du risque", *Econometrica*, 269–290.

Arrow KJ. (1953): "Le rôle des valeurs boursières pour la répartition la meilleure des risques", *Colloques Internationaux du CNRS. XL, Paris*, 41–88.

Baudier E. (1968): " Minimax behaviour and price prediction", in: Borch K, Mossin J, eds. *Risk and Uncertainty*, London: Macmillan 283–305.

Bernoulli D. (1954): "Specimen theoriae novae de mensura Sortis", St. Petersburg, 1738. English translation *Econometrica*, 23–36.

Böhm-Bawerk E. (1881): *Rechte und Verhältnisse vom Standpunkte der Volkswirtschaftlichen Güterlehre*, Innsbruck.

Borch K, and Mossin J. (1968): *Risk and Uncertainty*, London: Macmillan.

Czuber E. (1902): *Wahrscheinlichkeitsrechnung*, Teubner, Leipzig.

Hirshleifer J. (1970): *Investment Interest and Capital*, Prentice-Hall Englewood Cliffs (N.J.).

Marshall A. (1890): *Principles of Economics*, London: Macmillan.

Neumann J von, and Morgenstern O. (1947): *Theory of Games and Economic Behavior*, 2nd edition, Princeton University Press.

Ramsey FP. (1931): "Truth and probability", *The Foundation of Mathematics and other Logical Essays*, Kegan Paul, London.

Rudin W. (1970): *Real and Complex Analysis*, New York: MacGraw-Hill.

Schwartz L. (1957): *Théorie des distributions*, Paris: Hermann.

Walras L. (1875–1877):*Éléments de l'Économie Politique pure*, Lausanne.

7. A Theory of Insurance Premiums*

1. Introduction

1.1 The buyer of an insurance contract buys security, and the seller accepts a risk. The premium charged by the seller must give him adequate compensation for the risk bearing service he provides, and of course be acceptable to the buyer.

It is useful to see an insurance contract as a contingent claim. The buyer pays a premium in advance, and will get a random amount in return — as settlement of the claims he can make under the contract. Formally the transaction is of the same type as the purchase of a share in a risky business. The price of such shares is presumably determined by supply and demand in the market, and it is natural to assume that insurance premiums are determined in the same way. Economic theory has taken a long time to develop satisfactory models for the pricing of contingent claims. The breakthrough came just over thirty years ago, with the work of Arrow (1953). In the following three decades a number of models have been developed, i.a. the so-called "Capital Asset Price Model" (CAPM) due to Sharpe (1964), Lintner (1965) and Mossin (1966), which has found extensive applications in practice.

1.2 Actuaries have of course been busy computing insurance premiums for more than a century. The more recent achievement in economics and finance do not seem to have had much influence on the work of actuaries. A recent survey volume of the theory of insurance premiums by Goovaerts et al. (1983) contains no references to highly relevant results in economic theory. One of the few exceptions is Bühlmann (1980) and (1984), which contain no references to actuarial literature.

One explanation of why actuaries have ignored economics may be that they consider CAPM — a one-period model depending only on expectation and variance — as too primitive for their purposes. Instead of adapting CAPM and similar models, they have continued the development of the "actuarial theory of risk", which places the focus on a class of stochastic process in continuous time. There is much pretty mathematics in this theory, but one inevitably feels that most contacts with economic reality have been lost. It is tempting to borrow a term from Mac Lane (1983), and tell actuaries that they tend to take "too much of a Hungarian view of mathematics — that the science consists not in good answers. but in hard questions". One purpose of this paper is to induce actuaries to provide some answers.

1.3 The next section gives a short presentation of a model of an insurance market, and shows that a full generalization of CAPM is fairly simple. Section 3 gives some examples, and indicates how the model can be applied in practice. Section 4 reviews a model due to De Finetti, which makes it possible, in theory to determine the utility functions used in section 2. Section 5 presents a modified, and possibly more realistic version of De Finetti's model. The last section contains some comments on the realism of the models, and possible applications.

2. A model of an Insurance Market

2.1 The model presented in this section is essentially a special case of Arrow's model from 1953.

It is convenient to interpret the model as a reinsurance market, in which n insurance companies trade among themselves. We shall take as given:

(i) The risk attitude of company r, represented by the Bernoulli utility function $u_r(\cdot)$, with the properties $u_r' > 0$ and $u_r'' < 0$.

(ii) The initial portfolio of company r, represented by the stochastic variable, x_r. $r = 1, 2, \ldots, n$.

In the market these n companies exchange parts of their initial portfolio among themselves. As a result of these exchanges company r obtains a final portfolio, represented by the stochastic variable, y_r. $r = 1, 2, \ldots, n$.

If the companies cannot trade with outsiders, we have

$$\sum_{r=1}^{n} y_r = \sum_{r=1}^{n} x_r = x \tag{1}$$

where x is the sum of the stochastic variables representing the initial portfolios.

At this stage it is necessary to make an assumption of *homogeneous beliefs*, i.e. that all companies hold the same opinion on the joint density $f(x_1, \ldots, x_n)$, and hence on $f(x)$. The assumption appears reasonable for a reinsurance market, where trade is supposed to take place under conditions of *uberrimae fidei*, and no information is hidden.

2.2 Any set of exchanges which satisfies (1) is feasible. The subset of Pareto optimal exchanges is determined by (1) and the conditions

$$k_r u_r'(y_r) = k_s u_s'(y_s) \qquad r, s = 1, 2, \ldots, n \tag{2}$$

where k_r, and k_s are arbitrary positive constants. The result has been proved explicitly by Borch (1962), but is really contained in earlier work by Arrow.

It is easy to see that (1) and (2) will determine the Pareto optimal exchanges as n functions $y_1(x), \ldots, y_n(X)$ of the stochastic variable x. These functions will contain arbitrary constants $k_1, \ldots, k_n$, as parameters, and $y_r(x)$ must be interpreted as payoff to company r, if total payoff is x.

It is easy to see that (2) can be written in the form

$$k_r u_r'\big(y_r(x)\big) = u'(x) \tag{3}$$

where the function $u'(x)$ in a sense represents aggregate marginal utility in the market. It will of course depend on the parameters $k_1, \ldots, k_n$.

To facilitate the interpretation of $u'(x)$ we differentiate (3) and obtain

$$k_r u_r''\big(y_r(x)\big) y_r'(x) = u''(x)$$

Division by (3) gives

$$\frac{u_r''\big(y_r(x)\big) y_r'(x)}{u'\big(y_r(x)\big)} = \frac{u''(x)}{u'(x)}$$

which we shall write

$$\frac{y_r'(x)}{R(x)} = \frac{1}{R_r\big(y_r(x)\big)}$$

where $R = -u''/u'$ stands for absolute risk aversion.

From (1) it follows that $\sum y_r'(x) = 1$, and hence that

$$\frac{1}{R(x)} = \sum_{r=1}^{n} \frac{1}{R_r(y_r)}$$

The inverse of absolute risk aversion is some times called "risk tolerance". Thus we obtain the attractive result that in a Pareto optimum the risk tolerance of the market as a whole is equal to the sum of the risk tolerances of the participants. If one participant is risk neutral, his risk tolerance will be infinite, and hence that of the market. This corresponds to the obvious, that a Pareto optimum implies that all risk should be carried by the risk neutral participants.

The result has also been found by Bühlmann (1980) for the special case of exponential utility functions.

2.3 To determine the competitive equilibrium of the market in the usual way, we need two assumptions:

(i) The market is complete, in the sense that it will assign a unique value $P\{y\}$ to an arbitrary final portfolio, described by a stochastic variable y.

(ii) The value operator $P\{\cdot\}$ is a linear functional of $y(x)$.

From the Riesz representation theorem it then follows that there exists a function $G(x)$ such that

$$P\{y\} = \int_{-\infty}^{+\infty} y(x)\, dG(x)$$

Any actuary worth his salt believes that he can compute the premium for any risk with known stochastic properties, so to him the first assumption will be trivial. Some economists, i.a. Hirshleifer (1970) seem to doubt that markets in the real world are complete, and the study of "incomplete markets" has become fashionable. These studies are however not relevant in the present context, since no restrictions are placed on the exchange arrangements which the companies are allowed to make.

If a derivative of $G(x)$ exists, we can without loss of generality write $G'(x) = V'(x)\, f(x)$, so that the formula above takes the form:

$$P\{y\} = \int_{-\infty}^{+\infty} y(x)\, V'(x)\, f(x)\, dx = E\{y(x)\, V'(x)\} \tag{4}$$

In (4) y represents a Pareto optimal portfolio, and hence it is a function $y(x)$ of the variable x. A non-optimal initial portfolio is described by the variable x_r, which is stochastically dependent on x. Analogy with (4) suggests that we can write

$$P\{x_r\} = E\{x_r V'(x)\} = \int_{-\infty}^{+\infty} x_r V'(x)\, f(x, x_r)\, dx\, dx_r \tag{5}$$

Clearly (4) is a special case of (5).

2.4 To find the competitive equilibrium in the conventional way, we note that the problem of company r is:

$$\max E\{u_r(y_r)\} \qquad r = 1, 2, \ldots, n$$

subject to

$$P\{y_r\} = P\{x_r\} \qquad r = 1, 2, \ldots, n \tag{6}$$

Conditions (6) say simply that the market value of a portfolio must remain constant if all exchange transactions are settled at market prices.

The problem is equivalent to

$$\max \int_{-\infty}^{+\infty} \left[u_r\left(y_r(x)\right) + \lambda_r \Big(E\{x_r V'(x)\} - y_r(x)\, V'(x) \Big) \right] f(x)\, dx$$

which can be seen as a problem in the calculus of variation. The Euler equation is

$$u_r'\left(y_r(x)\right) = \lambda_r k_r V'(x) \tag{7}$$

and from (3) it follows that this can be written as

$$u'(x) = \lambda_r k_r V'(x)$$

There is no loss of generality if we take $\lambda_r = k_r^{-1}$ and write $V'(x) = u'(x)$. It then follows that the assumption that the function $G(x)$ is differentiable is equivalent to assuming that the aggregate utility function is differentiable.

We can now sum up the results:

Conditions (1) and (3) determine the form of the functions $y_r(x)$.

The equations (6) determine the parameters $k_1, \ldots, k_n$ in the functions $y_r(x)$.

For the market value of an arbitrary portfolio we find

$$P\{x_r\} = E\{x_r u'(x)\} \tag{8}$$

2.5 We have so far discussed only market values of portfolios. To obtain market premiums for insurance contracts, we note that the initial portfolio of company r consists of assets R_r, and of liabilities under the insurance contracts held by the company. Let the non-negative stochastic variable z_r represent claim payments under the contracts, and write

$$x_r = R_r - z_r$$

If for the sake of simplicity we assume that the assets are risk-free, we have

$$P\{x_r\} = R_r - P\{z_r\} \tag{9}$$

Formula (9) says simply that the market value of the company's portfolio is equal to risk-free assets, less the market premium for insurance of the liabilities. The formula makes it easy to translate results expressed in terms of portfolio values into insurance premiums.

3. Examples and Applications

3.1 As a simple example we shall take

$$u'_r(x) = \operatorname{sgn}(c_r - x) \mid (c_r - x)^\alpha| \qquad r = 1, \ldots, n$$

The condition $u'_r > 0$ is satisfied only when $x < c_r$, so the analysis is valid only in this domain. If α is an odd integer we can take $u'_r(x) = (c_r - x)^\alpha$. We shall use this simpler notation, and fall back on the complete notation only when it is necessary to avoid misunderstanding.

In the example (3) takes the form

$$k_r(c_r - y_r)^\alpha = u'(x) \tag{3'}$$

which can be written

$$c_r - y_r = \left(k_r^{-1} u'(x)\right)^{1/\alpha}$$

Summing these equations over all r, and using (1), we obtain

$$\sum_{r=1}^{n} c_r - x = \left(u'(x)\right)^{1/\alpha} \sum_{r=1}^{n} k_r^{-1/\alpha}$$

Here we write

$$\sum_{r=1}^{n} c_r = c \qquad \text{and} \qquad \sum_{r=1}^{n} k_r^{-1/\alpha} = K^{-1/\alpha}$$

so that the equation takes the form

$$u'(x) = K(c - x)^\alpha$$

From (3′) we then find

$$k_r\left(c_r - y_r(x)\right)^\alpha = K(c - x)^\alpha$$

and the explicit expression for $y_r(x)$

$$y_r(x) = c_r - (c-x)(Kk_r^{-1})^{1/\alpha} = c_r - (c-x)h_r$$

where $h_r = (Kk_r^{-1})^{1/\alpha}$, and $\sum h_r = 1$.

The equations (6) then take the form

$$KE\Big\{\big(c_r - (c-x)h_r\big)(c-x)^\alpha\Big\} = KE\{x_r(c-x)^\alpha\} \tag{6'}$$

and the parameters are determined by the equations

$$h_r = \frac{E\,\{(c_r - x_r)(c-x)\}^\alpha}{E\,\{(c-x)^{\alpha+1}\}} \qquad r = 1, 2, \ldots, n$$

3.2 The right-hand side of (6′) gives the market value of an arbitrary portfolio, so we can write

$$P\{x_r\} = KE\{x_r(c-x)^\alpha\} \tag{10}$$

The special case $\alpha = 1$ has led to models which are widely used in practical financial analysis, so it may be useful to discuss this case in some detail.

For $\alpha = 1$ the equation (10) takes the form:

$$P\{x_r\} = KcE\{x_r\} - KE\{xx_r\} = K\,(c - E\{x\})\,E\{x_r\} - K\mathrm{cov}\,xx_r$$

If we here take $x_r = x$, we obtain in the same way

$$P\{x\} = K\big(c - E\{x\}\big)E\{x\} - K\,\mathrm{var}\,x$$

Combining these two equations, we obtain

$$P\{x_r\} = KAE\{x_r\} + \big(P\{x\} - KAE\{x\}\big)\frac{\mathrm{cov}\,xx_r}{\mathrm{var}\,x} \tag{11}$$

where $c - E\{x\} = A$.

It is worth noting that the arbitrary constant K can be interpreted as a risk-free rate of interest in the market.

Formula (11) is of course CAPM, which has found widespread applications in practice, and is discussed in virtually every textbook in finance — in spite of its obvious shortcomings.

We derived (11) by assuming that marginal utilities were linear, i.e. that all utility functions were quadratic. This assumption seems to be too strong for most economists. The equivalent assumption, implied by (11), that values are determined by the two first moments of a stochastic variable, seems however to be acceptable. A multivariate normal distribution is completely described by means and covariances. If the variables z_1, z_2, $\ldots$, z_m are normally distributed, the variable $z = t_1 z_1 + \cdots, t_m z_m$ defining a portfolio, is also normally distributed. This seems to be the current justification for the practical application of CAPM.

The normal is the only distribution with finite variance which has the "stability" property sketched above. This means that strictly speaking CAPM can assign a value only to portfolio defined by normally distributed variables, and that may be the explanation of the interest in "incomplete" markets.

3.3 Actuaries seem to consider CAPM as too primitive for their purposes. They may find some support for this view in a statement by Cramér (1930) who wrote: "... in many cases the approximation obtained by using the normal function is not sufficiently good to justify the conclusions that have been drawn in this way". The statement has led to a number of hard questions which must delight any actuary who takes the "Hungarian" view. In their efforts to answer Cramér's questions these actuaries have made contributions of some importance to the development of probability theory. It is however doubtful if their work has had any noticeable effect on insurance practice.

Economists working on finance seem to have taken the opposite attitude. They have found an easy answer in CAPM, which may not be a particularly good one, and put it to application. One can discuss how useful this model really has been in practice. It is however certain that the applications of CAPM has led to deeper insight into the functioning of financial markets.

3.4 Let us now return to the more general version of CAPM given by (10). From (9) it follows that we have

$$P\{z_r\} = R_r - P\{x_r\} = R_r - KE\{x_r(c-x)^\alpha\}$$

Here we substitute

$$x_r = R_r - z_r \qquad \text{and} \quad x = R - z$$

and find the following expression for the premium

$$P\{z_r\} = R_r R_r\Big(1 - KE\{(c - R + z)^\alpha\}\Big) + KE\{z_r(c - R + z)^\alpha\}$$

where $R = \sum R_r$ and $z = \sum z_r$.

For the degenerate case $z_r \equiv 0$, consistency requires that $P\{z_r\} = 0$, so that we must have

$$K^{-1} = E\{(c - R + z)^\alpha\}$$

Hence the premium formula takes the form

$$P\{z_r\} = KE\{z_r(c - R + z)^\alpha\} = \frac{E\{z_r(c - R + z)^\alpha\}}{E\{(c - R + z)^\alpha\}}$$

or written full

$$P\{z_r\} = K \int_0^\infty \int_0^\infty z_r(c - R + z)^\alpha f(z, z_r)\, dz\, dz_r \tag{12}$$

Formula (12) shows how the premium for a risk which can lead to losses represented by the stochastic variable z_r, depends on:

(i) The stochastic properties of the risk itself.

(ii) The stochastic relationship between the particular risk and claims in the market as a whole, described by the joint density $f(z, z_r)$.

(iii) The attitude to risk in the market as a whole, represented by c.

(iv) The total assets of all insurance companies in the market, R.

A realistic theory of insurance premiums must of course take all these four elements into account. This is however rarely done in actuarial risk theory. The recent book by Goovaerts et.al. covers only the first of the four elements.

One could consider as a fifth element the interest earned on the premium before claims are paid. This is regularly done in financial theory, but is rather trivial in the present context. One has just to multiply the premium by the appropriate discount factor.

3.5 As another simple example we shall take

$$u_r'(x) = \exp\left\{-\frac{x}{\alpha_r}\right\} \qquad r = 1, 2, \ldots, n$$

Equation (3) then takes the form

$$k_r \exp\{-y_r \alpha_r^{-1}\} = u'(x)$$

Taking logarithms on both sides, we obtain

$$\log k_r - y_r \alpha_r^{-1} = \log u'(x)$$

Multiplication by α_r and summation over all r gives

$$\sum \alpha_r \log k_r - x = \log u'(x) \sum \alpha_r$$

Writing

$$\sum_{s=1}^{n} \alpha_s \log k_s = K \quad \text{and} \quad \sum_{s=1}^{n} \alpha_s = A$$

we obtain

$$u'(x) = \exp\left\{-\frac{L-x}{A}\right\}$$

and

$$y_r(x) = \frac{\alpha_r x}{A} - \alpha_r \log k_r - \frac{\alpha_r K}{A}$$

We can then proceed as in the first example. From (8) we determine the value of an arbitrary portfolio in the market, and hence also the market premium for an arbitrary insurance contract.

3.6 The two preceding examples are fairly simple because the "sharing rules" are linear, i.e.

$$y_r(x) = q_r x + c_r$$

where

$$\sum q_r = 1 \qquad \text{and} \qquad \sum c_r = 0$$

The sharing rules have this form only if all utility functions belong to one of the following two classes:

$$u_r'(x) = (x + c_r)^{\alpha}, \quad \text{or} \tag{i}$$

$$u_r'(x) = e^{-\alpha_r x} \tag{ii}$$

The result is well known, and has been proved by many authors, i.a. by Borch (1968).

If the sharing rules are linear, it is possible for the companies to reach a Pareto optimum through proportional reinsurance arrangements. Other forms of reinsurance are widely used, so there should be a need for studying utility function which do not lead to linear sharing rules. The problem is difficult, and it is surprising that it has only occasionally been taken up by those who cherish "hard questions" for their own sake. We shall not discuss the problem in any detail, but it may be useful to study a simple example.

Consider 2 persons with the utility functions

$$u_1(x) = 1 - e^{-x}, \qquad \text{and} \qquad u_2(x) = \log(c + x).$$

Condition (2) then takes the form

$$k_1 e^{-1} = \frac{k_2}{c + y_2}$$

As $y_1 + y_2 = x$, we can write this as

$$(c + y_2)e^{-\alpha - y_2} = k$$

Clearly we must have $y_2 > -c$. Hence under a Pareto optimal rule of loss-sharing, person can under no circumstances pay more than c, so that the rule will correspond approximately to a stop loss insurance arrangement.

3.7 Let us now return to the general case (3), and consider a risk described by the stochastic variable z.

From (8) it follows that the insurance premium for this risk is

$$P\{z\} = \int_0^\infty \int_0^\infty z\, u'(x)\, f(x, z)\, dx\, dz \tag{13}$$

Here we have written x for total claims in the market, and we have not brought the assets explicitly into the utility function.

It is convenient to write (13) in the form:

$$P\{z\} = \int_0^\infty u'(x) \left\{ \int_0^\infty z\, f(x, z)\, dz \right\} dx$$

Let us now write $z = z_1 + z_2$, where $z_1 = \min(z, D)$ and $z_2 = \max(0, z - D)$.

For the two components we find the following premiums

$$P\{z_1\} = \int_0^\infty u'(x) \left\{ \int_0^D z\, f(x,z)\, dz + D \int_D^\infty f(x,z)\, dz \right\} dx$$

$$P\{z_2\} = \int_0^\infty u'(x) \left\{ \int_0^D (z - D)\, f(x,z)\, dz \right\} dx$$

These two formulae can be given a number of different interpretations, i.a.:

$P\{z_1\}$ can be seen as the reduction in the premium offered to a buyer, if he will accept a deductible D.

$P\{z_2\}$ can be seen as the reinsurance premium for a stop loss contract, under which the reinsurer pays all claims in excess of the limit D.

We now write $P\{z_2\} = P\{D\}$, and differentiate twice with respect to D. This gives:

$$P'(D) = -\int_0^\infty u'(x) \left\{ \int_D^\infty f(x,z)\, dz \right\} dx$$
$$P''(D) = \int_0^\infty u'(x)\, f(x,D)\, dx \tag{14}$$

If a reinsurer is willing to quote premiums for a number or stop loss contracts, with different limits, the left-hand side of (14) can be estimated for an arbitrary D. If the joint density $f(x,z)$ is known, at least approximately it may be possible to obtain an estimate of the kernel function $u'(x)$. With this estimate, we can then compute the premium for an arbitrary insurance contract in the market.

It is obviously impossible to determine the function $u'(x)$ from (3), i.e. from the preferences of all companies, and then use (8) to calculate the market premium for an arbitrary insurance contract.

It is however clear that $u'(x)$ plays an important part in determining market premiums. Since premiums are observable, we can turn the problem around, and estimate the function $u'(x)$ from observations. This approach is widely used in economics. Demand curves and underlying utility functions cannot be observed, but must be estimated from observed behaviour. This approach is some times referred to as the "principle of revealed preference".

4. A Dynamic approach to Utility

4.1 In the preceding sections we have studied simple one-period decision problems, and assumed there was a utility function behind the decision. In practice it may often be difficult to specify this utility function — for good reasons. The utility a company assigns to the profits earned in one period will presumably depend on how that profit can be applied in future periods. This suggests that the problem should be studied in a dynamic or multi-period frame-work. If the company has an overall, long-term objective, this must contain the utility functions which govern the decisions in each period. This overall objective may often be simpler to specify than the Bernoulli utility function.

One of the first to study this problem in an insurance context was De Finetti (1957) in one of his pioneering papers. As a long-term objective he suggested that an insurance company should seek to maximize the expected present value of its dividend payments. In the following decades this problem has been discussed by several other authors, i.a. by Borch (1967) and (1969), Bühlmann (1970), and Gerber (1979).

De Finetti made his observation in a critical study of the now obsolete "collective risk theory". This theory placed the focus on the probability that an insurance company shall remain solvent forever, provided that it does not change its operating procedures. This probability of achieving eternal life will inevitably be zero, unless the company allows its reserves to grow without limit. De Finetti pointed out that an insurance company could not really be interested in building up unlimited reserves, and argued in fact that the marginal utility of accumulated profit *(vincite utili)* must be decreasing. He illustrates his argument with a very simple example, based on a two-point distribution. In the following we shall consider a simple, slightly more general example.

4.2 Consider an insurance company which in each successive operating period underwrites identical portfolios, and take the following elements as given:

S = the company's initial capital

P = the premium received by the company at the beginning of each operating period

$f(x)$ = the probability density of claims paid by the company in each operating period.

If S_t is the company's capital at the end of period t, and x_{t+1} the claims paid by the company during period $t+1$, the company's capital at the end of period $t+1$ will be:

$$S_{t+1} = S_t + P - x_{t+1}$$

Assume now that the company operates under the following conditions:

(i) If $S_t < 0$, the company is insolvent, or "ruined", and cannot operate in any of the following periods.

(ii) If $S_t > Z$, the company pays a dividend $s_t = S_t - Z$. It is natural to assume that Z is chosen by the management, because accumulated profits beyond Z has lower utility than a paid out dividend.

The dividend payments $s_1, s_2, \ldots, s_t, \ldots$ is a sequence of stochastic variables, and we shall write $V(S, Z)$, or when no misunderstanding is possible $V(S)$ for the expected discounted sum of the dividend payments which the company makes before the inevitable ruin, i.e.

$$V(S) = \sum_{t=1}^{\infty} v^t E\{s_t\}$$

where r is a discount factor. We shall assume that the company seeks the value of Z which maximizes $V(S, Z)$.

4.3 To study the function $V(S)$, we first note that for $S < Z < S + P$ it must satisfy the integral equation

$$\begin{aligned} V(S) = v \int_z^{S+P} & (x - Z + V(Z)) f(S + P - x)\, dx \\ + v \int_0^Z & V(x)\, f(S + P - x)\, dx \end{aligned} \tag{15}$$

The equation says that if claims x are less than $S + P - Z$, a dividend $S + P - Z - x$ will be paid at the end of the period, and the company will begin the next period with a capital Z.

If $S + P - Z \leq x \leq S + P$ the company will pay no dividend, and begin the next period with a capital $S + P - x$. If $S + P < x$, the company is ruined, and cannot operate in any of the following periods.

In the interval stated (15) is an integral equation of Fredholm's type, and it is known that is has a unique continuous solution. For $S < Z - P$, no dividend can be paid at the first period, and some modifications are necessary.

On the whole (15) is difficult to handle, and unless one holds a strong "Hungarian" view on mathematics, a general solution appears uninteresting. The optimal dividend policy is given by the value of Z, which maximizes $V(S, Z)$. The existence of an optimal policy poses some hard questions, which we shall not take up.

4.4 The main idea behind De Finetti's paper can be presented as follows:

Assume an insurance company with equity capital S is offered a premium Q, if it will underwrite a one-period insurance contract described by the claim density $g(x)$. If the company accepts the contract, expected present value of future dividend payments will be

$$U(S) = \int_0^{S-Q} V(S+Q-x)\,g(x)\,dx \tag{16}$$

Hence, given the company's long-term objective, the contract will be acceptable if and only if $U(S) \geq V(S)$. This means that $V(S)$ serves as the utility function which determines the company's decision, and that in (8) $u'(x)$ can be replaced by $V'(x)$. This assumes of course that the company receives the offer after it made its reinsurance arrangements, or that it takes the reinsurance possibilities into account when deciding about the particular offer.

De Finetti did not elaborate his suggestion, but went instead on to discuss other functions of an arbitrary upper limit to accumulated profits, which could serve as alternative objectives. His paper was generally ignored for a decade, even in actuarial circles. The influential paper on the subject is by Shubik and Thompson (1959), who independently developed a model which is virtually identical to that of De Finetti, but not interpreted in terms of insurance.

4.5 De Finetti's model implies that an insurance company is basically risk-neutral. This may at first sight seem surprising, but it makes some sense if one considers the alternatives. It seems artificial to assume that the board of a company will consider different utility functions, and possibly take a vote, to pick one which adequately represents the company's attitude to risk. It seems more natural to assume that a board will settle for some simpler rule, such as that of maximizing expected present value of dividend payment. With this rule the company will behave as if it were risk-averse in its underwriting and reinsurance transactions.

At this stage we can see dimly the outline of an attractive unified theory of insurance:

(i) Premiums and reinsurance arrangements are determined by the methods sketched in Section 2.

(ii) The utility functions which play all important role in Section 2, can be determined by the methods indicated in this Section.

A number of hard questions must be answered before a complete theory can take form. Before taking up the challenge, it may however be useful to pause, and ask if it really is necessary to answer these questions.

5. A modification of the De Finetti's Model

5.1 De Finetti's innovation consisted in removing the ruin probability as part of the objective of the insurance company. Instead he put the emphasis on the dividend payments, and placed an upper limit on the reserves which the company would accumulate. His model presented actuaries with a number of new hard questions, and seems to have given the collective risk theory a *coup de grâce.*

It is natural also to consider a lower limit on the equity capital which the company will hold at the beginning of a new operating period. This means that the company will have to obtain new equity capital after an unfavorable underwriting period. If capital markets function efficiently, this should be possible. If the insurance company is owned by a holding company, one must expect that the owner will see that the subsidiary enters each period with an optimal equity capital, i.e. that the owner will risk the optimal amount of capital in the insurance business. This leads us to consider an insurance company which initially holds an equity capital Z, and has adopted the following policy:

If claims in a period amounts to x

(i) The company pays out a dividend $\max(P-x,0)$

(ii) an amount $\min(x-P,Z)$ is paid into the company as new equity capital.

This policy implies that if the company is solvent at the end of a period, it will enter the next period with an equity capital Z.

5.2 Under the policy outlined expected present value of the dividend payment at the end of the first period is

$$W_1(Z) = v \int_0^{P+Z} (P-x)\, f(x)\, dx$$

The probability that the company shall be solvent at the end of the period, and hence be able to operate in the second period is

$$\Pr\{x \leq P+Z\} = F(P+Z)$$

it then follows that the expected present value of all payments is

$$W(Z) = v \int_0^{P+Z} (P-x)\, f(x)\, dx \sum_{n=0}^{\infty} \left[vF(P+Z)\right]^n$$

or

$$W(Z) = \frac{v \int_0^{P+Z} (P-x) f(x)\, dx}{1 - vF(P+Z)} = \frac{v\left\{\int_0^{P+Z} F(x)\, dx - ZF(P)Z\right\}}{1 - vF(P+Z)} \tag{17}$$

5.3 The problem of the company is now to determine the value of Z which maximizes (17), i.e. to find the optimal amount of capital which the owners should put at risk in their company.

The first order condition for a maximum, $W'(Z) = 0$, takes the form

$$Z\left\{1 - vF(P+Z)\right\} = v \int_0^{P+Z} (P-x) f(x)\, dx \tag{18}$$

From (18) Z can be determined, and comparison with (17) shows that for the optimal Z we have we have

$$Z = W(Z)$$

This simple condition expresses the obvious, that the optimal capital to put into a venture is equal to the expected present value of the return.

In the discount factor $v = (1+i)^{-1}$ which occurs in (17) and (18), i must be interpreted as the return on competing investments. This invites some conventional comparative static analysis. Differentiation of (18) gives

$$\frac{dZ}{dv}\left(1 - vF(P+F)\right) = \int_0^{P+Z} F(x)\, dx > 0$$

This again expresses the obvious. If return on competing investments decreases, i.e. if v increases, more capital will now into the insurance industry. In the opposite case insurance companies may be unable to attract new equity capital.

Clearly $F(P+Z)$ is the probability that an insurance company shall be able to pay its claims. In most countries government regulations require that this probability shall be close to unity. In practice this means that an insurance company is only allowed to operate if it satisfies a solvency conditions of the form $F(P+Z) \geq \alpha$. If there is a general increase in returns on investments, it is evident that insurance companies must increase their premiums, in order to attract the capital necessary to satisfy the solvency condition. This may be a useful result. It shows that the government cannot decree both high solvency and "reasonable" premiums in a free capital market. The result should be obvious, but does not always seem to be so.

6. The Models and the Real World

6.1 The model presented in Section 2 was interpreted as a reinsurance market, and we determined the equilibrium premiums. One must expect that these premiums, at least in the longer run, will have some influence on the premiums in direct insurance.

Insurance markets are far from perfect, and a company may well — for some time — be able to charge premiums above those determined by the model. This company can however earn a risk-free profit if it reinsures its whole portfolio in the market, so the situation cannot be stable in the long run. One must also expect that the customers of this company eventually will discover that they can buy their insurance cheaper elsewhere.

Similarly an insurance company may charge lower premiums than those determined by the model. This company will probably find that reinsurance costs more than it is worth, and carry most of the risk itself. With good luck this may go on for quite some time, and with ample reserves the company will be able to satisfy the solvency conditions laid down by the government. When luck runs out, as it eventually must, the company may well find itself insolvent, when its liabilities are valued at market prices.

6.2 In Section 2 it was proved that a Pareto optimum could be reached only if every insurer participated in every risk in the market. This does not happen in practice, and it is natural to seek the explanation in transaction costs. This is however not entirely satisfactory, since it should not be prohibitively expensive to carry out the calculations necessary to divide a risk in a Pareto optimal way. It seems more likely that some elements of moral hazard enter. It is always stressed that reinsurance is carried out under conditions of the "utmost good faith". In practice this means that a reinsurer accepts the ceding company's report on the stochastic properties of the risk covered, without a costly checking of the statistics. The possibility that the ceding company cheats is always there, so the reinsurer has the choice of either expenses, or of being exposed to moral hazard. It is therefore natural that reinsurers should try to cover a medium sized risk within a fairly small group, and this may lead to some segmentation of the market.

One way to model this would be to assume that there are cost c involved in checking the portfolio offered by a would-be ceding company. If n companies participate in an exchanges arrangement, each checking the other, total costs will be $n(n-1)c$. With increasing n there will clearly be a point where increasing costs will offset the gain by wider diversification of the risk

6.3 In Section 4 we have in a sense banished utility and risk aversion from the supply side of the insurance market. There are however some reasons for assuming that insurance companies should be risk-neutral. Insurance companies are intermediaries between those who want to buy insurance, and those who are willing to risk their money in the underwriting of insurance contracts. If these two parties are risk-averse, a set of Pareto optimal arrangements exists. The parties may however be unable to reach a Pareto optimum, if the transactions have to be carried out through an intermediary that imposes its own risk aversion. The problem has been discussed in economic literature, i.a. by Malinvaud (1972). We shall not discuss it further here, since a complete discussion will require detailed specification of the institutional framework.

On the demand side risk aversion remains essential, since a buyer of insurance is by definition risk-averse. When he is faced by a market which can quote a premium for any kind of insurance contract, he can compute or program his way to the contract which is optimal according to his preferences.

References for Section 7

Arrow KJ. (1953): "Le rôle des valeurs boursières pour la répartition la meilleure des risques". *Colloques Internationaux du CNRS 40*, 41–48. Translated in 1964 as "The role of securities in the optimal allocation of risk-bearing". *Review of Economic Studies 31*, 91–96.

Borch K. (1962): "Equilibrium in a reinsurance market", *Econometrica 30*, 424–444.

Borch K. (1967): "The theory of risk", *Journal of the Royal Statistical Society, Series B 29*, 432–452.

Borch K. (1968): "General equilibrium in the economics or uncertainty", in *Risk and Uncertainty*, Borch and Mossin (Eds.), London: Macmillan.

Borch K. (1969): "The static decision problem in its dynamic context", *Colloques Internationaux du CNRS 171*, 53–62.

Bühlmann H. (1970): *Mathematical Methods in Risk Theory*, Springer-Verlag, Berlin.

Bühlmann H. (1980): "An economic premium principle", *The ASTIN Bulletin 11*, 52–60.

Bühlmann H. (1984): "The general economic premium principle", *The ASTIN Bulletin 14*, 13–21.

Cramér H. (1930): "On the mathematical theory of risk", *Skandia Jubilee Volume 7*, 84, Stockholm.

De Finetti B. (1957): "Su un impostazione alternativa della teoria collectiva del rischio", Transactions of the XV International Congress of Actuaries 2, 433–443.

Gerber HU. (1979): *An Introduction to Mathematical Risk Theory*, Huebner Foundation Monograph No. 8. Homewood Illinois: Richard D. Irwin Inc.

Goovaerts M, F. De Vylder, and Haezendonck J. (1983): *Insurance Premiums*, North-Holland, Amsterdam.

Hirhsleifer J. (1970): *Investment, Interest and Capital*, Englewood Cliffs, Prentice-Hall, New Jersey.

Lintner J. (1965): "The evaluation of risky assets and the selection of risky investments in stock portfolios and capital budgets", *Review of Economics and Statistics 47*, 13–37.

Mac Lane S. (1983): "The health of mathematics". *The Mathematical Intelligencer 5*, 53–55.

Malinvaud E. (1972): "The allocation of individual risks in large markets", *Journal of Economic Theory 4*, 312–328.

Mossin J. (1966): "Equilibrium in a capital asset market", *Econometrica 34*, 768–783.

Sharpe W. (1964): "Capital asset prices", *Journal of Finance 19*, 425–442.

Shubik M. and Thompson G. (1959): "Games of economic survival", *Naval Research Logistics Quarterly 6*, 111–123.

CHAPTER 4

LIFE INSURANCE

1. Early Development of Life Insurance

1.1 Life insurance includes two different basic forms of insurance contracts

(i) Life annuities paying fixed amounts at specific dates, provided that the recipient is alive.

(ii) Life insurances paying a fixed amount at the death of the insured.

All life insurance contracts on the life of one person can be built up as combinations of these two component.

The history of both forms of life insurance can be traced back at least to the days of the Roman Empire.

1.2 In the Middle Ages it was possible to retire into a monastery, and be assured of the means of subsistence for life against an advance payment. This payment was usually made by donating property to the monastery, and the subsistence was paid in kind, so the arrangement was in modern terms an inflation-proof pension plan.

Some medieval guilds imposed special dues on their members, and the amounts collected were paid to the dependents of the members who had died during the past year. The sums involved were usually modest, and the main objective seems to have been to secure a decent funeral for the departed member.

Neither of the two early forms of life insurance can be said to have had any real importance in the economy.

1.3 From the 16th century the sale of life annuities or pensions became an important element in government borrowing. Then as now governments found it difficult to repay their debts on schedule, and some loans were floated without any redemption plan. This meant that the lender really bought a perpetual annuity, as one can still do by buying British consuls. If it was agreed that annuity payments should cease with the death of the lender, the loan would eventually be liquidated. The annual payments would however be higher than if interest on the principal was to be paid in perpetuity.

To a scientist in the 17th century who specialized in the new subject known as "political arithmetics" it was no easy task to determine how much higher the annual payments should be under a life annuity than under a perpetual annuity. The compilation and analysis of mortality statistics was a popular subject of study at the time, but it was not clear how this was related to the price of life annuities. There are a number of examples that the sale of annuities turned out to be a disastrously expensive way of borrowing money. Sometimes lifelong annuities were sold at a fixed price, independent of the buyer's age.

1.4 The theoretical problem was solved by Jan de Witt. He argued that the price to be paid for an annuity contract must be equal to the expected present value of the payments. This has become known as the "principle of equivalence", and is the foundation of modern actuarial calculations.

De Witt presented his conclusion in 1671 in a report (De Vardye van de Lif-renten) to the States General of the Netherlands. De Witt's result became quickly known in interested circles, but the original of his report seems to have been lost. Apparently Todhunter (1865) had not seen it, and he reports that Leibnitz tried repeatedly, without success to get hold of a copy of de Witt's report.

According to Neuburger (1974) de Witt argued that the price of a lifelong annuity to a child of 3 years should be 16 to 18 times the annual payment. He was however overruled by the politicians, who decided that the price should be 14. This may be the first, but certainly not the last time that a mathematician had to give in to politicians, who had their own ideas as to what constituted an "affordable" price for insurance.

1.5 A special form of governmental borrowing was the sale of "tontines", named after Lorenzo Tonti, who proposed the scheme to Cardinal Mazarin, the Prime Minister of Louis XIV. Under a tontine a large number of tickets or bonds were sold to buyers who were divided into age-groups. The government paid the agreed interest on the total amount raised by each group, and the amounts paid were divided among the surviving members of the group. When all members of a group had died, payments stopped and the debt owed to the group was liquidated. The tontines brought an element of gambling into the purchase of life annuities, and this seems to have been appreciated by investors and lenders at the time. A recent survey of the tontines in France, the country where they originated, is given by Jennings and Trout (1982). The tontines had a certain success also in some countries outside France. Tontines survived until well into the 19th century both in Europe and the U.S.A.

1.6 In the 17th and 18th centuries mutual or "friendly societies" were formed in several European countries to offer life insurance for modest amounts, on principles similar to those used by the medieval guilds. The technical basis of calculation was shaky in most of these societies, and few of them survived for any length of time. It is generally agreed that modern life insurance began in 1762 with the formation of the Equitable Society in London. This society which still is in active operation, used the proper scientific methods in its premium calculation. The book by Ogborn (1962) gives a very readable account of the motives behind the foundation of The Equitable, and of early British life insurance.

In the following decades life insurance societies were established in most major countries, but growth was slow. The founders of these societies were often idealists who wanted to make safe and fair life insurance available to those who wanted it, and they sometimes seemed disappointed that not more use was made of the opportunities offered.

The active selling of life insurance began in the middle of the 19th century, and led to rapid growth. This development did to some extent associate life insurance with high pressure salesmanship and led to the maxim that "life insurance is sold, not bought". It is not easy to explain why this should be so, and here is not the place to speculate over the subject. Be it sufficient to observe that preachers who urge people to save for their old age, or to provide for dependents in case of premature death, rarely have found a responsive audience.

2. Elements of Actuarial Mathematics

2.1 The basis of actuarial mathematics is the "principle of equivalence", which can be traced back to the report of Jan de Witt in 1671. To compute the present expected value of payments under an insurance contract one needs assumptions about mortality and interest rates in the future. Forecasts of interest rates are of importance to almost any kind of economic activity, and will not be discussed here.

Forecasts of mortality is usually based on a mortality law which traditionally is described by the "death rate" q_x. The rate q_x can be interpreted

Table 4.1: Death rates: 1000 q_x under some mortality laws.

x	H^M	1980 CSO Male	1980 CSO Female
10	4.90	0.75	0.68
30	7.72	1.75	1.37
50	15.95	7.00	5.13
70	62.19	47.37	23.16
90	279.45	228.43	198.85

as the probability that a person of age x shall die before he reaches the age $x+1$. The death rates are estimated from observations, and usually graduated. Table 4.1 gives the values of q_x for some widely used mortality laws.

H^M is a life table from 1869 based on the experience for Healthy Males of 20 British life insurance companies. In some countries this table was used well into the present century.

CSO stands for Commissioners' Standard Ordinary, and is the life table prepared by the National Association of Insurance Commissioners.

From the death rates one calculates the mortality table ℓ_x by the formula

$$\ell_{x+1} = \ell_x(1 - q_x)$$

The ratio

$$\frac{\ell_{x+t}}{\ell_x} = {}_tP_x = \pi(t)$$

can be interpreted as the probability that a person of age x shall still be alive after a time t. In the following this probability will be denoted by $\pi(t)$ when it is not necessary to emphasis how it depends on the person's age.

2.2 The simplest life insurance contract is the "pure endowment". Under this contract an amount of one unit is paid to the insured if he is alive at time t. The expected present value of this payment is $\pi(t)e^{-\delta t}$, where δ is the "force of interest". From the principle of equivalence it follows that the single premium which the insured has to pay is ${}_tE_x = \pi(t)e^{-\delta t}$

If ℓ_x is differentially, it is convenient to write $d\log \ell_x/dx = -\mu_x$, so that

$$\pi(t) = \frac{\ell_{x+t}}{\ell_x} = \exp\left(-\int_0^t \mu_{x+s}\, ds\right)$$

The single premium for the pure endowment insurance then becomes

$$_tE_x = \pi(t)e^{-\delta t} = \exp\left(-\int_0^t (\delta + \mu_{x+s})\, ds\right) \tag{1}$$

Formula (1) shows that the forces of interest and mortality enter the calculation in a completely symmetric way. If either force increases, the premium will be reduced.

The pure endowment with single premium rarely occurs as a separate insurance contract, but it is an important building block in more complicated contracts. A life-long annuity — a pension — is the sum of pure endowments, i.e.

$$a_x = \sum_{t=1}^{\infty} {_tE_x} = \sum_{t=1}^{\infty} \pi(t)e^{-\delta t}$$

2.3 In theoretical work it is often convenient to assume that the annuity is paid as a continuous stream, and write

$$\bar{a}_x = \int_0^\infty \pi(t)e^{-\delta t}\, dt$$

for the single premium.

Under a typical pension plan the insured will pay a constant, or "level" premium P up to the time of retirement n, and from then on he will receive an annuity B as long as he lives. The principle of equivalence gives the following relationship between premium and benefit:

$$P\int_0^n \pi(t)e^{-\delta t} dt = B\int_n^\infty \pi(t)e^{-\delta t}\, dt$$

In the standard actuarial notation this is written

$$P\bar{a}_{x:\overline{n}|} = B(\bar{a}_x - \bar{a}_{x:\overline{n}|}) \tag{2}$$

The symbol $\bar{a}_{x:\overline{n}|}$ is a "temporary annuity" which terminates after a time n.

2.4 The function $\pi(t)$ is non-increasing, $\pi(0) = 1$ and $\pi(\infty) = 0$, so that $F(t) = 1 - \pi(t)$ is a cumulative probability distribution. If a derivative exists, $F'(t) = -\pi'(t)$ will be the probability density of the event that the person shall die at the time t. The present value of a unit payable at this time is $e^{-\delta t}$. From the principle of equivalence it follows that the single premium for an insurance contract paying one unit when the insured dies is:

$$\bar{A}_x = -\int_0^\infty \pi'(t)e^{-\delta t}dt = 1 - \delta \int_0^\infty \pi(t)e^{-\delta t}\,dt$$

or

$$\bar{A}_x = 1 - \delta \bar{a}_x \tag{3}$$

This insurance contract is called *Whole life insurance.*

Formula (3) gives the expected present value of the rights of the insured under the contract, which according to the principle of equivalence must be equal to the single premium he has to pay. The right-hand side of (3) shows that these rights are equivalent to paying out the sum right away, provided that the insured accepted to pay interest on this "loan" as long as he lives.

Two other forms of widely used life insurance contracts are:

Term insurance. The single premium is given by:

$$\bar{A}^1_{x:\bar{n}|} = -\int_0^n \pi'(t)e^{-\delta t}dt = 1 - \delta \bar{a}_{x:\bar{n}|} - \pi(n)e^{-\delta n} \tag{4}$$

From (4) it is seen that under this contract the sum is paid only if the insured dies before time n.

Endowment insurance. The single premium is given by

$$\bar{A}_{x:\bar{n}|} = -\int_0^n \pi'(t)e^{-\delta t}dt + \pi(n)e^{-\delta n} = 1 - \delta \bar{a}_{x:\bar{n}|} \tag{5}$$

Under this contract the sum insured is paid at death, or at the latest at time n. From the formulae it is easy to see that this contract is a sum of term insurance and a pure endowment.

Relatively few insurance contracts are paid by single premiums. The usual practice is that the insured pays a level premium over a period $k \leq n$. This premium P is for an endowment contract determined by

$$P\bar{a}_{x:\bar{k}|} = \bar{A}_{x:\bar{n}|}$$

The right-hand side gives the expected present value of the insured's entitlements under the contract, and the left hand side the expected present value of his obligations — i.e. to pay the premium over the period k, if he is alive. By the principle of equivalence the two must be equal.

For the whole life policy the level premium payable as long as the insured is alive, is determined by $P\bar{a}_x = 1 - \delta\bar{a}_x$, or

$$P = \frac{1}{\bar{a}_x} - \delta$$

2.5 Most life insurance contracts contain an important element of saving. For the pension plan described by (2) this is obvious, and it also holds for the insurance contracts (3)–(5), if they are paid for by a level premium.

As an illustration consider a whole life policy paid for by a level premium. This premium P is determined by the principle of equivalence, i.e. by the condition

$$\int_0^\infty \big(P\pi(s) + \pi'(s)\big)e^{-\delta(s)}\,ds = 0 \tag{6}$$

For any value of t one has

$$\int_0^t \big(P\pi(s) + \pi'(s)\big)e^{-\delta s}\,ds = -\int_t^\infty \big(P\pi(s) + \pi'(s)\big)e^{-\delta s}\,ds \tag{7}$$

As the premium is constant and the mortality risk increases with t both sides of (7) must be positive.

In (6) expected present value is computed from time 0. Multiplying (7) by $e^{\delta t}/\pi(t)$ one finds $V(t)$ given by

$$\int_0^t \left(P\frac{\pi(s)}{\pi(t)} + \frac{\pi'(s)}{\pi(t)}\right) e^{\delta(t-s)} ds = -\int_t^\infty \left(P\frac{\pi(s)}{\pi(t)} + \frac{\pi'(s)}{\pi(t)}\right) e^{\delta(t-s)} ds\,.$$

As
$$\frac{\ell_{x+s+t}}{\ell_x} = \frac{\ell_{x+s}}{\ell_x}\frac{\ell_{x+s+t}}{\ell_{x+s}}\,,$$

it follows that

$$\pi(s+t) = \pi(s)\pi(t)\,.$$

The latter condition says that the probability that a person shall be alive after a time $s+t$ is equal to the probability that he shall be alive at time s, multiplied by the probability that he is alive t years later.

Using this, $V(t)$ can be written as

$$V(t) = -\int_0^\infty \big(\pi'(s) + P\pi(s)\big)e^{-\delta s}\,ds\,.$$

Reintroducing the age of the insured, and recalling that he has now reached the age $x + t$, one has

$$V(t) = \bar{A}_{x+t} - P\bar{a}_{x+t} \tag{8}$$

The first term on the right-hand side of (8) gives the remaining rights of the insured under the contract — to receive one unit when he dies. The second term represents his remaining obligations — to pay the premium, determined by (6) as long as he lives.

2.6 In life insurance $V(t)$ is called the "premium reserve", since it represents the part of the premiums received which the insurer must keep in reserve to meet expected future obligations. The premium reserve is entered as a liability in the balance sheet of the insurance company.

The premium reserve also represents the accumulated savings of the insured. Usually he will at any time have the right to cancel the contract and receive the "surrender value" of the policy in cash. The surrender value is as a rule equal to the premium reserve, less a deduction for expenses incurred by the insurer. A life insurance contract which states that the insured will forfeit all rights if he fails to pay the agreed premium, will in most countries not be legally enforceable.

The way the premium reserve was derived from the right-hand side of (7) is called the "prospective" method. This method implies that one looks forward and computes the premium reserve as the difference between the expected present values of the insured's entitlements and his obligations, as given by (8).

Similarly one can compute the premium reserve from the left-hand side of (7) as the compounded value of the premiums paid by the insured less the insurance protection he has received. This method of computing the premium reserve is called the "retrospective" method.

2.7 A life insurance contract can be of very long duration, and once the contract is concluded the insurer can usually not change the terms. When the insurer quotes a premium, his quotation must be based on forecasts of interest and mortality rates several decades into the future. It is natural, and indeed necessary that these forecasts should include considerable safety margins. This means however that the insurance contract can be expected to — although not certain to — yield a substantial "surplus", or profit to the insurer. Under most life insurance contracts this surplus is paid back to the insured, once it has been realized. The surplus can be returned to the policy holders in cash, in the form of lower premiums in the future, or in the form of higher face values of the policies.

2.8 Until the end of World War II practically all life insurance contracts were of one of the three forms discussed above, i.e. with single premiums given by (3)–(5), and paid for by level premiums. This gave a very rigid system, although the insured could obtain some flexibility by surrendering and buying different combinations of term and endowment contracts as his needs changed.

A more general insurance contract can be described by two functions $C(t)$ and $P(t)$, defined as follows:

(i) $C(t)$ = the amount payable at the death of the insured, if death occurs at time t. $C(t)$ must clearly be non-negative.

(ii) $P(t)\,dt$ = the premium paid by the insured in the time interval $(t, t+dt)$, if he is alive at the time. $P(t)$ may be negative for some values of t, as in the pension plan described by (2).

The principle of equivalence requires that

$$\int_0^\infty C(t)\pi'(t)e^{-\delta t}\,dt + \int_0^\infty P(t)\pi(t)e^{-\delta t}\,dt = 0 \tag{9}$$

Any pair of functions which satisfy (7) may represent a feasible life insurance contract. In practice it is however also necessary to require that the premium reserve never shall be negative.

There is no need for fixing $C(t)$ and $P(t)$ in advance. They can be changed at any time, with the changing needs of the insured. As an illustration assume that the insured has accumulated a positive amount of savings, i.e. his premium reserve is positive. He can then let his insurer know how much he wants to pay as premium for the next year, and what amount he wants paid as benefit if he should die during the year. The insured may even withdraw money, and use his insurance policy practically as a pass book. In principle any choice should be possible, as long as the premium reserve does not become negative. There are however some additional restrictions to prevent adverse selection. For instance substantial increases in the death benefit, without any other changes in the policy, will not be allowed, for obvious reasons.

2.9 The actuarial mathematics found its definite form about the turn of the century. There are a large number of textbooks on the subject. One of the most recent in English is Neil (1977). One of the most complete is Wolff (1970). The book by De Vylder and Jaumain (1976) gives a presentation of the subject in terms of modern mathematics. These texts all make extensive use of the special actuarial symbols and notation, and this makes the subject unnecessarily difficult to a reader who is not familiar with this terminology. In the presentation above the use of the special terminology has been reduced to a minimum. This should make it clear to the non-actuarial reader that the underlying ideas are very simple.

3. Life Insurance, Consumption and Saving

3.1 Life insurance is essentially a form of saving, and in the market it competes with other forms of saving. It is therefore necessary to study more conventional forms of saving. Assume that a person's income rate can be represented by a continuous function of time $y(t)$. Similarly one can assume that his planned expenditure rate on consumption is represented by a function $c(t)$. Whether a particular consumption plan can be carried out with a given income stream, will in the first place depend on the facilities for saving and borrowing, i.e. on the possibilities of using income in one period to cover expenditure on consumption in another period.

The simplest assumption about these credit facilities is that the consumer can save or borrow any amount at the same force of interest δ. For a given income stream and an arbitrary consumption plan the consumer's net savings (positive or negative) at time t will be:

$$S(t) = e^{\delta t} \int_0^t e^{-\delta s} \big(y(s) - c(s)\big)\, ds \tag{10}$$

One can assume that the person wants to consume as much as possible, so every consumption plan that satisfies (10) cannot be feasible. It is natural to impose some constraints of the form

$$S(t) \geq a(t) \qquad \text{for some or all } t$$

If $a(t) < 0$, the consumer is allowed to be in net debt at time t.

There may be only one single constraint

$$S(T) \geq B \geq 0 \tag{11}$$

where T is some planning horizon. The condition (11) implies that the consumer must settle his debts and be solvent at time T.

3.2 A natural planning horizon is the time when the consumer's income ceases, because he retires or dies. In the case of retirement one can take B in (11) to be so large that the interest will provide an income sufficient for the rest of the consumer's life.

The time of death is uncertain, and must be represented by a random variable with the density $f(t) = -\pi'(t)$, in the notation introduced earlier. Taking the expectation of (10) and discounting, one finds

$$-\int_0^\infty e^{-\delta t} S(t)\pi'(t)dt = -\int_0^\infty \left[\int_0^t (y(s) - c(s))e^{-\delta s} ds\right] \pi'(t)\, dt$$
$$= \int_0^\infty \pi(s)e^{-\delta s}(y(s) - c(s))\, ds$$

If debts eventually must be paid, the last term must be non-negative. If the consumer desires the highest possible consumption this term must be zero. Hence

$$\int_0^\infty \pi(s)e^{-\delta s}(y(s) - c(s))\, ds = 0 \tag{12}$$

From (1) it follows that (12) can be written as

$$\int_0^\infty \exp\left(-\int_0^t (\delta + \mu_{x+s})\, ds\right)(y(t) - c(t))\, dt = 0$$

This expression shows that saving through life insurance takes place at a higher rate of interest than conventional saving.

3.3 If we take $y(t) = 0$ for $t > n$, we obtain from (2) and (9)

$$\int_0^n \pi(t)e^{-\delta t}(y(t) - c(t))\, dt = \int_n^\infty \pi(t)e^{-\delta t} c(t)\, dt$$

This means that until he retires the person's expenditure on consumption at time t is $c(t)$. The rest of his income $y(t) - c(t)$ is paid into a pension plan, which pays the rate $c(t)$ as long as the person is alive. The income is paid as long as it is needed, but only if it is needed. This makes it possible to compound payments at a higher rate of interest.

3.4 The formulae above give the possibilities of transferring income from one period to another under different forms of saving. In order to determine the optimal consumption plan one needs some assumptions about the consumer's preferences over consumption patterns. In a discrete model these preferences can be represented by a utility function of the form $U(c_1, c_2, \ldots, c_T)$. This is a little too general, and it is often assumed that

$$U(c_1, c_2, \ldots, c_T) = \sum_{t=1}^{T} e^{-\gamma t} u(c_t) \tag{13}$$

Here γ is a measure of the person's "impatience" for early consumption.

In a discrete model accumulated saving at time t is

$$S(t) = e^{\delta t} \sum_{s=1}^{t} e^{-\delta s}(y_t - c_t)$$

A meaningful problem is to maximize (13) subject to $S(T) = 0$, i.e. that the consumer is not allowed to be in debt at the planning horizon. The classical Lagrange method then leads to the problem

$$\max \left[\sum_{t=1}^{T} e^{-\gamma t} u(c_t) + \lambda \sum_{t=1}^{T} e^{-\delta t}(y_t - c_t) \right]$$

The first order conditions for a maximum are:

$$e^{-\gamma t} u'(c_t) = \lambda e^{-\delta t}, \qquad t = 1, 2, \ldots, T$$

and

$$\sum_{t=1}^{T} e^{-\delta t}(y_t - c_t) = 0$$

The first conditions can be written

$$u'(c_t) = \lambda e^{t(\gamma - \delta)}$$

Hence the marginal utility of consumption will decrease or increase steadily with t, according to the sign of $\gamma - \delta$, i.e. the difference between the consumer's impatience and the market rate of interest.

3.5 In a world of complete certainty this result may not be unreasonable, and it seems difficult to refute it by observations from the real world. It is easy to find people who have enjoyed steadily increasing or decreasing consumption for years. Whether they planned it this way must remain an open question.

Pension plans presumably represent planned consumption after retirement. Practically all pension plans are designed to give a level pension until the end of life. It is of course possible that all these plans are "irrational", but it may also indicate that the result is suspect. The cause of the trouble seems to lie in the representation (13). It is easy to show that once uncertainty is introduced, the right-hand side does not satisfy the consistency requirements of the expected utility theorem.

3.6 Life insurance is sometimes sold to persons who want to provide for their dependents in case of premature death. It is difficult to find any authoritative or generally accepted statement as to how much life insurance a supporter of a family should carry.

One rule which has been strongly advocated by Solomon Huebner (1964) is that life insurance should provide a death payment equal to the insured's future earnings. This means that if death occurs at time t, the amount payable is

$$B(t) = \int_t^{\infty} e^{\delta(t-s)} y(s)\, ds$$

The idea behind this suggestion is obviously analogy with non-life insurance. A person's future earning is called his "human capital". A prudent man should keep this asset fully insured as he would any physical asset. His death would then leave the family's net worth unchanged.

References for Sections 1–3

De Vylder F, Jaumain C. (1976): *Exposé moderne de la théorie mathématique des opérations viagères*, Office des Assureurs de Belgique.

Huebner SS. (1964): "Human Life Values — Role of Life Insurance" in *Life Insurance Handbook*, 2nd edition, Richard D. Irwin, Homewood, III.

Jennings RM, Trout AP. (1982): *The Tontine: From the Reign of Louis XIV to the French Revolutionary Era.* Huebner Foundation Monograph 12, Richard D. Irwin.

Neil A. (1977): *Life Contingencies*, London: Heineman.

Neuburger E. (1974): "Die Versicherungsmathematik von vorgestern bis heute", *Zeitschrift für die gesamte Versicherungswissenschaft 63*, 107–124.

Ogborn M. (1962): *Equitable Assurances, The Story of Life Assurance in the Experience of the Equitable Life Assurance Society*, London: Allen & Unwin.

Todhunter I. (1865): *A History of the Mathematical Theory of Probability*, Cambridge. Reprinted 1965 by Chelsea Publishing Company, New York.
Wolff KH. (1970): *Versicherungsmathematik*, Springer-Verlag.

4. Optimal Life Insurance*

1. Introduction

1.1 A person who wants to arrange his life insurance in the best possible manner will probably be bewildered by the many different offers available from insurance companies. The literature which should guide him through this jungle of offers is usually of little help. Much of it is plain sales talk, although it may be of high technical quality, particularly when it comes to explaining the tax advantages offered by life insurance in different countries. There is certainly literature which seeks to offer unbiased advice, but this does not help much, since the authors and would-be experts seem to disagree among themselves.

1.2 Much of the theoretical literature on life insurance is based on Huebner's concept of "human life value". This is essentially the present value of the future income which will not be realized if the person dies. This is an asset — presumably an intangible one — which, according to Huebner, a rational person should cover by insurance.

This is however controversial. According to Denenberg (1970) "Huebner's "human life value" ideas have been endorsed and enshrined by the life insurance texts and prominently featured in the training materials of the American College of Life Underwriters". On the other hand, Josephson (1970) states flatly: "I believe it can be said unequivocally that the Huebner concept did not influence the marketing philosophy of a single life insurance company".

We shall not try to settle this dispute, but we should note that the idea of Huebner has its origin in property insurance. Both authors seem to overlook that the real problem in this field is not to evaluate the property, but to decide if the owner should carry some of the risk himself. Clearly this decision will depend on the cost of insurance cover, and calls for an economic analysis.

---

* Reprinted from *The Geneva Papers on Risk and Insurance*, 1977; 6:3–16, copyright (c) Association International pour l'Étude de l'Economie de l'Assurance, Geneva.

1.3 Life insurance has obvious relations to economics, since it is essentially a form of saving. One gives up consumption at the present time, in order to provide for one's own old age, or for dependents one may leave at death. If a person wants to know by how much he should cut down current consumption in order to provide better for the future, he will get little help from economic literature. Economic theory is based on "consumer's sovereignty", and leaves it to the individual to decide for himself how he will evaluate current needs in relation to the need for providing for future contingencies. In the theory one does however study how this evaluation is made, since such information is essential in the construction of general models for predicting saving and investment in the economy as a whole. An economist is more likely to observe, than to preach thrift and frugality with the enthusiasm of a good insurance salesman.

1.4 As life insurance is a form of saving, it will have to compete with other forms of saving. The growing interest in portfolio theory over the last two decades has brought much attention to insurance. Life insurance policies obviously should have a place in an optimal portfolio. How prominent this place should be will clearly depend on the nature of the alternative investments, and this leads to a number of interesting problems, which recently have been studied by several authors, i.a. by Fischer (1973) and Richard (1975). We shall not take up these problems in their full generality, and we shall find it convenient to begin our discussion by considering some older models.

2. The Simplest Saving — Consumption Models

2.1 The models we shall study go back to the neo-classical schools, and were studied in detail by Marshall (1890) and by Fisher (1930), who dedicated his book to Böhm-Bawerk (1889), "who laid the foundation upon which I have endeavored to build". The purpose of these studies was to determine the theoretical relationships between savings and interest rates in the economy. The notation used by these writers appears cumbersome to a modern reader, and in the following we shall use a notation which is due to Yaari (1964) and (1965).

2.2 The given element in the models we shall study is the consumer's income stream $y(t)$, a function of time t. The problem is to determine the optimal stream $c(t)$ for his expenditure on consumption. It is convenient to refer to the function $c(t)$ as a *consumption plan.* Any plan which can be carried out for a given income stream will be called a feasible plan.

If the consumer can neither borrow money, nor save money for future consumption, the feasible consumption plans will be defined by the inequality

$$c(t) \leq y(t)$$

This simply says that the consumer cannot at any time spend more than his income. Among the feasible plans, the plan $c(t) = y(t)$ will appear as the optimal one, under the usual assumption of non-saturation, i.e. if we assume that the consumer prefers to spend his income on consumption, rather than letting it be wasted.

2.3 In order to arrive at less trivial models, we must assume that the consumer has some possibilities of transferring money from one point of time to another, i.e. that he can reallocate his income over time. The simplest assumption of this kind is that the consumer can borrow or save any amount at the same rate of interest. For an arbitrary consumption plan, his accumulated savings at time t will then be

$$S(t) = e^{\delta t} \int_0^t e^{-\delta s} \big(y(s) - c(s)\big)\, ds$$

where δ is the force of interest.

It is natural to assume that there are some restriction on the consumer's borrowing. One restriction of this kind would be a condition:

$$S(T) \geq 0 \tag{1}$$

which says that the consumer must be solvent at time T. We can interpret T as his "planning horizon" — or that of his creditors.

A stricter condition would be:

$$S(t) \geq 0 \qquad \text{for } 0 \leq t \geq T \tag{2}$$

If this condition is imposed, the consumer is never allowed to be in debt, and it is not necessary to assume that interest rates are the same for borrowing and saving.

Either of the conditions (1) or (2) will give a set of feasible consumption plans, and it is evident that (2) will give the more restricted set. If no value is assigned to consumption beyond the horizon, we will have $S(T) = 0$ for the optimal plan — under the non-saturation assumptions.

2.4 It is not necessary to assume that $y(t)$ and $c(t)$ are continuous flows. We can define $Y(t)$ and $C(t)$ as accumulated income and consumption up to time t. Accumulated savings at time t will then be

$$S(t) = e^{\delta t}\left(\int_0^t e^{-\delta s}\, dY(s) - \int_0^t e^{-\delta s}\, dC(s)\right)$$

There is little to be gained by this trivial generalization, and it will not be used in the following discussion.

2.5 To select the optimal plan, we need a preference ordering over the set of feasible consumption plans. It is convenient if this ordering can be represented by a utility functional, i.e. a mapping from the set of feasible plans to the real line, which can be expressed in a simple analytical manner.

In economic theory one usually assumes that the utility assigned to an arbitrary consumption plan is given by an expression of the form:

$$U(c) = \int_0^T e^{-\gamma t} u\big(c(t)\big)\, dt \qquad (3)$$

Here γ represents the consumer's "impatience", i.e. his preference for consumption early rather than late in the planning period. For the instantaneous utility function $u(c)$ one usually assumes:

$$u'(c) > 0 \qquad \text{and} \qquad u''(c) < 0$$

Expression (3) dearly contains a number of "heroic assumptions", and the main merit of models of this type may be that they lead to problems which can be solved by relatively simple mathematical methods. One should however note that it is difficult even to describe other, and possibly more realistic preference orderings over sets of consumption plans.

2.6 We have now arrived at the problem of maximizing (3), subject to some condition, such as (1) or (2), which will keep the maximal finite. From the definition of accumulated savings $S(t)$ we find

$$S'(t) = \delta S(t) + y(t) - c(t)$$

or

$$c(t) = y(t) + \delta S(t) - S'(t)$$

Substituting this in (3) we arrive at the problem of maximizing:

$$\int_0^T e^{-\gamma t} u\big(y(t) + \delta S(t) - S'(t)\big)\, dt$$

This expression is of the form

$$\int_0^T F\big(t, x(t), x'(t)\big)\, dt$$

so the problem is reduced to a problem in the classical calculus of variation. A solution to the problem must satisfy the Euler equation

$$\frac{\partial F}{\partial x} = \frac{d}{dt}\left(\frac{\partial F}{\partial x'}\right)$$

2.7 In our problem the Euler equation takes the form

$$\delta e^{-\gamma t} u'\big(c(t)\big) + d\Big[e^{-\gamma t} u'\big(c(t)\big)\Big]$$

which reduces to

$$c'(t) = (\gamma - \delta)\frac{u'\big(c(t)\big)}{u''\big(c(t)\big)} \tag{4}$$

or

$$u'\big(c(t)\big) = Ke^{(\gamma-\delta)t} \tag{4'}$$

Here K is an arbitrary positive constant, which occurs because the solution of the problem remains the same if the utility function is multiplied by a positive constant.

From (4) it follows that $c(t)$ will be constant if $\gamma = \delta$, i.e. if the rate of impatience is equal to the rate of interest. If $\gamma > \delta$, $c(t)$ will be monotonic decreasing, and if $\gamma < \delta$, $c(t)$ will be monotonic increasing.

If by pure chance the solution of the problem should be $c(t) = y(t)$, the consumer will neither borrow nor save. In general it will however be to his advantage to transfer income from one period to another.

2.8 It may be useful to give a simple example to illustrate the results above. Let $u(c) = \log c$. The differential equation (4) then becomes

$$c'(t) = (\delta - \gamma)c(t)$$

with the solution

$$c(t) = Ae^{(\delta-\gamma)t}$$

The constant of integration $A = c(0)$ must be determined so that condition (1) is satisfied, with equality, i.e. we must have

$$\int_0^T e^{-\delta t} y(t)\,dt = \int_0^T e^{-\delta t} c(t)\,dt = A \int_0^T e^{-\gamma t}\,dt$$

Let us further assume $y(t) = y =$ constant for $0 \leq t \leq T$.

If in this case $\delta > \gamma$, we will have $c(t) < y$ in the beginning of the period, and $c(t) > y$ towards the end. This plan will be feasible, also if the stricter condition (2) is imposed.

If on the other hand $\delta < \gamma$, we have $c(t) > y$ in the beginning of the period, and this plan is not feasible under condition (2). The optimal feasible plan will then be $c(t) = y$. In this case the introduction of credit facilities would relax the condition (2), and allow the consumer to adopt a better consumption plan.

3. Models with Uncertainty and Insurance

3.1 In a world of complete certainty there are no compelling reasons for not giving credit to a consumer, provided that his future income is sufficient to repay the debt with interest. If however there is a possibility that the income stream may be cut off at any time, potential creditors may impose the strict condition (2), and not allowing the consumer to be in debt.

To formulate this idea in a simple manner, we shall assume that the income stream $y(t)$ is given, but that it at any time can drop to zero for the rest of the planning period. Let $\pi(t)$ be the probability that the income stream flows at time t. We have $\pi(0) = 1$.

As a concrete interpretation we can think of situations in which the income ceases because the consumer becomes permanently disabled, or unemployed. The traditional purpose of saving is just to build up a reserve for such events.

3.2 The problem of the consumer must now be reformulated, and it is natural to assume that he will maximize expected utility:

$$\int_0^T e^{-\gamma t} \Big[\pi(t) u\big(c(t) + y(t)\big) + \big(1 - \pi(t)\big) u\big(c(t)\big) \Big]\,dt \tag{5}$$

subject to some conditions such as (1) or (2).

As in para 2.6 we can find a differential equation which accumulated savings must satisfy, and solve a problem in the calculus of variation.

This solution to the problem seems inefficient, since it may lead to an accumulation of savings which will not be "needed" if the income stream is maintained until time T, i.e. until the end of the planning period. The introduction of insurance will make it possible for the consumer to obtain an income $c(t)$ for consumption if, and only if, his earnings $y(t)$ stops. This possibility may then help the consumer, just as credit facilities did in para 2.8.

3.3 To make things simple, we shall assume that he hands his whole income $y(t)$ over to an insurance company. In return he receives a stream $c(t)$, which he can use for consumption.

The principle of equivalence implies that we must have

$$\int_0^T \pi(t)y(t)e^{-\delta t}\,dt - \int_0^T c(t)e^{-\delta t}\,dt = 0 \qquad (6)$$

This condition which defines the feasible consumption plans, plays the same role as condition (1) in the previous section.

The prospective reserve of the insurance arrangement at time t is:

$$V(t) = e^{\delta t}\int_t^T c(s)e^{-\delta s}\,ds - e^{\delta t}\int_t^T \pi(s)y(s)e^{-\delta s}\,ds$$

For any insurance contract one usually requires that the reserve shall be non-negative, i.e. that

$$V(t) \geq 0 \qquad (7)$$

This is obviously equivalent to condition (2), and the conditions (2) and (7) are usually imposed for similar reasons.

3.4 Insurance has removed the uncertainty, so the problem of the consumer is now

$$\max \int_0^T e^{-\gamma t}u\big(c(t)\big)\,dt \qquad (8)$$

subject to condition (6), or to the stricter condition (7).

From the definition of the reserve we find

$$V'(t) = \delta V(t) + \pi(t)y(t) - c(t)$$

We can use this to substitute for $c(t)$, and obtain a problem in the calculus of variation.

To compare the two problems (5) and (8), we note that expected income at time t is

$$E\{y(t)\} = \pi(t)y(t)$$

Hence the former problem can be written

$$\max \int_0^T e^{-\gamma t} E\{u(\delta S - S' + y)\}\, dt \tag{5'}$$

and the second

$$\max \int_0^T e^{-\gamma t} u\Big(\delta V - V' + E\{y(t)\}\Big)\, dt \tag{8'}$$

Formally the two problems are identical, and they will have identical solutions, provided that the stricter conditions (2) and (7) do not become effective.

As we have assumed that $u(c)$ is concave, it follows from Jensen's inequality that we have

$$E\{u(y)\} < u(E\{y\})$$

so that problem (8) gives a higher utility than problem (5).

3.5 We have introduced insurance in a rather artificial way. A more conventional way would be to assume that the consumer agrees to pay a stream of premiums $p(t)$ as long as his income flows. In return he receives an income stream $c(t)$ if the stream $y(t)$ should stop. The problem is then to determine an insurance plan which will make it possible to carry out the best possible consumption plan. Formally the problem is as before to maximize

$$\int_0^T e^{\gamma t} u(c(t))\, dt$$

Under this plan accumulated savings at time t will be:

$$S(t) = e^{\delta t} \int_0^t \big(y(s) - c(s) - p(s)\big) e^{-\delta s}\, ds$$

The retrospective reserve under the insurance contract at time t will be:

$$V(t) = e^{\delta t} \int_0^t \pi(s)p(s)e^{\delta s}\, ds - e^{\delta t} \int_0^t \big(1 - \pi(s)\big)c(s)e^{-\delta s}\, ds$$

Differentiating these two equations, and eliminating $p(t)$, we obtain an expression for $c(t)$ which can be substituted into the maximal. The problem then takes a familiar form. If we impose no other conditions on $S(t)$ and $V(t)$ than simple boundary conditions, such as

$$S(0) = S(T) = 0$$

and

$$V(0) = V(T) = 0$$

the problem can be solved by classical calculus of variation.

It can be shown that under the optimal plans $c(t) + p(t) = y(t)$ i.e. $S(t) = 0$, so that all saving takes place by building up reserves in the insurance company. This result should not be surprising, since insurance does not lead to any savings which may not be needed.

3.6 The premium is determined by the principle of equivalence, i.e. the equation

$$V(T) = 0 \quad \text{or} \quad \int_0^T \pi(t)p(t)e^{-\delta t}\, dt = \int_0^T \big(1 - \pi(t)\big)c(t)e^{-\delta t}\, dt$$

Any function $p(t)$ which satisfies this equation represents a feasible premium plan, although one would usually also require that $V(t) \geq 0$.

In conventional insurance contracts the function $p(t)$ is usually of a simple form, for instance $p(t) = p =$ constant. In such cases the difference $y(t) - p(t) - c(t)$ will be saved, or if negative must be covered from accumulated savings. Hence an inflexible plan for paying premiums may force the consumer to save in the conventional way. The point may have some practical interest. Why should a consumer have to put money into the bank in order to pay future "level premiums" to his insurance company?

4. Life Insurance

4.1 Let us now assume that the income stream ceases only with the consumer's death. If we assume that his need for consumption dies with him, the models in the preceding section do no longer apply. The upper limit T in the integral in the objective function (3), was interpreted as the consumer's planning horizon. His life time is a very natural planning horizon indeed, so let us interpret T as the time of the consumer's death. Clearly T is a stochastic variable, and its probability density is

$$f(T) = \frac{\ell_{x+T}}{\ell_x}\mu_{x+T}$$

Here ℓ_x is the mortality table, and μ_x is the force of mortality. It is really unnecessary to introduce the symbol x, representing the consumer's age, but it is convenient to do so, since this makes it possible to use the standard actuarial notation.

4.2 The expected utility of the lifetime consumption is then obtained from (3)

$$U = \int_0^\infty \left[\int_0^T e^{-\gamma t} u\big(c(t)\big)\,dt\right] \frac{\ell_{x+T}}{\ell_x}\mu_{x+T}\,dt = \int_0^\infty e^{-\gamma t}\frac{\ell_{x+t}}{\ell_x}u\big(c(t)\big)\,dt$$

Hence the problem is to maximize

$$\int_0^\infty e^{-\gamma t}\frac{\ell_{x+t}}{\ell_x}u\big(c(t)\big)\,dt \tag{9}$$

subject to some conditions.

The principle of equivalence requires that the expected discounted value of income must be equal to that of the expenditure on consumption, i.e.

$$\int_0^\infty e^{-\delta t}\frac{\ell_{x+t}}{\ell_x}\big(y(t) - c(t)\big)\,dt = 0 \tag{10}$$

As in para 3.3 we can assume that the consumer agrees to pay his whole income $y(t)$ to an insurance company, and in return receives funds $c(t)$ for consumption. The prospective reserve for this insurance contract is

$$V(t) = e^{\delta t}\int_t^\infty e^{-\delta s}\frac{\ell_{x+s}}{\ell_{x+t}}\big(c(s) - y(s)\big)\,ds$$

and we find

$$V'(t) = (\delta + \mu_{x+t})V(t) + y(t) - c(t) \tag{11}$$

It is usual to require that the reserve for an insurance contract must be non-negative, i.e. that

$$V(t) \geq 0 \tag{12}$$

4.3 We have now arrived at the problem of maximizing (9) subject to the condition (12). If we carry out the maximization under only the weaker condition (10), we can determine $c(t)$ from (11), substitute in (9), proceed as in Subsection 2, and arrive at the same result. We find that the optimal consumption plan is determined by the differential equation

$$c'(t) = (\gamma - \delta)\frac{u'\big(c(t)\big)}{u''\big(c(t)\big)}$$

As $u'(c) > 0$ and $u''(c) < 0$ it follows that $c'(t) < 0$ if $\gamma > \delta$. This is Fisher's case of high impatience. The consumer will be eager for early consumption, and his optimal plan will be represented by a decreasing function $c(t)$.

This is not a reasonable result. It may of course happen that a person has a high consumption early in life, and that his consumption decreases steadily. It is however difficult to accept that a consumption pattern of this form should be the outcome of deliberate lifelong planning. Most people seem to plan for progress, and to improve their lot.

The case $\delta > \gamma$ does not appear much more reasonable, although a person may conceivably plan so that he can enjoy an increasing consumption all through his life.

4.4 To throw more light on the two questions raised above, we shall study a simple special case. Let as in para 2.8 $u(c) = \log c$. The differential equation which determines $c(t)$ then has the solution

$$c(t) = c(0)e^{(\delta-\gamma)t}$$

Let us further assume that $y(t) = y$ for $0 \leq t \leq n$, and $y(t) = 0$ for $n < t$. This is a case of a typical old age pension.

The initial value $c(0)$ is determined by (10), i.e.

$$y \int_0^n e^{-\delta t}\frac{\ell_{x+t}}{\ell_x}\,dt = c(0)\int_0^\infty e^{-\gamma t}\frac{\ell_{x+t}}{\ell_x}\,dt$$

The premium to be paid for this pension plan is

$$p(t) = y - c(t) \qquad \text{for } 0 \leq t \leq n$$

Under condition (12), the plan will not be feasible if $c(0) > y$. In this case it may be optimal to consume the whole income early in life, with good intentions of beginning to pay into a pension plan at some later date.

It is difficult to accept that the consumption plan we have found is superior to the more conventional plan with $c(t) = c =$ constant. The feasible constant consumption level will then be determined by

$$y\bar{a}_{x:n} = c\bar{a}_x$$

and it will be paid for by the level premium $p = y - c$ up to time n.

The paradoxes we have found are due to our rather arbitrary assumptions about the utility function. We shall however not study utility functions which lead to more reasonable results. Instead we shall discuss a more real paradox.

4.5 Let us assume that the consumer has no income in the first part of the planning period. He may then borrow money for consumption, and secure the loan by life insurance. Let $c(t)$ and $p(t)$ be the flow functions representing respectively consumption and premium payment.

At time t the accumulated debt of the consumer will be

$$S(t) = e^{\delta t} \int_0^t \big(c(s) + p(s)\big) e^{-\delta s}\, ds \tag{13}$$

The premium must be sufficient to pay for a life insurance with an amount $S(t)$ payable if the consumer dies at time t. The principle of equivalence then gives the relation

$$\int_0^t p(s) \frac{\ell_{x+s-\delta s}}{\ell_x}\, ds = \int_0^t S(s) \frac{\ell_{x+s}}{\ell_x} \mu_{x+s} e^{-\delta s}\, ds$$

We see that this equation is satisfied for $p(t) = S(t)\mu_{x+t}$. This corresponds to a pure risk insurance, or a "renewable term" contract. The reserve for this insurance is zero, so that the non-negativity condition (12) is satisfied. Substituting the expression for $p(t)$ in (13), we obtain

$$S(t) = e^{\delta t} \int_0^t \big(c(s) + \mu_{x+s} S(s)\big) e^{-\delta s}\, ds$$

Differentiating we obtain the differential equation

$$S'(t) = (\delta + \mu_{x+t}) S(t) + c(t)$$

which has the solution

$$S(t) = \int_0^t c(s) e^{-\int_s^t (\delta + \mu_{x+r})\, dr}\, ds$$

or in the standard actuarial notation

$$S(t) = \int_0^t \frac{D_{x+s}}{D_{x+t}} c(s)\, ds$$

4.6 In the problem discussed above there are no obvious limits neither to $c(t)$ nor to t. Hence a person with no prospective income should be able to maintain an arbitrary high level of consumption for any finite period of time, if he is allowed to play the "insurance game" we have outlined.

Apparently nobody loses in the game. The insurance company will receive the premiums, and pay the corresponding amount on the death of the consumer. The lender will receive the loan back, with compound interest when the consumer dies. There are no obvious institutional difficulties. There should for instance be no legal objections if the lender himself takes out life insurance on the consumer, pays the premiums and adds them, with interest to the loan.

Yaari (1965) recognizes the paradox, but dismisses it with an assumption that the "company will refuse to issue life insurance after the consumer reaches a certain age". This is correct, but the age limit is in most countries between 70 and 90, so this is not a very satisfactory explanation. To a man in his early twenties, half a century of no work and unrestrained consumption, even if a day of reckoning is bound to come, may seem an attractive prospect.

4.7 Fisher (1930) does not discuss the paradox explicitly, but he recognizes the legitimacy of "consumption loans to anticipate improvement in financial condition". It is however clear from his book that Fisher would have tried to explain the paradox by macro-economic arguments. Nobody can consume more than his income, unless somebody else is willing to save a part of his income and lend it to the impatient consumer. In Fisher's world consumers who want to play the "insurance game" may be unable to find lenders.

This is however not a complete explanation. The interest rate should bring about equilibrium between demand from borrowers and supply from lenders, but it is clear that higher interest would not deter a consumer who wanted to play the game. An increase in the interest rate would just drive out of the market those who want to borrow for investment purposes.. Hence life insurance backing for consumer loans must create some inflationary pressure, simply because it makes possible consumption which otherwise would have to be postponed.

The real paradox behind these observations may be that life insurance companies, whose very existence seems to be threatened by inflation, contribute to the inflation by selling term insurance to cover loans which may accelerate consumption. We shall not discuss this question further, since it seems to merit a separate paper. It may however be of interest to mention that Fisher observes that "such loans are made perhaps most often in Great Britain" (Fischer (1930, p. 358)), a country which has the world's most developed insurance institutions, and also an unenviable rate of inflation.

5. *Insurance for the Benefit of Survivors*

5.1 We have so far considered life insurance only as a mean to smother a fluctuating income stream over an uncertain life time. The solution to the problems considered made certain that the consumer left no unspent savings at his death. Much life insurance is however written for the explicit purpose of leaving liquid assets as "bequests" to heirs. We must therefore conclude that some people assign utility to leaving such bequests.

To bring this element into the model we can assume that the person's consumption insurance plan consists of two elements:

(i) a consumption plan for his life time $c(t)$;

(ii) an amount $B(t)$ payable as bequest to the consumer's heirs if he should die at time t.

With given resources, i.e. when the income stream $y(t)$ is given, a set of pairs $\big(c(t), B(t)\big)$ will appear as feasible. The first problem is then to establish a preference ordering over a set of such pairs.

With the assumptions we have made earlier, it is natural to assume that the utility assigned to an arbitrary pair is

$$\int_0^\infty e^{-\gamma t}\frac{\ell_{x+T}}{\ell_x}u\big(c(t)\big)\,dt + \int_0^\infty \beta(t)\frac{\ell_{x+T}}{\ell_x}\mu_{x+T}w\big(B(t)\big)\,dt \tag{14}$$

Here we have written $\beta(t)$ rather than $e^{-\beta t}$, because it seems a little artificial to assume that bequests should be discounted at a constant rate.

The function $w(B)$ represents the utility of a bequest B. Expression (14) is Yaari's criterion function in standard actuarial notation.

5.2 In order to determine the feasible pairs, we can again assume that the consumer pays his whole income $y(t)$ to an insurance company, which in return gives him a pair $\big(c(t), B(t)\big)$. The principle of equivalence then requires that

$$\int_0^\infty e^{-\gamma t}\frac{\ell_{x+T}}{\ell_x}y(t)\,dt = \int_0^\infty e^{-\gamma t}\frac{\ell_{x+T}}{\ell_x}\big(c(t)+\mu_{x+T}B(t)\big)\,dt \tag{15}$$

The prospective reserve of this insurance contract is

$$V(t) = e^{\delta t}\int_t^\infty e^{-\delta s}\frac{\ell_{x+s}}{\ell_{x+t}}\big(c(s)+\mu_{x+s}B(s)-y(s)\big)\,ds \tag{16}$$

From this we obtain

$$V'(t) = (\delta+\mu_{x+t})V(t) + y(t) - \big(c(t)+\mu_{x+t}B(t)\big)$$

We can use this to find an expression for $c(t)+\mu_{x+t}B(t)$, and substitute in (14). The problem of maximizing (14) is then reduced to a problem in the classical calculus of variation. The problem becomes more complicated if we impose the natural condition:

$$V(t) \geq 0$$

5.3 It is not possible to discuss the shape of the solution in any detail, without making some assumptions about the functions $u(c)$, $w(B)$ and $\beta(t)$. It is however not easy to decide which assumptions one should reasonably make, and the literature we have referred to has little to say about this question.

If the purpose of the insurance is to provide income for a surviving widow, it may be natural to put $B(t) = b\bar{a}_{z+t}$, where z is the age of the wife when the insurance arrangement is made. The function $c(t)$ and b must satisfy (15), and be determined so that (14), or some other criterion function is maximized.

This arrangement will give the widow a lump sum, sufficient to buy a life-long annuity for an amount b.

5.4 The arrangement we have outlined may be inefficient for two reasons:

(i) if the widow does not want a constant consumption plan, she will after the death of the husband have to solve the problem discussed in Section 4, and determine her own optimal consumption-insurance plan;

(ii) the wife may die before the husband, and in this case the bequest will be "wasted" in the same way as the conventional savings discussed in Section 2.

The more general approach would consist in specifying three consumption plans $c_1(t)$, $c_2(t)$ and $c_3(t)$ for respectively the couple, the surviving widow, and the surviving widower. The principle of equivalence will then give the feasible plans, which must satisfy the condition

$$\int_0^\infty y(t)\frac{D_{x+t}}{D_x}\,dt = \int_0^\infty \big(c_1(t) - c_2(t) - c_3(t)\big)\frac{D_{x+t,z+t}}{D_{xz}}\,dt + \int_0^\infty c_2(t)\frac{D_{z+t}}{D_z}\,dt + \int_0^\infty c_3(t)\frac{D_{x+t}}{D_x}\,dt$$

The optimal triplet must then be determined so that some criterion function is maximized.

It does not seem realistic to assume that a family shall be able to specify its preferences for future consumption in the form of a criterion function, even more complicated than (14). Such assumptions must however be made by those who design or sell pension plans for group of families. Governmental plans are usually established through a democratic process, and private plans are sold, so we must assume that the plans we find in real life, in some sense are close to optimal. These plans do however differ considerably from one country to another, and from one group to another. If they all are optimal, there must be wide differences in the underlying preferences. If we don't accept this conclusion, we should examine existing plans critically. It may be possible to improve them, without violating the principle of equivalence, which simply says that you pay for what you get.

5.5 To generalize our model, we can consider the family as the unit, and introduce the notation:

$\pi_s(t)$ = the probability that the family shall be in state s at time t. Here

$$\sum_{s=1}^{n} \pi_s(t) = 1$$

$y_s(t)$ = the family's income at time t, if it is in state s.

$c_s(t)$ = the family's consumption at time t, if it is in state s.

The principle of equivalence then gives

$$\sum_{s=1}^{n} \int_0^\infty e^{-\delta t} \pi_s(t) \big(y_s(t) - c_s(t) \big) \, dt = 0$$

This equation gives the set of feasible consumption plans $c_s(t)$ for the different states. The given elements are the income streams $y_s(t)$ and the state probabilities $\pi_s(t)$. In order to determine the optimal plan, we need information about the family's preferences, and this may be difficult to obtain in an articulate form.

If the purpose of life insurance is to provide income for the family in different states, there is no need for the conventional insurance contract with a lump sum payable at death — or more generally — when the family makes a transition from one state to another. This contract is however flexible in the sense that it makes it possible for the family to readjust its consumption plan after a change of state. The flexibility may be worth some theoretical loss in efficiency, at least to the normal family unable to specify a complete preference ordering over future consumption in all possible states.

References for Section 4

Bøhm-Bawerk E. (1889): *Positive Theorie des Kapitals*, Vienna.

Denenberg HS. (1970): "Author's Reply", *The Journal of Risk and Insurance*, 648–654.

Fischer S. (1973): "A Life Cycle Model of Life Insurance Purchasing", *International Economic Review*, 132–152.

Fischer I. (1930): *The Theory of Interest*, Macmillan.

Josephson HD. (1970): "A New Concept of the Economics of Life Value and the Human Life Value: Comment", *The Journal of Risk and Insurance*, 641–643.

Marshall A. (1890): *Principles of Economics*, Macmillan.

Richard SF. (1975): "Optimal Consumption, Portfolio and Life Insurance. Rules for an Uncertain Lived Individual in a Continuous Time Model", *Journal of Financial Economics*, 187–203.

Yaari ME. (1964): "On the Existence of an Optimal Plan in a Continuous Time Allocation Process", *Econometrica*, 576–590.

Yaari ME. (1965): "Uncertain Lifetime, Life Insurance, and the Theory of the Consumer", *Review of Economic Studies*, 137–150.

5. Life Insurance and Consumption*

The main purpose of life insurance is to provide income for consumption. The ordinary life policy provides a lump sum or a guaranteed income to dependents when the breadwinner dies. Pension insurance or life annuities provide income to the retired and to other who obtain no income from their own work. Life insurance is thus a form of saving for the rainy day, and it is usually superior to the conventional forms of saving. The reason is simply that the consumer's savings must be sufficient to cover only his expected, or average needs, and not his needs under the most unfavorable circumstances.

In the following it will be argued that life insurance may do its job a little too efficiently, and that this may have some undesirable effects. The letter contains no results which are really new. Most of them have been found by many authors, apparently first by Yaari and Hakansson, who studied the optimal strategies of savers and investors. In the discussion below the focus is shifted to the effects which these optimal strategies may have on the rest of the economy.

A convenient starting point is the usual consumption — saving model. A person's plan for future expenditure on consumption can be represented by a continuous function of time, $c(t)$. Whether a plan is feasible or not will depend on the person's income, represented by a function $y(t)$. Feasibility will also depend on the facilities for saving and borrowing, i.e., on the possibilities of transferring income from one period and use it for consumption in another.

One will get the simplest case by assuming that the consumer can save or borrow any amount at the same rate of interest δ. In this case it is reasonable to assume that a plan is feasible if it satisfies the condition

$$\int_0^T e^{-\delta t}\big(y(t) - c(t)\big)\, dt \geq 0 \tag{1}$$

where T is some planning horizon. Essentially (1) implies that the consumer must settle his debts before the time T.

If there is a possibility that the income stream will terminate, for instance at the death of the consumer, his creditors may suffer a loss. They may

---

* Reprinted from *Economics Letters*, 1980; 6(2):103–106, copyright (c) North-Holland, Amsterdam.

therefore impose the stronger condition

$$\int_0^t e^{-\delta s}\big(y(s) - c(s)\big)\, ds \geq 0 \tag{2}$$

for all t. The condition (2) is natural if the consumer has no assets which can be offered as collateral for a loan.

To consider life insurance, introduce $\Pi(t)$ = the probability that the consumer shall be alive at the time t. The probability density of the event that he dies at time t is then $-\Pi'(t)$.

The consumer's lifetime is a natural planning horizon. The time of death must however be represented by a stochastic variable, so one is led to require that condition (2) holds only as an expectation, i.e.

$$-\int_0^\infty \int_0^t e^{-\delta s}\big(y(s) - c(s)\big)\, ds\Pi'(t)\, dt \geq 0\,,$$

or, assuming $\Pi(\infty) = 0$

$$\int_0^\infty e^{-\delta t}\big(y(t) - c(t)\big)\, \Pi(t)\, dt \geq 0 \tag{3}$$

The condition (3) says that the expected discounted expenditure on consumption cannot exceed the expected discounted income of the consumer. It will apply if a group of consumers join — or form — an insurance company selling life annuities. The company will usually require

$$\int_0^t e^{-\delta s}\big(y(s) - c(s)\big)\, \Pi(s)\, ds \geq 0 \tag{4}$$

for all t. This corresponds to condition (2), and implies that the consumer's net saving, or his 'premium reserve' is not allowed to be negative.

Under the strict condition (2) the consumer cannot die insolvent, which implies that he can be expected to leave some positive assets when he dies. Under the weaker condition (4) he will leave nothing behind. This shows that life annuities are superior to conventional saving, since no money which the consumer would like to spend, is 'wasted' by being left to his heirs.

To study the effect of ordinary life insurance, consider a whole life policy for an amount b. The single net premium for this insurance contract is

$$p = -b\int_0^\infty e^{-\delta t}\Pi'(t)\, dt = b\left(1 - \delta\int_0^\infty e^{-\delta t}\Pi(t)\, dt\right)$$

A fully paid insurance policy of this kind is usually an acceptable collateral for a loan, even if it was not bought for such purposes. Hence this use of life insurance will release the consumer from the severe restrictions imposed by condition (2). For an arbitrary consumption plan the accumulated debt at time t is

$$a(t) = e^{\delta t} \int_0^t e^{-\delta s} \big(c(s) - y(s) \big)\, ds$$

The plan will be feasible if the creditors accept the life insurance contract as collateral for the loan. Assuming that the consumer borrows money also to pay for the premium, one is led to the condition

$$b \geq a(t) + p$$

for all t. The condition can be written in the form

$$b\delta \int_0^\infty e^{-\delta t} \Pi'(t)\, dt \geq \int_0^t e^{-\delta s} \big(c(s) - y(s) \big)\, ds \tag{5}$$

This is clearly a condition far weaker than (2). In fact for any finite consumption plan, and for any finite t, one can find a sum insured b, so that (5) is satisfied. This is possible even when the consumer has no income, so this simple insurance arrangement should allow a person to carry out a consumption plan virtually independent of his income — if any.

The arrangement is not as farfetched as it may seem, and this can be illustrated by a numerical example. With the actuarial tables used in most industrialized countries, and with 4 percent interest, the net single premium for a man at age 25 will be about 0.2 per unit of sum insured. Taking $c(t) = 1$ and $y(t) = 0$ the accumulated debt after 20 years will, with 4 percent interest, be about 30, and this gives the condition

$$b \geq 30 + 0.2b \qquad \text{or} \qquad b \geq 37.5$$

The situation will not be substantially different in the real world, although a loading will be added to the net premium, and 4 percent seems today a low rate of interest for a consumer's loan. It is not usual that a young man with only vague prospects of future income, buys a whole life policy with a face value of about 40 times his desired annual consumption, but most companies will be delighted to sell it to him. They may inquire about his health, but not into his financial circumstances, as long as he is ready to pay the single premium on the spot.

Evidently a day of reckoning will come to this young man, when his debt exceeds the amount covered by his life insurance. At that time the only ways out seem to be death or bankruptcy, and the choice should be easy in a society where bankruptcy is not considered a fate worse than death.

The example above may be extreme, but it clearly represents a use of life insurance which will allow consumption to exceed income over long periods. In a world plagued by inflation this could be the cause of some concern.

References for Section 5

Hakansson NH. (1969): Optimal investment and consumption strategies under risk, and uncertain lifetime and insurance. *International Economic Review 10*, 443–466.

Yaari ME (1965): Uncertain lifetime, life insurance, and the theory of the consumer. *Review of Economic Studies 32*, 137–150.

CHAPTER 5

BUSINESS INSURANCE

1. Insurance bought by Business Enterprises

1.1 Business insurance is of course the insurance that businessmen buy for themselves or on behalf of their corporations. There are many different lines of business insurance, and traditionally these are treated separately in the insurance literature.

The oldest line of business insurance is marine insurance. In Roman law bottomer loans (*foenus nauticum*) played an important part. These loans made it possible for a merchant to borrow money to buy and equip a ship for an expedition. Under a loan of this kind the owner of the ship repaid the loan, with interest only if the vessel returned safely from its voyage. If the ship was lost, the loan was not repaid. Under this arrangement the lender carried a considerable risk, and he naturally charged an appropriate rate of interest. Some historians maintain that the origin of marine insurance is the Catholic Church's ban on usury. Be this as it may, but the bottomer disappeared, and these loans with interest adjusted to the risk involved, were replaced by lending at the "risk-free" rate, and insurance, that is by pure risk-bearing with a high expected reward.

The rate of interest on a bottomer bond sometimes called "maritime interest", could be very high. As an illustration assume that the risk-free rate is r, and the probability that the ship shall be lost is p. Let the lender's utility function be $u(\cdot)$. He will then give the loan only if the rate of return R is such that the following condition is satisfied

$$u\big(L(1+r)\big) \leq pu(-L) + (1-p)u\big(L(1+R)\big)$$

Assume for simplicity that the lender is risk neutral. The condition then reduces to

$$1 + r \leq -p + (1-p)(1+R)$$

or

$$R \geq \frac{r + 2p}{l - p}$$

It seems that in many cases it was the lender, and not the owner who insured the ship. It is not likely that medieval markets were perfect, so such arbitrate operations might give handsome risk-free profits.

Marine insurance covers both the ship (hull) and the cargo, and it has been extended to include *over-land* transportation. In the U.S. marine insurance proper is usually referred to as "ocean marine", and insurance of goods transported by rail or road is referred to by the curious term "inland marine", because the first extension was to inland waterways. Transportation by air, as a recent arrival, is usually treated separately as Aviation insurance.

1.2 The second oldest branch of business insurance is "Fire insurance and allied lines". The "allied lines" have been extended to include any damage to business property, with special lines as Boiler and Machinery insurance. The branch also includes consequential losses, such as loss of profits caused by business interruption due to fire and other accidents.

Other lines of insurance which are important to business are liability insurance, and in some countries workers compensation.

In all industrial countries workers who are injurers on the job are entitled to compensation, and it is the employer who pays. Usually he pays through compulsory membership in some government operated insurance scheme, often affiliated with the national social security system. In many countries — countries with economies as different as Finland and U.S.A. — employers cover their liability to injured workers by insurance with private companies.

Liability insurance is important to business firms, and can be expected to increase in importance in the future, since there seems to be a trend towards stricter liability legislation. Product liability insurance in particular seems to cause problems in many countries.

1.3 The lines of insurance discussed above all present their particular problems, and special expertise is required in any of the lines both to set premium rates, and to settle claims. Historically most of the lines were first introduced by small specialized insurance companies, confining their underwriting to only one line. Gradually these companies extended their field of activity, or merged with other companies writing related lines. This led to the situation which we have known for at least one generation, where any major insurance company can offer any kind of insurance needed by a business corporation.

These insurance companies are operated by people who usually consider themselves as businessmen, and the owners, that is the share-holders have made their investment in order to make profits. Hence business insurance can be seen as an instrument for risk-sharing within the business community, and it is natural to analyse the situation with the methods discussed in Chapters 2 and 3. An analysis along these lines might lead to results which could be useful in practice.

1.4 Should it turn out that the insurance arrangements made within the existing institutional framework do not appear to be Pareto optimal, something might be wrong. It is then tempting to conclude that it must be possible to find another arrangement that would be better for all parties involved. Some caution is however required. Well established business practices may be due just to conventional thinking, but they may also have more subtle justifications that are not immediately obvious to the eager young MBA.

It may also happen that an arrangement which is Pareto optimal, seems to cost too much to certain participants, i.e. they pay more than the equilibrium premiums determined in Chapter 3. Again some caution is called for. In Chapter 1 we discussed the decomposition of an insurance premium into three components:

$$P = E\{x\} + A + R$$

It was observed in business insurance the last term, the risk premium might be substantial, but that the second term on the right-hand side could be insignificant. This may be the case in some well-established line of insurance, such as covering a jumbo jet. This insurance contract will be risky, but the transaction costs will not be important. There will usually be a market rate for this kind of insurance, and an insurer who quotes a premium can be reasonable certain that he can obtain reinsurance "on original terms". Things may be different for any new type of insurance contract, say cover for a new kind of off-shore oil installation. For this contract extensive technical studies may be required to arrive at a premium rate acceptable to reinsurers, and hence the administrative expenses A is likely to be high.

2. Risk Sharing in Business

2.1 The oldest form of risk-sharing is probably to find partners in a risky venture. The Merchant of Venice, long before he was made immortal by Shakespeare, might have felt uneasy about using all his wealth to equip one ship and send it on a risky expedition to the Orient. He would probably feel much better if he owned a fractional interest of $1/n$ in n ships. If he was risk-averse this would give him a higher expected utility.

Assume that the probability that the ship will be lost is p, and that the expedition then will give a zero profit. The probability that the ship shall return safely from the voyage is $q = 1 - p$, and assume that the profit in this case will be 1.

The expected utility assigned to owning just one ship outright will then be

$$E\{u_1\} = pu(0) + qu(1)$$

As utility is determined only up to a positive linear transformation, one can take $u(0) = 0$ and $u(1) = 1$.

Hence we can write

$$E\{u_1\} = q \tag{1}$$

2.2 If the probability that a particular ship shall return safely is independent of the fate of the others, the expected utility of owning a fraction $1/n$ of n ships will be

$$E\{u_n\} = \sum_{k=0}^{n} \binom{n}{k} p^{n-k} q^k u\left(\frac{k}{n}\right) \tag{2}$$

If $u(k/n) = k/n$, the right-hand side of (2) takes the form

$$\frac{1}{n}\sum_{k=0}^{n} \frac{n!}{k!} p^{n-k} q^k k = \sum_{k=1}^{n} \frac{(n-1)!}{(k-1)!} p^{n-k} q^{k-1} = q = E\{u_1\}$$

If $u(k/n) > k/n$ for $k = 1, 2, \ldots, n-1$, the utility function is concave, and

$$E\{u_n\} > E\{u_1\}$$

Hence it is always advantageous to diversify investment in assets which are stochastically independent. For large n the risk can virtually be "diversified away". It is easy to see that

$$\lim_{n \to \infty} E\{u_n\} = u(q)$$

Since $u(\cdot)$ is assumed concave, it follows that $u(q) > q$ for $0 < q < 1$.

2.3 Another way of risk sharing is to organize a risky business as a company with limited liability. This means that the risk is shared between those who have provided the equity capital and those who have acquired claims against the company. If the company should go bankrupt, the former will lose their investment, and the latter will not have their claims completely settled. If the claims are acquired simply by lending money to the company this may be reasonable, as one must assume that the lenders have evaluated the risk and charged the appropriate rate of interest.

The situation may be different if the claims have arisen because the company has incurred product liability, for instance by manufacturing and selling food or drugs which have harmful or even fatal effects. In most countries there are laws which prevent businessmen from escaping such liabilities by establishing companies with limited liability. The law may for instance require such companies to carry sufficient liability insurance. In some cases the legislation opens possibilities of making the real owners, or the executives of the company personally liable for the claims.

2.4 In the following we shall discuss a simple example which may give some insight into the possibilities of risk-sharing in real life. A similar example has been discussed by Borch (1979).

Let the cost of building a ship be X, and let Y be the net revenue earned from operating the ship. Hence the profit obtained by ordering an operating the ship is $Y - X$.

Assume that the *Operator* orders the ship from the *Builder*, and that they agree on the price K. The Operator has an initial wealth W, and borrows $K - W$ from the *Banker* to pay the Builder. The rate of interest on the loan is r. This arrangement gives the following division of the profits among the three parties:

The Builder: $K - X$

The Banker: $r(K - W)$

The Operator: $Y - (1 + r)K + rW$

An arrangement of this kind is usually reached after bargaining or negotiations, and must include agreement on the values of the two "free" variables K and r. In this oversimplified, risk-free example it is not possible to say much about the outcome of the negotiations, except that a negative profit will not be accepted, i.e. the following conditions must hold: $K \geq X$ and $r \geq 0$.

2.5 As a first step toward generalization, assume that there is a positive probability that Y will take the value zero, for instance because the ship is lost at sea. This will make the Operator insolvent, and unable to repay his debt to the Banker. The cautious Banker may then require that the Operator insures his ship for at least the amount required to repay the loan $(1+r)(K-W)$. Assume that the Operator can insure the ship for an amount H, by paying a premium $P(H)$ to the *Insurer*. This arrangement will give the following division of the profits

	The ship is lost	The ship returns safely
Builder	$K - X$	$K - X$
Banker	$r(K - W)$	$r(K - W)$
Insurer	$P(H) - H$	$P(H)$
Operator	$H - P(H) - (1 + r)K + rW$	$Y - P(H) - (1 + r)K + rW$

Here it is assumed that $H \geq (1 + r)K - rW$, so that the Banker runs no risk. All risk is carried by the Insurer and the Operator. If the ship is insured for $H' = (1 + r)(K - W) + W + P(H')$, the whole risk is carried by the Insurer, and the Operator will escape with his initial wealth intact, also if the ship is lost.

The arrangement outlined above seems to correspond to the conventional thinking in marine insurance, and models of this kind seems to be behind the discussion of the subject in many textbooks. If all the four parties to the arrangement are risk averse, it is clearly not optimal that one of them should carry all the risk. The optimal arrangement must be of a form similar to the ones discussed in Chapter 2.

2.6 Before elaborating this point, it is useful to introduce two more generalizations:

(i) Assume that X, the building cost, is a random variable, so that the builder runs some risk by quoting a fixed price when the contract is signed. Further it is realistic to assume that the Builder grants some credit to the Operator, and that this is repaid a few years after the delivery of the ship.

(ii) Assume further that Y is a random variable which can take any value on the non-negative half-line, possibly only up to an upper limit.

With these assumptions it becomes natural to analyse the situation with the methods discussed in Chapter 2. The four parties to the arrangement have to agree *ex ante* on how the total profits $Z = Y - X$ shall be divided among themselves.

The situation is however not quite so symmetric as those discussed in Chapter 2. The Builder is obviously in a position to influence building costs X, and an efficient sharing rule must give him some incentive to keep these costs as low as possible.

Similarly the Operator may be able to influence Y, the net earnings of the ship by efficient management. The sharing-rule must contain incentives which keep him on his toes.

One of the pioneers in the study of incentives is Stiglitz (1974) and (1983). His starting point was an analysis of share-cropping, which can be seen as a special case of the model outlined above. Stiglitz has generalized the model, and has laid the foundations of a more general approach to the study of economic incentives.

2.7 If a group of businessmen is not satisfied with the offers received from insurance companies, the members of the group could set up a mutual insurance scheme of their own. All that is needed is really an informal agreement on how losses caused by specific random events and hitting some member, shall be shared by all. An arrangement of this kind can be described by a set of functions $y_r(x)$, $r = 1, 2, \ldots$, where $y_r(x)$ is the amount member r shall pay if total losses amount to x. Clearly one must have $\sum_r y_r(x) = x$, and it is natural to require that the functions $y_1(x)$, $y_2(x)$, $\ldots$, should satisfy the conditions of Pareto optimality given in Chapter 2.

An informal arrangement may work well for a small group, but in a larger group there might obviously be problems in collecting the contributions and enforcing the agreement. It was then natural to incorporate the informal risk-sharing agreement as an insurance company, a mutual, or a joint stock company, with members of the group as share owners.

According to Clayton (1971) the first group of businessmen to choose this course of action was the English sugar refiners. After years of dissatisfaction with the insurance offered by existing fire companies, the refiners formed an association in 1781, which in 1782 established the Phoenix Fire Office.

In the following two centuries many groups have followed the example of the sugar refiners. Taxi-owners and racehorse breeders have formed mutual companies to insure the risks special to their trades. In Norway the railway employees in 1895 formed their own mutual fire insurance company. Most of these employees had their homes situated close to the railway, and the established fire insurers maintained that this constituted an extra fire hazard and charged an extra premium in addition to the standard one.

Many of the insurance companies which have been set up in this way have had short lifes. Often the major insurance companies have admitted that the dissident group had a justified complaint, and have offered insurance on acceptable terms.

In other cases these companies have come to stay. They have somehow expanded their activity, and have gained access to international reinsurance markets. It is possible that these companies have some competitive advantages, and have been able to survive because they have as a base a group of fairly homogeneous risks.

2.8 An important group of insurance companies which have been set up for such special purposes are the *P&I Clubs* which offer "Protection and Indemnity" insurance to ship owners. The old standard marine policy of Lloyds covered only three-fourths of the liability which a ship could incur in a collision, and left a number of other liabilities completely uncovered. To cover these risks ship-owners formed the *P&I Clubs*, which in reality are mutual insurance companies.

It should be possible to include the risks covered by the *P&I* policy in an ordinary marine insurance contract, but it seems that the Clubs have certain advantages. The members are shipping companies, and their number is, even on a world-wide basis fairly limited. This means that some simplifications and some informality is possible. The premium paid is proportional to the gross tonnage of the vessel, and the number of votes a member can cast is proportional to the number of gross tons he has registered in the Club (See Winter (1952)).

2.9 The conclusion of this section is that businessmen don't really need insurance. It is always possible for them to get together, and go it alone. The market for business insurance depends above all on how imaginative insurers are in devising risk-sharing arrangements which are superior or more attractive than the arrangements a group of businessmen can carry out alone.

3. Captive Insurance Companies

3.1 Between the two World Wars some major European corporations set up "captive" insurance companies as wholly owned subsidiaries. The background seems to have been the following: A large corporation which owned plants and property at many different locations, and even in different countries, could rely almost completely on self insurance. At most the corporation might need insurance against accidents which could cause catastrophic losses. Under the lax systems of taxation which prevailed before World War I, the corporation could set aside reserves in an "insurance fund" to meet such losses.

Under the stricter taxation of corporate profits which emerged in the years following the War, corporations were not always allowed to deduct money from taxable income and use it to build up such emergency funds. Some corporations then decided to incorporate their "insurance fund" as an insurance company. According to the laws this company had to be placed under government supervision, and premiums paid to a supervised insurance company were deductible from taxable income — without question.

The captive insurance company was first seen as a technical device to avoid "unreasonable" taxation of a corporation that had decided to self-insure. Self-insurance can however lead to inconvenient fluctuations in the results of even a very large corporation. It is possible to reduce these fluctuations if the captive buys reinsurance in the market. This naturally leads to consideration of the possibility that the captive should also accept reinsurance from others, and in general act as a reinsurance company, taking part in the exchanges in the international market.

3.2 One of the oldest captive insurance companies in Europe is *Industriforsikring A/S* which began its operations in 1920. The company is a wholly owned subsidiary of Norsk Hydro, the largest industrial corporation in Norway. The shares of this corporation are quoted on all major stock exchanges in the world. The captive is licensed to write all kinds of property-casualty insurance, and all risks of the corporation are in the first instance insured with the captive. The captive company has no other customers than Norsk Hydro and its subsidiaries.

Table 5.1 shows Industriforsikring's portfolio of fire insurance contracts over the last 15 years. Column (3) shows considerable fluctuations in the loss ratio for the captive's direct insurance, so that the number of contracts is too small for the law of large numbers to apply. After reinsurance transactions the loss ratio becomes remarkably stable as is seen from column (6).

Table 5.1: Industriforsikring A/S: Fire insurance, premiums and claims, 1000 Norwegian Kroner.

	Direct Norwegian Insurance			Retained on own account		
	Premiums received (1)	Claims paid (2)	Loss Ratio (3)	Premiums received (4)	Claims paid (5)	Loss Ratio (6)
1983	63215	8815	0.14	73474	40227	0.55
1982	71790	55725	0.78	60405	32366	0.53
1981	65976	18105	0.27	46764	23697	0.51
1980	99870*	3775	0.04	44604	22829	0.51
1979	39134*	9449	0.24	30731	15709	0.51
1978	34261	26222	0.76	25727	14360	0.56
1977	24044	3303	0.14	18342	9779	0.54
1976	21365	29956	1.40	16935	9537	0.56
1975	18094	2426	0.13	14693	7627	0.52
1974	11379	1589	0.14	14056	7526	0.54
1973	9118	839	0.09	12991	7160	0.55
1972	6934	1255	0.18	13629	7880	0.57
1971	6757	4100	0.61	12801	7064	0.55
1970	5549	1827	0.32	11183	5929	0.53
1969	6185	4649	0.75	9619	5210	0.54

Source: *Sociétés d'assurance, 1983*, Oslo 1985
*In 1979–80 Norsk Hydro changed its accounting year, so the entries under direct insurance for these two years are not comparable with other entries.

In the direct insurance the average loss ratio for the 15 years is 0.40. Hence one can see the table as an example of how a risk-averse insurer trades expected profit against reduced variance. An enthusiast on portfolio models may even be led to — with some heroic assumptions — to use the table to estimate the insurer's risk aversion.

The average loss ratio is higher after reinsurance than before. This does not mean that the company has exchanged good business for bad. It is possible that a disastrous fire would lead to a loss more than ten times the annual premium. No such fire occurred in the 15 years covered by the table, but it could occur, say once in a century. Had it occurred, the average loss ratio of the direct insurance for the next 20 years would more than double, but the loss ratio for the retention on own account might have been practically unchanged. The very purpose of reinsurance is to give protection against such catastrophic losses.

Industriforsikring A/S is a success story, and it is not unique. There is however also a number of sad stories about inexperienced managers of captive insurance companies who have been badly burnt by their dealings in reinsurance markets.

3.3 In the 1960's there was another surge of captive insurance companies which now seems to have subsided. There are however still more than 1000 captive companies registered in Bermuda alone. The background for this second wave seems to have been different from that of the first one.

In modern management theory decentralization is considered an advantage, i.a. to avoid excessive corporately bureaucracy. One seeks to give each division of a corporation freedom to make its own decisions on investment, production, marketing etc. within budgetary limits set at the corporation's head-office. It would seem natural to leave the divisions free to establish their own policy also with regard to insurance, but this would be contrary to an overall corporate objective of self-insuring to the largest extent possible. One can then set up separate accounting unit at the corporate headquarters. This unit will charge each division with a premium corresponding to the risks which it represents. Should the division suffer losses due to fire or other accidents the accounting unit will automatically credit the budget of the division with the amount lost.

This system means of course that the corporation relies entirely on self-insurance. Usually even a very large corporation will buy some insurance from outsiders, for instance to cover catastrophic accidents. It is natural to let the accounting unit, which has rated the risk for internal purposes, handle the buying of insurance in the market. From here it is a relatively small step to incorporate the internal accounting unit as an insurance company. This will make it possible for the captive company to accept reinsurance from other insurers, for instance by reciprocal arrangements with other similar companies. The net effect of such arrangements will reduce expected cash outflow from the corporation, but there are obviously some risks involved.

3.4 It is of some interest to note that insurance in the countries in Eastern Europe has been built up with a similar motivation. In these countries practically all plants and production equipment as well as banks and financial institutions belong to the state, so the state must necessarily act as self-insurer. Most of these countries do however have active insurance companies. The main function of these companies seems to be to secure prompt settlement of compensation for losses suffered by producing units in the centrally directed economy.

3.5 A relatively new development is the captive reinsurance company. Some multinational corporations have found some advantages in insuring their assets with local insurers. To retain some control over the risks, the corporation will then require that the local insurance companies reinsure with a reinsurance company that is a wholly owned subsidiary of the corporation. The captive reinsurance company will then deal in the international reinsurance market.

The Swedish-based Electrolux Corporation established the captive *Electrolux Re.* in 1978. This company has during the last years received an annual premium of about Swedish Kronor 10 million.

References for Sections 1–3

Borch K. (1979): "Mathematical Models for Marine Insurance", *Scandinavian Actuarial Journal*, 25–36.

Clayton G. (1971): *British Insurance*, London: Elek.

Stiglitz J. (1974): "Incentives and Risk in Sharecropping", *Review of Economic Studies* *41*, 219–255.

Stiglitz J. (1983): "Risk, Incentives and Insurance", *The Geneva Papers 8*, 4–33.

Winter W. (1952): *Marine Insurance: Its Principles and Practice*, 3rd edition. McGraw-Hill.

4. Application of Game Theory to some Problems in Automobile Insurance*

Introduction

In this paper we shall study the problem of determining "correct" premium rates for sub-groups of an insurance collective. This problem obviously occurs in all branches of insurance. However, it seems at present to be a really burning issue in automobile insurance. We shall show that the problem can be formulated as a conflict between groups which can gain by co-operating, although their interests are opposed. When formulated in

* Reprinted from *The ASTIN Bulletin* 1962; 2(2):208–221.

this way, the problem evidently can be analysed and solved by the help of the "Game Theory" of Von Neumann and Morgenstern (1944).

1. Discussion of a Numerical Example

1.1 We shall first illustrate the problem by a simple example. We consider a group of $n_1 = 100$ persons, each of whom may suffer a loss of 1, with probability $P_1 = 0.1$. We assume that these persons consider forming an insurance company to cover themselves against this risk. We further assume that for some reason, government regulations or prejudices of managers, an insurance company must be organized so that the probability of ruin is less than 0.001.

If such a company is formed, expected claim payment will be

$$m = n_1 P_1 = 10$$

and the standard deviation of the claim polymers will be

$$\sigma = \sqrt{n_1 P_1 (1 - P_1)} = 3$$

If the government inspection (or the company's actuary) agrees that the ruin probability can be calculated with sufficient approximation by assuming that the claim payments have a normal distribution, the company must have funds amounting to

$$m + 3\sigma = 10 + 9 = 19$$

This means that the company must collect the following amount from the 100 persons:

	A net premium	10
+	a safety loading	9
=	Total premium	19

Hence each person in this group, which we shall call *Group* 1, must pay a premium of 0.19.

1.2 We then consider Group 2, which consists of $n_2 = 100$ persons for whom the probability of a one unit loss is $P_2 = 0.2$. If these persons form an insurance company, they will have to pay:

	Net premium	20
+	Safety loading	12
=	Total premium	32

in order to reach the security level required, i.e. each person will have to pay a premium of 0.32.

Assume now that the two groups join, and form one single company. In order to ensure that the ruin probability shall be less than 0.001, this company must have funds amounting to

$$n_1P_1 + n_2P_2 + 3\sqrt{n_1p_1(I - P_1) + n_2P_2(I - P_2)} = 10 + 20 + 15 = 45$$

1.3 We see from this example that it is to the advantage of the two groups to form one single company. Total payment of premium will then be 45, whilst it will be $19 + 32 = 51$ if each group forms its own company.

The open question is how this advantage shall be divided between the two groups. The classical actuarial argument is that each group shall be charged its "fair" premium. However, this principle has meaning only as far as the net premium is concerned, it does not say anything about how the safety loading should be divided between the two groups. The orthodox method would be to divide the safety loading *pro rata* between the two groups, i.e. to let them pay total premium of 15 and 30 respectively. The "fairness" of this rule is certainly open to question, since it gives Group 1 most of the gain accruing from the formation of one single company. In any case the rule is completely arbitrary.

The Theory of Games has as its purpose just to analyse such situations of conflicting interests. In some cases the theory will enable us to find a solution without resorting to arbitrary rules. In other cases the theory will make it clear that the problem in its very nature is indeterminate, and that some "additional assumption" or "arbitrary rule" is indeed required.

1.4 In the example we have analyzed, most actuaries will reject as "unfair" the suggestion that both groups should pay the same premium of 22.5, i.e. that each person should pay 0.225. The game theory also rejects this suggestion, but not on the basis of some arbitrary rule of fairness. In game theory one notes that Group 1 by forming its own company will have to pay a premium of 19. If the joint company demands a premium of 22.5, Group 1 will then break out and form its own company. This will increase the premium for Group 2 from 22.5 to 32. Hence it will be to the advantage of this group to offer some concession in order to keep Group 1 in the company. For instance if Group 1 is charged a premium of 18, it will lose if it breaks out and forms its own company. Group 2 will in this case have to pay a premium of 27, which is considerably less than 32, the premium Group 2 will have to pay if it cannot persuade Group 1 to stay in the joint company.

1.5 The considerations in the preceding paragraph do not give a determinate solution to our problem.

Let P_1 and P_2 be the amount of premium paid by the two groups. If the groups act "rationally" and form a joint insurance company, we have

$$P_1 + P_2 = 45$$

The groups will stay in this company only if $P_1 \leq 19$ and $P_2 \leq 32$, hence we must have

$$13 \leq P_1 \leq 19$$

$$26 \leq P_2 \leq 32$$

Any pair of premiums which satisfy the equation and the inequalities in this paragraph, will constitute an acceptable solution to our problem.

1.6 We now assume that a Group 3 enters the picture. Let $n_3 = 120$ and $p_3 = 0.3$. It is easy to see that if this group forms its own insurance company, the group will have to pay a total premium of

$$n_3 P_3 + 3\sqrt{n_3 p_3 (1 - p_3)} = 36 + 15 = 51$$

in order to keep the ruin probability under 0.001. If the three groups join to form one company, the total amount premium will be

$$10 + 20 + 36 + 21 = 87$$

As in the preceding paragraph we find the indeterminate solution, given by

$$P_1 + P_2 + P_3 = 87$$

$$4 \leq P_1 \leq 19$$

$$17 \leq P_2 \leq 32$$

$$36 \leq P_3 \leq 51$$

It may seem surprising that one of the two first groups actually may be charged an amount less than the net premium. However, this is not complete nonsense. If for instance Group 1 pays only 7, the two other groups together will have to pay 80, which is less than $32 + 51 = 83$ which they would have to pay if each of them had to form its own company.

1.7 The rather surprising result in the preceding paragraph cannot materialize if Groups 2 and 3 can form an insurance company without Group 1. If they form such a company, the amount of premium to be paid will be

$$n_2P_2 + n_3P_3 + 3\sqrt{n_2p_2(1 - P_2) + n_3P_3(1 - p_3)} = 20 + 36 + 19.2 = 75.2$$

It is then clear that the two groups will admit Group 1 into their company only if this will reduce their own premium, i.e. lead to a solution where $P_2 + P_3 < 75.2$. This means that Group I will have to pay a premium $P_1 > 11.8$. However, it will be to the advantage of Group 1 to accept this, as long as $P_1 < 19$, the premium the group must pay if it forms its own insurance company.

Similar considerations of the companies which can be formed by groups 1 and 2 and by groups 1 and 3 gives

$$P_1 + P_2 < 45$$

$$P_1 + P_3 < 63.4$$

Hence we get the final solution

$$P_1 + P_2 + P_3 = 87$$

where

$$11.8 \leq P_1 \leq 19$$

$$23.6 \leq P_2 \leq 32$$

$$42 \leq P_3 \leq 51$$

1.8 This simple example should be sufficient to illustrate the power of game theory when it comes to analyzing some of the essential problems in insurance. The basic idea is that a group will have to pay a premium which depends on the alternative actions available, if the group should decide to reject an offer from other groups, i.e. from an insurance company. In other words, the *bargaining strength* of the group will determine the premium. There can be little doubt that this is a more realistic approach to the problem than one based on more orthodox actuarial considerations of "fairness".

During the last decade we have seen that a number of groups, civil servants, physicians, teetotallers etc. have felt strong enough to form their own, usually mutual, automobile insurance companies. A number of authors deplore this development, which they consider a danger to the whole insurance industry. For instance Thépaut (1962) states:

> Ces groupements ou mutuelles qui bouleverseraient complètement la distribution de l'assurance automobile et partout de l'assurance tout court, paraissent de nature à mettre en question l'existence même des réseaux d'Agents Généraux des Sociétés.

It is possible to find even stronger statements. It seems, however, that these authors, as long as they argue in the terms of more orthodox actuarial concepts, have difficulties, both in explaining the development, and in proposing remedies.

2. A more General Case

2.1 In this Subsection we shall try to build a more general theory on the basis of our discussion of the example above.

We shall now consider m groups. Group i ($i = 1, \ldots, m$) consists of n_i persons who are exposed to risk of a unit loss with probability p_i. We shall refer to this set of groups as M. Let S be an arbitrary subset of M.

We assume that the groups in any subset can form an insurance company to protect the members of the groups against the losses, and we assume further that the safety requirements are the same as in the example of the preceding Subsection (i.e. probability of ruin < 0.001).

If the groups in the subset S form an insurance company, the amount of premium they have to pay will be

$$v(S) = \sum_S n_i p_i + 3\Big(\sum_S n_i p_i (1 - P_i)\Big)^{1/2}$$

where summation is over all members of S.

Our problem can then be formulated as follows: Which of the $2^m - 1$ possible subsets will form their own insurance companies, and what premium will be paid by each of the groups which belong to these sets?

2.2 Let us consider a set S consisting of s groups, and let $\bar{S}$ be the set consisting of the $m - s$ groups which are not members of S.

It is easy to prove by elementary arithmetics that for any S we have

$$v(S) + v(\bar{S}) > v(M)$$

This inequality states the rather obvious, namely that the total amount of premium will be lowest, if all groups join to form one single insurance company.

Hence, if the groups act rationally, we should expect this company to be formed. We have thus found the answer to the first question in the preceding paragraph. The second question can only be answered in part, all we can conclude so far is that we must have:

$$\sum_{i=1}^{m} P_i = v(M) \tag{1}$$

where P_i is the premium to be paid by Group i.

If Group i refuses to co-operate with any other group, it will have to pay a premium

$$v(i) = n_i p_i + 3\sqrt{n_i p_i (1 - p_i)}$$

If the group acts rationally, it will not co-operate with other groups, if such co-operation gives a higher premium than it can obtain by forming its own insurance company. Hence we must have

$$P_i \leq v(i) \qquad \text{for all } i \tag{2}$$

2.3 Any set of values $P_1 \ldots P_m$ which satisfy the two conditions (1) and (2) constitute in the terminology of Von Neumann and Morgenstern a *solution* to the n-person game. The conditions are obviously a generalization of those found in para 1.5.

The solution is indeterminate, in the sense that it gives only an interval in which the premium for each group must lie. We see this if we write

$$P_i = v(i) - t_i$$

where t_i is non-negative and satisfies the condition

$$\sum_{i=1}^{m} t_i = \sum_{i=1}^{m} v(i) - v(M)$$

$\sum_{i=1}^{m} t_i$ represents the gain obtained collectively by the groups if they co-operate and form one single insurance company. How this gain should be divided among the groups is left undetermined.

2.4 The solution concept of Von Neumann and Morgenstern is obviously not entirely satisfactory. A number of devices or additional assumptions have been proposed in order to make the solution completely, or at least more determinate.

A fairly innocent looking assumption is that for any set S contained in M we shall have

$$\sum_{j \in S} P_j \leq v(S) \tag{3}$$

This is the same assumption which we made in para 1.7. It implies that no set of groups will stay in the joint company, if the total amount of premiums to be paid by those groups will be lower if they form their own company. All sets of values $P_1 \dots P_m$ which satisfy the conditions (1), (2) and (3) is referred to as the *core* of the game. This term is due to Gillies (see Luce (1957), page 194). The core is obviously contained in the *solution* defined by Von Neumann and Morgenstern.

2.5 As we did for a special case in para 1.7, we shall use the core to obtain narrower limits for P_i.

Let $M-i$ stand for the set consisting of all groups except Group i. Under our assumptions we have

$$\sum_{j=1}^{m} P_j = v(M)$$

$$\sum_{j \neq k} P_j \leq v(M-k)$$

By subtracting the inequality from the equation we obtain

$$P_k \geq v(M) - v(M-k)$$

Hence we get the following interval for P_i

$$v(M) - v(M-i) \leq P_i \leq v(i)$$

2.6 We now introduce the symbols

$$\pi_j = n_j p_j$$

$$\pi = \sum_{j=1}^{m} \pi_j$$

$$u_j = n_j p_j (1 - p_j)$$

$$u = \sum_{j=1}^{m} u_j$$

i.e. π_j and u_j are the mean and variance of the losses in Group j. With this notation we have

$$\sum_{j=1}^{m} P_j = \pi + 3\sqrt{u}$$

It is easy to see that if u_j is small in relation to u the inequality in the preceding paragraph can approximately be written in the following form:

$$\pi_i + 3\frac{u_i}{2\sqrt{u}} \leq P_i \leq \pi_i + 3\sqrt{u_i}$$

We see from this that a P_i which belongs to the core cannot be smaller than the net premium π_i. The inequality when written in this form, indicates that it will not be possible to obtain a determinate solution by some limiting process.

If $n = \sum_{j=1}^{m} n_j$ increases towards infinity, it is of course trivial that each person will have to pay a premium approximately equal to the net premium. However, the group to which he belongs will still have to pay a non-zero safety loading.

2.7 It is clear that in order to get a determinate solution we need stronger assumptions than the three conditions which define the core. These assumptions must state something about how the groups negotiate their way to a final arrangement, how they make offers and counter-offers, and how they compromise or break off negotiations.

Let us first assume that Group 1 forms its own company, i.e. that

$$P_1 = v(1)$$

Let us then assume that the manager of this company wants his company to grow at all costs, and that he persuades Group 2 to join the company on the condition the group is charged the lowest possible premium, i.e. that Group 1 shall get no reduction in premium owing to Group 2 joining the company. This means that Group 2 will pay

$$P_2 = v(1, 2) - v(1)$$

If similarly Group 3 joins the company on the same conditions, we get

$$P_3 = v(1, 2, 3) - v(1, 2)$$

If Group m is the last to join the company, it will be charged a premium

$$P_m = v(M) - v\big(M - (m - 1)\big)$$

2.8 The premiums $P_1 \dots P_m$ which we determined above satisfy the conditions (1), (2) and (3), and hence constitute an acceptable solution. However, we cannot accept this as the final unique solution to our problem, unless we know that the m groups can join the company only in the particular order we assumed.

Altogether the groups can join the company in $m!$ orders. If we consider all these orderings as equally acceptable, it is reasonable that Group i shall pay the average of the premium it will be charged in those ordering. Hence we get

$$P_i = \sum_S \frac{(s-1)!(m-s)!}{m!}[v(S) - v(S-i)]$$

where summation is over all subsets S in M, and where s stands for the number of groups in S.

This solution is due to Shapley (1953). It certainly appears reasonable, although one may hesitate in accepting it as the final correct solution to the rating problem in automobile insurance. One may for instance accept that the differences $v(S) - v(S-i)$ are the essential strategic elements which must determine the premium of Group i, but one may suggest a different set of weights, for instance a set giving less weights to the extremes $v(M) - v(M-i)$ and $v(i)$.

It is hard to argue against such suggestions from the rather arbitrary way in which we have derived the solution. However, the Shapley solution can be derived in a number of different ways which may be more convincing than the one we have followed.

2.9 In his original proof Shapley (1953) took a quite different approach. He first proved that the set function $v(S)$, usually referred to as the *characteristic function* of the game, can be written as a linear combination

$$v(S) = \sum_R c_R \frac{v_R}{r}$$

Here summation is over all subsets R of M, c_R are constants, and $v_R(S)$ are characteristic functions of symmetric games. His basic assumptions are, in our symbols:

(i) The premium of each group is determined by the characteristic function, i.e. $P_i = P_i(v)$

(ii) In a symmetric game, the participants will divide the gain equally among themselves.

(iii) $P(v)$ is additive, i.e. $P_i(v + w) = P_i(v) + P_i(w)$.

From these assumptions it follows that

$$P_i(v) = \sum_R c_R \frac{v_R}{r}$$

where r are the number of players, or groups in the subset R. It is then easy to show that this reduces to the expression which we found in para 2.8.

2.10 Harsanyi (1959) has obtained the Shapley solution as a special case of a far more general game. In the game studied by Harsanyi each player attaches a *utility* to the gain, and this utility may be different from the monetary value of the gain. The starting point is the Nash (1950) solution to the two-person game, according to which two rational players will agree on the solution which maximizes the product of the gains in utility. Harsanyi generalizes this to n-person games, and finds that his solution reduces to the Shapley solution if utility is equal to monetary value.

2.11 If the Shapley solution is applied to the two numerical examples in Section 1, we find: For the two group example:

$$P_1 = 16 \qquad \text{and} \qquad P_2 = 29$$

and for the three group example:

$$P_1 = 14.5\,, P_2 = 26.9 \qquad \text{and} \qquad P_3 = 45.6$$

Whether these premiums are more "reasonable" than those found by more intuitive arguments, is of course open to discussion. However, our premiums have been derived from a few simple assumptions about rational behaviour, which seem to have a fairly general validity. This should at least mean that those premiums ought not to be rejected outright in favour of other premiums derived from necessarily arbitrary considerations as to what constitutes actuarial fairness.

2.12 In our model we have assumed that each group of persons behaves as one "rational player" in the sense given to this term in game theory. With our present knowledge of group behaviour it is difficult to say much either for or against this assumption.

Our assumption implies, however, that each group attaches the same utility to a given gain, i.e. to a given reduction in the total amount of premium payable by the group. It may be more natural to assume that the utility which the group attaches to a certain reduction in total premium is equal to the reduction obtained for *each member* of the group. Under this assumption the gain t_i of Group i will have the utility

$$u_i(t_i) = \frac{t_i}{n_i}$$

If groups in fact behave in this way, the Shapley solution will no longer be valid. We will then have to analyze the problem either with the more general method of Harsanyi, or use Shapley's approach to a game between n persons instead of a game between m groups. This will require some very heavy arithmetics, and we shall not in the present paper pursue the matter any further.

3. Another Numerical Example

3.1 The difference between the traditional approach of fairness and the game theory solution is brought out most clearly if the groups are of very unequal size.

If in the example studied in Subsection 1, we assume

$$n_1 = n_2 = 10 \qquad \text{and} \qquad n_3 = 300$$

we find

$$P_1 = 2.20\,, \quad P_2 = 3.70\,, \quad P_3 = 111.39$$

Hence the Shapley solution gives the following premiums per person in the three groups:

$$q_1 = 0.220\,, \quad q_2 = 0.369\,, \quad q_3 = 0.371$$

The traditional method of making the safety loading proportional to the net premium would give

$$q_1' = 0.126\,, \quad q_2' = 0.252\,, \quad q_3' = 0.378$$

3.2 Groups 1 and 2 do not get "fair" treatment if we accept the Shapley solution. However, they can do little about this. If the two groups each form their own company, they will have to pay the following premiums

$$q_1'' = 0.385 \qquad \text{and} \qquad q_2'' = 0.572$$

If the two minority groups join and form one company, they do better. If the gain resulting from this co-operation is divided equally, the premiums per person become

$$q_1''' = 0.294 \qquad \text{and} \qquad q_2''' = 0.481$$

To Group 3 it does not matter much whether the two other groups co-operate or not. If Group 3 has to form a company alone, the premium per member of the group will be

$$q_3''' = 0.379$$

Hence Group 3 can afford to refuse the demand for actuarial fairness from the other groups.

3.3 If all three groups form one company, and if this company charges the same premium to all members, this common premium will be $q = 0.367$.

This means in practical terms that if the Shapley solution is accepted, Group 2 will not be able to obtain its own rating, since q_2 and q_3 above are practically equal.

Group 1 will, on the other hand, be recognized as a group of particularly good risks, and will get its own rating. However, the group will have to pay a premium which probably will be considered as "unfair" by any actuary the group may consult.

4. Conclusion

4.1 The particular results which we have arrived at in the preceding sections obviously depend on our very arbitrary assumptions about the safety requirements of insurance companies. It is, however, clear that the whole argument could be carried through with safety requirements or equivalent restrictions in a different form.

It might have been more realistic if we had considered administrative costs instead of safety loading. We can for instance assume that these costs in an insurance company depend on the number of policies n, and on the number of claim payments m.

If we assume that the cost function is of the form

$$a\sqrt{n} + b\sqrt{m}$$

the expected cost of an insurance company formed by Group 1 will be

$$C_1 = n_1p_1 + a\sqrt{n_1} + b\sqrt{n_1p_1}$$

If this group forms a company together with Group 2, expected cost will be

$$C_{12} = n_1p_1 + n_2p_2 + a\sqrt{n_1 + n_2} + b\sqrt{n_1p_1 + n_2p_2}$$

It is easy to see that

$$C_{12} < C_1 + C_2$$

Hence this model is substantially the same as the one we have studied in the preceding sections. The gain will in this case be a saving in administrative cost.

4.2 In a general analysis we would have to consider the *utility* of the different groups. It has been argued in a previous paper (Borch (1961)) that a utility concept is essential to deeper studies in the theory of insurance. However, the concept is not strictly necessary for our present purpose which is to illustrate how the theory of n-person games can be applied to some of the central and most controversial problems in insurance.

4.3 The problem we have studied seems at present to have particular importance in automobile insurance. However, the problem obviously exists in all branches of insurance.

For instance, a number of fires are caused by careless smokers and children playing with matches. Hence non-smoking and childless home owners could with some right demand lower fire insurance premiums. When they have neither obtained, nor even claimed this, the reason may be that as a group they are not strong enough to form their own insurance company. If they were sufficiently strong, it is likely that the existing companies would offer this group concessions which would balance any advantages the group could gain by forming its own company.

4.4 Our problem may have some real importance in life insurance. During the last decades most companies have become more and more "liberal" in accepting at normal premium, risks which previously were considered as "sub-standard". The game theory indicates that there may be limits to how liberal a company can be if it wants to avoid a revolt among the "standard" risks, who in the and pay for the company's liberal policy.

References for Section 4

Borch K. (1961): "The Utility Concept applied to the Theory of Insurance", *The ASTIN Bulletin*, 245–255.

Harsanyi JC. (1959): "A bargaining model for the cooperative n-person game", *Annals of Mathematical Studies*, Princeton, 325–355.

Luce RD, Howard R. (1957): " *Games and Decisions*", John Wiley & Sons.

Nash JF. (1950): "The bargaining problem", *Econometrica* 155–162.

Neumann von J, Morgenstern O. (1944): *"Theory of Games and Economic Behavior"*, Princeton.

Shapley LS. (1953): "A value for n-person games", *Annals of Mathematical Studies*, Princeton, 307–317.

Thépaut A. (1962): "Quelques réflexions sur la réforme du tarif français d'assurance automobile", *The ASTIN Bulletin*, 109–119.

CHAPTER 6

HOUSEHOLD INSURANCE

1. Administrative Expenses

1.1 In Chapter 1 we discussed the premium formula

$$P = E\{x\} + A + R$$

and observed that for the insurance bought by the ordinary consumer the second term in the formula, A = administrative expenses tended to be substantial. In many cases the last term, the risk premium could be ignored, because the amounts insured were modest.

To the "little man" there is usually no alternative to insurance if he wants to be relieved of the risks he carries. It is in his interest that there should be real competition between the insurers who offer to cover these risks. It is of course also in his interest that the insurers should remain solvent, so that they are able to meet their obligations, even if the number and size of claims should exceed the expectation by considerable amounts. On the latter point it is generally accepted that it is the task of the government to see that the insurers have sufficient funds to offer adequate security. The "little man" cannot be expected to study the balance sheet of an insurance company and decide how likely it is that the company shall be able to keep the promises made in the policy. The government's role in maintaining the solvency of insurance companies will be discussed in Chapter 8.

It is traditionally considered as "normal" that one third of the total premium is used for administrative expenses. In its balance sheet an insurance company must enter "Unearned premiums" as a liability. In many countries the Law lays down that this liability must be at least one third of premium receipts during the accounting year. If $A = P/3$ and $R = 0$, it follows that $E\{x\} = 2P/3$. If the expire dates of the one-year insurance contracts are evenly distributed over the calender year, it follows that at the end of the year the expected claim payments under unexpired contracts are just $P/3$.

1.2 If insurers shall be able to compete by offering lower premiums, they must reduce their administrative expenses. This can be done by better or simpler management, but there are obvious limits to how much one can achieve by this approach. Methods of premium rating have been greatly simplified. In the early days of fire insurance a number of factors were taking into account when premiums were set for a particular residential building, for instance fire hazards in the neighborhood, the efficiency of the local fire service, and of course the nature of the building itself. The so-called "conflagration" risk was considered as important, and wooden houses in densely built up areas were charged a substantially higher premium than isolated houses in open country.

Gradually the rating become simpler, and today most residential buildings are insured at the same rates, possibly with some differences depending on geographical location, or whether the house is built of wood or of fireproof material. This development means that some "fairness" is sacrificed in order to reduce expenses, and offer insurance at lower premiums.

1.3 The most efficient way to reduce *relative* administrative expenses is to cover as many risks as possible under a single insurance contract. Until the 1950's a home owner needed a whole bundle of insurance policies to be covered against all the risks to which he was exposed. During the following decades his insurance problems have become much simpler. In all industrial countries one has developed "comprehensive" or "multi peril" policies for home owners, and other private citizens. The coverage of such policies differs, but they can include:

(i) Fire insurance on the house, the furniture and other household goods. Often the insurance covers replacement costs, whatever that may be, and the premium is adjusted by a price index. Earlier the insured had to take the initiative to increase the face value of his policy with increasing price level.

(ii) Other damage to or loss of property caused by burglary, vandalism, bursting waterpipes etc.

(iii) Damage caused by natural disaster, such as flooding, landslide or hurricane. In many countries this is compulsory.

(iv) Liability one can incur as a home owner, or more generally as a private person.

(v) Personal accident insurance for the home owner and his family.

(vi) Travel insurance on vacations (Lost property and accidents) for the home owner and his family.

(vii) Legal assistance. This is a fairly recent development, which can be seen as a result of market analysis of risks left uncovered by conventional insurance. Any person runs a risk of having to defend himself in a frivolous suit, or of having to initiate legal action, and the costs involved can be substantial.

1.4 The last four covers are strictly limited to private activities. Liability, accidents or travels connected with the exercise of a profession or business activities are excluded, and must be covered by separate insurance contracts.

All the seven covers included in the comprehensive "package" were at one time considered as separate lines of insurance, and often sold only by companies specializing on these lines. One must assume that insurers writing only a particular line of insurance have the know-how required to estimate expected claims correctly, and hence set "fair" premiums. The expenses involved in this division of labour among specialists are however considerable. It seems to have turned out that the competitive solution is to have one insurer covering as many risks as possible under one single insurance contract. This may lead to fairly rough rating of some components of the total premium, but the net result is savings for all.

Until the first decade after World War II one attached great importance to the fairness of premiums. Liability incurred as owner of a dog was covered only if the insured accepted a rider to his policy and paid an additional premium. Other riders covered liability incurred in the exercise of relatively harmless sports, as golf, fishing and shooting. Today such trivial riders have virtually disappeared. The civil liability is covered against the same premium, whether the insured keeps a pet and plays golf or not.

1.5 The standard marine insurance policy has for almost two centuries covered all losses caused by the "perils of the sea". The multiple peril policies developed during the last decades for home-owners — and for people living in rented apartments — come close to cover all losses caused by the perils of living in a modern society. In most countries these policies have developed as extensions of the old fire insurance contract, but the traditional fire insurance of the building may be only a minor part of the package.

Any activity beyond just living leads to new hazards and additional needs for insurance. Business activities and the insurance of the risks involved were discussed in Chapter 5.

Table 6.1: Household Insurance Premiums in U.S.A. in 1984. $ millions

Home-owner's Multiple Peril	13213
Automobile Liability	24809
Automobile Damage (collision insurance)	18498

Source: *Insurance Facts 1985–86*, Insurance Information Institute.

By far the most important risky activity a private person can undertake is to drive his own automobile, and in all industrial countries automobile insurance is the most important line of household insurance. This is illustrated by Table 6.1.

1.6 Automobile (third party) liability insurance is compulsory in all countries in Western Europe, and in most of them it is unlimited. In the U.S. it is compulsory in more than half of the states, but usually for very modest amounts. Hawaii is the only state which has adopted the European pattern of compulsory unlimited liability insurance. In practice automobile liability insurance is however essential in all the states, since most states have "financial responsibility laws", which require that a person involved in an automobile accident furnish proof of financial responsibility up to a certain amount. The most convenient way — and for many people the only way — of giving such proof is in the form of an insurance policy.

U.S.A. is unique in setting low limits for compulsory automobile liability insurance. No state, except of course Hawaii, has a higher limit than $50000 for bodily injury. This is of course quite insufficient to meet the liability which may result from a serious automobile accident, so people who have some assets to lose, will usually — or should — have liability insurance for higher amounts than those required by the law.

1.7 Collision insurance is naturally optimal. A person is free to decide if he wants to insure his property or not, whether it is a house, a yacht or a car. If however he has a mortgage on his house or has bought his car on instalments, the lender will usually require that the collateral is insured. This illustrates how insurance can eliminate the lender's risk, and thus makes it easier to obtain credit. It can also be used the other way round.

Young drivers have a bad accident record in most countries, and this particularly goes for those who ride powerful motorcycles. Many insurers refuse to write collision insurance for these drivers, or will do so only at prohibitive premiums, and some insurers justify this discrimination as a contribution to road-safety.

1.8 Table 6.1 shows that the American public spends about four times more on automobile insurance than on comprehensive insurance related to their home and household. The premiums for automobile insurance will thus be a non-negligible part of the budget for most American families. Hence it is important that the premiums should be fair. The rough and ready methods which sometimes are used for the minor components of the multiple peril policy will not do.

It will clearly not be fair to charge the same premium to all cars and all drivers. The frequency of automobile accidents varies widely from one area to another, so the geographical area in which the car is usually driven should be taken into account for the sake of fairness.

In the analysis of the problem it is convenient to separate the frequency of accidents, and the size of the claim resulting from an accident. It is often believed that the frequency depends primarily on the driver, and the size of the claim on the type of car, but Table 6.2 shows that the two elements cannot be separated quite so neatly.

The average claim frequency for all cars in the survey is set equal to 100, and the table gives the deviation from the average for some models

L = large — wheelbase more than 11 inches
C = compact — wheelbase 106–111 inches
SC = subcompact — wheelbase 101–106 inches
SS = small subcompact — wheelbase less than 96 inches.

1.9 It is hardly practical for an insurer to operate with separate premiums for each make and model for automobiles. In practice one will group the vehicles according to a few characteristics, such as wheelbase and cylinder volume. As mentioned above it may also be necessary to group the policies according geographical area, and statistics indicate that the accident frequency also depends on the age of the driver, the use of the vehicle and the occupation of the owner. A farmer and a schoolteacher may have very different driving patterns.

If one groups the policies according to all criteria that seem to influence accident frequencies and claim size, one might easily arrive at groups which contain so few policies that no reliable statistical estimates can be made. This is the main problem of rating premiums in automobile insurance. The problem will not be discussed further in the present study. A recent book by Lemaire (1985) gives a detailed survey of the rating methods used in the U.S.A., Quebec and seven European countries. Two papers by Hallin

Table 6.2: U.S.A.: Best and worst loss experience 1981–1983. Personal injury liability for some automobile models.

	Car size	Claim frequency	Claim freq. by size of claim Over $250	Over $500	Over 1000
Oldsmobile Delta 88	L	59	58	58	59
Oldsmobile Cutlass	C	60	50	44	
Mercedes Benz 300SD	L	61			
Volvo 245	SC	70	58		
Datsun Corolla	SS	132	136	140	137
Nissan Pulsar	SS	148			
Pontiac 1000	SS	156	149	145	

Source: *Insurance Facts 1985–86*, Insurance Information Institute.

and Ingenbleek (1981) and (19S3) give a complete background of the rating methods used in Sweden.

1.10 It may be worth while noting that the desire for a fair premium tariff is not founded exclusively on pure idealism. It is actually a necessity. The two occupational groups mentioned earlier, farmers and teachers, usually have strong organizations. If it can be established by statistical analysis that one group is subsidizing the automobile insurance of the other, either group is capable of establishing its own insurance company.

In the beginning of this chapter it was observed that the amounts involved in household insurance usually were modest, so that the risk premium could be ignored. This is certainly the case for collision insurance, as the highest possible claim is the total value of the car. Lemaire (1985) gives an example which he considers as the "world record" of claim settled under automobile liability insurance.

In the evening of 18 March 1976 a young French school teacher drove home with his girlfriend in his small Citroën, when he skidded on the wet road and hit the railroad crossing at Bar-le-Duc. The visible damage to the car was slight, the back was crushed and a fender was bent. It was only when the teacher tried to start the car again that he realized that the car was stuck, and that there was no way to get it loose. When he tried frantically to call the nearest railroad station, a freight train arrived at a speed of more than 100 km per hour. The train swept the Cirtroën away and came to a stop on the bridge over the Rhine-Marne canal. The 21 freight cars, loaded mainly with bottled beer became derailed and piled up on the locomotive, and eventually fell into the canal. Six cranes and forty barges were required to clear away the debris, and for ten days all railway traffic between Paris and Strasbourg had to take a 200 km detour. Nobody was injured by the accident, but settlement of all claims — including compensation to the association of fishermen of the canal — came to about $5 million. The premium the schoolteacher had paid for this liability insurance was about $70.

This may not be quite the world record as claimed by Lemaire. A very similar accident happened in Sweden a few years earlier. A Volkswagen stalled at a railroad crossing and caused an express train to be derailed. The settlement under the automobile liability insurance was of the same order of magnitude as the settlement after the accident at Bar-le-Duc.

It is not certain which of these two accidents should be entered in Guiness Book of Records, but it is certain that the two accidents made European automobile insurers review their reinsurance arrangements.

2. No-Claim Bonus and Merit Rating

2.1 When a person applies for a large life insurance policy, the insurer will usually require that he should go through medical examination. The purpose is to find out if the applicant is a "normal" risk, so that the premium calculation can be based on the standard mortality table. If the health of the applicant appears to be sub-standard, he may be offered life insurance at a premium higher than the normal.

In theory one could use a similar procedure to a person who applies for automobile insurance. It is conceivable that one could develop a battery of psychological on physiological tests which would make it possible to evaluate the driving ability of the applicant, and hence make predictions about his future driving record. This procedure would however be very costly, and given the importance of administrative expenses in household insurance, a scheme of this kind has never been seriously considered in practice.

2.2 As an alternative one can give a person who wants automobile insurance the benefit of doubt, and charge the standard premium. As the person develops a driving record, one lets the record speak for itself. If the record is better than the average, the premium is reduced, and if the record is worse

Table 6.3: Probability distribution of premiums in the first four years.

Premium	Probabilities			
	year 1	year 2	year 3	year 4
P_0	1	p	p	$2p^2 - p^3$
P_1	0	$1-p$	$p-p^2$	$p^3 - 3p^2 + 2p$
P_2	0	0	$1-2p+p^2$	$1-2p+p^2$

than average, the premium is increased. This method of rating is usually referred to as a *No-claim bonus* system. In some European countries it is called a "bonus-malus system". In North America where this method of rating is not widely used, it is usually called "experience rating", a term borrowed from marine insurance, or "merit rating". The latter term will probably appeal to a potential insurance buyer who believes he is a good driver, and can argue that his driving record shows this to be true.

Some insurance companies in Europe have practised no-claim bonus in automobile insurance since before World War II, and now the system is almost universally applied on the continent, in some countries a no-claim bonus is even mandatory under government regulation.

2.3 To illustrate how a no-claim bonus works it may be useful to consider an extremely simple example with three premium levels.

Let p be the probability that a driver shall have one or more accidents during a year. Assume:

(i) All new drivers are insured against a premium P_0.

(ii) If no claim is made during the first year, the premium for the second year is reduced to P_1.

(iii) After two consecutive years without claims the premium is reduced to P_2.

(iv) If a claim occurs, the premium for the following year is increased to the level immediately above. If the premium already is P_0, it remains unchanged.

If the accident probability p is constant, and if claims in different years are stochastically independent, the probability distribution of the premiums in future years can be found by elementary manipulations. The distributions for the first four years are given in Table 6.3.

2.4 To analyse the situation further, it is useful to interpret the model as a Markov chain, described by the following matrix of transition probabilities:

$$A = \begin{pmatrix} p & 1-p & 0 \\ p & 0 & 1-p \\ 0 & p & 1-p \end{pmatrix}$$

The element in row r and column s gives the probability that an insured who in year 1 paid the premium P_{r-1} shall pay the premium P_{s-1} in the following year.

It is easy to verify that the elements in the matrix A^n will give the corresponding probabilities of the premium to be paid in year $n+1$.

The eigenvalues of the matrix A are determined by the equation:

$$\begin{vmatrix} p-\lambda & 1-p & 0 \\ p & -\lambda & 1-p \\ 0 & p & 1-p-\lambda \end{vmatrix} = 0$$

and are found to be

$$\lambda_1 = 1, \qquad \lambda_2 = \sqrt{p(1-p)} \qquad \text{and} \qquad \lambda_3 = -\sqrt{p(1-p)}$$

The spectral representation of the matrix is

$$A = \lambda_1 S_1 + \lambda_2 S_2 + \lambda_3 S_3$$

The spectral matrices have the properties $S_i^2 = S_i$ and $S_i S_j = 0$ for $i \neq j$.

Using these properties it is easy to show that

$$A^n = \lambda_1^n S_1 + \lambda_2^n S_2 + \lambda_3^n S_3$$

As $|\lambda_2| = |\lambda_3| < 1$ and $\lambda_1 = 1$, it follows that

$$\lim_{n\to\infty} A^n = S_1$$

The matrix S_1 corresponds to the "steady state" of the Markow chain. S_1 is the matrix of eigenvectors corresponding to the eigenvalue $\lambda_1 = 1$. One can show that this matrix is given by

$$S_1 = \frac{1}{1-p+p^2} \begin{pmatrix} p^2 & p(1-p) & (1-p)^2 \\ p^2 & p(1-p) & (1-p)^2 \\ p^2 & p(1-p) & (1-p)^2 \end{pmatrix}$$

This means that when the steady state is reached, an arbitrary driver will pay a premium

$$P_0 \text{ with probability } \frac{p^2}{1-p+p^2} = \pi_0$$

$$P_1 \text{ with probability } \frac{p(1-1)}{1-p+p^2} = \pi_1$$

$$P_2 \text{ with probability } \frac{(1-p)}{1-p+p^2} = \pi_2$$

regardless of which of the three premiums he paid in year 1. The premium depends only on his driving record.

A more direct method to find the stationary probabilities π_i, $i = 0, 1, 2$ is the following: Denote the elements of the matrix A by p_{ij}. Also let $p_{ij}^{(n)} = \Pr\{X_{n+1} = j \,|\, X_n = i\}$ where X_n represents the premium class after n years. Here it is possible to show that $\lim_{n\to\infty} p_{ij}^{(n)}$ exists, and is independent of i, for all i and j. Let us call this limit π_j, $j = 0, 1, 2$. Notice that $p_{ij}^{(n)}$ are the elements of A^n, that is, A raised to the n-th power.

From the above it is easy to argue that the π_j's must satisfy the following system of linear equations:

$$\pi_j = \sum_{i=0}^{2} \pi_i p_{ij}\,, \qquad j = 0, 1, 2$$

$$\sum_{j=0}^{2} \pi_j = 1$$

From this simple system it follows directly that S_1 has the above given form, and that the limiting probabilities are as indicated. A Markov chain $(X_n, n \geq 0)$ with the above properties is called *ergodic* (see for example Ross (1985)).

2.5 As a numerical example take $p = 0.1$. The row vectors in S_1 is then equal to $(\pi_0,\ \pi_1,\ \pi_2)$, and the values are

$$(0.011, 0.099, 0.890)$$

For $p = 0.5$ one finds the vector $(\pi_0,\ \pi_1,\ \pi_2)$ to be

$$(0.333, 0.333, 0.333)$$

This is almost obvious on intuitive reasons. There is a fifty-fifty chance that a driver shall have an accident in any year, and one can then expect that in the long run the drivers will be equally distributed over the premium classes.

Assume now that an insurance company has a portfolio consisting of:

1000 good risks with accident probability 0.1

1000 bad risks with accident probability 0.5

The company knows only that the overall accident frequency is 0.3, and charges the same premium to all drivers.

Assume for the sake of simplicity that the size of any claim payment is equal to 1. Expected claim payments in the portfolio will then amount to $0.3 \times 2000 = 600$. If the company shall break even in the long run, it must collect this amount in premiums. From the two row vectors above, it follows that there are respectively 344, 432 and 1224 drivers in the three premium classes. Hence the following condition must hold:

$$344P_0 + 432P_1 + 1224P_2 = 600 \tag{1}$$

Any triple (P_0, P_1, P_2) which satisfies (1) will be a possible scale for no-claim bonus.

One possibility would be

$$P_0 = 0.76\,, \qquad P_1 = 0.5 \qquad \text{and} \qquad P_2 = 0.1$$

This scale may have a certain sales appeal. A prospective buyer who believes he is a good driver can be assured that he will be charged the "correct" premium as soon as he can prove by his record that he really is good. Actually the scale is unfair to good drivers, since they on the average will pay a premium of 0.147 instead of 0.1. The bad driver benefits, since on the average he will pay 0.453.

A more dramatic scale as $P_0 = 0.9$, $P_1 = 0.5$ and $P_2 = 0.06$ will actually be fairer, since it will give average premiums of 0.113 and 0.487 to good and bad drivers respectively.

2.6 The bonus systems used in practice are of course far more complicated than this simple example. One of the simplest systems seems to be that of Sweden which reduces the premium to $0.25P_0$ after six consecutive years of accident-free driving. In Sweden there is no automatic malus. The premium can be increased to $2P_0$ only in exceptional circumstances, for instance if a driver who already pays P_0 has three accidents within a year, or if he is sentenced by a court for reckless driving. One must assume that this system is unfair to good drivers.

It seems easier to arrive at a system which is both fair and practicable if one has an automatic malus built into the scale. Switzerland has a bonus-malus scheme with 22 steps. New drivers enter at step 9, corresponding to a premium level of 100. After nine years of claim-less driving he reaches step 0, with a level of 45. For each claim he moves up three steps, and if he is unlucky — or really bad — he may reach step 21, with a premium level of 270.

3. The Market for Household Insurance

3.1 *Theory*

By household insurance it is natural to understand the insurance bought by the ordinary consumer, or by the "little man". He is rarely in the position to bargain with the insurance company, but he is usually offered a fairly wide choice of different insurance contracts.

These insurance contracts are clearly sold in a mass market, and there is usually a strong competition among the sellers. This should indicate that the standard theory of competitive markets could be used to analyse this class of insurance. There are however a number of difficulties. One of these is that there is no obvious natural unit of insurance cover. If a client chooses a higher deductible, he clearly buys less insurance, but it is not easy to state how much less, and it is not clear how one shall formulate the familiar demand relation between price and quantity bought. This dependence between quantity bought (or sold) and price is the starting point of most conventional economic analysis, and it seems that a different approach is required.

3.2 The premium is relatively low for most household insurance policies. This means that transaction costs will be relatively high, i.e. the companies' expenses on sales and administration constitute an important part of the premiums charges to the public.

Returning to the equation

$$P = E\{x\} + A + R$$

it is natural to assume that the term A is substantial. On the other hand R — the charge the insurer makes for his risk-bearing services — may be insignificant. This means that one can assume that the insurance company is approximately risk neutral. It has been proved by many authors, most generally by Arrow (1974), that in this case the Pareto optimal solution has the form

$$y(x) = 0 \qquad \text{for} \qquad x < D$$

$$y(x) = x - D \qquad \text{for} \qquad x \geq D$$

Here $y(x)$ stands for the compensation the consumer will receive if his loss is x. The interpretation is that he will carry losses less than the deductible himself, and have all excesses completely covered by the insurance policy.

3.3 Competition has forced companies to make every effort to reduce administrative expenses and this has led to a tendency towards standard contracts and standard premiums. This again means that companies knowingly underwrite good and bad risks at the same premium, simply because it would be too expensive to examine all risks and classify them correctly. This leads to a new and fascinating set of problems, which first were examined by Rothschild and Stiglitz (1976).

The simplest model studied by Rothschild and Stiglitz can be described as follows:

A person with initial wealth W is exposed to a risk which can lead to a loss x with probability π.

The person can pay a premium cP, $c \leq 1$ to an insurance company, which in return undertakes to pay a compensation cx if the loss occurs.

If the person's preferences can be represented by the utility function $u(\cdot)$, his problem is to determine the value of c which maximizes expected utility:

$$U(c) = (1 - \pi)u(W - cP) + \pi u(W - cP - x + cx)$$

The first order condition for a maximum is

$$(1 - \pi)Pu'(W - cP) = \pi(x - P)u'(W - cP - x + cx)$$

It is easy to see that $c = 1$ is a solution if $P = \pi x$. For $P > \pi x$ one will have $c < 1$ if $u'' < 0$, i.e. a risk averse person will not buy full cover.

This result may be surprising. The premium must cover the company's administrative expenses, so in general one will have $P > \pi x$, but casual observation indicates that most people take full cover, if they buy insurance at all.

3.4 If administrative expenses can be ignored, and there is perfect competition in the insurance market, it can be argued that one must have $P = \pi x$, which implies that the company's expected profits is zero.

Assume now that there are two types of risks in the market, good and bad, with claim probabilities respectively π_G and π_B, and $\pi_G < \pi_B$. Assume further for the sake of simplicity that the number of risks in each group are equal, and take $x = 1$.

If the company can distinguish the two types of risk, there is no problem. Each group will be charged the premium $P_G = \pi_G$ and $P_B = \pi_B$ respectively, and they will both buy full insurance cover.

The problems occur when the insurance company is unable to, or not allowed to, distinguish between the two groups and quote different premiums. These problems are essential in insurance, and are particularly relevant in household insurance. The premiums are small and it will be prohibitively expensive to make them fair for each group of customers — i.e. to examine each risk and determine the fair premium which it should be charged.

3.5 In household insurance it is necessary to sacrifice some fairness in order to reduce administrative expenses. This means the same premium will be charged to each member of a group of heterogeneous risks. In the example above this implies that the same premium P will be charged for both good and bad risks. It is natural to assume $\pi_G \leq P \leq \pi_B$.

The customers representing the bad risks will in this case buy full cover. Those representing the good risks will take a cover $c < 1$, determined by the equation

$$(1 - \pi_G)Pu'(W - cP) = \pi_G(1 - P)u'(W - cP - 1 + c)$$

If there is perfect competition in the market, the insurance company's profits will be zero. This gives the equation

$$c(P - \pi_G) + P - \pi_B = 0$$

or

$$(1 + c)P = c\pi_G + \pi_B$$

3.6 If the two equations above have a solution in c and P, this will constitute an equilibrium. It is however not obvious that the equations have a meaningful and unique solution.

If the equations give a solution with $c < 0$, the only meaningful equilibrium is obviously $c = 0$ and $P = \pi_B$. In this case only the people representing bad risks will buy insurance, and they will take full cover. This arrangement can hardly be said to be optimal in any usual sense of the word.

Thus in the model presented by Rothschild and Stiglitz it is doubtful if a competitive equilibrium exists, and if it exists it may not be Pareto optimal. This shows that some of the central results in conventional economic theory do not seem to hold in the market for household insurance. The reason is clearly that one party to the transactions has imperfect information about the risks insured.

3.7 The insurance company may not know *ex ante* if a customer represents a good or a bad risk. In the model the company will however know *ex post* when the customer has made his decision. If the customer chooses full cover, i.e. $c = 1$, he must represent a bad risk, and should have been charged a premium $P = \pi_B$. If on the other hand the choice is $c < 1$, the customer represents a good risk, and could have been offered full cover at a lower premium.

The new idea emerging from these observations is that the customer, when making his decision must send a "signal", or convey some information to the insurance company. The problem of the company or more generally of the other party to the transaction — is then to interpret the signal correctly, and make appropriate use of the information.

3.8 One suggestion made by Rothschild and Stiglitz, and developed further by Wilson (1977) is that the insurance company offer two standard contracts defined by the pairs (c_1, P_1) and (c_2, P_2). The former offers a compensation c_1 against a premium P_1, and correspondingly for the second. If these pairs are chosen so that customers representing good risk prefer the former contract, and those representing bad risks prefer the latter, one can obtain some fairness. There will however still be difficulties about the existence of a competitive equilibrium, and about the Pareto optimality of the equilibria.

3.9 The fairly recent results outlined above represent an approach to essential problems in economic analysis of household insurance. The results are however obtained for extremely simple examples, and it is not easy to see how they can be generalized to more realistic models.

A more realistic case would be to assume that the loss is represented by a stochastic variable with a density $f(x)$. One can then assume that an insurance contract specifies that a compensation cx is paid if the loss is x, and that the premium to be paid is cP. The problem of the customer is then to determine the value of c which maximizes

$$U(c) = \int_0^\infty u(W - x + cx - cP) f(x)\, dx \tag{1}$$

The first order condition for a maximum is

$$U'(c) = \int_0^\infty (x - P) u'(W - x + cx - cP) f(x)\, dx = 0$$

It is easy to see that

$$U'(1) = \int_0^\infty (x - P) u'(W - cP) f(x)\, dx = \big(E\{x\} - P\big) u'(W - cP)$$

From this it follows that $c = 1$ can give a maximum only if $E\{x\} = P$. It is easy to show that if $P > E\{x\}$ the maximum is obtained for some $c < 1$, i.e. the customer will not buy full insurance cover if the premium exceeds the expected loss.

3.10 The example above seems to indicate that the results in this section can be generalized fairly easily. This is however deceptive, since the maximizing was carried out under the arbitrary assumption that the compensation should be proportional to the loss, i.e. $y = cx$. In a more general formulation the insurance contract could specify that a compensation $y(x)$ should be paid if the loss amounts to x. This leads to the problem

$$\max_{y(x) \in Y} \int_0^\infty u\big(W - Py - x + y(x)\big) f(x)\, dx\,,$$

where Y is the set of permissible compensation functions.

If Y consists of all functions such that $0 \leq y(x) \leq x$ the solution is as mentioned earlier an insurance contract with full cover above a fixed deductible D. By the maximization described earlier one assumes that $y(x) = cx$, and this must lead to a sub-optimal solution.

The examples above illustrate the limitations of the simple model introduced by Rothschild and Stiglitz. In this model, based on a two-point claim distribution, it is not possible to distinguish between a policy with a deductible, and one with a compensation proportional to the loss. If the loss can take several non-negative values, the two contracts become different, and this leads to new problems, which seem to merit further research.

3.11 *Practice*

The most striking conflict between theory and practice in household insurance may be that a consumer should never buy full insurance cover. It would indeed be surprising if a traveller deliberately insured his baggage for say 80 per cent of its value but this is what he would do if he solved his problem by maximizing (1). One explanation may be that there is some element of "impulse buying" in insurance, and that a consumer does not really bother to maximize his expected utility when small amounts of money are involved. Another may be that the problem represented by (1) does not lead to an optimum. If the consumer was offered a choice of different deductibles, he might have been able to reach a more rational decision.

3.12 Insurance is usually the only way in which the ordinary consumer can be relieved of the risks he carries. Hence the market for household insurance is in a sense self-contained. Insurance companies compete among themselves to cover the insurance needs of a large, but finite number of households. The market will evidently expand with general economic growth, but further expansion may be possible only if the public at present is underinsured. One should of course not rule out the possibility that insurance companies through innovations can find ways of insuring risks which households at present must carry themselves. One example is the legal assistance insurance which has become very popular in some countries. The origin of this form of insurance seems to be market studies which revealed that one of the few important risks which is uncovered in a modern society is the risk of becoming involved in a law suit, without any fault of one's own.

3.13 There are elements which indicate that the market for household insurance many shrink in the future. Then tendency to stricter liability legislation may reduce the apparent need for personal accident insurance, and hence transfer some insurance from the household — to the business class. It is debatable if this is a desirable development. A good personal accident policy should secure adequate compensation to the victim, without forcing him to go to court. If liability is involved, the settlement could be arranged out of court, between the insurance companies of the victim and the one responsible for the accident.

3.14 In most countries the government has taken special action to protect the buyer of household insurance — because he is assumed to be the weaker party to the insurance contract. With the rise of the consumers' movement there has been increasing pressure for stricter governmental control and supervision of insurance companies and their operations. The organized consumers want low premiums and generous claim settlements, and often seem to have the political strength necessary to obtain legislation assumed to have this effect.

It is obvious that pressure for low premiums can lead to conflicts with solvency requirements. Good insurance cannot be cheap. If the solvency requirements are not relaxed, it may be tempting to seek solutions outside the insurance industry. An automobile manufacturer, or a car dealer with good repair facilities can offer to do any necessary repairs to the cars they sell, against a premium paid in advance. This will probably be cheaper to the buyer than conventional collision insurance, and the question has come up in some countries, i.a. in Scandinavia. The governments have stood firm, and insisted that such guarantees can be given only by companies under the same supervision as insurance companies, and this again has led to the formation of at least one captive company.

References for Sections 1–3

Arrow KJ. (1974): "Optimal insurance and generalized deductibles", *Scandinavian Actuarial Journal 1*, 1–42.

Borch K. (1981): "The three markets for private insurance", *The Geneva-papers on Risk and Insurance*, 20.

Hallin M, Ingenbleek JF. (1981): "Etude Statistique de la Probabilité de Sinistre en Assurance Automobile", *The ASTIN Bulletin 12*, 40–56.

Hallin M, Ingenbleek JF. (1983): "The Swedish Automobile Portfolio in 1977", *Scandinavian Actuarial Journal*, 49–64.

Lemaire J. (1985): *Automobile Insurance: Actuarial Models*, Kluwer-Nijhoff.

Ross SM. (1985): *Introduction to probability models* (3rd ed.). Academic Press, Inc.

Rothschild M, Stiglitz J. (1976): "Equilibrium in competitive insurance markets: An essay on the economics of imperfect information", *Quarterly Journal of Economics 90*, 629–649.

Wilson, C. (1977): "A model of insurance markets with incomplete information", *Journal of Economic Theory 16*, 167–207.

4. The Optimal Insurance Contract in a Competitive Market*

In this letter we shall consider a person who is exposed to a risk which can cause a loss, represented by a stochastic variable with the distribution $F(x)$. We shall assume that this person by paying the premium $P\{y\}$ can

* Reprinted from *Economics letters*, 1983; 11(4):327–330, copyright (c) North-Holland, Amsterdam.

buy an insurance contract which will pay a compensation $y(x)$, if the loss amounts to x. The insurance buyer's problem is then to determine the function $y(x)$, which maximizes his expected utility:

$$\int_0^\infty u\big(W + y(x) - x - P\{y\}\big)\, dF(x) \tag{1}$$

In (1) W is the person's initial wealth, and $u(\cdot)$ is his utility function,which we shall assume concave. The maximization will have to be carried out over some set of admissible y-functions.

If the premium $P\{y\}$ is given in a competitive market, it is natural to assume that it must be a continuous linear functional of $y(x)$, i.e. that

$$P\{ay_1 + by_2\} = aP\{y_1\} + bP\{y_2\}$$

From the Riesz representation theorem it then follows that there exists a function $V(x)$, such that

$$P\{y\} = \int_0^\infty y(x)\, dV(x) \tag{2}$$

Hence the problem is the maximize (1) subject to (2). If the distribution is discrete, i.e. if $F(x)$ is a step function, the problem reduces to

$$\max \left[\sum_r f_r u(W + y_r - x_r - P) + \lambda \Big(P - \sum_s v_s y_s \Big) \right]$$

Here λ is a Lagrange multiplier, and f_r, and v_r, are the jumps of $F(x)$ and $V(x)$ at $x = x_r$. The solution of the problem is given by

$$u'(W + y_r - x_r - P) f_r = \lambda v_r \tag{3}$$

If the distribution is continuous, we are led to a problem in the calculus of variation, and (3) takes the form (3′), which can be derived as the Euler equation of the problem

$$u'\big(W + y(x) - x - P\big) f(x) = \lambda v(x)\,, \tag{3′}$$

where $f(x) = F'(x)$ and $v(x) = V'(x)$. If there is no loading on the premium, i.e. if $P = E\{x\} = \bar{x}$, and $f_r = v_r$, (3) reduces to

$$u'(W + y_r - x_r - P) = \lambda \tag{4}$$

In (4) the right-hand side is independent of r, so it follows that $y_r = x_r$, i.e. that it is optimal to buy full insurance cover. The result has been found by many authors, i.a. by Arrow (1963 and 1974), and by Mossin (1968), who have generalized it in different directions.

Arrow and Mossin both assume that there is a proportional loading on the premium, i.e. that $P = (1 + \alpha)E\{x\}$, where $\alpha > 0$. In (4) there is no loss of generality if we choose the utility scale so that $\lambda = 1$, so that the solution to the more general problem is given by

$$u'(W + y_r - x_r - P) = (1 + \alpha) \tag{5}$$

Mossin assumed that the only permissible compensation functions are of the form $y(x) = kx$, and that the corresponding premium is $k(1+\alpha)E\{x\}$. He then shows that for $a > 0$ it is optimal to buy an insurance contract with $k < 1$. This result seems to be contradicted by observations. If a traveller insures his baggage at all, we will expect him to take insurance for its full value.

In (5) Arrow (1974) makes the additional assumption that $y_r \geq 0$, i.e. that the compensation cannot be negative. By Kuhn-Tucker methods he then shows that the optimal insurance contract is of the form

$$y(x) = 0 \qquad \text{for } x \leq D\,,$$

$$y(x) = x - D \qquad \text{for } x > D\,.$$

Here D is the familiar deductible which occurs in many insurance contracts.

It is clear that under weak assumptions (5) will have a solution of the form $y_r = x_r - c$. It makes no sense to buy insurance contracts which imply a negative "compensation" for small losses, but the amount c can well be added to the premium. This simply means that the insurer charges a flat fee c to cover his expenses, which generally can be assumed independent of the form of contract chosen by the buyer. If the fee can be expected to yield some profits, the insurer may forgo the proportional loading.

If $P\{kx\} = kE\{x\} + c = k\bar{x} + c$, Mossin's problem takes the form: Determine the value of k which maximizes $U(k) = E\{u(kx - x - k\bar{x} - c)\}$. It is then easy to show that $U'(1) = 0$, and that full cover is optimal.

It follows that if the premium is $P = \bar{x} + c$, the client will buy full cover if and only if $E\{u(W - x)\} < u(W - \bar{x} - c)$, otherwise he will take no insurance at all.

Deductibles do not seem very relevant in a theory of risk bearing, which assumes that insurers are risk neutral. This follows almost trivially from earlier work, i.a. by Borch (1960) and Arrow (1963) on Pareto optimal risk sharing. If the insurer is risk neutral, i.e. if he is interested only in expected profits, there must exist a premium, $P > E\{x\}$, which will induce a risk averse buyer to take full insurance cover. Deductibles should be seen as a practical device for avoiding the expenses involved in checking and paying compensation for negligible losses.

As a slightly more general application of (3′) we shall consider the premium function $v(x) = (1 + \alpha x)f(x)$. This implies that the insurer is risk averse, and corresponds to premium formulae used in practice. (5) is then replaced by

$$u'\Big(W + y(x) - x - E\{(1+\alpha x)y\}\Big) = 1 + \alpha x \qquad (5')$$

This equation will under weak assumptions determine the optimal contract as a function $y(x)$.

Consider now the case of quadratic utility, and write $u'(z) = K(a-z)$ for $z \le a$. Here the scale factor K, must be determined so that $u'(W - \bar{x}) = 1$, i.e. $K = (a - W + \bar{x})^{-1}$. Taking $W = 0$ for the sake of simplicity, we see that (5′) will take the form:

$$a - y + x + E\{(1+\alpha x)y\} = (1+\alpha x)(a + \bar{x}) \qquad (6)$$

which reduces to

$$(y - \bar{y}) - (x - \bar{x}) - \alpha E\{xy\} + \alpha(a + \bar{x})x = 0$$

Taking the expectation of this equation, we find

$$E\{xy\} = (a + \bar{x})\bar{x}$$

Substitution in (6) then gives the optimal contract:

$$y(x) = \big(1 - \alpha(a + \bar{x})\big)x + \bar{y} - \big(1 - \alpha(a + \bar{x})\big)\bar{x}$$

Under this contract the insured will pay a premium $P = \bar{y} - \big(1 - \alpha(a + \bar{x})\big)\bar{x}$, to which a fee c may be added, and he will receive a compensation $\big(1 - \alpha(a + \bar{x})\big)x$, if his loss amounts to x. The function $y(x)$ is linear only because we have assumed that the buyer's marginal utility is linear, and will of course be different for other preferences.

References for Section 4

Arrow KJ. (1963): Uncertainty and the welfare economics of medical care, *American Economic Review 53*, 941–973.

Arrow KJ. (1974): Optimal insurance and generalized deductibles. *Scandinavian Actuarial Journal*, 1–42.

Borch K. (1960): The safety loading of reinsurance premiums, *Skandinavisk Aktuarietidskrift*, 163–184.

Mossin J. (1968): Aspects of rational insurance buying, *Journal of Political Economy 76*, 553–568.

CHAPTER 7

UNINSURABLE RISKS

1. Conditions that a Risk is Insurable

1.1 Older insurance texts often gave a lengthy discussion of the conditions a risk must satisfy in order to be insurable. Among these conditions was the requirement that it must be possible to make reliable estimates of the relevant probabilities from statistical observations. The implication is really that a risk is insurable only if one can apply the law of large numbers.

This seems to be too strict, although a recent book by an insurance executive Berliner (1982) takes this attitude. Most modern authors tend to take the pragmatic attitude that if two parties agree on an insurance contract, the risk covered is by definition insurable. The saying *Ab esse ad posse valet consequentia* expresses good common sense.

1.2 In marine insurance war risk in any part of the world is covered as a routine. It may not always be clear how premium rates are set, but they seem acceptable to both parties to the insurance contract.

Commercial telecommunication satellites are regularly insured. In the beginning there was practically no statistical information available, but technical analysis of the possibility that different components could malfunction made it possible for insurers to quote premiums, and these premiums seemed in general to be acceptable to the buyers of insurance.

When the commercial jet airliners started to fly there was little experience available. Military jet planes had flown for years but their record was presumably neither available to insurers, nor considered as relevant by them. The dismal record of the "Comet", the British-built jet liner was something which insurers hoped would turn out to be irrelevant, and which airlines hoped would be forgotten.

When the first of the new jet liners were insured the premium for hull insurance was set at 8% of the value, and this was accepted by the airlines. It soon turned out that the premium was much too high. It was gradually reduced and sometimes the premium was less than one per cent.

1.3 A risk can be insured also when no statistics is available, and even when no theoretical analysis seems possible. This is brought out by the following case reported by Brown (1973):

In 1971 the whisky distillery Cutty Sark offered an award of one million pounds for the capture of the monster assumed to live in Loch Ness. Apparently Cutty Sark had second thoughts about the liability this promise could lead to, and approached Lloyd's about insurance. As usual Lloyd's was obliging, and agreed to cover the risk against a premium of £2.500. From the insurance contract or "slip", reproduced in Brown's book, it is evident that Lloyd's observed all the proper forms. It is stated that the risk is covered only if the monster is captured alive between 1st May 1971 and 30th April 1972. Further the slip says:

"As far as this insurance is concerned the Loch Ness Monster shall be deemed to be:

1) In excess of 20 feet in length
2) Acceptable as the Loch Ness monster to the curators of the Natural History Museum, London".

As a last condition the underwriters added the standard clause in marine insurance that if the sum insured should be paid, the monster would become the property of the underwriters at Lloyd's. This condition should make the insurance contract virtually risk-free to the underwriters.

1.4 One must assume that there were a number of underwriters at Lloyd's who were firmly convinced that there was no monster in Loch Ness, and hence should be willing to accept the whole risk at a nominal premium. They were however cautious. The leading underwriter accepted to cover only 7.5% of the risk, and none of his colleagues accepted a higher share. The explanation of this caution may be that at the time there was a committee at Lloyd's which monitored the underwriting of members. If this committee found that an underwriter had accepted risks which were not commensurate with his resources, it would give him a polite warning. It is possible that there was some member of this committee who did not believe that the insurance cover given to Cutty Sark was risk-less, and hence might suggest that the underwriters should reduce their engagement in other risks.

As for Cutty Sark, somebody in the top management of the company must have believed that there might be a monster in Loch Ness, and that the probability that it should be captured during the next twelve months was not negligible.

1.5 The example above may lead one to believe that every risk is insurable. In theory this may be true, but in practice it is not. There are at least two elements which can make a risk uninsurable, and usually referred to as "Adverse Selection" and "Moral Hazard". They will be discussed in some detail in the next two sections.

(i) *Adverse selection* occurs mainly in household insurance when it is prohibitively expensive to rate every risk correctly. In such cases the insurer may have to charge the same premium to all risks in a group, based on his general knowledge of the average losses caused by risks of the type considered. Some prospective buyers who represent low risks may find the premiums based on averages too high, and decide to go without insurance. This will increase the average loss on the risks insured, and may lead to further increases in the premium, which again may induce more people to do without insurance. It is easy to see that this may start a chain reaction, with the result that the risk eventually turns out to be uninsurable. In some cases one can deal with such situations by introducing a scheme of no-claim bonus of the form discussed in Chapter 6.

(ii) *Moral hazard* occurs when the insured can cheat on his obligations under the insurance contract without being discovered. It may be possible for the insurer to check and make sure that the insured really observes his obligations — of taking proper care to prevent accidents, and limit the damage if an accident occurs. Such checking does however cost money, and the costs must be born by the insured. If these costs are very high, the insurance contract may become unacceptable to the prospective buyer, and hence the risk will become uninsurable.

A business insurance contract will usually cover a number of different risks, and some of these can simply be excluded, if they lead to expensive checking measures.

1.6 There is obviously a fairly close connection between adverse selection and moral hazard, and often it is difficult to distinguish between the two.

The present interest in moral hazard among economists springs from a paper by Arrow (1963). In his terminology moral hazard is present if: "The insurance policy might itself change incentives and therefore the probabilities upon which the insurance company has relied. Thus, a fire insurance policy for more than the value of the premises might be an inducement to arson or at least to carelessness".

This definition seems to capture the essential elements of a concept which many authors have tried to define in general terms. The example may help a reader to get an intuitive grasp of the concept, but from an insurance point of view it is slightly misleading. In most countries the law will prevent a person from making a profit by over-insuring his property. This holds whether the property is destroyed by accidental fire or a fire set by the owner himself. It is also doubtful if a person becomes careless if he has adequate fire insurance on his property. He may however be less heroic in his efforts to fight the fire and limit the damage, than he would have been if the property was uninsured. Hence the existence of the insurance contract may affect the probability distribution of the loss. A better example may be found in automobile insurance. The owner of an automobile usually has the right to lend his car to anybody who has a valid driver's license. If however his insurance does not cover collision risk, he may be reluctant to lend his car to others, and this may reduce the probability of accidents.

1.7 The definition of moral hazard outlined by Arrow implies that claim payments under an insurance contract are given by a conditional probability density $f\big(x|y(x)\big)$, where $y(x)$ is the "compensation function" introduced in Chapter 2. For a given function $y(x)$ there should be no particular problems involved in quoting a premium for insurance to cover of this risk, so it is insurable, if the premium is acceptable to the would be buyer of insurance. One can clearly compute the premium for any function $y(x)$, and let the prospective insured choose which compensation function he prefers — if any, costs considered.

Arrow studied the welfare economics of health care. In this context the density function above must be interpreted as the density of expenditure x on health services, given that insurance will cover a part $y(x)$ of the expenditure. In most cases people do not pay for their health insurance themselves. The premium is often paid — in part or in full — by an employer, or by the government under some social security scheme. If the premium is paid by the employer, and covers all expenditure on health care, health services become a "free good" to the insured, and one must expect his consumption of this good to be excessive. With a system of deductibles and co-insurance, one may be able to keep the demand for health services "reasonable", or at least within the capacity of the existing health services. This system seems to work for a similar line of insurance, that of legal assistance. This line does however not carry the same ethical and emotional overtones as health insurance. In any case it should be clear that the mere fact that the claim distribution depends on the insurance cover is not sufficient to make a risk uninsurable.

2. Adverse Selection

2.1 The concept of adverse selection was first studied in connection with life insurance. In the early days of life insurance the insurers were very concerned over the possibility that people who applied for life insurance might be in poor health, and likely to die earlier than assumed in the standard mortality table. In the middle of the 19th century a medical examination was virtually mandatory before a life policy was issued. At the time a medical examination was simpler and cheaper than today, and presumably had less predictive power.

Today practically anybody can get life insurance, but if there is anything unfavorable in his medical history he may have to pay a higher premium than the normal one. This higher premium will of course include a medical examination, fees to consulting physicians and statisticians, and all the expenses necessary to determine the correct premium for a "sub-standard life", to use the technical term.

2.2 Adverse selection can clearly occur in any kind of insurance. A person who is exposed to a risk and worries about it, is likely to seek insurance. It is however not obvious that the worry also implies that the person represents a risk higher than the average. Further it is not certain that he is so price conscious that he will cancel the insurance if the premium is increased, and thus start the chain reaction described in the preceding section.

These observations seem to indicate that adverse selection is not a particularly useful concept in the study of general insurance. In life insurance the concept is however in daily use. In Chapter 4 it was observed that a current life-long pension to a person of age x represented an accumulated saving of $\bar{a}_x$. The recipient cannot change the contract and receive the amount $\bar{a}_x$ in cash. One assumes that a person who wants to convert a life-long income into a lump sum of cash must believe that he is in poor health, and hence that his choice represents adverse selection.

An analysis of this kind is applied to any proposed change in the insurance contract. Consider for instance a whole life insurance, to be paid for by a level premium during a period n. The level premium P is determined by the condition

$$P\bar{a}_{x:\bar{n}|} = \bar{A}$$

At any time $t < n$ the insured can stop premium payments and demand the surrender value of the policy in cash. An alternative is to stop payments and let the contract continue as a paid-up policy with a lower face value. As the accumulated savings of the insured at time t is $\bar{A}_{x+t} - P\bar{a}_{x+t:\overline{n-t|}}$, the new face value is

$$F = \frac{\bar{A}_{x+t} - P\bar{a}_{x+t:\overline{n-t|}}}{\bar{A}_{x+t}}$$

Assume now that instead of any of these two alternatives, the insured wants to continue the insurance with the face value unchanged, but he wants to pay a lower premium over a longer period — say as long as he is alive. The new premium P_1 is then determined by the relation

$$P\bar{a}_{x+t:\overline{n-t|}} = P_1\bar{a}_{x+t}$$

This proposed change will however immediately put the actuary on the alert against adverse selection, and the change will probably not be permitted.

2.3 One of the first studies of adverse selection in nonlife insurance is by Rothschild and Stiglitz (1976). They study the existence of a competitive equilibrium in an insurance market, and base their presentation on an extensive use of diagrams. In analytical terms their model can be described as follows.

A person with initial wealth W is exposed to a risk which can cause a loss x with probability π. The person can pay a premium cP, $c \leq 1$ to an insurance company, which in return undertakes to pay a compensation cx if the loss occurs. If the persons preferences can be represented by the utility function $u(\cdot)$, his problem is to determine the value of c which maximizes his expected utility:

$$U(c) = (1 - \pi)u(W - cP) + \pi u(W - c\pi x - x + cx) \quad (1)$$

Rothschild and Stiglitz ignore administrative expenses, and argue that competition between insurers will drive the premium down to $P = \pi x$, the point where the expected profit of insurers is zero. This means that (1) can be written as

$$U(c) = (1 - \pi)u(W - c\pi x) + \pi u(W - c\pi x - x + cx)$$

The first order condition for a maximum

$$U'(c) = -(1-\pi)\pi x u'(W - c\pi c) + \pi(1-\pi)xu'(W - c\pi x - x + cx) = 0$$

which reduces to

$$u'(W - c\pi x) = u'(W - c\pi x - x + cx)$$

This holds only if $c = 1$. Hence the person will buy full insurance cover if the insurer's expected profit is zero, a result found i.a. by Mossin, and discussed in Chapter 2.

2.4 Assume now that there are two types of risks in the market, "high" and "low", with claim probabilities of respectively π_H and π_L, with $\pi_H > \pi_L$, and take for the sake of simplicity $x = 1$. If the insurance company can distinguish the two types of risk without incurring any costs, there is no problem. Each group will be charged its proper premium, i.e. $P_H = \pi_H$ and $P_L = \pi_L$ respectively, they will both buy full cover, and the insurance company can be expected to break even.

The problem of adverse selection occurs if it is impossible or prohibitively expensive to examine each risk and set the correct premium. The insurer may then have to charge the same premium for each risk. It is natural to assume that this premium P lies in the interval $\pi_L \leq P \leq \pi_H$. In that case the customers representing the high risk will all buy full insurance, i.e. choose $c = 1$. Those who represent the low risks will buy an insurance cover $c < 1$, where c is determined by the first order condition

$$(1-\pi_L)Pu'(W - cP) = \pi_L(1-P)u'(W - cP - 1 + c) \tag{2}$$

This means that for the insurer there is

an expected loss of $\pi_H - P$ on each high risk
an expected profit of $c(P - \pi_L)$ on each low risk

The zero expected profit condition takes the form

$$c(P - \pi_L) + P - \pi_H = 0$$

or

$$P = \frac{\pi_H + c\pi_L}{1 + c} \tag{3}$$

If (3) has meaningful solutions in c and P, one or more equilibria of some kind will exist. They may even be considered as "competitive" and "Pareto optimal" within the restrictions imposed by the model.

2.5 The paper by Rothschild and Stiglitz has indeed proved to be seminal, also by throwing new light on older problems. There is for instance the one which once was known as the "problem of the discriminating monopolist". If a monopolist producer knows how much each of the customers is willing to pay for his product, he can earn a profit in excess of what he would gain if he was forced not to discriminate, by law or by lack of information.

The Rothschild-Stiglitz paper also gives new insight into the more recent subject of "signaling" developed by Spence (1974). When the insurance buyer makes his decision, he inevitably conveys some information, or sends a "signal" to the insurer. If the buyer does not take full insurance cover he sends a signal which can be interpreted to mean that he (believes) he represents a lower risk than the one which corresponds to the premium he pays. If the insurer interprets the signal in this way, he may lower the premium, and the customer may buy full insurance cover.

It is however possible to send a false signal. By buying less than full insurance cover the customer may lead the insurer to believe that he represents a low risk, and charge a lower premium. It may take a considerable time before the insurer accumulates enough statistics to conclude that the customer must belong to the high risk category.

Theoretical analysis of this situation leads to a number of interesting problems, which can be brought together under the heading of "asymmetric information". These problems are clearly important in economics, since it usually will be unreasonable to assume that all parties to a transaction have access to the same relevant information. Insurance should in some sense be an exception, since the insured is supposed to provide the insurer with all relevant information. People do however not always do what they are supposed to do, nor do they accept uncritically all information they receive from other parties to a contract under negotiation. Hence asymmetric information is of importance in insurance, and a comprehensive survey of its implications are given in a recent book by Cresta (1984).

Practically oriented studies of how to deal with these problems lead to methods similar to the no-claim bonus systems discussed in Chapter 6.

2.6 To illustrate how adverse selection can make a risk uninsurable it is useful to discuss an example. Consider a group of n persons, each exposed to a risk which can cause a loss equal to 1. Assume that the probability that person r shall suffer a loss is p_r $(r = 1, 2, \ldots, n)$, and assume for the sake of simplicity that $p_1 > p_2 > \ldots > p_n$.

If an insurance company covers all persons in the group against the losses, expected claim payments will be $\sum_r p_r$. If the company charges the same net premium to the members of the group, this premium will be

$$P(n) = \frac{1}{n}\sum_{r=1}^{n} p_r$$

Assume now that person r is risk averse, and that he has some idea of his own probability of suffering a loss. Assume further that after some analysis of expected utility he decides that he will buy the insurance only if

$$P(n) < (1+\lambda)p_r \tag{4}$$

The condition (4) represents a convenient simplification. The highest premium person r is willing to pay P_r is determined by

$$u_r(W_r - P_r) = (1 - p_r)u_r(W_r) + p_r u_r(W - 1)$$

If the utility function is concave, it follows from Jensen's inequality that $P_r > p_r$.

As a concrete interpretation of the model one can think of insurance against natural disaster, say avalanches in the Swiss Alps or riveting flooding in the Mississippi Valley. If the premium is low, the insurance may be bought by most property owners in the area. If on the other hand the premium is high, it is likely that only owners of the most exposed property will be interested in insurance.

2.7 If the insurance company charges the premium $P(n)$, and the inequality (4) holds only for $r \leq k < n$, insurance will be bought by the owners of the k highest risks. The company will then receive a total premium $kP(n)$, and this amount will be insufficient to pay expected claims from the k highest risks. To see this, write

$$kP(n) = \frac{k}{n}\sum_{r=1}^{n} p_r < \sum_{r=1}^{k} P_r$$

Division by k gives

$$P(n) = \frac{1}{n}\sum_{r=1}^{n} p_r < \frac{1}{k}\sum_{r=1}^{k} P_r = P(k) \tag{5}$$

The meaning of (5) is the obvious, that higher premium is required if only the k highest risks join the insurance scheme. The higher premium may lead more property owners to drop their insurance, and the chain reaction will go on.

If the relation

$$(1+\lambda)p_{k+1} < P(k) < (1+\lambda)p_k \tag{6}$$

holds for some number k, it is possible to cover the k highest risks, without any expected loss to the insurer. If (6) holds only for small k's, it is reasonable to say that the risk is uninsurable. The condition (6) can hold for many different values of k, and any k which satisfies (6) will represent an equilibrium of some kind, but it will not have the optimality properties associated with a competitive equilibrium.

The model outlined above seems to capture the essential elements of the situation studied by Rothschild and Stiglitz, and it gives a simpler and less technical explanation of the implications of their result.

2.8 If it is desirable that a risk should be insured, although the risk is inherently uninsurable, insurance may be made compulsory. In some cantons in Switzerland insurance against damage caused to buildings by avalanches and fires is compulsory.

In the 18th century fire insurance of property in some towns in Northern Europe was made compulsory. This may have been out of concern for the welfare of the citizens, but the main motive of the authorities seems to have been protection of the tax-base. It is interesting that this should have been thought necessary. In England voluntary fire insurance was developed successfully on a commercial basis after the great fire in London in 1666.

Kunreuther (1978) has studied several schemes for government subsidized insurance against damage to property caused by natural disaster in the U.S.A. These schemes were not particularly successful. People were not anxious to buy the insurance, even if they knew that the price was heavily subsidized. This seems to contradict most of the results derived in this section, and a number of explanations are possible. One is that people systematically underrate the probabilities of disastrous events. Another explanation discussed by Kunreuther is that people believe that if hit by disaster, they will receive relief from public funds, whether they have insurance or not.

3. Moral Hazard

3.1 There is no doubt that the concept of moral hazard has its origin in marine insurance. The old standard marine insurance policy of Lloyd's — known as the S.G. (Ship and goods) policy — covered "physical hazard", more picturesquely described as the "perils of the sea". The "moral hazard" supposed to be excluded, but it seemed difficult to give a precise definition of this concept.

One of the leading British writers on marine insurance in this century, Victor Dover (1957, p. 189–190) writes: "It is often said that whereas physical hazard can be rated, where there is pronounced moral hazard the risk should be declined by the underwriter. "Moral hazard" is somewhat difficult to define precisely. It may be said to be some element in the nature of the insurance, either with regard to the assured's interest, or the surrounding conditions, which makes — the happening of a casualty a means of benefit to the policy-holder". Half a page later he writes: "Moral hazard is sometimes associated with particular parts, countries or even flags. In such circumstances, underwriters attempt to meet the position by imposing extra premiums. Such discrimination is usually difficult to maintain. For example, vessels of Greek nationality and/or management have sometimes been subjected to such treatment by the marine insurance market. — In the past investigations have usually demonstrated that discrimination on grounds of flag alone cannot be justified. The alternative would appear to be the compilation of so-called "Black Lists" of owners having a bad record, but even this approach presents difficulties".

3.2 Dover's view seems to be that if moral hazard is present, a higher premium should be charged, but he is somehow at loss to give advice as to when and by how much the premium should be increased. His difficulty with giving a general definition is understandable. The SG-policy covers as a peril of the sea "barratry", an antiquated term which the Oxford dictionary defines as "fraud or gross negligence of master or crew to prejudice of ship's owners". Most modern economists, not familiar with Lloyd's SG-policy will probably consider this as a typical example of moral hazard. The insured, i.e. the owner should confide his ship only to a competent and reliable crew.

An insurance executive Page (1957) takes a simpler view. He offers the definition: "Taken as a whole, moral hazard may be defined as that condition that exists in a risk, either physically or mentally, which is a departure from the standards of conduct acceptable to society, which in turn increases the likelihood of loss". Ten lines later he explains the implications: "When insurers are permitted to establish varying rate levels based on their own qualitative judgements on the seriousness of the moral hazard, it is probable that insurers will be willing to voluntarily insure most risks".

An insurer is of course free to exercise his subjective judgement in the rating of a risk which he keeps on his own account. If however he wants reinsurance for parts of the risk, it is important that the potential reinsurers agree with his subjective judgement. Some consensus must be reached, and this may mean that each reinsurer makes his own evaluation of the risk. This will involve some expenses, and hence the existence, or the possibility of moral hazard will lead to higher insurance premiums.

3.3 It may be useful to give a third and short definition from a widely used British textbook. Dinsdale (1949) writes: "Moral hazard mainly concerns the *bona fides* of the proposer and is therefore dependent upon his character and business integrity. It is essential that the insured be scrupulously honest in all his dealings with his insurers so that he will act with the same prudence as he would do if uninsured". This is essentially a definition in the same spirit as the one given by Arrow (1963).

The same idea is behind the following remarks by a leading American writer on marine insurance, William Winter ((1952), p. 108–109): "... the whole fabric of marine underwriting is based on good faith and fair dealing between underwriter and assured. This element in the marine contract is little talked of but is ever present and is known as *moral hazard*".

3.4 It is possible to cite a number of other definitions which seem to confirm that moral hazard in general is an elusive concept. This is neither useful nor original observation. It is therefore desirable to try to be more concrete and consider a simple example due to Borch (1982), which can be analysed by methods from game theory.

If the baggage of an air traveller is lost or damaged, the airline will under international rules have to pay a compensation. Usually an airline will take insurance to cover this liability, and the insurance contract will oblige the airline to take all reasonable steps to prevent loss or damage of the passengers' baggage.

The baggage is exposed to many risks, and one of these is that it can be stolen on arrival in the claim area. The airline can make certain that this does not happen, by checking the tag on every suitcase against the ticket stub. Assume that in the insurance contract the airline undertakes to do just this, as a part of taking reasonable care to prevent losses. It is clear that such complete control will be a costly procedure, and the airline may be tempted to cut costs, by doing only some spot checking. The insurer is aware of this, and may decide to do some random checking on his own, to satisfy himself that the airline has control of who picks up whose suitcases.

3.5 The situation described can be considered as a two-person game, described by the following payoff table:

		Airline (Player A)	
		No check	Check
Insurer	No check	$-G, 0$	$0, -C$
(Player I)	Check	$P - D - G, -P$	$-D, -C$

G = the value of baggage stolen in the absence of any checking. This amount must be paid by player I.
C = the cost of carrying out the complete checking which player A has undertaken to do in the insurance contract.
D = the cost to player I of controlling that player A always keeps his contractual obligations.
P = the penalty which player A must pay to player I, if it is discovered that the checking is not in accordance with the insurance contract.

The table implies that the insurer can only check the control measures of the airline, and cannot prevent theft.

3.6 Assume now that both players decide to do their checking in a random manner:

Player I checks on a fraction x of the arrivals.

Player A checks on a fraction y of the arrivals.

If both players make their choices independently, and in a random manner, there will be a probability $x(1 - y)$ that the inspector from the insurance company discovers that the airline does not carry out a complete checking. If this happens, player A pays the penalty P, and player I receives a net amount $P - D - G$.

The payoffs for the other combinations are easily established, and we find the expected payoffs to the two players:

$$v_I(x,y) = -1(1-x)(1-y)G + x(1-y)(P-D-G) - xyD$$
$$= -(1-y)G + x(P-D-yP)$$
$$v_A(x,y) = -x(1-y)P - yC = xP - y(c - xP)$$

A pair of mixed strategies ($\bar{x}$, $\bar{y}$) is an equilibrium point of the game if:

$$v_I(\bar{x},\bar{y}) \geq v_I(x,\bar{y}),$$

and

$$v_A(\bar{x},\bar{y}) \geq v_A(\bar{x},y)$$

The meaning is that a player cannot gain by departing from his equilibrium strategy, if the opponent uses his equilibrium strategy.

3.7 In the game between the insurer and the airline, it is easy to see that the only pair of equilibrium strategies is

$$\bar{x} = \frac{C}{P} \quad \text{and} \quad \bar{y} = \frac{P-D}{P}$$

The corresponding payoffs to the two players are

$$v_I(\bar{x},\bar{y}) = -\frac{DG}{P} \quad \text{and} \quad v_A(\bar{x},\bar{y}) = -C \tag{7}$$

The solution is meaningful only if

(i) $P > D$: The insurer will only check if the penalty he can collect exceeds checking costs. If this is not the case, the equilibrium strategies will be that $\bar{x} = \bar{y} = 0$, and the corresponding pair of payoffs $(-G, 0)$.

(ii) $P > C$: The airline will only check if the penalty it must pay exceeds checking costs. Otherwise the equilibrium strategies will be $\bar{x} = 1$ and $\bar{y} = 0$, and the payoff pair is $(P - D - G, -P)$.

If the inequalities $P > C$ and $P > D$ both hold, it follows from (7) that it will never pay for the airline to cheat. The expected savings from less than complete checking, will be equal to the penalty which must be paid if the airline is caught cheating. The expected cost to the airline will be equal to C, the cost of complete checking, provided of course that both players use their equilibrium strategies.

From (7) it also follows that the insurer will incur expected costs of DG/P, because he finds it necessary to check that the airline observes the conditions of the insurance contract. This will be the real cost of moral hazard, and it will of course be added to the premium that the insured must pay. It is worth noting that this extra charge does not reflect on the morale of the insured. He may have no intention of cheating, but he has the opportunity. A prudent insurer will consider this as an additional risk, and add a charge to the premium.

If the penalty is very high, the risk due to the presence of moral hazard may become insignificant. Often legislation or competition will set limits to the harshness of the conditions that an insurer can write into the insurance contract. A possible penalty may be $P = G$, which means that the insurance contract is declared void, so that the airline has to pay the compensation to passengers who lose their baggage. The additional premium will then be D, i.e. the cost of complete checking by the insurer.

3.8 It is easy to find other examples of how this model can be applied to calculate the extra premium that an insurer must charge, when moral hazard is present.

A manufacturer may obtain a reduction in the premium for his fire insurance, if he undertakes to install sprinklers and fire extinguishers, and arranges regular fire drills for his employees. The insurer may however, from time to time send an inspector to check if the sprinkler actually works, and that the extinguishers are in place, and that the employees know how to use them. This inspection will cost money, and the costs must be paid by the insured, i.e. in this case by the manufacturer.

Product liability insurance protects a producer against claims made those who buy or use his product. An insurer who agrees to cover this risk, will naturally want to satisfy himself that the producer has effective control of his production, and that proper care is taken to prevent defective products from reaching the market. In order to achieve this the insurer will have to inspect the producer's routines for quality control. The cost of this inspection has to be paid by the producer, as an additional premium, even if he takes the utmost care to maintain the quality of his product.

3.9 In a major paper on moral hazard Stiglitz (1983) stresses the importance of incentives, and argues that insurance contracts should be designed so that they induce the insured to take good care of his property. This is an important point, but the importance of incentives is brought out much more clearly in his earlier work, Stiglitz (1974) on share-cropping.

A landowner can work his land in several ways:

(i) He can hire labour at fixed wages to do the work. This arrangement means that all the risk is carried by the landowner, and will usually imply some costs of supervision of the workers.

(ii) He can rent his land to the workers. This means that all risk is carried by the workers, who should have strong incentives to work efficiently.

(iii) The landowner and labour can share the risk, for instance by a share-cropping contract. If both parties are risk adverse, they will prefer this arrangement to any of the two first ones. For the landowner it is however important that the contract gives the workers incentives to work the land efficiently.

References for Sections 1–3

Berliner B. (1982): *Limits of Instability of Risks*, Prentice-Hall.

Borch K. (1982): "Insuring and Auditing the Auditor", *Games Economic Dynamics and Time Series Analysis*, Deistler, Fürst and Schwödiauer, eds. Physica Verlag 117–127.

Brown A. (1973): *Hazard Unlimited. The Story of Lloyd's of London.* London: Peter Davies Ltd.

Cresta J.P. (1984): *Théorie des Marchés d'Assurance.* Paris: Economica.

Dinsdale W.A. (1949): *Elements of Insurance*, London: Pitman & Sons.

Dover V. (1957): *A Handbook to Marine Insurance.* Fifth edition. London: Witherby.

Kunreuther H. (1978): *Disaster Insurance Protection*, John Wiley & Sons.

Page R.H. (1957): "Underwriting", *Multiple-Line Insurers*, Michelbacher and Roos, eds. McGraw-Hill.

Rothschild M., Stiglitz J. (1976): "Equilibrium in Competitive Insurance Markets", *Quarterly Journal of Economics 90*, 629–649.

Spence M. (1974): *Market Signaling*, Harvard University Press.

Stiglitz J.E. (1974): "Incentives and Risk Sharing in Share-cropping", *Review of Economic Studies 41*, 219–255.

Stiglitz J.E. (1983): "Risk, Incentives and Insurance: The Pure Theory of Moral Hazard", *The Geneva Papers on Risk and Insurance 26*, 4–33.

Winter W.D. (1952): *Marine Insurance: Its Principles and Practice*, Third Edition, McGraw-Hill.

4. The Monster in Loch Ness*

In 1971 the whisky producer Cutty Sark offered an award of one million pounds for the capture of the monster assumed to exist in Loch Ness. The author does not know what led the firm to make this offer, nor does he know how the offer affected the firm's share of the whisky market. His only source of information is a recent book by Anthony Brown (1973).

Apparently somebody in the higher echelons of Cutty Sark got cold feet after the offer had been made, and approached Lloyd's in London. As usual Lloyd's was obliging, and agreed to cover the risk for a premium of £2500. The case was appropriately handled by marine underwriters.

The insurance contract or "slip" is reproduced in Brown's book, and it is of interest that Lloyd's observed all the proper forms. The contract specifies that the risk is covered only if the monster is captured alive between 1st May 1971 and 30th April 1972. Further the slip says:

"As far as this insurance is concerned, the Loch Ness Monster shall be deemed to be:

1) In excess of 20 feet in length
2) Acceptable as the Loch Ness Monster to the curators of the Natural History Museum, London.

In the event of loss hereunder, the monster shall become the property of the underwriters hereon".

Presumably Cutty Sark found that this wording gave the firm adequate protection. The possibility of selling "Nessie", once captured, should make the contract virtually risk free from the underwriters' point of view, and was probably overlooked in the first place by Cutty Sark.

A Bayesian could make many interesting observations in connection with this insurance contract. If he or she knows something about insurance, s/he will note that the premium is fairly high, considerably higher than the premium for fire insurance on good residential buildings. The rate may be of the same order as the fire insurance premium which Cutty Sark pays for its plant and inventories and should indicate that the managers of Cutty Sark assign about the same probabilities to the capture of the monster and to a major fire in the firm. This is considered a fairly safe conclusion, but some reservations are in order. A market exists for fire insurance, and possibly the firm would be willing to pay much more than the going rate

---

* Reprinted from *The Journal of Risk and Insurance*, 1976; 33(3):521–525, copyright (c) The American Risk and Insurance Association.

for its insurance. If a strong risk aversion is behind all decisions made by the firm, it may buy insurance against events which can occur only with infinitesimal probabilities.

The probability P_e that a monster in Loch Ness exists can of course not be smaller than the probability P_c that the same monster shall be captured in a single season, i.e. we must have $P_e \geq P_c$. From this probability relationship it follows that

$$P_e = 0 \Rightarrow P_c = 0$$

If the latter of the probabilities is positive, Nessie is certain to be captured in an infinite sequence of trials, and hence that he (or she) exists. This means that

$$P_c > 0 \Rightarrow P_e = 1$$

Patently the inverse of the two relations does not necessarily hold. A person may be convinced that the monster exists, because he "believes his own eyes", but he or she may still assign a zero probability to the event that Nessie shall be captured. We would expect that no series of unsuccessful attempts to capture the monster can shake the prior beliefs of this person.

From such observations a complete Bayesian model could be built for the decision process which led Cutty Sark to take insurance in London. The author shall not do this, since his knowledge of the firm is limited to some samples — too few and too small — of its main product. Noted, however is that the managers of the firm evidently assigned a non-negligible probability to the event that Nessie should be captured alive during the 1971–1972 season. This observation leads to the inevitable conclusion that some influential distillers in the glens of Scotland are firmly convinced that a monster is in Loch Ness.

Now turn to Lloyd's of London where there are more than 7000 members. One would expect that some of these — or rather some of their underwriters — would be convinced absolutely that no monster exists in Loch Ness. Also expected is that a good broker, with his or her client's interests at heart, would seek out these underwriters and bring down the premium, by making the disbelievers compete for the slip from Cutty Sark.

This scenario did not happen, and it seems that the broker had some difficulty in having the slip covered. Apparently no underwriter was willing just to sign the slip, pocket a profit of a few thousand pounds, and forget about it. The slip was covered in a cautious manner, with a number of underwriters accepting from 1 to 10 per cent of the risk.

Given these facts, the temptation is to conclude that all underwriters at Lloyd's must be convinced that a monster does exist in Loch Ness. Life usually is more complicated than the mathematical models which can be handled with ease. Therefore the elements which have been assumed away should be examined in order to reach a clear-cut conclusion.

Expenses are associated with any underwriting, and the broker is entitled to his or her commission. Possibly, although not likely, the premium paid by Cutty Sark was just sufficient to cover the cost of negotiating an unorthodox insurance contract.

Also possibly the underwriters at Lloyd's recognized the slip for what it was, a gift from Heaven. For ethical reasons the leading underwriter may then have felt that friends and other colleagues should be let in on a good thing.

Neither of these explanations is satisfactory, and a third explanation which has some mathematical foundation may be outlined.

Underwriters at Lloyd's operate under strict, although mainly self-imposed rules, and are not allowed to over-extend their underwriting. Each underwriter will have to keep below a limit, say M, which can be thought of as the maximum possible loss under the contracts in his or her portfolio. Let the stochastic variable x, with the distribution $F(x)$ represent the claim payments under these contracts, and let P be the premium received by the underwriter. His expected profit will be

$$E = \int_0^M (P - x)\, dF(x)$$

where $F(M) = 1$.

Let now N be the amount payable if Nessie is captured, and Let Q be the premium offered for insurance against this risk. If the underwriter does not believe in the existence of the monster, he can increase his (subjective) expected profit by an amount qQ by accepting a fraction q of the slip from Cutty Sark. In doing so he or she however will exceed his or her limit, so only a fraction p of the portfolio can be retained, determined by the equation:

$$pM + qN = M \qquad \text{or} \qquad p = 1 - q\frac{N}{M}$$

The expected profit of the underwriter will then be

$$E_q = pE + qQ = E - q\left(\frac{N}{M}E - Q\right)$$

This equation produces the following: $E_q > E$ if $NE > MQ$. Hence if the underwriter wants to maximize expected profits, he or she will either refuse to touch Nessie at all, or s/he will be prepared to accept the whole risk. It can be shown that a similar "all or nothing" conclusion will be reached if the underwriter also assigns a positive probability to the event that the monster will be captured.

In order to explain the observed behaviour of the underwriters at Lloyd's one can introduce risk aversion, represented by the utility function $u(x)$. If the underwriter seeks to maximize the expected utility of profits, his or her problem will be to determine the value of q which maximizes

$$\int_0^M u\big(p(P-x)+qQ\big)\,dF(x) = \int_0^M u\left[P-x-q\left(\frac{N}{M}(P-x)-Q\right)\right]dF(x)$$

This problem obviously can have a meaningful solution for suitable utility functions, and for suitable values of M, N, P and Q. Hence the observed behaviour of disbelieving underwriters can be explained as the outcome of a rational optimizing process.

With this explanation, the real Bayesian appears to be the Committee of Lloyd's. The members of this committee may have been convinced that no monster exists in Loch Ness, but they were prepared to revise this opinion when Cutty Sark assigned a positive probability to the event that Nessie should be captured. This conclusion may be an example of the principle that the customer is always right. As a result of the revision, underwriters had to count the slip from Cutty Sark when they computed their limits. Whether this risk was counted in the same way as any other marine risk is an open question. Bayesians however are broad-minded, and underwriters had some room for using their discretion, i.e. for acting on their prior beliefs.

When a paper like this is published in a serious Journal, some excuses are in order, and now shall be offered:

(i) Much of the literature on decision theory is based on introspection. Readers are asked to explain how they will choose between a gift of one million and the chance of receiving ten millions if a red ball is drawn from an urn. Few have encountered such choices in real life, and no way exists to test if true answers are given to questions of this kind. On rare occasions real life presents decision problems which are as outlandish as anything which can be dreamed up at a philosopher's desk. These problems deserve particular attention, because they actually happened, and they represent unique chances of learning how responsible people make decisions in extraordinary situations.

(ii) Most elementary textbooks on insurance contain a chapter explaining to the student when a risk is insurable. Usually it is required that the risk must be random in nature, and that it must be possible to estimate the relevant probabilities from available statistics. The same question was discussed on a higher level at an international congress of actuaries in 1954. On this occasion learned actuaries presented 20 papers which together included 400 pages laying down different conditions which a risk must meet in order to be insurable. All these sets of conditions make it impossible to insure against the capture of a monster in Loch Ness, but still the insurance was written.

A suitable conclusion seems to be "*Ab esse ad posse valet consequentia*", although that proverb may be non-Bayesian in spirit.

References for Section 4

Brown A. (1973): *Hazard Unlimited. The Story of Lloyd's of London.* London: Peter Davies.

5. Ethics, Institutions and Optimality*

1. Introduction

1.1 As a suitable introduction to our subject we shall consider two competing firms. We shall assume that their situation can be represented by the game known as the "Prisoners" Dilemma', and that it can be described by the following double matrix

---

* Reprinted from *Decision Theory and Social Ethics: Issues in Social Choice*, H.W. Gottinger, W. Leinfellner, eds. 1978: 237–249, copyright (c) Kluwer Academic Publishers, Dordrecht, Holland.

		Firm 2	
		Maintain Price	Cut Price
Firm 1	Maintain Price	1, 1	−2, 2
	Cut Price	2, −2	−1, −1

The elements of the matrix can be interpreted as the profits of the two firms. The only equilibrium point in this game is the pair $(-1, -1)$.

1.2 Under the usual assumptions about economic behaviour each firm will seek the decision which maximizes profit, without knowing the decision made by the competitor. This will lead both firms to cut the price, and they will both suffer a loss.

Even casual observations of economic activity in the real world indicate that things don't happen in quite this way. Firms do not usually engage in this kind of cut-throat competition, which eventually will drive their competitors out of business. In most countries it is illegal for the firms to collude and agree to maintain prices, but there seems to be some tacit agreement to "live and let live". If the firms do not break the law and collude, it is natural to assume that there are some ethical motives which prevent them from engaging in all out competition. My interest in ethical questions springs from observations that firms often seem reluctant to make full use of their competitive advantages, and this is the question which will be discussed in the following.

1.3 The problem I have outlined can be approached in several ways:

(i) We can try to formalize the ethical considerations which keep firms away from aggressive or "unfair" competition. This approach,which has been taken i.a. by Baier (1977), implies that we try to change the game so that one of the equilibrium points becomes Pareto optimal, or at least approximately so.

(ii) We can make experiments, in the first stage to find out how people actually play the game and in a second stage we can then construct formal models, which can be tested statistically by further experiments. The most penetrating studies along these lines seem to be those of Rapoport (1965) and Selten (1978).

The subjects in such experiments are usually students, and it is doubtful if the ethical restraints they observe in the games carry over to economic and political decisions in the real world.

(iii) A third possible approach would be to interview businessmen, and ask them to state the reasons why they do not engage in the unrestrained profit maximization assumed in standard economic theory. From these statements we may be able to spell out formally the ethical rules which are observed in economic life, although few authors seem to have found this approach promising.

1.4 In this paper I shall take none of these three approaches. Instead we shall discuss other economic situations which seem to have some properties similar to the situations which can be represented by the game of the "Prisoners" Dilemma'. The study of these situations may reveal something about the ethical considerations behind the observable economic decisions.

The problem will be presented in the next subsection and a number of examples will be discussed in the two following subsections.

2. Presentation of the Problem

2.1 Social scientists will some times observe that groups of persons in the real world agree on arrangements which seem to be far from optimal. As outside observers, we can see other perfectly feasible arrangements which appear better from the points of view of all persons concerned, and it is natural to ask why the persons we observe do not agree on one of these arrangements. The three most obvious answers to the question seem to be:

(i) The people we observe may simply be stupid, an explanation which should not be dismissed out of mere politeness.

(ii) The people may have incomplete information, and believe they have reached the best possible arrangement. In this case they are simply not aware of the possible arrangements which the outsider can see.

(iii) Ethical or institutional considerations may prevent the persons from reaching an arrangement which seems the ideal one to an outside observer.

2.2 In the following we shall discuss problems related only to the last of the three explanations. We shall as we would expect, find it natural to use some concepts from game theory.

The "solution" of a game can be defined as the expected outcome if the game is played by "rational" players. If we want to be precise at this point, we run into some difficulties since there are many different solution concepts. Most of them — as for instance the "core" — will however be included in the set of Pareto optimal arrangements, or in the set of "imputations", to use the term from game theory.

To reach agreement on a Pareto optimal arrangement, it is usually necessary that the players cooperate and coordinate their strategies. If there is no possibility of coordinating the decisions, the game may be played in a non-cooperative manner. This means that each player will look exclusively after his own interest, and use a minimax strategy. Any non-cooperative game has at least one equilibrium point in mixed strategies. In general this point will not be an imputation, i.e. it will be sub-optimal. In many cases equilibrium points represent likely outcomes of the game, and it may be natural to include them, by definition in the "solution". For instance the different "bargaining sets" will contain both the core, and some equilibrium points, and it is natural to expect that the outcome of the game will be within some set of this kind.

Some problems arise if it is optimal to use mixed strategies. In such cases, it will not be single observations, but their average which will be optimal.

2.3 When a situation in real life can be represented by a game-theoretical model, we will usually have some indications as to whether it is possible or not for the players to cooperate. The two most interesting cases which can occur in such situations seem to be:

(i) Cooperation between the players appears possible, but the observed outcome is sub-optimal. It is then natural to look for conventions or *institutional* elements which prevent the players from reaching an optimal arrangement.

(ii) It seems impossible for the players to communicate and coordinate their decisions, but they still arrive at an outcome which is close to the optimum. Such observations should lead us to look for some ethical considerations which induce the participants to play in a cooperative manner.

These two cases form a convenient starting point for our explorations. We shall not try to give any precise definitions of the terms "institutional" and "ethical", which in our context stand for different kinds of constraints in an optimizing problem. Loosely we can apply "ethical" to constraints observed as binding by individuals, and "institutional" to those binding for the persons as a group.

2.4 Before we discuss our examples, it may be useful to restate some of the basic results from the economics of uncertainty. They are not very complex, and can be considered as part of the general knowledge. Formal proofs have been given in Borch (1960) and Borch (1962).

We shall consider n persons who have to share an uncertain prospect. Payoff from the prospect will be x, a stochastic variable with the distribution $F(x)$. Let the attitude to risk of person i be represented by the utility function $u_i(x)$. The most general arrangement the persons can agree upon can be described by n functions $y_1(x) \ldots y_n(x)$, where $y_i(x)$ is payoff to person i, if payoff from the prospect is x. The assumption that the persons have to share the whole prospect implies that

$$\sum_{i=1}^{n} y_i(x) = x \tag{1}$$

The arrangement will give person i the utility

$$\int u_i\big(y_i(x)\big)\, dF(x)$$

One can prove that the Pareto optimal arrangements are given by the n-tuple of y-functions which satisfies (1) and condition (2) below:

$$u'\big(y_i(x)\big) = k_i u_i'\big(y_1(x)\big) \tag{2}$$

where $k_1 = 1$ and $k_2 \ldots k_n$ are arbitrary positive constants.

2.5 The functions which satisfy (1) and (2) will usually have a complicated form. They will be linear, i.e. we will have $y_i(x) = a_i x + b_i$ only if all utility functions belong to one of the following three classes:

$$u_i(x) = 1 - e^{-\alpha_i x} \tag{i}$$

$$u_i(x) = (x - c_i)^{\alpha} \tag{ii}$$

$$u_i(x) = \log(x - c_i) \tag{iii}$$

Positive linear transformations of these functions will of course not change the Pareto optimal arrangements.

These classes do not seem rich enough to accommodate the different attitudes to risk which we would expect to find in most groups of people.

Class (i) allows for differences in risk aversion — measured by α_i — but implies that preferences are independent of "initial wealth".

Classes (ii) and (iii) imply that all persons have the same risk aversion function. Differences in preferences can be explained by differences in initial wealth.

3. Some Examples from Economics

3.1 As our first example we shall consider *fixed wages versus profit sharing.* Let:

x = a stochastic variable representing the gross profit which a contractor (Person 1) will get from a certain job

w = the wages he pays the labour (Person 2) necessary for doing the job

The risk sharing arrangement will then be:

$$y_1(x) = x - w$$

$$y_2(x) = w$$

with some obvious modification if there is a possibility that the contractor can go bankrupt and become unable to pay the agreed wages.

It is clear that an arrangement of this simple linear form cannot in general be optimal. It should be possible to devise some scheme of risk- and profit-sharing, which would be considered better by both parties, and it is difficult to explain why the fixed-wage agreement seems to dominate in our economies.

3.2 The two main exceptions to the fixed wage contract seem to be:

(i) Pay by piece rates, a system which seems to be on the way out in industry.

(ii) Share-cropping, a system usually associated with primitive agriculture.

Both these forms of payment appear to be more flexible than the fixed wage system, and should make it possible to reach an arrangement closer to the optimum. Piece-rates and share-cropping are often associated with unethical exploitation of labor, and this may be the explanation of the dominating role played by the fixed wage contract.

A widely accepted ethical principle is that the entrepreneur should carry the whole business risk. This does of course lead to fixed wages, and there is some evidence that labor wants to push the principle further and press for fixed monthly salaries, and for job security. The latter demand may force the government to bail out entrepreneurs whose firms run into difficulties. This may turn the government into the ultimate risk-carrier, and in a sense lead to socialism, since the risk-taking entrepreneur will be eliminated.

Under socialism it may be possible to reach a Pareto optimal division of the risks inherent in society, but we shall not pursue this intriguing question in the present paper.

3.3 As another example we shall consider the financing of a risky business. We shall first consider an ordinary loan. Let:

x = a stochastic variable representing the payoff from a venture which person 1 wants to undertake

K = the capital required for the venture

r = the interest rate demanded by person 2 (the banker) for lending the capital to person 1.

The conventional loan arrangement implies that the banker will take over the assets of person 1 if he should default on the loan. The payoff functions will then be

$$\begin{aligned} y_1(x) &= 0 && \text{if } x \leq (1+r)K \\ &= x - (1+r)K && \text{if } x > (1+r)K \\ y_2(x) &= x && \text{if } x \leq (1+r)K \\ y_2(x) &= (1+r)K && \text{if } x > (1+r)K \end{aligned}$$

It is clear that an arrangement of this form will not in general be optimal, even if the interest rate r is adjusted to the risk of default. In many cases this seems to be recognized. When the financing of an important project is discussed, we can frequently observe that the parties seek some arrangement between the conventional loan scheme and the 50–50 risk-sharing involved in a joint venture. Presumably they seek an arrangement which will satisfy the two conditions in para 2.4.

3.4 Ethics does not seem to play any important part in negotiations over the financing of risky business enterprises. It is however clear that institutional elements may prevent the parties from reaching a Pareto optimal arrangement. Banks are often not allowed to take an equity interest in a risky venture, and may be able to offer only conventional loans — against suitable collateral. Such restrictions on the actions of banks and financial institutions can obviously in some cases lead to non-optimal arrangements.

The restrictions themselves may of course have ethical origin. They may for instance have been designed to protect depositors or share holders.

Risk sharing is only one (possibly a minor) aspect of the two examples discussed in this section. Arrangements which seem far from optimal from a risk sharing point of view, may be fairly close to an optimum when all aspects are considered. In the next section we shall therefore discuss a few examples which in some respects are simpler.

4. Examples from Insurance

4.1 In insurance we can study risk sharing arrangements virtually under laboratory conditions, and it is worth studying the optimality of the arrangements which we can observe. As a first step we shall study the simplest possible case.

Assume that person 1 is exposed to a risk which can cause him a loss represented by the stochastic variable x.

Assume further that an insurance company — person 2 — is willing to take over the risk against a premium P.

This arrangement gives the payoff functions

$$y_1(x) = -P$$

$$y_2(x) = P - X$$

This arrangement may of course be sub-optimal, and this seems to be generally recognized. In insurance we find a very wide variety of different contracts, which presumably bring both parties closer to the optimum rather than the simple contract with fixed premium and full cover. The simple contract seems to be used principally when the premium and the amount at risk are small, i.e. when transaction costs make it unprofitable to seek a better, but more complicated arrangement.

4.2 Normally a person who seeks insurance against a non-trivial risk will have a number of options. Let us first assume that by paying a premium kP he becomes entitled to a compensation kx if his loss amounts to x. This arrangement will give him the expected utility

$$U(k) = \int_0^\infty u(S - kP - x + kx)\, df(x)$$

Here S stands for the "initial wealth" of the person.

The problem is now to determine the value of k which maximizes this expression, under the natural condition that $0 \leq k \leq 1$. We find

$$U'(k) = \int_0^\infty (x - P)u'\big(S - x + k(x - P)\big)\, df(x)$$

and

$$U''(k) = \int_0^\infty (x - P)^2 u''\big(S - x + k(x - P)\big)\, dF(x)$$

If our person is a risk averted, so that $u''(x) < 0$, it follows that $U''(k) < 0$, and hence $U'(k)$ is a decreasing function. We have

$$U'(1) = u'(S - P) \int_0^\infty (x - P)\, dF(x) = (\bar{x} - P)u'(S - P)$$

As $u'(S - P) > 0$, it follows that $U'(1) < 0$ if $P > \bar{x}$, i.e. if the premium is greater than the expected payments under the insurance contract. This will normally be the case, and hence we must conclude that $U(k)$ cannot have a maximum for $k = 1$, i.e. it will never be optimal to take full insurance cover. It is possible that the equation

$$U'(k) = 0$$

has a non-negative root $k < 1$. If so, the equation will give the optimal quota which our person should insure.

4.3 The result above, which is due to Mossin (1968), is clearly contradicted by observations. If a person takes fire insurance on his house, he does not insure it for 60 or 80 per cent of its value. He will take insurance for the full value, and often add something as a safety margin. This is demonstrated by virtually all insurance statistics, so that Mossin's result calls for an explanation. It may be tempting to just reject the consistency assumptions behind the expected utility theorem, and the assumption that the underlying utility function is concave. This implies however that we throw overboard a good deal of contemporary decision theory, so it is advisable to study possible explanations with less drastic implications, before jumping to conclusions.

In the early days fire insurance was almost invariably made on the basis of assessed value. Persons who suffered losses should receive full compensation, and neither more nor less; and they should pay fair premiums. These are of course ethical principles, and they seem to survive as conventions, also in a commercial age, when an owner is free to insure his property for any value he chooses. This is at least a plausible explanation of the discrepancy, between theory and observations, found by Mossin.

4.4 In the example above we have assumed that the insured would receive a compensation proportional to his loss. The obvious generalization is to assume that he can conclude an insurance contract which will pay him a compensation $y(x)$ if the loss amounts to x. His problem is then to determine the function $y(x)$ which maximizes the expected utility

$$\int_0^\infty u\big(S - P - x + y(x)\big)\, dF(x)$$

where the premium P depends on the function $y(x)$.

Arrow (1974) assumes that the premium is proportional to the expected compensation, i.e.:

$$P = (1 + \lambda) \int_0^\infty y(x)\, dF(x)$$

where $\lambda \geq 0$. He then proves that the optimal insurance contract is defined by the function

$$y(x) = 0 \qquad \text{for } x \leq D$$

$$y(x) = x - D \qquad \text{for } D < x$$

This means that the insured, himself, will pay all losses smaller than the "deductible" D. For larger losses, the excess will be fully covered by the insurance.

4.5 Many insurance contracts in the real world are of this form. It is comforting to note that this often holds for important contracts, which presumably have been concluded after careful considerations. This should indicate that existing arrangements are not too far removed from optimality.

In property insurance the maximum possible loss is necessarily finite. In medical insurance, and in many forms of liability insurance there is no upper limit to the possible loss. Insurance companies seem reluctant to accept unlimited liability, and the payoff function for insurance contracts of this kind will usually be of the form:

$$\begin{aligned}
y(x) &= 0 && \text{for } x \leq D \\
y(x) &= x - D && \text{for } D < x \leq M \\
y(x) &= M - D && \text{for } M < x
\end{aligned}$$

This arrangement is obviously non-optimal, and it means that the insurance is not effective when it is most needed.

For the insurance contracts bought by the ordinary household, the companies could without serious difficulties accept unlimited liability, and give the customer virtually full security. In fact insurance companies do this in the countries where the law requires unlimited cover for third person automobile liability.

The premium must of course be adjusted if the upper limit on the liability is removed. This should however be a simple matter. For large M, the difference between

$$\int_0^\infty (x - D)\, dF(x)$$

and

$$\int_0^M (x - D)\, dF(x) + (M - D) \int_M^\infty dF(x)$$

will be almost negligible.

4.6 Arrow's result depends on the assumption that the premium paid for an insurance contract is proportional to expected claim payments under the contract. This is often considered an ethical principle, defining the "fair" premium.

It is worth noting that Arrow's result can be obtained as a special case of the general result para 2.4, if we assume that the utility function of the insurance company is linear. This assumption implies that the insurance company must be risk neutral. The existence of reinsurance shows that insurance companies also have risk aversion, and this is probably the reason why they don't offer the customer the insurance contract which he considers as optimal.

5. Concluding Remarks

5.1 In this paper we have considered some economic situations in which the persons concerned seem to have arrived at a solution which is sub-optimal. We have tried to explain these observations by pointing out ethical and institutional factors which may play their part in the decision process. We have not tried to separate and analyse these factors, since they all seem to hang together. Ethical norms, once they are generally accepted, tend to be codified and become the conventions and institutional framework of the next generation. Institutions and conventions seem to have their inertia, and tend to remain unchanged for a long time after the ethical norms have changed.

5.2 The paper does not contain any basically new results. It is however hoped that some of our observations may help in locating new fields of empirical research in social sciences.

References for Section 5

Arrow KJ. (1974): "Optimal Insurance and Generalized Deductibles", *Scandinavian Actuarial Journal*, 1–42.

Baier K. (1977): "Rationality and Morality", *Erkenntnis.*

Borch K. (1960): "The Safety Loading of Reinsurance Premiums", *Skandinavisk Aktuarietidskrift*, 163–184.

Borch K. (1962): "Equilibrium in a Reinsurance Market", *Econometrica*, 424–444.

Mossin J. (1968): "Aspects of Rational Insurance Purchasing", *Journal of Political Economy*, 553–568.

Rapoport A, Chamman AM. (1965): *Prisoner's Dilemma*, University of Michigan Press.

Selten R. (1978): "The Equity Principle in Economic Behavior", *Decision Theory and Social Ethics: Issues in Social Choice*, H.W. Gottinger, W. Leinfellner, eds.

6. The Price of Moral Hazard*

6.1 In this note we shall show that a simple application of game theory makes it possible to determine the costs associated with the presence of moral hazard.

The concept "moral hazard" is usually connected with insurance. It seems difficult to give a general and really satisfactory definition, but the

* Reprinted from *Scandinavian Actuarial Journal*, 1980: 173–176, copyright (c) Almqvist & Wiksell International, Stockholm.

underlying idea is easy to grasp. It is brought out clearly in the following statement by Arrow: "The insurance policy might itself change incentives and therefore the probabilities upon which the insurance company has relied. Thus, a fire insurance policy for more than the value of the premises might be an inducement to arson or at least to carelessness (Arrow (1970)). Another example would be that people tend to make greater use of medical services than they otherwise would, if the costs are covered, fully or in part by health insurance.

6.2 Moral hazard is not necessarily "a product of the criminal mind", as it is some times alleged in insurance circles. It may be careless not to keep fire extinguishers in a factory, it becomes worse if the owner has promised to see that the factory is adequately equipped with fire extinguishers, but it becomes fraud only if the promise was made in order to obtain a reduction in the fire insurance premium. In general, if the insured can gain by breaking the insurance contract, moral hazard is present. In such cases the insurance company will often check that the insurance contract is observed. The checking will usually cost money, so it follows that the mere existence of moral hazard can lead to costs. The situation clearly invites analysis as a two-person game played — between the insurance company and its customer.

6.3 We shall consider an insurance contract, under which expected claim payments are K_0 and the premium P_0. We assume that if the insured spends an amount a on loss prevention measures, expected claim payments will be $K < K_0$. He should agree to make this expenditure if the premium is reduced to $P < P_0 - a$.

We assume further that the insurance company can check if the insured actually carries out the safety measures agreed upon, and that the checking will cost the company an amount b.

If the checking shows that the insured keeps the agreement, nothing happens. If however the checking reveals that he has cheated on the agreement, the insured must pay a penalty Q to the company.

6.4 Formulating the situation as a two-person non-zero sum game, we see that the first player, the insured, has two pure strategies. He can either keep or break the agreement.

Similarly the second player, the insurance company, has two pure strategies: To check, or to trust that the insured keeps the agreement without any checking.

The game is described by the following double matrix, where the entries give the payments to be made by the two players under different choices of strategies.

		Insurance company	
		Trust	Check
Insured	Keep	$P+a\,,K$	$P+a\,,K+b$
	Break	$P\,,K_0$	$P+Q\,,K_0+b-Q$

The insured pays the premium and the penalty to the company. If we rule out insurance of any third party's interest, we can assume that claim payments are made from the company to the insured. The only payments out of the system will then be a and b, and the game can be described by the double matrix below, where the entries give net payoffs to the two players.

		Insurance company	
		Trust	Check
Insured	Keep	$K-P-a\,,P-K$	$K-P-a\,,P-K-b$
	Break	$K_0-P\,,P-K_0$	$K_0-P-Q\,,P-K_0+Q-b$

The penalty Q is paid only if the insured tries to cheat, and is discovered when the company checks. It is easy to see that the penalty will have no deterrent effect unless

$$Q > a + K_0 - K$$

and that checking will not be worth while unless

$$Q > b$$

6.5 We now introduce mixed strategies, and assume that the insured decides to break the agreement and drop the safety measures, with a probability x. Further we assume that the insurance company decides to check that the agreement is observed, with a probability y.

Expected payoff to the players will then be:

To the insured:

$$\begin{aligned} v_1(x,y) &= (1-x)(1-y)(K-P-a) + (1-x)y(K-P-a) \\ &\quad + x(1-y)(K_0-P) + xy(K_0-P-Q) \\ &= K-P-a+x(a+K_0-K-yQ) \end{aligned}$$

To the insurance company:

$$\begin{aligned} v_2(x,y) &= (1-x)(1-y)(P-K) + (1-x)y(P-K-b) \\ &\quad + x(1-y)(P-K_0) + xy(P-K_0+Q-b) \\ &= P-K+x(K-K_0)-y(b-xQ) \end{aligned}$$

The pair of mixed strategies corresponding to

$$\bar{x} = \frac{b}{Q} \qquad \text{and} \qquad \bar{y} = \frac{a+K_0-K}{Q}$$

is an equilibrium point, since we have

$$K-P-a = v_1(x,\bar{y}) \le v_1(\bar{x},\bar{y}) = K-P-a$$

$$P-K-\frac{b(K_0-K)}{Q} = v_2(\bar{x},y) \le v_2(\bar{x},\bar{y}) = P-K-\frac{b(K_0-K)}{Q}$$

for $x, y \in (0,1)$. It is easy to show that this is the only equilibrium point in the game.

6.6 The insurance company is usually free to reject the contract, so we must expect that the premium P is set so that payoff to the company is non-negative. This leads to the condition

$$P \ge K + \frac{b}{Q}(K_0-K)$$

If we ignore administrative costs and payments to the company for its risk-bearing service, the equality sign is possible, and lowest acceptable premium will be

$$P = K + \frac{b}{Q}(K_0-K)$$

Here the first term on the right hand side represents the expected claim payments under the insurance contract, i.e. the net premium. The second term represents a "loading" which is necessary because some moral hazard exists. The term has the reasonable properties: It is proportional to the cost of checking b, and to $K_0 - K$, the gain to be obtained from the safety measures. The loading term is inversely proportional to the penalty Q, indicating that cheating can be prevented if penalties are severe.

It thus seems that the unique equilibrium point also is a "reasonable" solution of the game.

6.7 When the premium is determined as above, payoff to the company is zero. The expected net payments made by the insured will be:

$$a + \frac{b(K_0 - K)}{Q}$$

The formula shows that the insured will have to pay the full cost of the safety measures, even if he occasionally cheats, and neglects to carry them out. In addition he will have to pay something because the company wants to check that the safety measures are carried out according to the contract. This amount must be paid simply because it is possible to cheat, and it represents the price he has to pay because an element of moral hazard is present.

It may be of some interest to note that severe penalties will be to the advantage of the insured. They will, like a strong oath, increase the credibility of his promise of not breaking the agreement.

References for Section 6

Arrow KJ. (1970): *Essays in the Theory of Risk-Bearing.* North Holland Publishing Company.

7. Insuring and Auditing the Auditor*

1. Introduction

1.1 Auditing of accounts is often based on sampling inspection, simply because it seems unnecessarily costly to check every voucher and every entry

* Reprinted from *Games, Economic Dynamics and Time Series Analysis*, Deistler, Fürst, Schwödiauer, eds. 1982: 117–127, copyright (c) Physica-Verlag, Heidelberg.

in the books. The possibility that any transaction may be checked in full detail is believed to have a deterring effect likely to prevent irregularities. A theoretical analysis of problems in this field naturally leads to a search for suitable sampling methods, and there exist handbooks of sampling techniques for the use of auditors. A short outline of these methods has been given by Kaplan (1973), who also gives references to relevant literature.

1.2 The sampling approach implies that the auditor believes he plays a game against nature, and that he finds it optimal to use a mixed strategy. It is not unreasonable to assume that in the real world the game is played against an intelligent opponent, who does his best to get away with fraud, or to steal without being discovered. This assumption leads to a non-zero-sum game of a type, which first seems to have been studied by Maschler (1966) and (1967). He called it the inspector's game, and in the following we shall discuss some varieties of this game.

In the next section we shall show that the sampling approach may be inappropriate, and in the following subsections we shall indicate how the situation can be analysed as a two- and three-person game.

2. The Sampling Approach — A Simple Model

2.1 We shall begin by studying a simple model of the type discussed by Kaplan (1973). Let the stochastic variable x_t represent the profits of the firm on day t. The profit becomes first known to an accountant, who can embezzle a non-negative amount c_t, and report a profit $y_t = x_t - c_t$ to the owner of the firm. If the owner finds the sequence $(y_1, \ldots, y_t, \ldots, y_n)$ suspicious, he may carry out an extra audit. The owner's problem is to determine when he should carry out the audit, i.e. for each n he must determine a critical region for the vector $(y_1, \ldots, y_n)$.

It is difficult to analyse this problem without assuming that the stochastic process generating the profits is completely known. The simplest assumption of this kind would be that the $x_1, \ldots, x_t, \ldots$ are stochastically independent and identically distributed.

2.2 The problem formulated above is too general to admit simple analysis. To simplify it we shall assume that n is given, for instance equal to the number of days in the month. If the owner finds the sequence $(y_1, \ldots, y_n)$ suspicious, he will audit the accounts for every day in the month. We shall assume that this will cost him an amount q.

We have

$$E(y_t) = E(x_t) - E(c_t)$$

If the accountant chooses c_t independently of x_t, we will have

$$\text{Var}\,(y_t) = \text{var}\,(x_t)$$

It is however evident that the accountant can choose the sequence $(c_1, \ldots, c_n)$ so that $\text{var}\,(y_t) \lesseqgtr \text{var}\,(x_t)$.

Kaplan suggests that the owner should choose a number r, and consider the y-sequence as suspicious if

$$y < E(x) - r\sqrt{\text{var}\,(x)} = E(x) - r\sigma$$

Here

$$x = \sum_{t=1}^{n} x_t \qquad \text{and} \qquad y = \sum_{t=1}^{n} y_t$$

Presumably the owner will choose r considerably lower than by the usual significance tests. If there is a probability of say 0.1 that an observed sequence has arisen when there is no embezzlement, a complete audit may be called for.

The test indicated is obviously crude, since it is based only on monthly profits, i.e. on the average of reported daily profits. To a statistician it may be tempting to design a more refined test to decide whether a reported sequence $(y_1, \ldots, y_n)$ differs in any suspicious way from the expected outcome.

2.3 Clearly an intelligent accountant will embezzle only if this can be done without resulting in a suspicious y-sequence. Such sequences can however arise naturally with a probability α. The owner will then audit the accounts for the corresponding months, without discovering any fraud. The average monthly cost of this auditing will be αq. To illustrate let the distribution of x be $F(x)$, and $E(x) = \bar{x}$, so that

$$\alpha = \Pr\{x < \bar{x} - r\sigma\} = F(\bar{x} - r\sigma) = F(z)$$

The expected amount which the accountant can steal each month will then be

$$\int_z^{\infty} (x - z)\, dF(x)$$

This is clearly less than the total amount x, which he could embezzle in the absence of any auditing, but the amount may still be substantial.

If $\Pr\{x_t = 0\} = \Pr\{x_t = 1\} = 1/2$ and $n = 25$, we have

$$E\{x\} = 12.5 \quad \text{and} \quad \operatorname{var}(x) = 2.5$$

and approximately

$$\Pr\{x \leq 9\} = 0.1$$

If the owner audits only the months showing a profit less than 10, an intelligent accountant can steal a day's profit in more than half the months, without being discovered, and possibly even without being suspected of dishonesty.

The owner might dismiss his statistical consultant, and decide to audit the accounts of arbitrary months selected at random with a probability α. This will give the same average auditing cost, and it will also give him a possibility of discovering fraud. If the accountant is unaware of the element of surprise introduced in the auditing, he may continue to steal at a fraction $1 - \alpha$ of the months. The probability that he shall not be caught is

$$1 - \alpha(1 - \alpha) = 1 - \alpha + \alpha^2 \geq 0.75$$

2.4 The assumption that the stochastic process is completely known is obviously unrealistic, and it is tempting to formulate the problem in a Bayesian manner. This will however place the owner in an even more disadvantageous position. The accountant can clearly manipulate his embezzlements so that the owner is led to believe that $E(x)$ is smaller and $\operatorname{var}(x)$ greater than in reality. Theoretically the embezzlements could continue until the Bayesian owner is convinced that his firm is unprofitable, and decides to close it.

We shall not discuss these long-term aspects of the situation. It is clear that a number of elements have been assumed away in order to formulate the situation as a simple two-person game. These elements are discussed in some detail in the papers by Maschler referred to. The problem of the accountant is obviously to gain the confidence of the owner, and then exploit it to his own advantage.

The application which Maschler has in mind is a nuclear test ban, with rights to inspect when certain seismic events are observed. These events can be due either to an earthquake, or to a nuclear test. Obviously an inspection will be carried out only if an event has occurred. If the two causes lead to more or less different seismic events, some statistical problems can occur.

One would then carry out an inspection only if the pattern of the seismic event indicated a fairly high probability that the cause was a nuclear test.

The conclusion of these considerations should be familiar from many applications of game theory. The solution to a difficult decision problem may be to draw lots or loss a coin.

3. A Two-person Game

3.1 To formulate the problem as a game, we shall consider an Accountant (player A) who works for a Businessman (player B). It is possible for the accountant to falsify the books and steal some money. The businessman is aware of this possibility, and has engaged an auditor to check the books. As a complete audit is expensive, the businessman has decided that some spot checks made at random will be sufficient. The accountant may try to outguess his employer, and conclude that if he steals on just some occasions, picked at random, he will have a fair chance of not being caught with his hand in the till.

To give a formal description of this situation, we shall introduce three symbols:

$G =$ the gain player A will make if he uses every opportunity of embezzlement, and is not discovered. We shall assume that the gain of A is the loss of B.

$C =$ the cost to player B of a complete audit, i.e. of checking every opportunity of fraud open to A.

$P =$ the penalty to be paid by player A if he is caught in fraud. If the penalty includes a jail sentence, we must think of P as the monetary equivalent of the punishment.The penalty does not constitute any gain for player B.

We can then summarize the options open to the two players in Table 1.

Each cell gives the gains of respectively player A and player B, corresponding to a pair of options, i.e. to a pair of pure strategies.

As indicated above, the players may find it advantageous to use mixed strategies. This will mean that:

Player A cheats on a fraction x of the opportunities.

Player B, or his auditor, checks a fraction y of the opportunities.

Table 1:

		Player B	
		Trust	Audit
Player A	Be honest	0, 0	0, $-C$
	Steal	G, $-G$	$-P$, $-C$

If both players make their choices independently, and in a random manner, there will be a probability xy that A shall be caught cheating. In this case player A will have to pay the penalty P, and player B will have the auditing cost C.

Similarly there will be a probability $x(1-y)$ that a theft is not discovered, and a probability $(1-x)y$ that an audit is made without discovering any irregularity.

3.2 If the two players use mixed strategies represented by the pair (x, y) the expected payoffs will be

Player A:

$$\nu_A(x, y) = x(1-y)G - xyP = x\big(G - (G+P)y\big)$$

Player B:

$$\nu_B(x, y) = -(1-x)yC - x(1-y)G - xyC = -xG - y(C - xG)$$

From the former of these expressions we see that if

$$y \geq \frac{G}{G+P} \qquad \text{we have} \qquad \nu_A(x, y) \leq 0$$

Hence by doing spot checking with sufficiently high frequency, the auditor can ensure that crime is not expected to pay.

A pair of mixed strategies $(\bar{x}, \bar{y})$ is an equilibrium point in the game if

$$\nu_A(x, \bar{y}) \leq \nu_A(\bar{x}, \bar{y}) \qquad \text{for all } x \in (0, 1)$$

$$\nu_B(\bar{x}, y) \leq \nu_B(\bar{x}, \bar{y}) \qquad \text{for all } y \in (0, 1)$$

It is easy to show that

$$\bar{x} = \frac{C}{G} \qquad \text{and} \qquad \bar{y} = \frac{G}{P+G}$$

satisfy the equilibrium conditions, and that the game has no other equilibrium points. For the equilibrium point we find:

$$\nu_A(\bar{x}, \bar{y}) = 0 \qquad \text{and} \qquad \nu_B(\bar{x}, \bar{y}) = -C$$

3.3 The equilibrium strategies give the same payoffs as the pure strategies of the point (0,1), corresponding to: "Complete audit" and "Complete honesty", as we have

$$\nu_A(0, 1) = 0 \qquad \text{and} \qquad \nu_B(0, 1) = -C$$

The point (0,1) is however not an equilibrium point. We have $\nu_A(x, 1) = -xP$, so that the Accountant can not expect to gain by cheating, but we also have $\nu_A(0, y) = -yC$, so that the Businessman can gain by spending less on auditing.

In the equilibrium point, the Businessman will spend $(GC)/(P+G) < C$ on auditing, but he will suffer an expected loss of $G\big(1-G/(P+G)\big)C/G = (PC)/(P+G)$, so that savings on auditing are just balanced by an increase in losses caused by embezzlement. Similarly the Accountant can expect to gain $(PC)/(G+P)$ from undiscovered embezzlement, but this is just offset by the expected penalty he must pay if he is caught.

3.4 If the problem we have discussed is analyzed as a cooperative game, it is trivial. The cooperative solution is obviously "No audit" and "Complete honesty". There is no real element of "threat" in the situation, since an accountant who threatens to steal presumably will be dismissed immediately. The possibility of embezzlement is however present, and this is clearly to the businessman's disadvantage. In real life the possibility seems to be used as an argument for higher remuneration of the accountant. Higher remuneration should have the same effect as an increase in the penalty P, since a part of the penalty may be the loss of a well paid job.

4. A Three-person Game

4.1 The Businessman can usually buy insurance to cover losses caused by the dishonesty of his employees. In the simple model we have studied there should be no need for insurance, because the Businessman could prevent such losses by strict auditing. This conclusion rests however on the assumption that the Accountant behaves rationally, and does not try to steal if it cannot be expected to be profitable. The assumption may be unrealistic, so we shall assume that the Businessman buys fidelity guarantee insurance, and brings in a player C, the insurance company.

Further we shall assume that the insurance contract obliges the Businessman to carry out a complete audit of his books, and we shall introduce the symbols:

$D =$ the cost to player C of checking that player B meets his obligations under the insurance contract.

$Q =$ the penalty which player B must pay to player C, if it is discovered that his auditing procedures are less strict than assumed in the contract.

There is of course a premium to be paid for the insurance, and this premium may depend on the auditing system of player B. We shall ignore this element for the time being. In practice the penalty, Q, may be that the insurance contract becomes null and void, or that B must pay the higher premium corresponding to a less satisfactory auditing system.

4.2 The Company may find it expensive to check the auditing system of all its clients. We shall assume that it settles for some random spot checking, so that there is a probability z that a check will be made of B. This assumption leads to a situation similar to the one considered in the preceding section, and it can be described by Table 2.

Table 2:

		Player B	
		Trust A	Audit A
Player C	Trust B	$0, -xG$	$-xG, -C$
	Check B	$Q - D, -Q - xG$	$-D - xG, -C$

Behind the table there is an assumption that only an audit can reveal an embezzlement. Hence if C checks, and finds that B's auditing is not in accordance with the insurance contract, B must pay the penalty Q, but a possible embezzlement will remain undiscovered.

4.3 If the three players in this game use mixed strategies represented by the triple (x, y, z), their payoffs will be:

Player A:

$$\nu_A(x, y, z) = x\big(G - (G + P)y\big)$$

Player B:

$$\nu_B(x, y, z) = y(xG + zQ - C) - (xG + zQ)$$

Player C:

$$\nu_c(x, y, z) = z(Q - D - yQ) - xyG$$

We see as before that for $y > G/(G + P)$ player A can only expect to lose by cheating. Further we see that for $y > (Q - D)/Q$, player C can only expect to lose by checking. It is easy to show that the game has a unique equilibrium point

$$\left(0, \frac{Q-D}{Q}, \frac{C}{Q}\right) \quad \text{if} \quad \frac{Q-D}{Q} \geq \frac{G}{G+P}$$

This gives the following expected gains for the three players:

$$\nu_A = 0\,, \nu_B = -C \qquad \text{and} \qquad \nu_C = 0$$

This case corresponds to high penalties, and the interpretation may be as follows: The risk of substantial penalties leads the Businessman to strict auditing, and this forces the Accountant to complete honesty. The Company spends some money on checking, but expects to collect an equal amount in penalty from the Businessman. The game also has a unique equilibrium point

$$\left(\frac{C}{G}, \frac{G}{G+P}, 0\right) \quad \text{if} \quad \frac{Q-D}{Q} < \frac{G}{G+P}$$

The corresponding gains are

$$\nu_A = 0\,, \nu_B = -C \qquad \text{and} \qquad \nu_C = \frac{-CG}{G+P}$$

The interpretation of this result is that low penalties lead the Accountant for fraud. He does not profit from this, but the fraud causes some losses to the insurance company. The company cannot recover these losses by checking on the Businessman's auditing system.

4.4 It is natural to assume that C, D and G are given, technical parameters.

The penalty for fraud, P represents a decision by society, and may be beyond the control of the three players.

The penalty for breaking the insurance contract, Q is essentially fixed by the insurance company, although it must of course be acceptable to the businessman, and within the law. It is in the interest of the Company to set Q so that

$$\frac{Q - D}{Q} > \frac{G}{G + P}$$

This leads to the first of the two cases considered in the preceding paragraph, and hence the Company is not expected to lose. It should induce a rational Accountant to be honest. An element of moral hazard may be present, since the Businessman may be tempted to be more lax in his auditing than assured in the insurance contract. The penalty Q does however prevent him from gaining, and the Company from losing by such violations of the contract.

In a very permissive society P may be close to zero, so that it is impossible to set Q high enough to satisfy the inequality above. This leads to the second of the two cases. The auditing will be so strict that crime does not pay, and the company will not find it necessary to check that the audits actually are carried out. Still the company will lose money. An insurance company will not usually make contracts which are expected to be unprofitable, so we must assume that the expected loss $CG(G + P)^{-1}$ is added to the premium paid by the Businessman. Hence we arrive at the fairly obvious conclusion that lower penalties for fraud lead to higher insurance premiums. The possibly surprising, remedy may be as indicated in para 3.4, to pay accountants really well.

4.5 Large risks are often reinsured. In such cases the reinsurers pay parts of the claims, but usually the direct insurer settles the claims. The reinsurers have the right to check that the claim settlements are in accordance with the insurance contract, so the situations we have considered may really be n-person games. In the insurance world it is always stressed that reinsurance arrangements are made in the "utmost good faith" (*uberrimae fidei*), and in the gentlemen's game which reinsurance is (or was), it is simply not done to check the books of a direct insurer. It may however be tempting for an insurer to make a generous settlement with a good client, knowing that reinsurers will cover a substantial part of the cost, and this possibility may be considered when reinsurance premiums are agreed upon.

5. Other Applications of the Model

5.1 In the example we have discussed it was assumed that a theft could be discovered only by the auditor. There are situations where an assumption of this kind does not hold, and a simple example can be found in traveller's baggage insurance.

An airline is responsible for lost baggage, and usually it will take insurance to cover this liability. The airline can make certain that no baggage is stolen in the claim area by checking the tag on every suitcase against the ticket stub, but this may be a costly procedure.

The insurance company may do some checking of its own, to satisfy itself that the airline has reasonable control of who pick up whose suitcases. This leads to a situation which can be described by the following table:

Table 3:

		Airline (Player B)	
		No check	Check
Insurer (Player C)	No Check	$-G$, 0	0, $-C$
	Check	$Q-D-G$, $-Q$	$-D$, $-C$

The notation here is the same as in Table 2, except that x, the probability of theft is not brought in explicitly. Hence C must be interpreted as expected loss due to theft, in the absence of any checking by the airline. The checking done by the insurer is assumed to have no effect on the expected loss. If the two players B and C check at an arbitrary arrival with probabilities y and z respectively, expected payments will be

$$\nu_B(y,z) = -zQ - y(C - zQ)$$

$$\nu_c(y,z) = -(1-y)G + z(Q - D - yQ)$$

The equilibrium strategies are found to be

$$\bar{y} = \frac{Q-D}{Q} \quad \text{and} \quad \bar{z} = \frac{C}{Q}$$

The corresponding payments are

$$\nu_B(\bar{y}, \bar{z}) = -C \qquad \text{and} \qquad \nu_C(\bar{y}, \bar{z}) = -\frac{DG}{Q}$$

5.2 The result above leads to two observations:

(i) The airline cannot make any savings by relaxing the checking. If the insurance company double-checks in an optimal manner, the airline must expect to pay an amount equal to the cost of complete checking.

(ii) The insurance company will not make a contract that is expected to lead to a loss. Hence the amount $(DC)/Q$ will be added to the premium, so that the airline will have to pay both the cost of a 100 percent checking, and the cost of the double checking of the insurance company. This situation, which is discussed in more detail in another paper (Borch, 1980), illustrates how the mere existence of moral hazard will lead to costs, even to those who have no intention of cheating. Actually $(DC)/Q$ is the expected cost of claim payments, if the airline cheats in an optimal manner.

5.3 The methods from game theory used in the preceding examples seem to have many potential applications in insurance. In any situation where the insured has undertaken to take special measures to prevent accidents and reduce losses, there is a risk — usually called moral hazard — that he may neglect his obligations. This may lead to more and larger claims against the insurance company, and usually the company reserves the right to inspect that the insured really carries out the safety measures foreseen in the insurance contract. This inspection costs money, and the insured must pay for it in the form of an addition to the premium.

It is not easy to estimate the increase in claim payments which will be the result of relaxed safety measures. A promising field for further studies may be product liability insurance. Often the quality of industrial products is controlled by sampling inspection, and the statistical methods used for this purpose give the probability that a defective product shall be delivered to the customer. This probability is obviously of interest for the setting of premiums for insurance of product liability. The insurance contract is usually written under the assumption that a specific control plan is followed. It may be tempting to the producer to cut costs by relaxing the control, and this will induce the insurer to do his own checking. This will cost money, and the costs must be paid by the K. Borch producer. The question has been discussed in some earlier papers (Borch (1978, 1979)) in a preliminary manner.

5.4 Sampling inspection in industry can naturally be considered as a game against nature. The purpose is to check that the production process is under control. Machines are not usually credited with intelligence or a vicious desire to deliver faulty products. The sampling approach discussed in Section 2 may therefore be more appropriate in industrial production than in financial auditing. It is however interesting to note that many inspection plans are based on minimax considerations of the same kind as those used in game theory. This may be unfair to the machines, but insurance people will tend to see this as a confirmation of Murphy's law: If something can go wrong, it will.

References for Section 7

Borch K. (1978): Product Liability, Quality Control and Insurance. *Rivista di matematica per le scienze economiche e sociali*, 89–98.

Borch K. (1979): Insurance and Loss Prevention: Producer's Liability. *Greek Economic Review*, 56–69.

Borch K. (1980): The Price of Moral Hazard. *Scandinavian Actuarial Journal.*

Kaplan RS. (1973): A Stochastic Model for Auditing. *Journal of Accounting Research*, 38–46.

Maschler M. (1966): A Price Leadership Method for solving the Inspector's Non-Constant-Sum Game. *Naval Research Logistics Quarterly*, 11–33.

Maschler M. (1967): The Inspector's Non-Constant-Sum Game: Its Dependence on a System of Detectors. *Naval Research Logistics Quarterly*, 275–290.

CHAPTER 8

RISK THEORY AND GOVERNMENT SUPERVISION

1. Is Regulation of Insurance Companies Necessary?*

To answer the question we must either know or make assumptions about what an insurance company will do in the absence of any regulation. There should be no need for governmental intervention unless the company, when left to its own devices, is expected to engage in unfair or socially harmful practices. In the following we shall study this problem with the help of some simple models, based on assumptions which seem reasonable. We shall find, not surprisingly, that if the company primarily is interested in making a quick profit, some regulation may be necessary. On the other hand we shall find that if the management of the company takes a long-term view, no regulation should be necessary, We shall also see that there are limits to what a government can achieve by regulation of private insurance companies which operate in a free economy.

1. The Basic Model

1.1 As our starting point we shall consider an insurance company which holds a portfolio of insurance contracts. The situation of the company can then be described by two elements:

P = the premiums which the company received when underwriting the contracts.

$F(x)$ = the probability distribution of the claims which the company will have to pay under the contracts in the portfolio. It is convenient to assume the existence of a density $f(x) = F'(x)$.

---

* Reprinted from *Geld, Banken und Versicherungen*, Göppl, Henn, eds. 1981: 103–112.

To obtain a simple dynamic model we shall assume that the insurance company in successive operating periods underwrites identical portfolios, and we shall assume that claims are settled at the end of each period.

These assumptions may appear unrealistic, but they are really fairly innocent. They can easily be relaxed, although at a certain cost in the form of a more complicated analysis.

A more serious assumption is that the company is not allowed to operate unless it is solvent, i.e. that at the beginning of any operating period the company must possess an equity capital $S \geq 0$. This is of course a "regulation", but not one which applies particularly to insurance. Usually it is illegal for a company of any kind to operate if it is insolvent.

1.2 Assume now that an insurance company at the end of an operating period finds itself with an equity capital, or a "surplus", $S \geq 0$. The company may then consider paying a dividend $s \leq S$, and enter the next operating period with an equity capital $S - s$.

A *dividend policy* can loosely be described as a rule for determining s for any given S. Any rule of this kind will generate a discrete stochastic process of dividend payments $s_0, s_1, \ldots, s_t, \ldots$ The optimal dividend policy will be the rule that gives the best of the attainable processes. Hence to solve its decision problem the company must know what it wants, i.e. it must be able to specify a preference ordering over a set of stochastic processes. This ordering represents the company's objective, and the optimal dividend policy will lead to the most preferred element in the set of attainable processes.

1.3 Models of the type described above was first presented by de Finetti (1957), who discussed different possible assumptions about the company's objectives. One of the assumptions he studied was that the company would seek to maximize the expected discounted sum of the dividend payments:

$$\sum_{t=0}^{\infty} v^t s_t$$

where $v \in (0.1)$ is the discount factor.

Let $V(S)$ denote the maximum, i.e. the expected discounted sum of the dividend payments, if the initial equity capital is S, and if the company follows an optimal dividend policy. It is easy to see that $V(S)$ must satisfy the functional equation:

$$V(S) = \max_{0 \le s \le S} \left(s + v \int_0^{S+P-s} V(S - s + P - x) f(x)\, dx \right) \tag{1}$$

Essentially early dividend payments are preferred, but a high dividend implies a low retained surplus, and hence a high probability of insolvency, i.e. that the payments will terminate.

Equation (1) can be solved by standard methods of dynamic programming. The problem is not really difficult, but the solution usually has a complicated form, and it is not easy to see how the solution depends on the given elements. Some simple examples can be found in Borch (1974), and they suggest that one should seek a different approach to the problem.

2. A Naive Dividend Policy

2.1 As an alternative approach we shall assume that at the end of a profitable operating period the company immediately pays the whole profit out as dividend. If the period has given a loss, no dividend is paid.

This policy in itself may not make much sense, but we shall see that it can help us to determine the shape of the solution to the problem given by (1).

Let $W(S)$ be the expected discounted sum of the dividends paid under the naive policy. The function $W(S)$ must clearly be a solution of the integral equation:

$$\begin{aligned} W(S) = \int_0^P (P - x) f(x)\, dx + vW(S) \int_0^P f(x)\, dx \\ + v \int_P^{S+P} W(S + P - x) f(x)\, dx \end{aligned} \tag{2}$$

This equation is evidently far simpler than the functional equation (1). Setting the first term on the right-hand side in (2) equal to C, rearranging the other terms, the equation takes the form

$$\bigl(1 - vF(P)\bigr) W(S) = C + v \int_0^S W(S - x) f(x + P)\, dx \tag{3}$$

2.2 Taking the Laplace transform of (3) we find.

$$(1 - vF(P)) \int_0^\infty W(S)e^{-tS}\, dS = \frac{C}{t} + \left(v \int_0^\infty W(x)e^{-tx}\, dx \right) \left(\int_0^\infty f(x+P)e^{-tx}\, dx \right)$$

If we write $1 - vF(P) = K$ and

$$\int_0^\infty f(x+P)e^{-tx}\, dx = \varphi(t)$$

the equation takes the form

$$t \int_0^\infty W(x)e^{-tx}\, dx = \frac{C}{K - v\varphi(t)} \tag{4}$$

For the left-hand side of (4) we have

$$t \int_0^\infty W(x)e^{-tx}\, dx = W(0) + \int_0^\infty W'(x)e^{-tx}\, dx$$

As $v\varphi(t) \geq \varphi(0) = 1 - F(P) < 1$, it follows that the right-hand side of (4) can be expanded in a convergent series. From (3) we see that $KW(O) = C$ so that we have:

$$\int_0^\infty W'(x)e^{-tx}\, dx = W(0) \sum_{n=1}^{\infty} \left(\frac{V}{K} \varphi(t) \right)^n \tag{5}$$

2.3 $(\varphi(t))^n$ is the Laplace transform of the n-th convolution of $f(x+P)$ with itself, which we shall denote by $f_n(x)$. Hence

$$f_n(x) = \int_0^x f_{n-1}(y) f(x+P-y)\, dy \qquad \text{for } n > 1$$

We shall write $f_1(x) = f(x+P)$.

Taking the inverse transform of (5), we find

$$W'(x) = W(0) \sum_{n=0}^{\infty} \frac{V}{K}^n f_n(x) \tag{6}$$

From (6) $W(x)$ itself can be found by integration:

$$W(x) = W(0) \sum_{n=0}^{\infty} \frac{V}{K}^{n} f_n(x)$$

This result can be verified directly. To show this, introduce a distribution $G(x)$ defined as follows:

$$G(0) = F(P)$$
$$G(x) = F(x + P) \qquad \text{for } x > 0$$

Substituting this in the calculations above, we find

$$W(x) = C\big(1 + vG(x) + v^2 G_2(x) \ldots\big)$$

$G_n(x)$ is the probability that accumulated losses in n periods shall not exceed the initial equity capital x. If this event occurs, the expected dividend is paid, and its discounted value is $v^n C$. The convolutions $G_n(x)$ have a complicated form, and we shall not use these functions in the following.

3. *The Form of the Optimal Dividend Policy*

3.1 The expansion (6) is, as we have noted convergent, and $W(x)$ as a discounted sum of distribution functions is a bounded and increasing function of x. We have already found from (3) that

$$W(0) = \frac{C}{1 - vF(P)}$$

Further it is easy to see, without any calculation, that

$$W(\infty) = \frac{C}{1 - v} = \sum_{t=0}^{\infty} v^t \int_0^P (P - x) f(x)\, dx$$

If the equity capital is infinite, the company will never be ruined, and the expected profit will be paid as dividend in all future periods.

From (6) it follows that

$$W'(0) = W(0) \frac{V}{K} f(P) \qquad \text{and} \qquad W'(\infty) = 0$$

3.2 Let Z be the solution of the equation

$$W'(Z) = 1 \tag{7}$$

If the company's capital at the end of an operating period is $Z + z$, with $z > 0$, we will have, at least for z sufficiently small

$$W(Z + z) < W(Z) + z$$

Hence the expected discounted sum of the dividends paid will increase, if the company departs from the naive policy, and immediately pays the amount z out as dividend.

Similarly, if the capital is smaller than Z, it will be optimal to retain profits until the capital has been brought up to Z, before paying any dividend. Hence the company can increase the expected discounted sum of its dividend payments if it departs from the naive policy, and adopts a dividend policy defined as follows:

$$s = S - Z \qquad \text{if } S > Z$$

$$s = 0 \qquad \text{if } S \leq Z$$

If this actually is the optimal one, the functional equation (1) reduces to an integral equation

$$V(S) = v \int_0^{S+P} V(S + P - x) f(x)\, dx$$

valid for $0 \leq S \leq Z$, with the boundary conditions

$$V(S) = 0 \qquad \text{for } S < 0$$

$$V(S) = S - Z \qquad \text{for } Z < S$$

The equation has a unique continuous solution, which usually is of a complicated form. It is therefore of some interest to determine the optimal dividend policy from (7), without solving (1) to find $V(S)$ itself.

3.3 If equation (7) has a unique solution, the optimal dividend policy will be of the form given above. This has been proved by many authors, and different proofs can be found in the references given at the end of the paper. With this policy there will be an optimal amount of capital which the company should seek to retain as reserves in future operating periods. This may not quite correspond to the dividend policies we can observe in the real world. After an exceptionally profitable period companies may tend to hold back some profits, in order to safeguard future dividend payments. This will however not be optimal under de Finetti's assumption about the preferences and objectives of the company. At present we shall not discuss whether it is the assumption or the management that is wrong. Such discrepancies between theory and practice must however be taken as a call for caution, and require an explanation.

3.4 Miyasawa (1962) and Morrill (1966) have shown that equation (7) may have more than one root, and this leads to dividend policies which do not seem reasonable on intuitive reasons. The two authors have given examples in which equation (8) has more than one root, but these are all based on discrete claim distributions of a rather artificial kind. It is clearly possible to construct similar examples with continuous distributions, and the question has been discussed recently by Hallin (1979). It is doubtful if these so-called "band strategies" have any relevance to insurance problems.

A sufficient condition that equation (7) has a unique non-negative root is $W(0) > 1$ and $W''(x) < 0$.

Differentiation of (6) gives

$$W''(x) = W(0) \sum_{n=1}^{\infty} \frac{V}{K}^n f_n'(x) \tag{8}$$

Differentiating the expressions for the convolutions, we find that the equation can be rewritten in the form

$$\begin{aligned} W''(x) = W(0)\frac{V}{K}\left(f'(x+P) + \frac{V}{K}f(P)f(x+P)\right) \\ + W(0)\sum_{n=2}^{\infty}\frac{V}{K}^n\left(\int_0^x f_{n-1}(y)f'(x+P-y)\,dy\right. \\ \left. + \frac{V}{K}f(P)f_n(x)\right) \end{aligned} \tag{9}$$

3.5 The first term in (9) is negative if

$$f'(x+P) + \frac{V}{K}f(P)f(x+P) < 0 \tag{10}$$

Substituting

$$f(x+P-y) = \frac{V}{K} f(P) f(x+P-y)$$

in the following terms, we see that they all vanish. Hence (10) is a sufficient condition that $W''(x) < 0$.

Condition (10) implies:

$$f(x+P) < f(P)e^{-VF(P)x/K}$$

Hence equation (7) will have a unique root if the claim density goes to zero at least as rapidly as an exponential.

A necessary, but not sufficient condition is that $f'(x+P) < 0$ for $x > 0$. For a unimodal distribution this condition will be satisfied when P is greater than the mode. The typical claim distribution will be skew, with a long tail. For such distributions the mean will be greater than the mode, and the premium P will again normally be greater than the mean, i.e. than expected claim payments.

If this condition is satisfied, the sufficient condition (10) appears as a mild regularity condition for the tail of the distribution, and the curious cases found by Miyasawa and Morrill may be dismissed as interesting but irrelevant.

3.6 Clearly the company will not find it optimal to maintain positive reserves unless

$$W'(0) > 1$$

Substituting the relevant expressions, we can write this condition in the form

$$vf(P) \int_0^P (P-x) f(x)\, dx > \left(1 - vF(P)\right)^2$$

Since the left-hand side will go to zero with P, it follows that the premium must be above a certain level to induce the company to risk some of its equity capital as reserves in the underwriting business. The company will not refuse to underwrite the portfolio, since it cannot lose unless it risks some of its own money.

$W(x)$ is clearly a function of P as well as of x, so it is natural to write equation (8) in the following form

$$\frac{\partial W}{\partial Z} = 1$$

The equation determines the optimal reserve Z as a function of the premium P. Differentiation of the equation with respect to P gives

$$\frac{\partial^2 W}{\partial Z \partial P} + \frac{\partial^2 W}{\partial Z^2}\frac{dZ}{dP} = 0$$

which can be used to study the relationship between Z and P. The connection can, as we shall show with an example in Section 5 be of a fairly complex nature. In general changes in P will have two different effects on Z:

(i) An increase in P will decrease the probability of insolvency, and hence reduce the size of the optimal equity capital.

(ii) An increase in P will make it more attractive to stay in business, and may lead to an increase in the optimal reserve in order to reduce the probability of insolvency.

4. Regulation and the Ruin Problem

4.1 A portfolio of insurance contracts will give a loss if claim payments exceed the premiums received. If claims exceed premiums plus the company's equity capital, the company will be unable to meet its obligations, or in the traditional terms, it will be ruined. The probability of this event is

$$\Pr\{x > S + P\} = 1 - F(S + P) = \alpha$$

The main objective of the governmental supervision is to see that this probability is very low. This is the purpose behind the different solvency conditions which the companies must satisfy, although it is difficult to find explicit statements as to what ruin probabilities should be considered as acceptable.

$F(S + P) = 1 - \alpha$ is a natural measure of the *quality* of the insurance contracts which the company offers to the public. The effect of the government's solvency conditions is to set a minimum quality standard for the insurance contracts which companies are allowed to offer in the market.

4.2 High quality insurance requires high equity capital, and to satisfy the government's quality requirement, the company must hold an equity capital at least equal to the value of S defined by an equation of the form

$$F(S + P) = 1 - \alpha \tag{11}$$

We have however seen that an insurance company will find it optimal to maintain an equity capital Z defined by the equation

$$W'(Z) = 1 \tag{7}$$

If $Z > S$ there is no need for solvency conditions laid down by the government. The company left alone will seek to maintain an equity capital more than sufficient to satisfy the quality standard set by the government. If however equations (7) and (11) give solutions such that $S > Z$, government supervision will be necessary to protect the insurance buying public.

It is not easy to decide which of the two cases prevails in the real world, and we shall not take this question up for discussion. It is however worth noting that it is often alleged that old and well established insurance companies are unduly conservative in their dividend policy, and tend to accumulate larger reserves than necessary.

4.3 Governmental supervision and regulation may often go beyond the mere checking that solvency conditions are satisfied. In many countries the government will specify the contents of the insurance contract, and thus virtually define the claim distribution $F(x)$. If the government also specifies the premium P which the company should charge for the contract, problems are bound to arise.

Together $F(x)$ and P will determine how attractive the insurance company will be as an investment, that is, how much equity capital it can obtain from a competitive capital market. The equity capital again determines the quality of the insurance contract, and the conflict between different regulatory objectives is obvious. Good quality insurance cannot be cheap, unless it is provided by a government guarantee. This observation has been made by many authors, i.a. in Borch (1974, Chapter 22). We shall however not discuss this question any further.

5. A Numerical Example

5.1 At this stage it may be useful to discuss a simple special case. We shall assume that the claim density is exponential, i.e.

$$f(x) = e^{-x}$$

Substituting this into the general formulae we find:

$$W(x) = \frac{C}{1-v}\left[1 - \frac{ve^{-P}}{1-v+ve^{-P}} \exp\left(\frac{-(1-v)x}{1-v+ve^{-P}}\right)\right]$$

and

$$W'(x) = \frac{Cve^{-P}}{(1-v+ve^{-P})^2} \exp\left(\frac{-(1-v)x}{1-v+ve^{-P}}\right)$$

These results can also be found by noting that in this special case the integral equation (3) can be reduced to a linear differential equation.

5.2 Equation (7) which determines the optimal reserves takes the form

$$\frac{1-v}{1-v+ve^{-P}} Z = ZnC + Znv - P - 2Zn(1-v+ve^{-P})$$

or by substituting the expression for C, and writing $v = (1+i)^{-1}$

$$\frac{iZ}{i+e^{-P}} = Zn(P-1+e^{-P}) - 2Zn(1+i) - P - 2Zn(i+e^{-P})$$

The table below gives the value of Z for some selected values of P, when $i = 0.1$.

Premium P	Optimal Reserve	Ruin probability e^{-Z-P}
1.0	Negative	–
1.2	"	–
1.3	0.166	0.23
1.4	1.052	0.086
1.5	1.42	0.054
2.0	2.28	0.014
3.0	2.14	0.0059
4.0	1.47	0.0042
7.0	0.0	0.0009

The table shows that increasing P will increase the quality of the insurance contracts, i.e. reduce the probability of ruin. It should not be surprising that Z will decrease with increasing P for large values of P. If the level of premiums is very high, there will be a very low probability that the underwriting shall lead to a loss, and the incentive to maintain additional reserves will be reduced.

5.3 It is easy to see that the results above are very sensitive to changes in the discount rate. For $v = 0.05$ and $P = 1.5$ we find $Z \approx 9$, which gives a ruin probability that should be acceptable in most circumstances.

This observation should lead us to consider the interpretation of the discount factor in the objective function. Generally this factor measures the stockholder's "impatience", i.e. his preference for early dividends rather than later ones. It seems natural to assume that this discount rate should be related to the market rate of interest, i.e. to the return which the stockholder could earn if he received the money and could invest it himself. It is however also natural to assume that some interest is earned on the reserves which the company maintains to keep the probability of ruin at an acceptably low level, and that these interest earnings are paid to the stockholders. In fact he could keep these reserves himself, and invest them as he sees fit, provided that he accepted a liability to cover the company's underwriting losses, up to a certain level. This would bring him into a situation similar to that of a member of Lloyd's.

Profits from insurance operations would come in addition to his normal investment income, as a reward for risk bearing.

It is not difficult to bring this element into the model, and show that under certain conditions it will have the same effect as less impatience. We shall however not explore this variety of the model. Instead we shall briefly mention another element in the company objectives, which also was studied by de Finetti.

5.4 De Finetti computed the expected life (i.e. expected time of ruin) of an insurance company under a given dividend policy. It does not make sense to assume that the company's objective is just to maximize expected life, since this would mean that no dividend would ever be paid. Nevertheless it is natural to assume that those who make the everyday decisions in an insurance company — executives and employees — will be more interested in job security and the expected life of the company, than in the expected discounted value of the dividend payments. This possible conflict of interest may lead to a conservative dividend policy, and to insurance of high quality.

6. Final Remark

The elaborate mathematical manipulations in this paper may — as often is the case — just have confirmed the conventional wisdom. Most insurance executives will maintain that they work for a responsible company, which takes the long-term view, so that there is no real need for supervision. They may however admit that there are some fly-by-night insurers, interested only in a quick profit, and that these should be carefully supervised, and their activity regulated.

References for Section 1

Borch K. (1974): *The Mathematical Theory of Insurance.* D.C. Heath & Co.
De Finetti B. (1957): "Su una Impostazione Alternativa della Teoria Collettiva del Rischio", *Transactions of the XV International Congress of Actuaries*, 433–443.
Hallin M. (1979): "Band Strategies: The Random Walk of Reserves", *Blätter der Deutsche Gesellschaft für Versicherungsmathematik*, 231–236.
Miyasawa K. (1962): "An Economic Survival Game", *Journal of the Operations Research Society of Japan*, 95–113.
Morrill J. (1966): "One-Person Games of Economic Survival", *Naval Research Logistics Quarterly*, 49–69.

2. Risk Theory and Serendipity*

1. Introduction

1.1 De Finetti (1959) was the first to use the word *serendipity* to characterize certain statistical activities. The word was coined by Horace Walpole in 1754 in some comments on the fairy tale "The Three Princes of Serendip". One of the ancient names of Sri Lanka is Serendip, and its three princes set out on a series of travels with very definite purposes in mind. For various reasons the princes never achieved what they set out to do, but by good luck or accident they made important discoveries and did many useful things.

The parallels between the fairy tale and risk theory in the twentieth century are obvious. The theory was developed to solve practical problems in insurance. Nobody can seriously claim that the actuaries who developed

---

* Reprinted from *Insurance Mathematics & Economics*, 1986; 5(1):103–112,

the theory were successful in this respect, but by pure serendipity they made discoveries which turned out to be useful in many unexpected ways. For instance, there is little doubt that the collective risk theory has brought modern mathematics into actuarial curricula, and this is useful, even if the theory is not.

1.2 One can look at the subject less kindly than De Finetti does. In a survey of contemporary mathematics Mac Lane expresses some fear that one may tend to take "too much of a Hungarian view of mathematics — that the science consists not in good answers but in hard questions". This remark could well have been addressed to actuaries working on risk theory. They may have come up with few good answers, but they have certainly formulated many hard questions. Some of these questions are such that it seems inconceivable that they could be asked by anybody from the insurance world, but they fascinate an esoteric group just because they are hard.

1.3 In the actuarial risk theory one usually studies risks completely detached from any economic context. It is then only to be expected that much of the work seems to lack any clear purpose. In this paper we shall try to connect the risk problems with economic reality, and thus give the theory a purpose.

The next section gives a brief presentation of the standard model of general economic equilibrium, in a form suitable for the study of insurance. Section 3 gives some examples of how the model can be applied and indicates how the results may be useful in practice. The following section presents a model due to De Finetti, which derives the utility functions essential in the equilibrium model, from a dynamic model. Section 5 gives a short discussion of the practical application of the different models.

2. A Model of the Insurance Market

2.1 An insurance contract is a contingent claim. When the contract is concluded an amount of cash, the premium is paid and the buyer will get a random amount in return — as settlement of the claims he can make under the contract. The transaction at this abstract level is of exactly the same form as the purchase of a share in a risky business. The price of such shares is presumably determined by supply and demand in stock markets, and it is natural to assume that insurance premiums are determined in a similar way. In the following we shall therefore give a brief outline of the standard equilibrium model, essentially due to Arrow (1953).

2.2 It is convenient to interpret the model as a reinsurance market, in which n insurance companies trade among themselves. We shall take as given (for $r = 1, 2, \ldots, n$),

(i) the risk attitude of company r, represented by the Bernoulli utility function $u_r(\cdot)$, with the properties $u_r' > 0$ and $u_r'' < 0$.

(ii) the initial portfolio of company r, represented by the stochastic variable x_r.

In the market these n companies exchange parts of their initial portfolios among themselves. As a result of these exchanges company r obtains a final portfolio, represented by the stochastic variable y_r, $r = 1, 2, \ldots, n$.

If the companies cannot trade with outsiders, we have

$$\sum_{r=1}^{n} y_r = \sum_{r=1}^{n} x_r = x \,, \tag{1}$$

where x is the sum of the stochastic variables representing the initial portfolios.

At this stage it is necessary to make an assumption of *homogeneous beliefs*, i.e., that all companies hold the same opinion on the joint density $f(x_1, \ldots, x_n)$, and hence on $f(x)$.

2.3 Any set of exchanges which satisfies (1) is feasible. The subset of Pareto optimal exchanges is determined by (1) and the conditions

$$k_r u_r'(y_r) = k_s u_s'(y_s) \,, \qquad r, s = 1, 2, \ldots, n \,, \tag{2}$$

where k_r and k_s are arbitrary positive constants. The result has been proved explicitly by Borch (1962), but is really contained in earlier work by Arrow.

It is easy to see that (1) and (2) will determine the Pareto optimal exchanges as n functions $y_1(x), \ldots, y_n(x)$ of the stochastic variable x. These functions will contain the arbitrary constants $k_1, \ldots, k_n$ as parameters, and $y_r(x)$ must be interpreted as payoff to company r, if total payoff is x.

It is easy to see that (2) can be written in the form

$$k_r u_r'\big(y_r(x)\big) = u'(x) \,, \tag{3}$$

where the function $u'(x)$ in a sense represents aggregate marginal utility in the market. It will of course depend on the parameters $k_1, \ldots, k_n$.

2.4 To determine the competitive equilibrium of the market in the usual way, we need two assumptions:

(i) the market is complete, in the sense that it will assign a unique value $P\{y\}$ to an arbitrary final portfolio, described by a stochastic variable y,

(ii) the value operator $P\{\cdot\}$ is a linear functional of $y(x)$.

From the Riesz representation theorem it then follows that there exists a function $G(x)$ such that

$$P\{y\} = \int_{-\infty}^{+\infty} y(x)\, dG(x)$$

Any actuary worth his salt believes that he can compute the premium for any risk with known stochastic properties, so to him the first assumption will be trivial. Some economists, i.a. Hirshleifer (1970), seem to doubt that markets in the real world are complete, and the study of "incomplete markets" has become fashionable. These studies are however not relevant in the present context, since no restrictions are placed on the exchange arrangements which the companies are allowed to make.

If a derivative of $G(x)$ exists, we can write, without loss of generality, $G'(x) = V'(x)\, f(x)$, so that the formula above takes the form

$$\begin{aligned} P\{y\} &= \int_{-\infty}^{+\infty} y(x)\, V'(x)\, f(x)\, dx \\ &= E\{y(x)\, V'(x)\} \end{aligned} \tag{4}$$

In (4) y represents a Pareto optimal portfolio, and hence it is a function $y(x)$ of the variable x. A non-optimal initial portfolio is described by the variable X_r which is stochastically dependent on x. Analogy with (4) suggests that we can write

$$\begin{aligned} p\{x_r\} &= E\{x_r V'(x)\} \\ &= \int_{-\infty}^{+\infty} x_r V'(x)\, f(x, x_r)\, dx\, dx_r \end{aligned} \tag{5}$$

Clearly (4) is a special case of (5).

2.5 To find the competitive equilibrium in the conventional way, we note that the problem of (3) company r is

$$\max E\{u_r(y_r)\}, \qquad r = 1, 2, \ldots, n,$$

subject to

$$P\{y_r\} = P\{X_r\}, \qquad r = 1, 2, \ldots, n \tag{6}$$

The conditions (6) say simply that the market value of a portfolio must remain constant if all exchange transactions are settled at market prices.

The problem is equivalent to

$$\max \int_{-\infty}^{+\infty} \Big[u_r\big(y_r(x)\big) + \lambda_r \big(E\{x_r V'(x)\} - y_r(x)\, V'(x)\big) \Big] f(x)\, dx,$$

which can be seen as a problem in the calculus of variation. The Euler equation is

$$u_r'\big(y(x)\big) = \lambda_r V'(x), \tag{7}$$

and from (3) it follows that this can be written as

$$u'(x) = \lambda_r k_r V'(x)$$

There is no loss of generality if we take $\lambda_r = k_r^{-1}$ and write $V'(x) = u'(x)$. It then follows that the assumption that the function $G(x)$ is differentiable is equivalent to assuming that the aggregate utility function is differentiable.

We can now sum up the results:

Conditions (1) and (3) determine the form of the functions $y_r(x)$.

The equations (6) determine the parameters $k_1, \ldots, k_n$ in the functions $y_r(x)$.

For the market value or an arbitrary portfolio we find

$$p\{x_r\} = E\{x_r u'(x)\} \tag{8}$$

2.6 We so far discussed only market values of portfolios. To obtain market premiums for insurance contracts, we note that the initial portfolio of company r consists of assets R_r, and of liabilities under the insurance contracts held by the company. Let the non-negative stochastic variable Z_r represent claim payments under the contracts, and write

$$x_r = R_r - z_r$$

If for the sake of simplicity we assume that the assets are risk-free, we have

$$P\{x_r\} = R_r - P\{z_r\} \tag{9}$$

Formula (9) says simply that the market value of the company's portfolio is equal to risk-free assets, less the market premium for insurance of the liabilities.

3. Examples and Applications

3.1 As a simple example we shall take The condition $u_r' > 0$ is satisfied only when $x < c_r$, so the analysis is valid only in this domain. If α is an odd integer we can take $u_r'(x) = (c_r - x)^\alpha$. We shall use this simpler notation, and fall back on the complete notation only when it is necessary to avoid misunderstanding.

In the example, (3) takes the form

$$k_r(c_r - y_r)^\alpha = u'(x)\,, \tag{3'}$$

which can be written

$$c_r - y_r = \left(k_r^{-1}u'(x)\right)^{1/\alpha}$$

Summing these equations over all r, and using (1), we obtain

$$\sum_{r=1}^{n} c_r - x = \left(u'(x)\right)^{1/\alpha} \sum_{r=1}^{n} k_r^{-1/\alpha}$$

Here we write

$$\sum_{r=1}^{n} c_r = r \qquad \text{and} \qquad \sum_{r=1}^{n} k_r^{-1/\alpha} = K^{-1/\alpha}\,,$$

so that the equation takes the form

$$u'(x) = K(c - x)^\alpha$$

From (3′) we then find

$$k_r\left(c_r - y_r(x)\right)^\alpha = K(c - x)^\alpha\,,$$

and the explicit expression for $y_r(x)$,

$$\begin{aligned} y_r(x) &= c_r - (c-x)\left(Kk_r^{-1}\right)^{1/\alpha} \\ &= c_r - (c-x)h_r\,, \end{aligned}$$

where $h_r = \left(Kk_r^{-1}\right)^{1/\alpha}$, and $\sum h_r = 1$.

The equations (6) then take the form

$$KE\Big\{\big(c_r - (c-x)hr\big)(c-x)^\alpha\Big\} = KE\big\{x_r(c-x)^\alpha\big\}\,, \tag{6'}$$

and the parameters are determined by the equations

$$h_r = \frac{E\big\{(c_r - c_x)(c-x)\big\}^\alpha}{E\big\{(c-x)^{\alpha+1}\big\}}\,, \qquad r = 1,2,\ldots,n$$

3.2 The right-hand side of (6′) gives the market value of an arbitrary portfolio, so we can write

$$P\{x_r\} = KE\big\{x_r(c-x)^\alpha\big\} \tag{10}$$

The special case $\alpha = 1$ has led to models which are widely used in practical financial analysis so it may be useful to discuss this case in some detail.

For $\alpha = 1$ the equation (10) takes the form

$$\begin{aligned} P\{x_r\} &= KcE\{x_r\} - KE\{xx_r\} \\ &= K\big(c - E\{x\}\big)\,E\{xr\} - K\operatorname{cov} xx_r \end{aligned}$$

If we here take $x_r = x$, we obtain in the same way

$$P\{x\} = K\big(c - E\{x\}\big)\,E\{xr\} - K\operatorname{var} x$$

Combining these two equations, we obtain

$$P\{x_r\} = KAE\{x_r\} + \big(P\{x\} - -KAE\{x\}\big)\frac{\operatorname{cov} xx_r}{\operatorname{var} x} \tag{11}$$

where $c - E\{x\} = A$.

It is worth noting that the arbitrary constant K can be interpreted as a risk-free rate of interest in the market.

Formula (11) is the well known "Capital Asset Price Model" or CAPM, due to Mossin (1966) and others. The model has found widespread applications in practice, and is discussed in virtually every textbook in finance — in spite of its obvious shortcomings.

We derived (11) by assuming that marginal utilities were linear, i.e. that all utility functions were quadratic. This assumption seems to be too strong for most economists. The equivalent assumption, implied by (11), that values are determined by the two first moments of a stochastic variable, seems however to be acceptable. A multivariate normal distribution is completely described by means and covariances. If the variables z_1, z_2, $\ldots$, z_m are normally distributed, the variable $z = t_1 z_1 + \cdots, t_m z_m$ defining a portfolio, is also normally distributed. This seems to be the current justification for the practical application of CAPM.

The normal is the only distribution with finite variance which has the "stability" property sketched above. This means that strictly speaking CAPM can assign a value only to portfolios defined by normally distributed variables, and that may be the explanation of the interest in "incomplete" markets.

3.3 Actuaries seem to consider CAPM as too primitive for their purposes. They may find some support for this view in a statement by Cramér (1930) who wrote: "... in many cases the approximation obtained by using the normal function is not sufficiently good to justify the conclusions that have been drawn in this way". The statement has led to a number of hard questions which must delight any actuary who takes the "Hungarian" view. In their efforts to answer Cramér's questions these actuaries have by serendipity made contributions of some importance to the development of probability theory. It is however doubtful if their work has had any noticeable effect on insurance practice.

Economists working on finance seem to have taken the opposite attitude. They have found an easy answer in CAPM, which may not be a particularly good one, and put it to application. One can discuss how useful this model really has been in practice. It is however certain that the application of CAPM has, possibly by serendipity, led to deeper insight into the functioning of financial markets.

3.4 Let us now return to the more general version of CAPM given by (10). From (9) it follows that we have

$$P\{z_r\} = R_r - P\{x_r\} = R_r - KE\{x_r(c-x)^\alpha\}$$

Here we substitute

$$x_r = R_r - z_r \qquad \text{and} \qquad x = R - z\,,$$

and find the following expression for the premium:

$$P\{z_r\} = R_r\Big[1 - KE\{(c - R + z)^\alpha\} + KE\{z_r(c - R + z)^\alpha\}\Big]\,,$$

where $R = \sum R_r$ and $z = \sum z_r$.

For the degenerate case $z_r \equiv 0$, consistency requires that $P\{z_r\} = 0$, so that we must have

$$K^{-1} = E\{(c - R + z)^\alpha\}$$

Hence the premium formula takes the form

$$P\{z_r\} = KE\{z_r(c - R + z)^\alpha\} = \frac{E\{z_r(c - R + z)^\alpha\}}{E\{(c - R + z)^\alpha\}}$$

or, written in full,

$$P\{z_r\} = K\int_0^\infty\int_0^\infty z_r(c - R + z)^\alpha f(z, z_r)\,dz\,dz_r \tag{12}$$

Formula (12) shows how the premium for a risk which can lead to losses represented by the stochastic variable z_r, depends on

(i) the stochastic properties of the risk itself,

(ii) the stochastic relationship between the particular risk and claims in the market as a whole, described by the joint density $f(z, z_r)$,

(iii) the attitude to risk in the market as a whole, represented by c,

(iv) the total assets of all insurance companies in the market, R.

A realistic theory of insurance premiums must of course take all these four elements into account. This is however rarely done in actuarial risk theory. The recent book by Goovaerts et al. (1983) covers only the first of the four elements.

One could consider as a fifth element the interest earned on the premium before claims are paid. This is regularly done in financial theory, but is rather trivial in the present context. One has just to multiply the premium by the appropriate discount factor.

3.5 As another simple example we shall take

$$u_r'(x) = \exp\left(-\frac{x}{\alpha_r}\right), \qquad r = 1, 2, \ldots, n$$

Equation (3) then takes the form

$$k_r \exp(-y_r \alpha_r^{-1}) = u'(x)$$

Taking logarithms on both sides, we obtain

$$\log k_r - y_r \alpha_r^{-1} = \log u'(x)$$

Multiplication by α_r and summation over all r gives

$$\sum \alpha_r \log k_r - x = \log u'(x) \sum \alpha_r$$

Writing

$$\sum_{s=1}^{n} \alpha_s \log k_s = K \qquad \text{and} \qquad \sum_{s=1}^{n} \alpha_s = A\,,$$

we obtain

$$u'(x) = \exp\left(-\frac{K-x}{A}\right)$$

and

$$y_r(x) = \frac{\alpha_r x}{A} + \alpha_r \log k_r - \frac{\alpha_r K}{A}$$

We can then proceed as in the first example. From (8) we determine the value of an arbitrary portfolio in the market, and hence also the market premium for an arbitrary insurance contract.

3.6 The two preceding examples are fairly simple because the 'sharing rules' are linear, i.e.,

$$y_r(x) = q_r x + c_r\,,$$

where

$$\sum q_r = 1 \qquad \text{and} \qquad \sum c_r = 0$$

The sharing rules have this form only if all utility functions belong to one of the following two classes:

$$u_r'(x) = (x + c_r)^\alpha , \tag{i}$$

or

$$u_r'(x) = e^{-\alpha_r x} \tag{ii}$$

The result is well known, and has been proved by many authors, i.a. by Borch (1968).

If the sharing rules are linear, it is possible for the companies to reach a Pareto optimum through proportional reinsurance arrangements. Other forms of reinsurance are widely used, so there should be a need for studying utility functions which do not lead to linear sharing rules. The problem is difficult, and it is surprising that it has not been taken up by those who cherish "hard questions" for their own sake. We shall not discuss the problem in any detail, but it may be useful to study a simple example.

Consider two persons with the utility functions

$$u_1(x) = 1 - e^{-x} , \qquad \text{and} \qquad u_2(x) = \log(c + x)$$

Condition (2) then takes the form

$$k_1 e^{-y_1} = \frac{k_2}{c + y_2}$$

As $y_1 + y_2 = x$, we can write this as

$$(c + y_2)e^{-(x-y_2)} = k$$

Clearly we must have $y_2 > -c$. Hence under a Pareto optimal rule of loss-sharing, person 2 can under no circumstances pay more than c, so that the rule will correspond approximately to a stoploss insurance arrangement.

3.7 Let us now return to the general case (3), and consider a risk described by the stochastic variable z.

From (8) it follows that the insurance premium for this risk is

$$P\{z\} = \int_0^\infty \int_0^\infty z u'(x) f(x, z)\, dx\, dz \tag{13}$$

Here we have written x for total claims in the market, and we have not brought the assets explicitly into the utility function.

It is convenient to write (13) in the form

$$P\{z\} = \int_0^\infty u'(x) \left(\int_0^\infty z f(x, z)\, dz \right) dx$$

Let us now write $z = z_1 + z_2$, where $z_1 = \min(z, D)$ and $z_2 = \max(0, z - D)$.

For the two components we find the following premiums:

$$P\{z_1\} = \int_0^\infty u(x) \left(\int_0^D z f(x, z)\, dz + D \int_D^\infty f(x, z)\, dz \right) dx\,,$$

$$P\{z_2\} = \int_0^\infty u'(x) \big((z - D)\, f(x, z)\, dz \big)\, dx$$

These two formulae can be given a number of different interpretations, i.a.,

- $P\{z_1\}$ can be seen as the reduction in the premium offered to a buyer, if he will accept a deductible D.
- $P\{z_2\}$ can be seen as the reinsurance premium for a stop-loss contract, under which the reinsurer pays all claims in excess of the limit D.

We now write $P\{z_2\} = P\{D\}$, and differentiate twice with respect to D. This gives

$$P'(D) = -\int_0^\infty u'(x) \left(\int_D^\infty f(x, z)\, dz \right) dx\,,$$

$$P''(D) = \int_0^\infty u'(x)\, f(x, D)\, dx \qquad (14)$$

If a reinsurer is willing to quote premiums for a number of stop-loss contracts, with different limits, the left-hand side of (14) can be estimated for an arbitrary D. If the joint density $f(x, z)$ is known, at least approximately, it may be possible to obtain an estimate of the kernel function $u'(x)$. With this estimate, we can then compute the premium for an arbitrary insurance contract in the market.

It is obviously impossible to determine the function $u'(x)$ from (3), i.e., from the preferences of all companies, and then use (8) to calculate the market premium for an arbitrary insurance contract.

It is however clear that $u'(x)$ plays an important part in determining market premiums. Since premiums are observable, we can turn the problem around, and estimate the function $u'(x)$ from observations. This approach is widely used in economics. Demand curves and underlying utility functions cannot be observed, but must be estimated from observed behaviour.

4. A Dynamic Approach to Utility

4.1 In the preceding sections we have studied simple one-period decision problems, and assumed there was a utility behind the decision. In practice it may often be difficult to specify this utility function — for good reasons. The utility a company assigns to the profits earned in one period will presumably depend on how that profit can be applied in future periods. This suggests that the problem should be studied in a dynamic or multiperiod framework. If the company has an overall, long-term objective, this must contain the utility functions which govern the decisions in each period. This overall objective may often be simpler to specify than the Bernoulli utility function.

One of the first to study this problem in an insurance context was De Finetti (1957) in one of his pioneering papers. As a long-term objective he suggested that an insurance company should seek to maximize the expected present value of its dividend payments. In the following decades this problem has been discussed by several other authors, i.a. by Borch (1967, 1969) and Bühlmann (1970).

De Finetti made his observation in a critical study of the now obsolete "collective risk theory". This theory placed the focus on the probability (14) that an insurance company shall remain solvent forever, provided that it does not change its operating procedures. This probability of achieving eternal life will inevitably be zero, unless the company allows its reserves to grow without limit. De Finetti pointed out that an insurance company could not really be interested in building up unlimited reserves, and argued in fact that the marginal utility of accumulated profits (*vincite utili)* must be decreasing. He illustrates his argument with a very simple example, based on a two-point distribution. In the following we shall consider a simple, slightly more general example.

4.2 Consider an insurance company which in each successive operating period underwrites identical portfolios, and take the following elements as given:

S = the company's initial capital,

P = the premium received by the company at the beginning of each operating period,

$f(x)$ = the probability density of claims paid by the company in each operating period.

If S_t is the company's capital at the end of period t, and x_{t+1} the claims paid by the company during period $t+1$, the company's capital at the end of period $t+1$ will be

$$S_{t+1} = S_t + P - x_{t+1}$$

Assume now that the company operates under the following conditions:

(i) if $S_t < 0$, the company is insolvent, or 'ruined', and cannot operate in any of the following periods,

(ii) if $S_t \geq Z$, the company pays a dividend $s_t = S_t - Z$. It is natural to assume that Z is chosen by the management, because accumulated profits beyond Z have lower utility than a paid out dividend.

The dividend payments $s_1, s_2, \ldots, s_t \ldots$ is a sequence of stochastic variables, and we shall write $V(S, Z)$, or when no misunderstanding is possible $V(S)$ for the expected discounted sum of the dividend payments which the company makes before the inevitable ruin, i.e.,

$$V(S) = \sum_{t=1}^{\infty} v^t E\{s_t\},$$

where v is a discount factor.

4.3 To study the function $V(S)$, we first note that for $S < Z < S + P$ it must satisfy the integral equation

$$\begin{aligned} V(S) = v \int_Z^{S+P} & (x - Z + V(Z)) f(S + P - x)\, dx \\ & + v \int_0^Z V(x)\, f(S + P - x)\, dx \end{aligned} \tag{15}$$

The equation says that if claims x, are less than $S + P - Z$, a dividend $S + P - Z - x$ will be paid at the end of the period, and the company will begin the next period with a capital Z.

If $S + P - Z \leq x \leq S + P$ the company will pay no dividend, and begin the next period with a capital $S + P - x$. If $S + P < x$, the company is ruined, and cannot operate in any of the following periods.

In the interval stated equation (15) is an integral equation of Fredholm's type, and it is known that it has a unique continuous solution. For $S <$

$Z - P$, no dividend can be paid at the first period, and some modifications are necessary.

On the whole, equation (15) is difficult to handle, and unless one holds a strong "Hungarian" view on mathematics, a general solution appears uninteresting. The optimal dividend policy is given by the value of Z, which maximizes $V(S, Z)$. The existence of an optimal policy poses some hard questions, which we shall not take up.

4.4 The main idea behind De Finetti's paper can be presented as follows:

Assume an insurance company with equity capital S is offered a premium Q, if it will underwrite a one-period insurance contract described by the claim density $g(x)$. If the company accepts the contract, expected present value of future dividend payments will be

$$U(S) = \int_0^{S+Q} V(S + Q - x)\, g(x)\, dx$$

Hence, given the company's long-term objective, the contract will be acceptable if and only if $U(S) \geq V(S)$. This means that $V(S)$ serves as the utility function which determines the company's decision, and that in (8) $u'(x)$ can be replaced by $V'(x)$. This assumes of course that the company receives the offer after it has made its reinsurance arrangements, or that it takes the reinsurance possibilities into account when deciding about the particular offer.

De Finetti did not elaborate his suggestion, but went instead on to discuss other functions of an arbitrary upper limit to accumulated profits, which could serve as alternative objectives. His paper was generally ignored for a decade, even in actuarial circles. The influential paper on the subject is by Shubnik and Thompson (1959), who independently developed a model which is virtually identical to that of De Finetti, but not interpreted in terms of insurance.

4.5 De Finetti's model implies that an insurance company is basically risk-neutral. This may at first sight seem surprising, but it makes some sense if one considers the alternatives. It seems artificial to assume that the board of a company will consider different utility functions, and possibly take a vote, to pick one which adequately represents the company's attitude to risk. It seems more natural to assume that a board will settle for some simpler rule, such as that of maximizing expected present value of dividend payment. With this rule the company will behave as if it were risk-averse in its underwriting and reinsurance transactions. This does, however, throw some doubt on the relevance of the model in Section 2, but the model may have been useful by serendipity, i.a. by providing a simple generalization of CAPM.

At this stage we can see dimly the outline of an attractive unified theory of insurance:

(i) premiums and reinsurance arrangements are determined by the methods sketched in Section 2,

(ii) the utility functions which play an important role in Subsection 2, can be determined by the methods indicated in this section.

A number of hard questions must be answered before a complete theory can take form. Before taking up the challenge, it may however be useful to pause, and ask if it really is necessary to answer these questions.

4.6 The model leading to (15) specified when a dividend should be paid, but not when the company's equity capital should be strengthened. Both questions are of equal importance to management, and at least if the insurance company is owned by a holding company, they will be considered together. Hence let us assume that the insurance company initially holds an equity capital Z, and consider the following policy:

If claims in a period amounts to x,

(i) the company pays out a dividend $\max(P - x, 0)$

(ii) an amount $\min(x - P, Z)$ is paid into the company as new equity capital.

This policy implies that if the company is solvent at the end of a period, it will enter the next period with an equity capital Z.

Expected present value of the dividend payment at the end of the first period is

$$v \int_0^{P+Z} (P - x)\, f(x)\, dx\,,$$

and the probability that the company shall be able to operate in the second period is

$$\Pr(x \leq P + Z) = F(P + Z)$$

It then follows that the expected present value of all payments is

$$W(Z) = v \int_0^{P+Z} (P - x)\, f(x)\, dx \times \sum_{n=0}^{\infty} (vF(P + Z))^n\,,$$

or

$$W(Z) = v \int_0^{P+Z} (P - x)\, f(x)\, dx / \big(1 - vF(P + Z)\big) \tag{16}$$

4.7 The problem of the company is now to determine the value of Z which maximizes (16), i.e., to find the optimal amount of capital which the owners should put at risk in their company.

The first-order condition, $W'(Z) = 0$, takes the form

$$Z\big(1 - vF(P + Z)\big) = v \int_0^{P+Z} (P - x)\, f(x)\, dx \tag{17}$$

From (17) Z can be determined. Comparison of (16) and (17) shows that for the optimal Z we have

$$Z = W(Z)$$

This simple condition expresses the obvious, that the optimal capital to put into a venture is equal to the expected present value of the return. In the discount factor $v = (1 + i)^{-1}$ which occurs in (16) and (17), i must be interpreted as the return on competing investments. This invites some conventional comparative static analysis.

Integration of the right-hand side of (17) shows that the equation can be written in the form

$$z = v \int_0^{P+Z} F(x)\, dx \tag{17'}$$

From (17′) we find

$$\frac{dZ}{dv}\big(1 - vF(P + Z)\big) = \int_0^{P+Z} F(x)\, dx > 0$$

This again expresses the obvious. If return on competing investments decreases, i.e., if v increases, more capital will flow into the insurance industry. In the opposite case insurance companies may be unable to attract new equity capital.

Clearly $F(P + Z)$ is the probability that an insurance company shall be able to pay its claims. In most countries government regulations require that this probability shall be close to unity. In practice this means that an insurance company is only allowed to operate if it satisfies a solvency condition of the form $F(P+Z) \geq \alpha$. If there is a general increase in returns on investments, it is evident that insurance companies must increase their premiums, in order to attract the capital necessary to satisfy the solvency condition. This may be a useful result. It shows that the government cannot decree both high solvency and 'reasonable' premiums in a free capital market. The result should be obvious, but does not always seem to be so.

5. The Model on the Real World

5.1 The model presented in Section 2 was interpreted as a reinsurance market, and we determined the equilibrium premiums. One must expect that these premiums, at least in the longer run, will have some influence on the premiums in direct insurance.

Insurance markets are far from perfect, and a company may well — for some time — be able to charge premiums above those determined by the model. This company can however earn a risk-free profit if it reinsures its whole portfolio in the market, so the situation cannot be stable in the long run. One must also expect that the customers of this company eventually will discover that they can buy their insurance cheaper elsewhere.

Similarly an insurance company may charge lower premiums than those determined by the model. This company will probably find that reinsurance costs more than it is worth, and carry most of the risk itself. With good luck this may go on for quite some time, and with ample reserves the company will be able to satisfy the solvency conditions laid down by the government. When luck runs out, as it eventually must, the company may well find itself insolvent, when its liabilities are valued at market prices.

5.2 In Section 2 it was proved that a Pareto optimum could be reached only if every insurer participated in every risk in the market. This does not happen in practice, and it is natural to seek the explanation in transaction costs. This is however not entirely satisfactory, since it should not be prohibitively expensive to carry out the calculations necessary to divide a risk in a Pareto optimal way. It seems more likely that some elements of moral hazard enter. It is always stressed that reinsurance is carried out under conditions of the "utmost good faith". In practice this means that a reinsurer accepts the ceding company's report on the stochastic properties of the risk covered, without a costly checking of the statistics. The possibility that the ceding company cheats is always there, so the reinsurer has the choice of either expenses, or of being exposed to moral hazard. It is therefore natural that reinsurers should try to cover a medium sized risk within a fairly small group, and this may lead to some segmentation of the market.

One way to model this would be to assume that there are costs c involved in checking the portfolio offered by a would-be ceding company. If n companies participate in an exchange arrangement, each checking the other, total costs will be $n(n-1)c$. With increasing n there will clearly be a point where increasing costs will offset the gain by wider diversification of the risk.

5.3 In Section 4 we have in a sense banished utility and risk aversion from the supply side of the insurance market. There are however some reasons for assuming that insurance companies should be risk-neutral. Insurance companies are intermediaries between those who want to buy insurance, and those who are willing to risk their money in the underwriting of insurance contracts. If these two parties are risk-averse, a set of Pareto optimal arrangements exists. The parties may however be unable to reach a Pareto optimum, if the transactions have to be carried out through an intermediary that imposes its own risk aversion. The problem has been discussed in economic literature, i.a. by Malinvaud (1972). We shall not discuss it further here, since a complete discussion will require detailed specification of the institutional framework.

On the demand side risk aversion remains essential, since a buyer of insurance is by definition risk-averse. When he is faced by a market which can quote a premium for any kind of insurance contract, he can compute or program his way to the contract which is optimal according to his preferences.

References for Section 2

Arrow KJ. (1953): Le rôle des valeurs boursières pour la répartition la meilleure des risques. *Colloques Internationaux du CNRS 40*, 41–48. Translated in 1964 as: The role of securities in the optimal allocation of risk-bearing. *Review of Economic Studies 31*, 91–96.

Borch K. (1962): Equilibrium in a reinsurance market. *Econometrica 30*, 424–444.

Borch K. (1967): The theory of risk, *Journal of the Royal Statistical Society 29, Series B*, 432–452.

Borch K. (1968): General equilibrium in the economics of uncertainty, in: K. Borch and J. Mossin, eds., *Risk and Uncertainty*. London: Macmillan.

Borch K. (1969): The static decision problem in its dynamic context, *Colloques Internationaux du CNRS 171*, 53–62.

Bühlmann H. (1970): *Mathematical Methods in Risk Theory.* Berlin: Springer-Verlag.

Cramér H. (1930): On the mathematical theory of risk, Skandia Jubilee Volume 7–84.

De Finetti B. (1957): Su un'impostazione altenativa della teoria colletiva del rischio, *Transactions of the XV International Congress of Actuaries 2*, 433–443.

De Finetti B. (1959): La probabilità e la statistica nei rapporti con l'induzione, *Centro Internazionale Matematico Estivo, Cremonese.* English translation as Chapter 9 in De Finetti (1972).

De Finetti B. (1972). *Probability, Induction and Statistics.* New York: Wiley.

Goovaerts M, De Vylder F, Haezendonck J. (1983): *Insurance Premiums.* North-Holland, Amsterdam.

Hirshleifer J. (1970): *Investment, Interest and Capital.* Englewood Cliffs, NJ: Prentice-Hall.

Mac Lane S. (1983): The health of mathematics, *The Mathematical Intelligencer 5*, 53–55.

Malinvaud E. (1972): The allocation of individual risks in large markets, *Journal of Economic Theory 4*, 312–328.

Mossin J. (1966): Equilibrium in a capital asset market, *Econometrica 34*, 768–783.

Shubik M, Thompson G. (1959): Game of economic survival, *Naval Research logistics Quarterly 6*, 111–123.

AUTHOR INDEX

SUBJECT INDEX